DOWRY MURDER

DOWRY MURDER

The Imperial Origins of a Cultural Crime

Veena Talwar Oldenburg

OXFORD
UNIVERSITY PRESS

2002

OXFORD
UNIVERSITY PRESS

Oxford   New York

Auckland   Bangkok   Buenos Aires   Cape Town   Chennai
Dar es Salaam   Delhi   Hong Kong   Istanbul   Karachi   Kolkata
Kuala Lumpur   Madrid   Melbourne   Mexico City   Mumbai   Nairobi
São Paulo   Shanghai   Singapore   Taipei   Tokyo   Toronto

and an associated company in Berlin

Library of Congress Cataloging-in-Publication Data
Oldenburg, Veena Talwar.
Dowry murder : the imperial origins of a cultural crime / by Veena Talwar Oldenburg.
p. cm.
Includes bibliographical references and index.
ISBN 0-19-515071-6; ISBN 0-19-515072-4 (pbk.)
1. Wives—Crimes against—India.   2. Uxoricide—Economic aspects—India.
3. Dowry—India—Criminal provisions.   4. Hindu women—Crimes against—India.
5. Hindu women—India—Economic conditions.   6. Caste—Political aspects—India.
7. India—History—British occupation, 1765–1947.   8. Great Britain—Colonies—India.
I. Title.
HV6250.4.W65 O43 2002
364.15'23'0820954—dc21   2001045770

1 3 5 7 9 8 6 4 2

Printed in the United States of America
on acid-free paper

For Mummy and Kaku

and in memory of my father, Baljit Singh,

whose intervention enabled

this work

In 1984, on a quiet spring afternoon in New York, the phone rang in my study and a television journalist asked me if I knew anything about "bride burning" or "dowry murder" in my native India. I did not, but I did offer some thoughts on sati, or widow burning, along with a reading list. No, the journalist insisted, an Indian documentary on this issue was to be aired as a segment of an important national weekly news show, and the television channel was looking for informed comment. My own memories of an experience in the summer of 1966 were still surprisingly fresh, but they appeared dated and so utterly unconnected with dowry that I said nothing. That denial and the subliminal provocation instigated this book.

I confess to having repressed my private suspicions about this wholly new yet chillingly remembered style of violence that appeared to have become a trend. The culprit (or culprits) used kerosene oil and a match to burn the woman to death; the motive was easily ascribed to marital conflict arising from demands for more dowry, in cash and/or as valuables, by the new husband and his family. These violent events were reported as kitchen accidents, involving the rather dangerous pressurized kerosene stoves in common use in Indian kitchens, from which other women, not just brides, and men as well frequently sustain accidental burns. Only in a very few cases of a young wife's death were the police actually summoned to the scene to file a report. Until the early 1980s, few such cases were investigated, and in even fewer was murder detected. Certainly no one had been convicted of the crime. Because violence in the home, even murder, was unofficially part of the private sphere, suspicion, innuendo, and speculation whispered in private conversations seldom became evidence in a court of law. There would be no reliable witnesses, since the mother-in-law was usually implicated as the perpetrator, often with a sister-in-law or even the husband himself as accomplice, and the crime occurred behind closed doors.

The day after the documentary was shown, colleagues and students at the small liberal arts college where I then taught besieged me with questions. They had seen the footage—a graphic depiction of a bride engulfed in flames, perhaps even the charred corpse—and they demanded answers. Appalling as the incident portrayed in the documentary might have been, it seemed clear that the U.S. media had seized an opportunity to make a spectacle of "the Orient," in this case India. I had become used to being brought to account for any Indian happening, good or bad (but chiefly bad). But never before had it been so difficult to deal with, because this time I had no satisfactory rebuttals. I tried to suggest that this could just be murder, an ordinary crime of passion or greed, as occurs against wives and girlfriends everywhere, and particularly here in the United States. No, they were quite sure that nothing they had seen could pass for a geographically or culturally neutral event. The burning death was perceived as fraught with deep Hindu religious and cultural significance. *Dahej* or dowry and its relationship to the Hindu caste system were portrayed as the key to understanding this crime. The narrator in the documentary had made it very clear that the Punjabi bride had been burned to death because she had not brought enough dowry to her husband's home, thus provoking a disappointed mother-in-law to douse her in kerosene and set her on fire.

Incidents of bargaining over dowry were not unheard of, but such behavior was customarily considered shamefully and unambiguously wrong. That matters had come to such a pass that brides were gruesomely immolated alive sounded like a postcolonial society's worst nightmare come true. This new crime against women was called "dowry death," and it was ironic that it made its appearance a quarter of a century after the passage of the Prohibition of Dowry Act in 1961. I vaguely remembered watching V. Shantaram's Hindi film *Dahej* from the late 1950s. It was a melodramatic tale, replete with singing, dancing, and pontificating, whose plot served as a vehicle to depict the evils of the dowry system. Though I was aware of the abuse of the custom, in the Indian context dowry also constituted a women's independent right to property and prestige. The burning of a bride to death for not bringing a dowry that satisfied the greed of a groom's family was a monstrous perversion of the meaning and function of the custom.

Culturally embarrassed, pedagogically nonplused, yet deeply stirred for reasons that will unfold, I knew the time had come for me to examine the alleged cultural roots of this crime. Yet the decision was not an easy one. The departure from my previous work—on the history of colonial Lucknow—into the relentlessly agrarian Punjab would require learning a whole new world. The differences between Oudh and Punjab in northern India were at least as acute as those a European historian might see between England and Ireland. Besides, the subject was morbid. Investigating and explicating women's powerlessness, rather than the opposite in which I so firmly believe, also angered me. After several false starts and setbacks and several intermittent spells of research and writing (between semesters with staggering teaching loads and the impositions of real life), this inner nag-ging eventually led to this book. My hope that the ordeal would at least be brief was also belied.

In writing this book, I have found it impossible to assume the persona of the omniscient historian-anthropologist and objective narrator who stands outside history and merely distills a clear and odorless account from what the documents, voices, and memories of events reveal. Neither can I be intimidated by the post-modernist critiques of ethnography and reject the genre of women's narratives entirely. My personal experience became inevitably and inextricably meshed with my research into "dowry murders," and the line between participant and observer faded. Therefore, I must disclose at the outset that I am deeply implicated in this history as one of its subjects—as a bride, as an academic and occasional activist, and as a witness to three decades of worsening violence against women—and I will rely not only on my training in the methods of history and anthropology but also on the self-conscious, feminist perspective I developed through my own en-counters with this pathology.

When I was growing up in a large extended family where four generations of women gathered almost daily, until I was fifteen, I became attuned to listening to, or rather overhearing, the conversations of women about their own and other women's happy or tragic betrothals and marriages and the conscious ideology that informed their judgments.

My *dadi* (paternal grandmother) and my *dada* (paternal grandfather) presided over a large extended family. *Dada* was a wealthy businessman—a cotton mill owner and hotelier—who permitted an apartment building he owned to be filled with the influx of *dadi's* relatives from the Punjab after the partition of India in 1947 and even managed to employ several of them in jobs in his various enter-prises. *Dada* and *dadi* had three sons, the eldest of whom was my father; the household included their wives and a daughter, with grandchildren added as time went on. I was the eldest grandchild of what was finally to be a brood of eleven. It was an assortment of *dadi's* three daughters-in-law, other female relatives, friends, and neighbors who gathered on winter afternoons and summer evenings to gossip, knit, and exchange recipes and folk wisdom.

A tragically ugly family partition and my admission to the hostel of Irish Catholic Loreto Convent College in 1962 began the second phase of my training for becoming a woman in an upper-class, convent-educated Indian milieu. The three and a half years of college were a lesson in coping with the mixed signals of a postcolonial society. We were to be chaste, segregated from men, in a convent's sense of sex segregation, and prepared by the curriculum to become very literate women but not quite career women. Neither needlepoint nor science and math-ematics were offered at the B.A. level, and rebelliousness was sternly crushed. All authoritarian institutions breed their own underworlds, and a few of us consti-tuted ours—we highlighted our subversion with forbidden Urdu couplets and love songs from Hindi cinema, and the occasional sly imbibing of gins and tonic. We were allegedly being prepared to fill the role of the good convent-educated wives that were in high demand in the marriage market beyond our walls, even as our strongest bonds of love and trust were with other women. Our role models lived in the fictional worlds of Jane Austen and George Eliot, and quotations from Keats, Shelley, and Tennyson peppered our conversations. The intense homosociability and Romantic poetry were a far cry from the compulsory destiny of arranged marriage that awaited most of us.

In 1965 I finished college and within months consented to an arranged marriage with a Punjabi man that proved disastrous. The misalliance, which lasted for ten stormy months, might have more easily ended in murder than in a legal annulment, as it did. This is arguably the best qualification I have for embarking on this project. The telling of my own story over time to disparate confidants, such as friends, relatives, and students, created different recensions. After it was over, I was compelled to tell the story to my mother, and finally I wrote an account of the events for my lawyer, who saw a devious legal route out of the mess. Each listener drew from me an untidy and disjointed narrative that varied in depth, detail, and emphasis, as I intuitively edited details and incessantly rearranged the pieces from the time they were first picked up. My listeners' questions framed and reframed the sequence of events that precipitated the breakup in that harrowing day-after-day conflict between my husband, his family, and myself.

Now, more than three decades from the horror of that first marriage and half a world away, I can dispassionately analyze the complications of the events and comprehend the sexual and psychosocial pathogens that infected the relationship. Having a story of my own sensitized my ear to the silences and subtexts in the stories of others. It became a habit to explore other people's meanings of being a wife. I was a primed sleuth who discovered the papered-over cracks and gently probed the layers of shame and concealment in the narratives of women similarly damaged by experiences in their married lives.

In the summer of 1984 in Delhi, when many more "bride burnings" were reported on the front pages of national newspapers, I was to make my first foray into the world of feminist activism. I spent the next academic year in India to explore what had by then become the best-known fact, after sati, about Indian women. At one level I was a "foreign" scholar whose project had to be approved severally by the Education, External Affairs, and Home Ministries of the Government of India. At another I was an Indian woman with a "complicated past." I knew that I had not come lightly to probe the problematic relationship of violence and gender in Punjabi households in northern India.

A clarification is essential at the outset: the burning of wives is neither an extension of nor culturally related to the notorious practice of sati (or "suttee," as the British called it), the voluntary self-immolation of widows on the funeral pyres of their husbands. The resonance may be confounding—the burning of women, the blurred line between suicide and murder—but the differences are significant, and they point to a serious devaluation of women in present-day India in spite of a century and a half of progressive legislation on women's rights. Sati was socially countenanced suicide because the widow perceived herself as having failed in her ritual duty to ensure the longevity of her husband by using her special power, or *shakti*. The rituals that a widow would follow to join her husband on his funeral pyre are adequately described and commented upon elsewhere; suffice it to say that it drew its cachet as a publicly witnessed act that generated social awe, status, and religious merit for the widow and made her the virtuous wife in death.

"Bride burning," on the other hand, is murder, culpable on social, cultural, and legal grounds, executed privately, and often disguised as an accident or suicide. Burning a wife is, perhaps, even more appalling than poisoning, drowning, strangling, shooting, or bludgeoning her, but it is patently chosen for the forensic advantage it has over the other methods, rather than for Hindu mythological or mystical reasons, as some reporters in the United States are fond of claiming. It is also relatively simple to execute. The crime occurs in the kitchen, where the lower- and middle-class housewife spends a lot of time each day. Kerosene stoves are in common use in such homes, and a tin of fuel is always kept in reserve. This can be quickly poured over the intended victim, and a lighted match will do the rest. It is easy to pass off the event as an accident since these stoves are, indeed, prone to explode (as confirmed by consumer reports). The now ubiquitous and inflammable nylon sari is only too wont to catch fire and engulf the wearer in flames. Signs of struggle do not show up on bodies with 90 percent or more third-degree burns. The young widower, who has equipped himself with a cast-iron alibi, is soon in the marriage market again looking for a new bride with perhaps an even handsomer dowry. Most often it is the mother-in-law, with or without her son as a direct accomplice, who obligingly does the deed. The reason for this, I would argue, is that the son (often the breadwinner for his widowed mother) must remain innocent of all suspicion and therefore eligible for remarriage as an unfortunate widower. His income-earning activities are also not interrupted, should the event actually be investigated as a crime. This poses difficult questions: Are Indian women victims of their culture or agents of a crime they inflict upon other women? Is dowry murder a cultural crime? This book sets out the equally complicated answers.

The search for answers and the attempt to write them down has been a long and involved one and not without mishaps. On the happier side of the ledger are the numerous intellectual and material debts I accrued, for which my gratitude is boundless. First and foremost I must thank the Social Science Research Council, for its generous and repeated support of my research in England in the summers of 1985, 1986, and the entire year in 1991–1992. The American Philosophical Society provided an enabling grant that supported my research on female infanticide in England on my two trips there in 1986–1987. For the extensive work in India I had a Senior Fellowship from the American Institute of Indian Studies at the University of Chicago and the Smithsonian Institution for a fellowship for research in India for ten months in 1985–1986. I spent an invaluable year among prominent feminist historians, with the inspiring leadership of Catharine R. Stimpson, as a Rockefeller Humanist-in-Residence in 1987–1988 at Douglass College of Rutgers University. In 1991–1992, a Baruch College Scholar Incentive Award and the City University of New York's Research Foundation's Out-of-Cycle Award allowed me the time and supplemented the necessary funds to complete the basic research on the historical aspects of this project.

All this was happening in the early days of the computer invasion into the average home. The Rockefeller fellowship paid for a state-of-the-art laptop computer and dot matrix printer (c. 1987) that revolutionized my typist-dependent ways. The leap from writing with a thick-nibbed fountain pen on notepaper to electronic production of text was liberating, although my spouse, Philip, was not spared phone calls in his office several times a day from my room in Briavel Holcomb's endlessly interesting home at Rutgers to demystify the workings of function keys or instruct me on the recovery of pages accidentally lost to the delete key, or hear me howl at the ether into which improperly named and saved items would vanish.

The India Office Library and Records with its helpful and knowledgeable staff made all this possible. It is hard to imagine how many long and tedious hours I would have expended squinting over the scores of Urdu tracts on dowry and marriage expenses had not Shabana Mahmud gone well beyond the call of desk duty to help me along and intersperse our work sessions with wine-enlivened discussions of love and marriage. The National Archives of India in New Delhi is a rather less organized treasure trove, but there encounters with fellow historians in the canteen more than made up for the long delays between the appearances of indented files. My several trips to Patiala to consult the Patiala State Archives during the Punjab insurgency, where I was often the lone scholar, would not have been possible without the cheerful, helpful, and commensal staff members who pulled out files from remembered locations, because the drawers of the catalogue had been looted. I found shelter with colleagues on days the police curfew ended work early in the afternoon. Every lunch and tea break turned into an informal seminar about the preference for sons and the military among Punjabi families; and these conversations found their way into the arguments I make in this study.

There were roadblocks too. In a panic to get to India, where my father's health was failing, I hastily left accumulated research notes in the care of the kindly manager of the Chelsea hotel where I had rented a room. The hotel changed hands while I was gone, and when I returned the entire place was under renovation, the manager had been fired, and the cartons had simply disappeared. This event and my father's death blanked out the project for a while. It was not until two years later, in 1988, that I returned to the India Office Library to recoup the information with diminished fervor. I thought I would go mad if I had to read another revenue settlement report. Yet, it was in going over this featureless terrain of bureaucratic paperwork again, and collecting and sifting through a mountain of red notebooks, graying photocopies, and yellowing newspaper cuttings that the reticulate argument that I make here painstakingly emerged. An abrupt change in jobs in 1990 led to another two-year delay, and it was not until another research trip to England and India in 1991–1992 that all the pieces were assembled for me to begin writing this work. The only positive aspect of these delays was that the fashion of deploying unintelligible academic jargon paled in the meantime and it was possible to write, without shame as an academic, in plain English.

My astonishingly brief ten months at Saheli, a women's resource center in Delhi, was probably the best immersion course I could have taken in feminist politics. I made some enduring friendships, learned the vocabulary of Indian feminist ideas and the legal constraints that prescribed the limits of action or self-expression. Sitting through the heat and the noise of the traffic bridge overhead, lubricating high-pitched discussions with sweet milky tea, the humor, pathos, heartbreak, and anger of the women mingled to make every day memorable. I am grateful that I could be there and be with Prabeen, Kalpana, Elizabeth, Savita, Gauri, Rukmini, and the many others who challenged, questioned, and taught me so much and reaffirmed my faith in laughter and song. Even our fierce disagreements were productive for me.

Students at Sarah Lawrence College, year after year, in my seminar on the "Second Sex in the Third World" questioned and refined ideas about women's history, about victims and agency, about the politics of the culturally benighted women in once colonized spaces. Preeta Law, who relocated to Delhi after graduating, tirelessly clipped news items on "dowry death" from journals and newspapers to keep me current; Heather Lewis, a mordantly philosophic research assistant, kept up a continuous interrogation that helped me refine my own views; Elizabeth Denlinger brought in fragments of poems and made me rethink things through. You have my love wherever you are today. A few of my colleagues at Sarah Lawrence were inspirational, gritty, and eloquent feminists—Grace Paley, Jane Cooper, Louise Merriwether, Amy Swerdlow, Judy Papachristou, Judy Seraphini Sauli—and their example and conversations are aglow in my mind.

There are many who read the first draft of this manuscript and offered detailed editorial and substantive comments, and to whom I would like to offer not just my thanks but also my abashed apologies for inflicting an untidy and unwieldy manuscript on them. Philip has borne the brunt of these many years when his life and his space were cluttered with this intermittent work-in-progress. Mandakini Dubey, a surrogate daughter, and Eileen Haas also combed through the then 500-odd pages of a hideously tangled first draft and gave me hope. Patricia Farr brought her editorial skills and knowledge of an editing program that trimmed the flab rather painlessly. Their questions made me acutely aware that the work needed more background information to become intelligible to nonspecialists and the larger audience I want to reach beyond the academy. Margaret Case's impeccable copyediting cleared the fog and bestowed clarity.

I was fortunate to have been invited to talk about parts of this work at several institutions and participate in seminars, colloquia, and conference panels, where particular chapters of the book were shaped and reshaped during the resultant interaction. Audiences at Brown University, Bryn Mawr College, University of California at Berkeley, University of Chicago, Columbia University, Cornell University, Dartmouth College, Delhi School of Economics, Harvard University, Hunter College, London University, Middlebury College, University of Minnesota, Oberlin College, Princeton University, Rutgers University, Sarah Lawrence College, Syracuse University, University of Texas at Austin, University of Wisconsin, University of Vermont, University of Virginia, and Wellesley College provided thoughtful questions that I hope are now answered.

Blair Kling and Douglas Haynes offered encouragement and expertise to sharpen my arguments. David Gilmartin read the first five chapters, and Bina Agarwal read the chapters on property rights and customary law, and offered thought-provoking critiques, much of which I have incorporated into the work. Una Chaudhuri and Rebecca Brown brought their keen literary sensibilities to the questions of autobiography and ethnography, respectively, in perusing the final chapter. Lloyd and Susanne Rudolph, Michael Fisher, and Paula Richman provided references and occasions for stimulating discussions. Dedi Felman of Oxford University Press in New York orchestrated the constructive review of this work by six—repeat six—anonymous readers from different disciplines that helped me to tighten and reorganize parts of this work. And to Doranne Jacobson, who has so sensitively photographed Indian women in all their diversity, I owe the cover picture of a north Indian woman humorously "veiling and peeking." This photographic double entendre suggested to me the quintessence of power and powerlessness in the condition of women that I explore.

And finally I have undying gratitude for those whose love and influence have always been there for me when real life intervened and spoiled my tidy plans to get this book over with. Pradip Krishen, Arundhati Roy, and Golak Khanduwal, with their unmatched friendship, hilarity, and hospitality, helped to salvage a parallel project that seriously hampered work on this manuscript: an unfinished brick and mortar hulk that took nearly four years to shape into a magical home in Gurgaon. My friends Susan Hambleton, Mary Bayes Ryan, Anita Shourie, Robin Tost, and Sandra Turner provided timely diversions and picturesque retreats, and eased the pain when I felt it acutely. It is futile, Arundhati reminds me, to calculate the "debit-credit" of friendship or to attempt "repayment." Virilocality-shirilocality; my father always knew where I belonged, and his untimely death robbed me of my chance to tell him one last story. My mother's quiet strength and unwitting feminism stirs me, as does the example of my three beloved but very dissimilar kinswomen, Chhoti Chachiji, Lakshmi, and Gitu, in ways that I cannot explain. I wish my three favorite uncles, Yogi, Minoo, and Babri, were still around to offer their mordant comments. And Philip, whose love has never flinched, might think this is getting too maudlin.

New York, 2001

CONTENTS

DOWRY MURDER

Seldom has there been so firm a consensus on a social issue in India as the one among scholars, journalists, feminists, politicians, legislators, and the police today that the custom of dowry has a causal relationship to prejudice and violence against women. The view that the murders of young wives are a special category of "cultural crime" linked to a high-caste Hindu cultural practice of dowry is unshakably entrenched. Women's organizations have designated the burning of wives baldly as "dowry murder." Although it is true that dowry — clothes, jewelry, household goods, cash, and property that a bride brings to a marriage — is neither new nor unique to India, just as violence against women is not an Indian cultural peculiarity, the view that dowry is a harmful, even dangerous institution has more credence in India than elsewhere.[1] Today the dowry system is also seen as the prime, if not the sole, explanation for two other practices akin to female infanticide that are increasingly prevalent in the subcontinent: the fatal neglect of female infants, and the selective abortion of female fetuses, made possible by the abuse of recent advances in fetal diagnostic technology.

The impugning of dowry as the causal force behind gendered crimes has its roots in the collusion of the imperial state and Punjabi men who reconfigured patriarchal values and manly ideals ever more strongly in nineteenth-century Punjab. The two became meshed in an unsurprising alliance against the customary rights of women, even though the avowed purpose of social reform legislation in this period was to uplift the status of women in Indian society. We must look beyond the statute book to comprehend a central paradox of colonial policy in India that persists in postcolonial India: although the legislative record is indeed impressive, and includes the outlawing of several customs that underscored the bias against women, there was in the colonial period a profound loss of women's economic power and social worth.[2] This was a direct consequence of the radical creation of property rights in land.

In precolonial India, dowry was not a "problem" but a support for women: a mark of their social status and a safety net. I demonstrate that dowry and associated wedding expenses neither caused the impoverishment of the Punjab peasant, which is what early colonial administrators claimed, nor were they the cause of the increase in violence against women, whether in the form of female infanticide or today's "bride burning." Rather, imperial policies created a more "masculine" economy and deepened the preference for sons that fostered the overt or hidden murder of girls. The establishment of property rights for peasants, inflexible tax demands and collection regimens, and a host of other imperial measures prepared the ground for worsening gender inequality which, in turn, increased the vulnerability of women to violence in both their natal and marital homes. The protective legislation passed for the benefit of women was aimed at protecting them from the presumed ill effects of their own cultural practices; it did little with respect to the ravages of new economic policies.

The scene of my investigation is the Punjab, in the northwestern part of the subcontinent, a varied and often partitioned space but representative of northern Indian marriage patterns and of an unabashed preference for sons. Delhi (historically part of the Punjab) became the obvious choice for the city I would concentrate on for the contemporary part of this project, for two reasons. The community most frequently implicated in these deaths consists of lower-middle-class and high-caste Punjabi Hindus and Sikhs, whose number in the capital swelled as they poured in as refugees after the partition of the Punjab in 1947. Second, the media, legal activists, and women's organizations are keenly at work there, and this affords convenient access to both historical and contemporary records.

My investigation of violence against women began in the present, but I was rapidly drawn to study its historical roots, and thereafter past voices and past policies intertwined with contemporary ones. I begin here with a preview of the arguments that emerged from on this long and convoluted journey.

INVESTIGATING THE CRIME

The daily news of "bride burnings" in Delhi beckoned me urgently. I was directed to Saheli, a women's resource center, where I spent the next ten months, gleaning from files and interviews with victims the fine-grained reality of violence against women, including their narrow escapes from death. Information gathered from reading newspaper reports, going to meetings, and antidowry protests, and interviewing potentially endangered women and the relatives of those who had died in the corridors of hospitals did not really explain *why* dowry had become such a scourge. And I did not trust the activists' obsession with dowry. I found the then-existing analyses of contemporary dowry murders ahistorical and counter-intuitive, and the scholarly treatments of female infanticide unsatisfactory. There was enough to suggest that the custom of dowry had been corrupted, but there was little to explain why or when. The "dowry problem" had indeed a deep but forgotten history that had to be disinterred from the volumes of imperial records in London, Delhi, and Patiala.

The explanations from archival and contemporary sources on dowry offered glaring contradictions. The colonial finger pointed at Hindu culture, whereas present-day Indian activists and media blamed Westernization, which increased materialism, greed, and a desire for consumer goods, and commercialized human relationships. Here was the puzzle. Was this violence against women related to the ancient custom of dowry, or was it a product of acculturation to Western and modern culture? In Europe, where dowries have all but disappeared, violence against women is still rampant. Modern industrial capitalism eroded the culture of dowry in the West, but did economic distortions peculiar to the colonial setting change it for the worse in India?[3]

In digging for the roots of the "dowry problem" to determine whether it had ever been associated with violence before 1980, I began to skim through annual compilations of administrative reports in the Punjab to see if, perhaps, a hundred years ago the custom of dowry had better press. And there it was, as a cause of the murder of females. But instead of the murder of brides, it was categorically indicted as the cause of female infanticide. The British had uncovered female infanticide in the Punjab 1851, a rampant crime that, they adduced, was directly related to the expense of wedding celebrations and dowry payments. Dowries, they reported, had impoverished Punjabi peasant families and brought them to the brink of ruin because they became heavily indebted in trying to marry off their daughters in the style demanded by upper-caste Hindu culture. It was logical, then, that the fear of future expenditure motivated peasants to kill their newborn daughters, and the imperial government, as the agent of a higher civilization, would make every effort to reform what they deemed to be culturally inbred habits engendered in a rude and ignorant people they had just conquered. Darkly, the same reports hinted at the true concern of the British: these same peasants who committed female infanticide were also defaulters on revenue payments and their lands were, therefore, up for auction by the government or foreclosure by local moneylenders. Infanticide was seen as what we might call preemptive dowry murder, with unmistakable cultural fingerprints at the site of the crime.[4] Given these allegations, could any historical investigation of "dowry murder" be complete without looking at female infanticide, particularly in the colonial period? It became a logical necessity to include female infanticide in the ambit of this project.

But as I studied female infanticide, the popular antidowry explanation I had thought I would deepen and endorse began to unravel. There was, indeed, abundant colonial documentation of female infanticide among high-caste Punjabi Hindus, but statistics on sex ratios in the subcontinent pointed to a serious anomaly in the logic that underpinned the colonial verdict on the dowry system, and made the British figures suspect. A startling contradiction emerged: several families from Hindu lower castes and Sikhs who received bride-price, and Muslims who did not follow the practice of dowry, were all found guilty of committing female infanticide. This made it more than a little awkward to insist on the "Hindoo" nature of the practice, and either extravagant dowries or upper-caste "pride" (as alleged in the case of the Rajputs, the powerful landowning and ruling castes in north India) as a cultural justification for so heinous a crime. Why would colonial bureaucrats stick so adamantly to the view that the culture of Hindu caste, rather than any other rationale, explained the undeniably widespread practice of killing female infants? So I began to investigate the beginning of British rule in the Punjab, and the trail led to the transformation of rights in property, particularly land. Fortunately for the historian, officialdom was not harmoniously one on this subject. The dominant discourse against culturally induced peasant "improvidence" (in extravagant weddings and dowries) was sharply rebutted by those who more honestly saw the havoc their own policies were visiting on peasant households.

In investigating dowry-related crimes on two temporal fronts I discovered a curious symmetry in the evidence spanning the past century and a half. I needed to look at the past to flesh out the overwhelming belief (which I share) that something somewhere had gone terribly wrong with the meaning and function of dowry, to the point when activist women would urge and achieve a legal ban of the practice in 1961. For the killing of brides I needed to recover the history of this corruption that would illumine the egregious present. But the converse was true with female infanticide, where present-day sex ratios and the increasing use of new diagnostic technology to determine the sex of the fetus prior to the decision to abort illumined the age-old desire for families to have more sons in a historically war-torn region. This need for a family with many more boys than girls was greatly intensified in the colonial period. The uninterrupted use of old and new methods of reducing the number of girl children in a family are reflected in the worst female-to-male sex ratios in the world today in the space that constituted the colonial Punjab. Only such a time span enables a conjoint exploration of the past and the present, and an attempt to understand the pattern of continuities and disjunctions in colonial and postcolonial periods in turn promises to lead to a more informed perspective on one of the most troubling social issues in the history of the subcontinent. Perhaps it will also point to where future legislation must be directed.

Juxtaposing archival and activist stints in my years in Delhi in 1985–1986 and 1991–1992, and the summers of all the years in between, allowed me to treat holistically what appeared as disparate problems in disparate eras. The tragic responses shaped in the past when the colonial state and educated natives colluded in matters of social reform were being replayed as farce in modern Delhi. To suppress the murder of female infants, the colonial government passed a law in 1870, and a few years later tried to restrict the value of dowries and curb wedding expenses by assembling all the important upper-caste Hindu chiefs from the forty-odd districts of the Punjab to have them pledge an end to their "improvidence" and thriftless ways. Yet the female sex ratios in India continued to decline, which leads to the questions of whether the government campaign was successful in reducing the cost of daughters' marriages—and, if it was, if there was, in fact, no causal relationship between dowries and female infanticide.

More than a century later, Indian news media, particularly the leading feminist journal *Manushi,* waged a vigorous campaign against dowry to prevent the murder of women in their marital homes. Activists working for women's causes demanded that the Prohibition of Dowry Act of 1961 be amended "to give it teeth." This push found passionate advocates among the Delhi intelligentsia. The most committed voice for this and other deep legal reforms has been the feminist lawyer and activist Lotika Sarkar. She profiled the average victim of a dowry death: "Such a person is always a woman . . . mostly in her twenties. She is a married woman [who has] already become a mother or is about to become a mother. . . . The woman is extremely unhappy by reason of demand for dowry. *She has no other reason or cause for unhappiness, except that resulting from, or connected with, the demand for dowry.* The demands are persistent, determined and oppressive" (Sarkar 1983: 2; emphasis added). The goal was duly accomplished in 1985, but neither dowry nor the violence blamed on it diminished, and the latter appeared steadily to rise. This raises the question of whether the unhappiness and the violence were, in fact, caused primarily by the dowry demands. In truth, the ban on dowries has had little meaning for the vast majority of the people for whom the custom has never caused serious friction, let alone provided the instigation to murder women either as infants or as brides. Yet the Delhi police proudly created a special "cell" to deal with "dowry deaths" in the late 1970s, as a model to be emulated in police departments in other major cities, and it was not until 1986 that the cell expanded its purview to deal with all violent crimes against women.

As I explored the etiology of dowry death and an increasingly masculine society (as measured by sex ratio), and continued to work with and listen to the women of Saheli, the experience of my own earlier marriage insistently came to the surface. It added one more case to the histories of women in the nineteenth and twentieth centuries that I was disentangling, but more important, it sharpened my vision and deepened my understanding.

PRESENTING THE CASE

This problem was initially literally my own, and I began this investigation in the present, working my way back in history to the mid-nineteenth century. My argument unfolds, however, more conventionally, in chronological order, with forward flashes from time to time.

I begin by discussing the scholarly and empirical meanings of "dowry" in chapter 1. Dowry, or *dahej* as it is called in Hindi and *daaj* in Punjabi, became the foundation on which explanations for the discrimination against women have been conveniently built because it has had the conceptual richness to satisfy a variety of analytical tastes since the mid-nineteenth century. British colonialists stressed its cultural roots in a benighted Hinduism with its rigid caste system; Marxists see it as a retrograde economic institution; and feminists see gender discrimination in it because women are given dowries but not a share in family property. A few scholars in the late 1980s and 1990s shifted from blaming dowry to looking for other causes for the violence against women in the sociocultural milieu in northern India. A rigorous historical treatment of dowry's relationship to the violence against women has not, however, been attempted before.[5]

The pervasive denunciation of dowry since the mid-1800s also underpins a host of corollaries that have blurred the thinking on the triangular relationship among marriage, gender, and property, which needs to be explored historically. It also pushes to the fore other, perhaps bigger, questions. Did imperial policies often create or aggravate the very problems they sought to ameliorate? For instance, were a host of new "social evils," such as accelerating chronic indebtedness and increasing drunkenness—and therefore domestic violence—in the Punjabi countryside the unwitting consequence of political economy of the new regime rather than of Hindu or Muslim cultural dictates?[6] And finally, what influence did the colonial enterprise of codifying custom into textual law and its implementation in the new courts in the Punjab have on various existing practices, particularly on the rights of women and the notions of *dahej* (dowry) and *stridhan* (women's wealth)?

The changes in the practice of dowry are uneven and ongoing, coexist in time and space, and can be best seen on a continuum rather than as sharply drawn opposites of "traditional" and "modern" dowry. Premodern dowry, I contend, was consonant with the premodern notions of rights in land. The modern notion of property that underlies the present-day pathology of dowry owes its origin to the exclusion of women from property rights in land as fashioned by the British. The social expectation that customs related to women would remain unchanged even as men's rights in property were transformed is naïve.

Dowry needs dynamic reformulation, defined neither as the timeless *stridhan* or women's wealth, as described in the third-century *Dharmashastra*, nor as the lethal custom that allegedly provokes the murders of several thousand young women annually. I therefore avoid defining dowry. Instead, I track the course of its changing perceptions and functions over time. In tracking these changes, the Punjab and northern India in general offer a dramatic contrast to parallel-cross-cousin marriages among many communities in the south, where women remain in close proximity and touch with their natal families. Both share the custom of dowry, but the south seems to be less prone to the pathological strain of the north, where the custom of virilocal marriages (that is, the bride leaves her own home to live in the household of her husband) cuts across caste and class lines. Demands for dowry affect only a small percentage of families even in northern India, but the murder even of a minuscule fraction of the number of married women makes the problem a crucial one to investigate.

A careful rereading of historical sources and a great many interviews with women who were connected with the present-day "dowry problem" led me to conclude that dowry could be called one of the few indigenous, woman-centered institutions in an overwhelmingly patriarchal and agrarian society. I would have used the word *feminist* to describe the institution of dowry, but in India the term is resolutely rejected in some quarters as a Western idea, so I avoid its use except in reference to some individuals who would describe themselves as feminists, including myself. The word *patriarchy*, however, is widely used by activists and scholars alike. In this study I use it as shorthand, for want of a better term, for families in which a preference for sons is marked, marriage is invariably virilocal, and property is inherited by sons or agnates (among the male kin in joint households, and from fathers to sons in nuclear households). I also examine dowry in contradistinction to bride-price, which allows us to sort out the bedeviled area of high- and low-caste cultures.

Gender lines in Punjabi society and by extension elsewhere in north India, I aver, do not create a neat binary of male and female power. The relationships of gender and power are complicated by factors such as kinship and age. For instance, a mother is more powerful than her sons and commands their obedience and loyalty; an older daughter or sister has the authority to participate in important decisions; and a wife accumulates power as she takes charge of the household and becomes a mother to the next generation. The fiercest competition for power is between the mother-in-law and her daughters-in-law, or among sisters-in-law, making gender solidarity within a multigenerational extended family difficult for women. The competition between brothers over property or other matters sunders the men in the family, too, and alliances are seldom found to run along gender lines. It is almost too facile to think that women qua women, not unlike workers of the world, can unite and eliminate the struggle for power and property.

In such a situation, dowry is an important asset for women. In the late nineteenth and early twentieth centuries, and even today, it is their economic safety net in a setting where women always marry outside their natal villages and where their rights in their natal home lapse when they leave for their marital homes. Dowry is a material resource over which a woman has had at least partial control, and her natal family has viewed it as providing her not only with goods for her use and pleasure but also with recourse in an emergency. In the absence of demands from the groom's family, a bride's dowry is reckoned as purely voluntary and comfortably within the means of her family; it serves as an index of the appreciation bestowed upon a daughter in her natal village, and the ostensible measure of her status in her conjugal village.

These parameters of the custom of dowry emerge with great clarity in the interviews conducted in Punjab villages in the 1870s to codify customary law, which are explored in chapter 5. None of the reports describes dowry as gifts demanded by the groom's family. Instead, those interviewed described it as a collection of voluntary gifts of clothes, jewelry, household goods, and cash bestowed on the bride by family and friends at the time of the wedding. In forty-nine separate volumes of customary law in an equal number of districts in the vast territory that constituted colonial Punjab—present-day Pakistan and Indian Punjab, Haryana, Jammu, Delhi, and Himachal Pradesh—this definition of dowry was reiterated. Nowhere was it treated as the prerogative of the groom and his family to demand specific consumer goods and large sums of cash for the groom's business, education, or mobility; it was voluntary and depended on the "pecuniary circumstances of the bride's parents." It also turns out that the charge of "improvidence" was not based on the expense for dowry—on what is given to the daughter—but on wedding feast and entertainment expenses for both daughters and sons. These costs were strictly itemized and evaluated in cash for three economic tiers in society and became part of the bureaucrats' handbook for enforcement. Wedding expenses did not mean only those for a daughter; many cases cited as evidence of profligacy in the handbooks refer to the weddings of sons.

Items for each daughter's dowry were, and to a lesser extent still are, accumulated gradually, not just by her immediate family but also by extended kin and friends in a village or urban neighborhood, those who share in an intricate network of reciprocal obligations.[7] Very few items were purchased; most of them were produced at home or received as part of the customary reciprocity prevalent among village families. Clothes, household furnishings, and jewelry were productive assets in terms of status (and jewelry served as collateral for loans); and cows, buffaloes, goats, and even camels, often more valuable than land, were given to daughters as income-generating assets. Cash and property began to play an increasing role in the composition of dowries as land became a marketable commodity in the colonial period and its value rose exponentially. The practical concern of families was to insure for each of their daughters a husband from a comparable family in which her life would be lived and her children would be raised; if there was unforeseen misfortune, the dowry would serve as a safety net. Why then was a strongly spun safety net twisted into a deadly noose?

FEMALE INFANTICIDE

A new historical understanding of the issue emerges when it is seen that as the East India Company "discovered" female infanticide they used this knowledge to further their own political ends by attributing purely traditional cultural reasons for the commission of this crime, which, in fact, had social and economic causes exacerbated by their own policies. The politics of imperial representation are far better understood today than previously, and female infanticide is a superb example to illuminate their workings.

The East India Company, originally chartered in 1600 only to trade, tasted the riches of the subcontinent by wresting the collection of revenue in the conquered province of Bengal from 1765. A century of aggressive empire building culminated in the conquest of the Punjab in 1849 and the annexation of Oudh in 1856. The company needed to make a compelling case to defend its ruthless actions to an increasingly critical Parliament and outraged public in Britain, even as it illegally assumed the substance and power of an imperial state. The development of explanations that described and blamed indigenous culture for some of its own miscalculations or the effects of misrule and greed, and justified its territorial expansion into two-thirds of the subcontinent, was perhaps the most widely deployed stratagem of the company to appease its jealous detractors at home. This stratagem is better known as Britain's "civilizing mission," with Hindu culture as its prime target. It might more aptly be called the state's alibi for its own unjust policies. For sound political reasons, imperial bureaucrats in mid-nineteenth-century Punjab reiterated the alleged causal connection between the expense of marrying a daughter and female infanticide that they had made in Bombay Presidency in the late eighteenth century. Replaying the cultural card, which had acquired a rich patina of moral superiority by the time the British conquered the Punjab in 1849, trumped most anti-imperial compunctions in Victorian England. Chapter 2 untangles the intricacies of the campaign against female infanticide and reconstructs the existential logic behind the practice.

The British used the prevalence of dowry as a litmus test for female infanticide; the corollary to this logic was that bride-price receivers must be innocent of the crime. This meant that the crime was noted and condemned only selectively. In 1851, for example, the Sikh Bedis were found guilty of female infanticide. This discovery became political capital for the British, who could retroactively justify the two unsanctioned bloody wars with the Sikhs that had led to the annexation of their rich and fertile kingdom only two years before. In their own estimation, the righteousness of their aggression was further underscored by the fact that Guru Nanak, the founder of the Sikh faith in the fifteenth century, was of the Bedi caste. In the same year, however, and in the course of the same investigation, the British judiciously overlooked the female infanticide prevalent among the Jats (a numerically preponderant agricultural caste that included Sikhs, Hindus, and Muslims), who were the favorite recruits of the British Indian Army and were in fact appreciated by the British for their strong physiques and martial qualities. Their exoneration hinged on a single, simple fact: Jats did not give dowries. On the contrary, they received bride-price for their daughters from the grooms' families. Their daughters worked in the fields, unlike Kshatriya and Brahmin daughters, and so must have been valued, and therefore they could not possibly be eliminated at birth.

The British also indicted dowry and wedding expenses as the main element of the "improvidence" that they claimed was at the root of the undeniable impoverishment of the Indian peasantry in the three decades after 1858, when the East India Company was dissolved and the Crown began its direct rule of India. As mortality from famines grew, the queries became more insistent; imperial officers generated questionnaires and reports to explain the horrifying immiseration of the victims as self-induced. It was simpler to exaggerate and condemn "wasteful" social expenditure—occasional feasts and gift giving, chiefly connected with wedding celebrations and dowry—than to acknowledge that governance by the British had created want among small landowners. Chapter 3 presents the evidence for this.

Chapter 3 also explores the reasons that, despite sumptuary regulations passed in 1853, the upward spiral in the costs of marriage in the colonial period continued. I argue that small quantitative changes added up to a big qualitative change. The British reduction or outright abolition of the customary subsidies given to village heads by Hindu, Mughal, and Sikh rulers for the maintenance of the village *chaupal* or guest house, oil lamps, the upkeep of shrines, and payment to itinerant musicians made hospitality offered during weddings more costly for individual families. The inflation that accompanied the steady rise in the price of land stood on their head the old equations of (movable) dowry for the daughters as against (immovable) property, based on virilocality, for the sons. And the increased circulation of cash and an ever-broadening range of consumer goods, chiefly British imports, generated a clamor for these items to be included in dowries.

CREATING PROPERTY TITLES, ERASING ENTITLEMENTS

The transformation of the basic relationship between peasants and their land and the simultaneous codification of customary law caused much of the infamous indebtedness of the Punjab peasant. These two intertwined events, which were inexorably in place by the 1860s, are dealt with in chapters 4 and 5, respectively. They became central in altering the texture of women's lives, their implicit rights and entitlements in their families as daughters, wives, and widows, by making men the sole proprietors. This in turn transformed the notions of women's wealth, property rights, and dowry. The new notion of peasant proprietorship produced new perceptions of gendered rights in land, and these were recorded as "customary." Colonial investment in the Punjab in the second half of the nineteenth century, while accomplished at no cost to the British, greatly expanded arable land and agricultural production. By clearing forests and building canals, communications, and railway lines in this fertile grain-producing region, the colonial authorities linked it to a thriving international market. The British extracted wealth from the countryside in the form of heavy taxation and exports of wheat and other raw materials to Europe, but did not consider sharing their own industrial development with a people who were forcibly contributing to Britain's prosperity.

This modernizing effort remained incomplete and inept because of a greater sin of omission: the deliberate suppressing of any indigenous efforts to import modern industry. An honest-intentioned state might have created general prosperity in their empire to match their own, instead of vast pockets of landlessness and unprecedented poverty in the various subregions of the Punjab. A million and a half Punjabis perished in the famine of 1876–1877, even when Punjab did not have the severity of food shortages experienced in Madras. The conflicting interests of modern capitalism and a colonial command economy produced a half-baked, deleterious version of capitalism for subsistence farmers and generated enormous social distortions that worked to the detriment of the interests of women. The new political economy with its ambivalent and hobbled capitalism created a deeper imbalance in power relations in the household. The evidence for this is carefully evaluated in chapter 4, and although no conspiracy is implied here, it emerges that the acute self-interest and racially inflected callousness that increasingly marked the imperial policies caused untold harm to the society that sustained its onslaught.

My own investigations and conclusions will make better sense if I clarify the politics of three key terms and their interrelationship on which my arguments rest: culture, imperialism (or colonialism, often used interchangeably to refer to British rule in India), and private property. The first is complicated because imperial officers used the word "culture" with deliberate political intent to create the linked pair of civilized ruler and barbaric Indian subject. In addition, there is the difficulty with what Richard Fox aptly calls "organismic conceptions of culture" (Fox 1985: 10), which render culture as static or structurally unchanging. Fox proposes that culture be viewed as a more historical and dynamic process. What is often taken as a consistent and long-lived cultural pattern, a coherent set of cultural meanings, he explains, is only the momentary and localized product of human action and contest—culture always "is," but it has always just become so. The British, for their part, had a paradoxical view of culture—they continually talked of timeless Hindu or Muslim culture, even though they believed that inferior cultures could evolve into higher ones. In their fascination with the structure of Punjabi castes and tribes, the British airbrushed historical contingency and human agency out of their voluminous descriptions of Punjabi society. Hindu culture—in contradistinction sometimes to Muslim culture but mostly to their own—was judged to be indubitably inferior. It was capricious, cruel, and barbaric, fostering criminal and amoral behavior. Thus cultural or religious motives were imputed for the crime of female infanticide. My purpose is to write the history of the political uses of "culture" in this respect.

Historians of the British Raj are well aware that colonialism (or imperialism) was a continually contested and negotiated set of power relations over time and space. In other words, it would be equally misguided to think of the 250-odd years of British rule in India as an unchanging structure uniformly imposed on the colonized as to construe Hindu culture or tradition as a timeless, frozen entity. Both continually changed in the process of interaction and acculturation.

But most significantly, to understand the changing meanings of dowry and the processes that underwrote the change, it is imperative to comprehend the centerpiece of this triptych—property—also as a *dynamic* category and to understand how rights in land were differently constituted in precolonial and colonial times. This profound change, glossed only briefly in studies of women's right to property, is a key element in my analysis of Punjabi women's relationship to land. In the colonial period, their historical customary entitlements to the produce of the land were translated into a lack of titular rights in ownership of the land. To go beyond what agrarian histories of the Punjab have already done (Ali 1988, Barrier 1966, Chowdhry 1989, Fox 1985, Kessinger 1974, Smith 1996, et al.), I have explored the brunt of the new colonial revenue policies and command economy on the dynamics of power within peasant families. With the creation of male individual property rights in land, the British decided to create the individual peasant owner as the centerpiece of their modern revenue policy. What was to be called the *ryotwari* settlement involved giving property titles to the land directly to the peasants (*ryots*) who tilled it. The policy might well have worked as well as its predecessors had the British not clung to two of its components: fixed amounts and inelastic dates for the payment of land revenue, with little room for contingency. These fixities, along with the newly created ability of peasant proprietors, especially those with smallholdings, to alienate their land through mortgage or sale, increased their vulnerability enormously; the government's unrelenting demand for revenue even in a bad year often led to forced alienation.

These new circumstances altered the generally symbiotic relationship between borrower and lender, perhaps even bringing out an unconscionable opportunism in the latter. In precolonial times moneylenders had advanced small loans; the object was never to let a debt be paid off entirely, in order to keep the debtor as a permanent client. The new breed of moneylenders, with an appetite for appropriating their debtors' land—the kind of villain who chills our blood as we encounter him in numerous Indian films and fiction—emerged as a scourge of the countryside in these changed circumstances. The critical difference was that land was now a commodity that could be alienated from the original proprietor and auctioned off by the government to recover their arrears of revenue. With his land as collateral and with the value of land rising, the peasant was able to borrow far more than ever before, up to 70 percent of the value of his land; the moneylender was equally eager to lend him far more than he formerly would have, in order to foreclose on the land. The peasant was forced to borrow in a bad year or a year when the harvest was late, chiefly to pay his taxes on time (rather than for riotous wedding parties or opulent dowries), because the dates and amounts had been clearly stipulated and there was little hope for mercy. Chronic indebtedness became the other side of the coin of prosperity for the vast majority of these small peasant proprietors.

Ironically, the price of land went up in this same period, as monetization of the economy proceeded apace with the building of canals, roads, railways, and market facilities, and as grain prices increased as exports rose. Apart from the colonial government, the grain merchant and the moneylender—not the peasant—benefited most directly from this. The merchants and moneylenders had no need to sustain the traditional symbiotic relationship with their peasant debtors; they now foreclosed on the mortgaged property as quickly as possible and hired the dispossessed proprietor as an ill-paid, wage-earning day laborer. The corollary to this was that indebtedness generated pressure to deploy women's resources—jewelry or cash—to rescue or enhance a family's holdings within the first score years of the *ryotwari* settlement, when approximately 40 percent of the traditional peasantry lost their lands.

Putting landed property in male hands exclusively, and holding the males responsible for payment of revenue had the effect of creating the Indian male as the dominant legal subject; this happened throughout British India and even in the independent princely states. The effects could be disastrous in the lives of women. When marital conflicts, a husband's violence, or drunkenness destroyed their marriages, the women were left landless with no legal entitlement to the land their husband or father-in-law owned. Meanwhile, their dowry might well have been spent on the husband's family's holdings. This created the very problem that has engaged feminist scholarship and activism from the late nineteenth century onward: the fight for women's rights to property.

The "masculinization" of the economy was one factor that made male children ever more desirable. In addition, the effects of recruiting the British Indian Army heavily from the ranks of Punjabi peasants, particularly the land-tilling Jats, generated a demand for strong young men who would be employed with a cash wage, awards of land, and eventually pensions. To achieve a "gender-targeted family" became vital, and in those medically primitive days it could only be done through selective female infanticide (DasGupta 1987). In chapter 4 I reevaluate the influence of these and other fundamental shifts in the relationship of the peasant to the land itself, and in the relationship of power and gender.

In telling this story, I rely on evidence in the critiques made by imperial civil servants of their own policies. These reports do not dabble in the cultural compunctions of Hindus and Muslims but quantify the distress experienced by hard-working peasants. They do this not out of sympathy for the peasants but to warn the government against sedition brewing in economically pressured regions. A serious evaluation of these blunt exposes of the new revenue policies is warranted. The epidemic of peasant indebtedness, they demonstrate, was generated by the inflexibilities in the revenue-paying arrangements enforced by the British rather than on "improvidence" and customary expenditure incurred for weddings by certain "thriftless tribes." That some of these reports had to be suppressed or their conclusions buried in larger overviews makes them all the more valid.

Credible testimony emerges from these discordant voices, particularly those of S. S. Thorburn, Malcolm Darling, and F. L. Brayne; their unassailable loyalty to British rule meant that their disagreement with revenue policies stemmed from their anxiety that such policies would provoke another widespread revolt against imperial rule. These powerful internal indictments begin to emerge in the last quarter of the nineteenth century and are the unexamined evidence that convincingly undercuts the coherence of imperial position on the question of cultural crimes and social evils.

It is a consistently reasoned strategy in this study to read some British reports against the grain and some as revelatory, for this was the complicated nature of the vast and variegated British colonial rule in India. The net result was that the one clear historical interpretation about the economically ruinous nature of the custom of dowry and its relationship to peasant indebtedness dissolved into a murky half-truth. Dowry in its menacing form, as we know it in some quarters today, was patently the artifact not of an organically unchangeable and permanently constituted Hindu or Sikh culture but a responsive and dynamic institution that adapted to changes in the new economic climate. It is this process of change —sporadic, uneven, and regrettably irreversible—that I endeavored to reconstruct from the very documents that purport to show its timeless and ruinous influence in peasant households.

THE PREFERENCE FOR SONS

The key to understanding the prejudice against women is to focus on reasons for the preference for sons. These are detailed in chapter 5.

Sons were the key to survival and prosperity in the relentlessly agrarian Punjab under the British. Acquiring land during auctions or sales, finding a jobs in the lower rungs of the imperial bureaucracy or the army, or finding a niche as a retailer in the expanding market were the new plums to fight over. The newly enhanced worth of sons with such prospects came to be reflected in the confidence of some families in demanding a consideration for a marriage alliance: specific amounts of cash (sometimes to recover the cost of the education that had qualified the groom for these jobs), jewelry, or expensive consumer durables. The competition for the best-qualified and best-employed grooms within an endogamous group was fierce—for there were but a tiny number of eligible males with proper employment or economic security—and mothers of daughters knew that a good dowry was now the net to secure "the catch." The idea that a groom's family could make demands slowly infiltrated other traditional gift-giving occasions reserved by parents for their married daughters and their children. This trend, which started in the colonial period, has steadily worsened, even occasioning violence: the suicides of prospective brides to save their parents from the expense and humiliation of such alliances, and the burning to death of wives whose dowries did not meet expectations. Such perverse transactions are unfairly perceived as "dowry problems"; it would be far more accurate to think of these shameless and amoral demands as "groom price." But they came to be countenanced in a world where the relationship of power and gender had been radically reordered.

The strategic and moral imperative for peasant and warrior families in precolonial times was not dictated by culture or religion but by the existential needs to reproduce the ideal family to defend their lands and their rulers, to subsist, to seek opportunities for advancement, and for economic security in old age through the labor of sons. Male children were critical to the prolonged well-being of the family; sons were future soldiers and farmers of the soil to which they belonged. Daughters also worked, but their crucial role as reproducers obliged them to marry at puberty and move to the village of their husbands, where they would "plan" their own families, again engineering the survival of fewer daughters than sons. Virilocal marriages cemented communities and far-flung villages in defensive political alliances. Both sexes were needed, but the struggle was to achieve the unnatural but logical mix of several more sons than daughters. Nature played an evenhanded role by holding "normal" birth ratios at 104 males to a 100 females, but endowing female infants with greater resilience against disease. Selective female infanticide then (and to a lesser extent now) was the only available method, albeit primitive and cruel, of achieving a *deliberately planned* family—with the numbers of sons and daughters appropriate for survival in a region plagued by continual political conflict. Philip Oldenburg (1992) finds an interesting correlation between the overall murder rate and high masculine sex ratios in north India, which bolsters my own argument that the preference for sons in the Punjab was related to its being a war zone and a popular recruiting ground for soldiers. The defense of land, rather than its tilling, made the presence of a strong defenders critical to the survival of the community.

The precolonial logic for female infanticide was to be unwittingly strengthened by imperial revenue and land-ownership policies, even as the British outlawed the practice in 1870 and charged heavy fines and imprisonment as penalties against its perpetrators. Their remedial measures to curb infanticide focused on apprehending culprits (including the surveillance of "infanticidal tribes" at their own cost), passing sumptuary laws to restrict dowries and expenditure at weddings, and imposing penalties such as fines and imprisonment. The British never found it worthwhile to examine the social effects of their own methods of governance and development that produced the milieu in which sons became even more preferred and dowry gradually acquired the very characteristics that the British purported to reform. Despite the legislation against infanticide, colonial policies gradually worsened the already adverse sex ratios over this past century.

PRESENT-DAY DOWRY DEATH

With the historical ground carefully prepared, it is possible, in chapter 6, to return to the contemporary problem that first drew me to write this book. In the years that I was trying to make sense of the historical material, scores of books have been published about dowry death, domestic violence, and the new women's movement. If I had been tongue-tied in 1985, not knowing what to say, I now feel that too much is now known and has been said about dowry murder. My historical research would undoubtedly add a missing dimension in most of these studies, but what could I possibly add to the accounts of the present?

What I have done is to knit together the conversations of the past, between colonial officials and their informants, with the conversations that I had with women: I connect the construction of colonial interpretations with the current discourse on dowry and dowry deaths. In the process I hope to displace this discourse with a feminist narrative and a feminist voice, to both view and comment on the dynamic nature of dowry and property, and their relationship to domesticated, gendered violence in a rural-urban continuum in the last century and a half. Through the use of conversations, memory, an analysis of my own experience as an nineteen-year-old bride who narrowly escaped the lethal consequences of a terrible marriage, and the stories collected in a women's resource center for ten months, I interrogate the role of dowry and dowry laws in the lives of women who sought help for dowry problems. I wish to have the reader discover the history and meaning of present-day violence against women without compromising the complexity of such meaning—and, more important, to conclude, along with the evidence I present from the stories of women, that their narratives and their actions are shaped by the legal imperatives that the ban on dowry has produced for those trapped in untenable marital relations. This last is, perhaps, a conclusion that is startling and deserves to be underscored. Yet in a way it is a conclusion that is also foregone, for the entire thrust of this study has been to demonstrate that "cultural crimes" were a legislated, imperial artifact. Violence against women is universal, and perhaps timeless, but much can be done to reduce its frequency and severity by reorienting the legal universe to address economic and social inequities founded on sex and gender, and let culture adjust to the new realities. The modern secular democratic Indian state, though worlds apart from its imperial forbear, is slowly acknowledging its duty to balance the ledger where women have always been in the debit column.

1

Conundrums and Contexts

What [was given] before the [nuptial] fire, what [was given] on the bridal procession, what was given in token of love, and what was received from her brother, mother or father, that is called the six-fold property of a woman.

[Such property], as well as a gift subsequent and what was given [to her] by her affectionate husband, shall go to her offspring [even] if she dies in the lifetime of her husband.
—*The Laws of Manu (c. 200 A.D.)*

After beating me senseless, my in-laws threw me out of the house for having argued with my husband who is a very *jealous* man. I dare not go back, I don't want to go back, but I want my dowry back. I have gold jewelry worth 40,000 of rupees, a sowing machine, utensils, furniture, a colour t.v. and 20,000 rupees in cash. I have found a job and I want to live independently without bothering my parents for long, but I must have my dowry back. Please get me help from a lawyer to get my dowry back; it is my right and I need my things desperately.
—*Statement made by a twenty-two-year-old Punjabi woman who came for help to Saheli, women's resource center, 10 December 1985. Emphasis added.*

Dowry is the wealth—money, goods or property—that a woman brings her husband at marriage.
—Indian Express, *New Delhi, 29 September 2000*

It is difficult to define contemporary dowry with the simplicity and clarity that Manu gave to the term *stridhan*, or the "sixfold property of a woman," almost two millennia ago; what he decreed has lingering echoes in the legal and moral worlds of colonial and contemporary India. *Stridhan* subsumed a woman's dowry— which he did not designate separately or name—and this aggregate term has been revived in legal discourse since the passage of the Hindu Code Bill in 1956.

It connotes much the same range of possessions as those mentioned by Manu, and increasingly surfaces in conversations in Delhi about women's right to property. Manu more notoriously did not believe in the sexual independence of women, as we know from his frequently cited words: "Her father protects [her] in childhood, her husband protects [her] in youth, and her sons protect [her] in old age; a woman is never fit for independence"(Muller [1886] 1964: 328). Yet in his eyes, a woman's right to own, control, and dispose of her own wealth, given to her by her family and her husband or his family, was unarguable. Her husband had neither control over nor the right to inherit this wealth if she predeceased him. This may appear to contradict Manu's own claim that "a woman is never fit for independence," but there is no confusion if we understand that Manu was referring to the sexual and not the economic control of women, though it has been misinterpreted by those who wish to prove that women are not permitted control over their own wealth.[1] Indeed, Manu could be seen as an influential lawgiver of his time who believed that women held wealth in their own right.

This is further affirmed in his little-known pandect describing in detail the unequal division of property among the sons of the deceased: the eldest son gets a somewhat larger and better share of animals, chattels, and so forth. It contains clear-cut instruction on what an unmarried sister's share of the estate is: "But to the maiden [sisters] the brothers shall severally give [portions] out of their shares, *each out of his share one-fourth part; those who refuse to give [it], will become outcasts*" (Muller [1886] 1964: 348; emphasis added). For a woman to continue to live unmarried on her father's estate was rare, however, since matrimony and virilocality were virtually compulsory. Muller notes that the authoritative commentator on the Dharmashastra, Meghatithi, "censures those commentators who think that one-fourth share need not be actually given, but only as much as will suffice to defray the marriage expenses" (ibid.: 349n). Thus a woman clearly had rights to a stipulated share of her father's estate if she remained unmarried. Nothing here is said of cattle or chattels, nor is a distinction made between movable and immovable types of property. The idea is that a woman who continued to dwell in her natal home would share with her brothers the inheritance of her father's estate. Clearly the tension between dowry and property is hoary, and suggests that brothers deemed it not only their sacred duty but also in their own material interest to see their sisters married off as early and quickly as possible. Marriage made woman the "movable" and man the "immovable" entity, and cattle and land and other resources were distributed according to this logic. Cattle often were by far the more valuable resource, and silver and gold ornaments might have often had greater value than mud huts and fields.

Much, of course, has happened to the notion of property (and entitlements) since the time of Manu and Meghatithi, and the most radical changes came in the colonial period. As large chunks of the subcontinent fell under the domination of the colonial government, a revolution in property rights transformed the social and economic world of the peasant. The introduction of the idea of land as a commodity and therefore entirely alienable, by sale or foreclosure, also gave men precise, titular ownership, at the cost of all subsidiary claims or entitlements that were traditionally ordained. The customary rights of women were the heaviest casualties of this transformation of a peasant economy into an unevenly modern and capitalistic one. Dowry, as a subset of *stridhan*, became vulnerable to the new market economy that abruptly replaced the old order of obligations and reciprocities among those who had shared the produce of the commonly controlled land. Indeed, the concept of a woman's right to property, even in its unequal and usufructuary way, seemed to have been entirely forfeited (and had to be fought for anew in the twentieth century), and dowry seemed to have become a matter for aggressive negotiation by the groom's family.

Since the late eighteenth century, when dowry was designated the causal factor of female infanticide, it has been consistently invoked as the single most compelling explanation of the widespread bias against women that is evidenced by adverse juvenile sex ratios and the strong preference for sons in the north and west of India. Dowry has also been redefined, I believe erroneously, in structural functional terms as compensation paid by the natal family to the conjugal family for a daughter who will not work in the fields. The meaning of dowry has shifted and darkened for women, and by 1961, well before we hear of dowry murders, dowry itself was prohibited by an act of parliament, allegedly to protect brides and their families from the greed and blackmail of the grooms' families. On 10 August 1983, the Law Commission of India published the *91st Report on Dowry Deaths and Law Reform: Amending the Hindu Marriage Act, 1955, the Indian Penal Code, 1860, and the Indian Evidence Act, 1872* (Sarkar 1983). The commission deemed it "desirable" that a "self-contained definition of 'dowry' . . . should be made applicable to all provisions that may come to be enacted as a result of our recommendations (wherever those provisions contain the word 'dowry'). We would recommend a definition somewhat in the following terms, for the purpose: 'Dowry' means money, or other thing estimable in terms of money, *demanded* from the wife or parents or other relatives, where such a demand is not properly referable to any legally recognized claim and is relatable only to the wife's having married into the husband's family."[2]

These many contested definitions—woman's right, gift, safety net, demand or payoff, and incentive to kill infants and brides—are all in play today, making dowry simultaneously "timeless" and historically changing, desirable and contemptible, and a scourge to abolish. However, before we reconstruct the narrative on this protean institution in the past century and a half in the Punjab (admittedly a space that has been politically divided and subdivided in this period), we have to consider the other form of marriage payment, namely *mul*, or bride-price. The cultural construction of dowry cannot be understood in isolation, particularly since the custom of dowry is infiltrating *mul*-paying communities, allegedly signaling a further spread of danger to women's lives.

It is widely believed that the *dahej* (or *daaj*, the Punjabi word for dowry) and *mul* systems represent opposite views on the value of women; that dowry (the system that allegedly devalues women) is rapidly replacing *mul* (the system that values women for their labor) in communities and regions that never knew it before, and that this in turn is leading to female infanticide and adverse sex ratios in these communities.[3] For more than two decades feminist scholars and activists have connected bride-price to women's worth in agricultural work. There is a concomitant belief that the practice is declining because women's representation in the workforce has seriously declined in many parts of India, making it possible for the practice of dowry to appear. I find these conclusions overly facile and the arguments presented partial and misleading. My own research in nineteenth-century records points to female infanticide having been widely practiced, and perhaps even more often, in communities that did not give dowries but accepted bride-price, as well as among Muslims. I will sketch an anachronistic backdrop by first briefly adumbrating the current (c. 1930–1990) meanings, definitions, and analyses of *daaj* and *mul*, in which the groom's family pays a negotiable price for his bride to her family.[4] It is imperative to appraise the two systems not only because marriage payments have been seen as the key to evaluating the "status of women" and gender violence but also because the widely distorted interpretations of these two systems as "mirror opposites" have, in my view, obscured the more complex construction of gender that underpins both systems.

The controversy over *mul* and *daaj* has also clouded the fact that the bride who is given a dowry also receives a *vari*, or a gift of clothes and jewels from the groom's parents, which frequently matches or exceeds what she receives as her dowry. This lesser-known counterpart of the *daaj* is difficult to explain unless it is acknowledged that the bride is instantly inducted as a productive member of her husband's family. She is the reproducer of its next generation and is therefore a pivotal member of the family, whose interests and status are now inseparable from her own, so it is only natural that the in-laws would bedeck their *nuh* or *bahu* (daughter-in-law) in clothes and ornaments that reflect their status. A wide circle of friends and relatives of the groom also contribute gifts to the *vari*, much as the bride's family, friends, and relations do for her *daaj*, and together these gifts constitute the woman's *stridhan*, over which she traditionally had complete control.[5] Oddly enough, *vari* is barely a footnote in anthropological studies that describe dowry, and certainly nothing can be learned about it from the newspaper accounts that report the escalation of *daaj*. It is true that this wealth does not cross over to the woman's family, nor does a bride make "*vari* demands" as her husband can make "dowry demands," but it certainly enhances the value of her personal *stridhan* and adds vastly to her status and leverage in the small world of the village.

This omission is puzzling enough, but even less comprehensible is the current view, especially prevalent among some Indian women scholars, that bride-price is a marker of the high evaluation of women in communities that practice it. The shift from bride-price to dowry payments, reported by ethnographers in all regions of India, is invariably regretted as a harmful condition for women. This idea—that bride-price–paying communities value their women more than dowry-paying ones—can be traced back to its antecedents in colonial reports that followed the discovery of infanticide in 1789 by British officers in the Banaras region. Their logic was simplistic (and antithetical to the logic of the status society they were dealing with): those parents who *receive* money for their daughters' weddings must value them more than those who have to *pay* dowries for their daughters for the same occasion. The reasoning was perpetuated by similar discoveries in the north and west of India as the East India Company's conquests and annexations brought the entire region under its sway. The Punjab, finally conquered in 1849, became an arena in which to eradicate the dowry system. The British held meetings with native chiefs, as we shall see, to make them agree to limit wasteful expenditure at weddings and on dowries, and the two appeared to have seen their partnership as the best means of destroying so entrenched a custom. By 1938 Altekar suggested that dowry, which had been "a voluntary gift of pure affection and presented no impediment in the settlement of a daughter's marriage" until the middle of the previous century, had for the past fifty years "begun to assume scandalous proportions," and it was now "high time to put an end to this evil custom" that had driven "many an innocent maiden to commit suicide." He feared that the custom "was becoming unpopular and odious," and exhorted youths to rise in rebellion against it (Altekar [1938] 1956: 21–22). Mahatma Gandhi, whose passion as a social reformer exceeded even his commitment to ridding India of the British, denounced the "evil custom" regularly in his newspapers, *Harijan* and *Young India*, and shamed men for agreeing to be purchased. He advocated that women wait to get married until they found grooms who would not demand gifts (Gandhi 1993: 71–72). The similarity of the rhetoric of these two men suggests that the adjective "evil" was inseparable from the noun "custom" in the writings of that time.

Since Independence, the state has continued to play the role of social reformer, and the "evil of dowry" continued to haunt the deliberations of the Hindu Code Bill in the early 1950s; these debates led to the separate Abolition of Dowry Act of 1961. Yet the practice continued to flourish, and dowry-related treacheries became the inspiration of films, novels, and political campaign speeches.

The publication in 1973 of Stanley Tambiah's classic on dowry, bride-price, and property identified dowry as a wider Eurasian practice and a premortem inheritance of a daughter in her father's estate (Tambiah 1973). He was clearly prepared to swim against the antidowry tide. Ever since then, anthropologists who have chosen to write about dowry have had to tackle this work and forcefully accept or reject its basic arguments. It has chiefly been the latter, as we shall see, but the debate rekindles itself periodically.

A year later, the publication of the government-sponsored, epoch-making *To-wards Equality* endorsed a strong antidowry position, but the report's own analysis, based heavily on Tambiah's work, tended to undercut it.[6] This state-of-the-art overview of the disabilities that women faced economically, socially, and legally reignited a feminist fervor that had dimmed after the passage of the Hindu Code in 1956, which had given Hindu women some startling new rights such as the right to divorce and inherit urban property (but not agricultural land) equally with their brothers, and generally to benefit from what seemed to be fairer laws for women. The committee that authored *Towards Equality* famously embraced the view that bride-price is a marker for the high value placed on women. It extrapolated that the bridegivers who receive bride-price from the bridetakers must operate in a cultural milieu that values daughters, since bride-price is compensation for the loss of value reckoned in the labor and the reproductive capacity of a daughter. Conversely, the argument ran, in societies that expect bridegivers to provide dowry for their daughters, they do so because they are obliged to compensate the bridetakers for accepting wives who will not be economically productive.

> Analytically speaking, payment in cash and kind to the bride's father by the bridegroom's father is made in exchange for the authority over the bride, which passes from her kin group to the bridegroom's kin group. The idea of compensation for the loss of a productive worker is also implicit in it. *This lends some status to the daughter. The data show that so far as the girl's status in her natal group is concerned, in the communities that follow the custom of bride-price, a daughter is not regarded as a burden, and parents do not have to dread the time when she will have to be married.* Birth of a daughter is, therefore, not regarded as some kind of a calamity. (*Towards Equality* 1974: 70; emphasis added)

This materialist reasoning is not so much a definition of bride-price as it is an implicit denunciation of dowry, which is defined as "compensation" demanded by or offered to the groom's family for taking on a wife presumed to be a net economic "burden." The report also noted that bride-price-paying communities were steadily switching to dowry. The cause was prosperity, which led to the withdrawal of women from the labor force along with their "absence of training in agricultural work," with the result that compensation or dowry had to be paid. This view influenced scholars and activists alike for a generation.

But *Towards Equality* is an amalgam of confusing pronouncements on dowry. The committee members make dowry stand for *status* and *contract,* in that it is a ncessary component of *kanyadan,* or the father's "gift of the virgin" to the husband. They also attempt, with bewildering results, to wed the utilitarian work-equals-worth argument to Tambiah's classic and controversial analysis of dowry "as a 'pre-mortem' inheritance of the daughter" and therefore "the notion of the female right to property" (p. 71). We also find dowry described as a safety net that parents provide for their married daughter. It is the parents' wish that their daughter "should have something to fall back on in times of crisis, and also for setting up her house." If it is indeed a parents' "genuine desire" to see their daughters at least as well off as their sons, then they must endow their daughters "with some property, generally moveables," with a component of gold, silver, and even precious gems, which are also viewed as the girl's "security" (p. 71).

The report goes on to define dowry "technically" as consisting of three clusters of gifts and expenses, the first of which is gifts given to the bride, frequently settled beforehand with the groom's family, which may or may not be regarded as the bride's exclusive property. The second category consists of the gifts given to the son-in-law or to his parents either in cash or in kind; and the third, the expenses incurred for travel and entertainment of the *baraat*, or bridegroom's party (which I consider an unacceptable inclusion). They further suggest that in the continuing relationship of the two families, the parents' gifts to their daughter, son-in-law, and grandchildren are made on several occasions, including visits and festivals and ceremonies that mark rites of passage such as the birth, naming, and initiation of their grandchildren. "These subsequent expenses," they assert, "are regarded *as making up for the deficiencies in the dowry* and can cause severe hardship to the girl's parents. In the first few years of marriage, the girl's treatment in her husband's house is linked to these gifts" (p. 71; emphasis added).

Once she is married, the daughter's relationship with her parents continues with strong but implicit rules and obligations for Punjabi families who believe in the ideology of *kanyadan*. For example, parents do not expect any material reciprocity from their married daughters and will not accept even a meal at their daughter's home. Even brothers, particularly older brothers, will not accept more than token gifts from their married sisters. These strictures are loosening with time and the ease of travel. Visits to a married daughter's home are now more common, but the food eaten in a daughter's home is still often compensated for in direct or subtle ways by the parents. These obligations extend to a daughter's daughters and a sister's daughters: on the occasion of their weddings, their maternal grandparents (*nana* and *nani*) and uncles (*mama*, or mother's brother) contribute a substantial and auspicious part of the gifts (*nanki shak*) that constitute their dowries. If anything, a residual matriliny seems to be at work in dowry-giving relationships, in the margins of the dominant patriarchal relationships. Yet, in another paragraph, forgetting Tambiah and reverting to the public mantra on the subject, the report's authors claim that "[t]echnically, dowry is what is given to the son-in-law or his parents on demand either in cash or in kind" (p. 71). The description of dowry again verges on the evil, and antidowry forces remain ascendant.

Several scholarly and activist voices have joined the chorus. Especially pertinent to my examination of the role of dowry and property in both female infanticide and dowry murder is Barbara D. Miller's monograph *The Endangered Sex*, not only because I find that its intellectual genealogy harks back to the reports of the scholar-bureaucrats in the colonial period but also because its influence in shaping the discourse on dowry in present-day India and among policy makers has been seminal. Miller strongly deplores what she sees as Tambiah's wish to impose what she calls a single predominantly Brahmanic form of marriage payment on the entire subcontinent and his "constant diminution of the significance of non-Brahmanical forms and practices" (Miller 1981: 137). She detects an unequivocal upper-class bias in considering bride-price to be "immoral," which belittles both the frequency and character of bridewealth. Tambiah, she asserts, ignores the actual statistical preponderance of marriages that involve no payment or the payment of bride-price; he also overlooks the north-south divide in gender relations and does not address the issue of social class. Although this particular point is well made, it does not make Miller's passionate objection to Tambiah's characterization of bride-price as mere high-caste prejudice any more acceptable, because, as we shall see, female infanticide was even more widespread among the lower social classes who actually practiced bride-price.

Miller's quest for the elusive grail of a universal theory is, like Tambiah's, beset with pitfalls in a terrain as notoriously varied and unyielding to tidy theories as that of the subcontinent. Using Tambiah's pioneering method of mining regional ethnographies for ready-made data, she produces deeply flawed results. She "discovers," not unlike the colonial investigators of the nineteenth century, the cause of adverse sex ratios and female infanticide embedded in the culture of dowry. This modern ethnographer's unwitting colonialist stance in this work spurred my own historical investigation of female infanticide.

To illustrate how the higher masculine ratios of the north and the balanced sex ratios of the south can be explained, Miller divides the subcontinent into two broad agrarian ecological zones: dry, wheat-growing north India, and south India, with its swidden agriculture and wet, rice-growing regions.[7] Her argument is that the intense preference for sons and discrimination against daughters in the north is driven by the following logic: dry-field and plow cultivation, with its low demand for female labor, leads to the exclusion of women from production and therefore from holding property. The high cost of raising several nonworking daughters, therefore, leads to discrimination against them, which in its most acute form consists of female infanticide. In south India, where swidden and wet-rice culture prevail, the high demand for female labor promotes women's inclusion in production and property holding. Dowries may include rights to land, and families calculate little disadvantage in raising several daughters (Miller 1981: 28). Thus, Miller avers, the appreciation of daughters leads to only a moderate preference for sons and therefore to balanced sex ratios. A closer look, however, at the ground realities renders this thesis unpersuasive.[8] It simply does not work for Bengal, and even less for Punjab and Haryana, the states from which Miller's data for the north are principally drawn and where the highest masculine sex ratios exist. Rice-growing communities in Bengal and elsewhere have a strongly entrenched dowry system and very high juvenile masculine ratios. Agriculturists in Punjab and Haryana (principally wheat-growing regions) are mainly Jats and lower castes, whose women are indispensable to agriculture and animal husbandry, participating in all stages of production except tilling the soil. Yet these groups have the highest masculine sex ratios in the country. Miller surprisingly asserts that the women of Haryana and Punjab play no active role in agriculture, and her use of the data has been strongly refuted by scholars who have worked in the same area (Freed 1982).

Although in the Punjab region both marriage-payment systems flourished side by side in the colonial period (1849–1957), an undeniable shift from *mul* to *daaj* has occurred on a large scale, and in post-Independence Punjab and Haryana *mul* appears to be fading as agriculturists have become more prosperous. An advantage of *daaj* over *mul* for women is evident in that all married women customarily leave the village of their birth and travel to their husbands' homes to become part of their conjugal households. The *daaj* accompanies the bride to her conjugal home and for the most part is considered her personal wealth, whereas *mul* is mainly intended not for the bride but for her natal family. The advantages of the former over the latter will become ever more obvious as we proceed.

Miller treats culture as the organically constituted thing that Fox deplores, and then proceeds to indict it roundly:

> It is culture that "invents" the reasons for which some children who are born are not desired. Second, it is culture that sketches the outlines of the group that is to be the target of infanticide: whether it is to be only boys, only girls, first sons, daughters beyond the first, children born on Thursday, children born with teeth, or children born with crippling deformities. Exactly *why* a certain target group is named within any culture cannot be answered, for in many cases it may be purely arbitrarily assigned. (p. 44)

Again, her assertions mystify. "Culture," however cruel or barbaric, ceases to be a meaningful category in explaining this phenomenon because female infanticide has been practiced widely among animal species and cross-culturally in human history—in the many subcultures of Europe (including England and Italy), in China, India, and Africa, in West Asia among the Arabs, in rice-growing and wheat-growing lands, and among nomads, pastoralists, and urban dwellers. Culture, ecology, and political economy all seem to be involved, and it appears not to be a wanton act. If "culture" arbitrarily targets specific groups for infanticide, then surely the elaborate north-south/dry-wet agricultural argument is an unnecessary embellishment. The agricultural theory also does not explain infanticide among urban trading and priestly groups or nonagricultural groups in other cultures. The argument is difficult to apply in the Punjab, since its "culture" was neither homogeneous nor shared by all the classes, castes, ethnicities, and religions. It is both a rice- and a wheat-growing region, its women are very hardworking, bride-price and dowry coexist, and the juvenile sex ratios are shockingly masculine. I contend that the north-south divide, difficult as it is to accept, can be better explained by historical contingency, such as intermittent warfare and grueling agrarian toil in the northwest. These contingencies, rather than an inherent culture-based devaluation of females, raised the demand for males.

Equally inexplicable is Miller's stout defense of bride-price, not to be confused with the African custom of paying bridewealth. Prem Chowdhry shows that the custom of bride-price gained ground in the first decade of the twentieth century and "that wide acceptance of the prevalent custom of sale and purchase of brides among the economically distressed peasantry" was perceived as a hardship by families who desperately needed the labor and reproductive capacity of a wife but did not have the means to pay for one. The price was tied closely to agricultural conditions, rising fourfold in the time of influenza in 1918 from 500 rupees to 2,000 and declining at the same rate during the drought of 1919–1921 (Chowdhry 1994: 66–69).

Bride-price was and still is existentially often tantamount to the sale of a daughter by a father to a husband. From *Towards Equality* we get a chilling sense of the "other ramifications" the practice of *mul* has had over the long term in a woman's married life. "[T]here is a flavor of buying a wife in the transaction of brideprice," the committee tells us, and the ideology that surrounds it is indeed that of the marketplace. The report goes on to say that because "wealth has been spent to bring her home it is not easily forgotten. When a woman leaves her husband and goes to another man, in the settlement of the amount to be paid by the latter, a reference to the amount of bride-price paid by the former husband comes up again" (p. 73). A wife for whom money has been paid can also be sold to another man (at a loss, from the husband's point of view, but doing so would give him the necessary capital to buy another woman) or be forced into prostitution to pay off the debt incurred to marry her in the first place. She may also be regarded as a kind of "family property," often serving several brothers among the polyandrous Jats. She can opt to leave her husband and return to her family, but her kin are liable for returning what they received for her.

It is imperative to emphasize that it is not upper-caste disdain for the custom, as Miller claims, but the equating of a woman's personal worth with the sum paid for her that makes bride-price objectionable. Lower-caste women resent this equation and prefer to receive dowries from their families rather than be sold to their husbands. This might explain the widespread shift from bride-price to dowry in the last fifty years; the assault has come from women themselves. The *Towards Equality* committee agrees that bride-price "certainly speaks for the relatively low status of the woman vis-à-vis the man" but suggests that a wife is so indispensable to a peasant household that she can find ways of asserting her rights. "[T]he woman has some bargaining power in regard to her relationship in the husband's house. The man cannot drive her too hard or else she will leave and he will have to pay bride-price to bring another wife. The compensation that he will get for her will not be the same as the bride-price that he will have to pay" (p. 70).

This, unfortunately, disproves the very point that the committee members are trying to make, because bride-price, as they describe it, is easily exploitable to become, in years of poor harvests, a thinly veiled form of trafficking in women. Given these conditions, it is not surprising, and ought not to be dismaying, that whole communities shift to dowry marriages as soon as their economic conditions enable this upward movement on the social ladder. Miller's position, however, becomes even more untenable.

What Miller and Tambiah share is their use of women's rights to property as the central explanatory variable in their theories, without ever defining "property"; they assume it to be a legally and culturally constituted category that has seen no changes over time in the subcontinent. For example, Miller emphasizes the distinction between movable and immovable property, disregarding the fact that gold and cash, which became important items in a bride's dowry in late nineteenth-century Punjab, could be readily changed into immovable acres of land, because land had become a commodity that could be bought and sold. Unless we think of property as a dynamic category that changed its entire meaning in the colonial period, we may never settle the question.

It is a challenge to review the storm of conflicting views on the subject of women's property published in monographs, journals, and newspaper editorials, and the influence of the conflict is vivid in recent work on dowry. Fortunately, other scholars have reviewed the literature adequately, which obviates a similar effort on my part. Bina Agarwal gives us a consummate recapitulation and a stimulating discussion of the dowry versus inheritance debate and a comprehensive and nuanced discussion of land rights and gender relations in the wider context of South Asia (Agarwal 1994: 133–52, 480–83). More recently, Srimati Basu has given us a rigorous discussion of the unequal balance between property and dowry and a review of the existing literature (Basu 1999: 61–77). Another fine review of this complicated literature, along with the most impressive qualitative analysis of dowry, is to be found in the work that Gloria Raheja has done. She based her evocative and substantive insights on the meanings of dowry that emerge in the songs and conversations of women themselves. "Why, then, do women speak so provocatively and profoundly of their ties to their natal place and to their kinsmen there?" she asks. "As I try to explicate women's words as they sing of gifts and of natal kin, I shall suggest that as women talk of *bhat* and *dahej*, and *milai* and *neg*, and of 'our [natal] land,' we hear not so much as a discourse on economy as a poetic discourse on power and the possibility of women's resistance to patrilineal authority on female identities." She goes on to say that in listening to some words spoken by rural and urban women alike, in north India, of dowry and gift giving, "we think of women gaining not just their share of the wealth but of contesting the power relations that make them so vulnerable when they marry and go away"

(Raheja 1995: 26). Her sensitive analysis puts us in direct touch with the feelings, contestations, and identities of women as it examines their songs on gift giving and sexuality—vital elements, Raheja points out, that are missing from the work of Tambiah or alliance theorists.

Dowry's direct link to "hypergamy," a term first used by colonial officials after the discovery by the British of female infanticide in 1789, became a common feature of all disquisitions on Hindu high-caste culture. "Hypergamy is based on consideration of status by birth. We find that caste groups following hypergamy have had a high incidence of dowry," say the magisterial authors of *Towards Equality* (p. 72). The almost mechanical invocation of hypergamy—their entire discussion of hypergamy is contained in those two sentences—as the ground on which the custom was founded is arguably based on a truism. The popular anthropological theory that hypergamy, rather than village exogamy, engendered the practice of dowry is rooted in the nineteenth-century colonial discourse on the role of hypergamy and dowry on female infanticide and has been espoused by ethnographers ever since. The authors insist that the prevalence of hypergamy among the upper castes (Brahmin, Khatri, and Bania) produced the highest incidence of dowry, and since upper-caste women traditionally were not expected to do gainful work outside the home, dowries had to be paid as "compensation," but this line of reasoning muddles their entire discussion. Why would the upper castes have expected compensation for accepting a nonworking bride when it was an important marker of status for women not to work? In fact, as we have seen, dowry, for the committee members, is all things at all times. But it cannot be a volitional gift to the daughter, and her birthright to a "premortem" share in her father's wealth, her own personal *stridhan*, and at the same time compensation to the bridetakers for accepting into their family an allegedly nonproductive woman who is consequently a financial burden. The authors seem not to notice their own contradictory assessments of a custom that they ultimately see as a sociological problem, an evil custom.

Fortunately several anthropologists have taken pains to demonstrate that hypergamy is not the norm in India, particularly in the Punjab. Marriages are preferably arranged within the same caste group, and between families roughly equal in status and income. In an impressive theoretical treatment of status relations in Indian culture, Murray Milner argues that since differences in status are very important in India, public acknowledgment of one's inferiority is no small matter—especially if the role as an inferior is a long-term one. This explains the strong tendency in India for caste endogamy and isogamy, or marriage between equals within the same caste group, particularly in areas such as the Punjab and Bengal (see chapters 3, 5, and 11 in Milner 1994). G. N. Ramu proposes that just as caste endogamy keeps marriage alliances from crossing caste lines, dowry might actually be a mechanism to promote isogamy, preventing lower-status persons from seeking alliances with higher-status persons (Ramu 1977: 31). I would add only one more theoretical wrinkle: even in the most carefully selected isogamous alliance, the bride and her givers are at a permanent disadvantage not because of caste status but because of the inherent inequality in the construction of gender. The idea of the bride being acquired either as a gift (along with her *daaj*) or after payment (*mul*) underscores the unambiguous construction of the woman as movable property in marriage. It is this reification of woman either as gift or as a wife by purchase that makes all bridetakers in some sense superior to all bridegivers. Punjabis and other north Indians, except Muslims, avoid exchange marriages, in which a brother and a sister of one family marry a sister and a brother of another family; such marriages, in effect, would level all difference in status.[9]

What further raises the ante for the bridegivers is their burden of looking for the best match among such equals; they seek the groom with the best job or earning potential, education, character, temperament, and appearance that caste endogamy and *gotr* or *got* (clan) and village exogamy can obtain for them. Such a quest is, at best, difficult because although the masculine sex ratios suggest a preponderance of eligible males in the population, the case is just the opposite. This apparent paradox can be easily explained: although there *are* more men in any given age group, there is a real shortage of eligible males because of deficiencies in educational qualifications, employment prospects (India has an overall unemployment rate of 40 percent), character, or appearance. This simple fact puts the less than socially ethical family of an eligible bachelor in a position to demand a big dowry from the families of prospective brides; the bride whose family succumbs is selected.[10] The other factor that makes the pool of brides larger is that men customarily marry women younger than themselves, making it possible for grooms to dip deep into the pool of ever-younger brides. The advantage that brides would have had by being numerically fewer is therefore wiped out; in reality the supply of educated, employed, attractive men "of good character" is shrinking even as the male population grows exponentially. Lack of physical attractiveness may be excused in a pinch, but few parents would want to marry their daughter to an unemployed youth with dim prospects or habits such as excessive drinking, smoking, gambling, or keeping bad company. Sex ratios have little impact in the world of arranged marriages.

Physical attractiveness has been far more important an attribute for women, because men can choose from the growing pool of younger women who need well-qualified husbands. A plain daughter becomes a liability in the marriage market; a beautiful one is so wanted that the dowry is completely incidental to clinching a match for her. Parents watch with despair the appearance of irregular teeth, pimples, or other signs of unattractiveness in their own daughters, and those who can afford it expend impressive sums on dental and dermatological services. Beauty, as we would all agree, is not common, and this imponderable alone adds to the preference for sons, plain or attractive. The important role that physical attractiveness, health, and sexuality play in the marriage arrangement is underestimated or ignored even in the best ethnographic accounts, and I will have occasion to consider it very briefly in the last chapter.[11]

The extent of a woman's control over her dowry in her marital home is also a matter of debate among scholars. It largely depends on the nature of the relationship that develops between a woman and her mother-in-law, if they live in the same extended family. A variety of ethnographic sources make it clear that often a woman has her own locked trunk (*patti* or *pitara*) in which she stores her jewels, cash, and other possessions "which will make the nucleus of her household equipment when she sets up her own home" (Hershman 1981: 213–14). Vatuk (1975: 165–66) confirms this type of control in the villages she studied, whereas Sharma (1980: 49–52) qualifies it somewhat without quite contradicting the view that women jealously guard their own jewelry. This is also borne out by my own investigations and experiences in a far larger and varied universe by the seventy-five women I queried on the subject while doing research in Delhi. These days in middle-class homes, steel almirahs are ubiquitous; bank lockers or safe deposit boxes are used by women to keep their jewelry and other valuables, and cash can be invested in interest-free bonds, saving schemes, and the stock market. By and large women keenly assert their right to control their own *stridhan*, and in Srimati Basu's sample about 75 percent of the women claimed that their gifts and jewelry remained with them (Basu 1999: 104–5). It is also not unusual for women from peasant and urban working-class families to wear their jewelry at all times, not only to keep it safe from pilferage but to have it under their direct control. Elaborately bejeweled women can be seen working on construction sites, as domestic servants, or itinerant vendors in the streets of villages and towns in northern India.

Srimati Basu's probing urban ethnography of three lower- and middle-class Delhi neighborhoods updates our view of urban women's notions of *stridhan*. She found that few women valued jewelry as a prime asset, but preferred to own land and property, or run a business and invest in savings schemes. Although women were fully apprised of their rights to an equal share in their natal property given by the Hindu Succession Act of 1956, Basu found this to be a nonevent because women often forfeited their right to retain support from their brothers in times of difficulty. Most commonly, though, women inherited affinal property, making marriage and widowhood the surer paths to property ownership. Even more significantly, women really looked to their own productive capacity to buy property in their own names and control it (Basu 1999: 41–77).

Culturally speaking, the fault line in a woman's existence is virilocal marriage; hypergamy and its alleged partner, dowry, are not the traits that turn lethal for married women. In order to show this, I concentrate on the crimes attributed to dowry—female infanticide in the mid-nineteenth century and dowry murders in the twentieth—rather than on the dowry system's everyday, nonviolent, and beneficial outcomes for the overwhelming majority of Indian women. I do this also because dowry as a workaday custom is amply discussed in the several fine ethnographies of the present-day Punjab, but the pathology of the system barely finds mention there. There was no female infanticide committed or brides burned, or even endangered, on account of dowry demands in the villages studied in the 1960s, 1970s, and early 1980s by ethnographers who were continuously resident.[12] Ursula Sharma developed her research interests as the daughter-in-law of a Himachal Brahmin family, and during many years of residence and fieldwork in the 1970s produced her excellent comparative study of Punjabi and Himachal villages. She does note that the value of dowries had escalated and that many families complained about the growing cost of a daughter's marriage. There were neither accidentally burned or murdered brides nor any suicide by a woman during her tenure. It was the brides rather than their in-laws who complained about disparities between their own *daaj* and those of their sisters (Sharma 1980: 48–49). Sharma also strongly and compellingly disputes the idea that dowry is ever given as compensation or bears any resemblance to it, particularly since in the Punjab there has been a total shift from bride-price marriage to *daaj*, while women's labor in the fields and at home has not changed noticeably (Sharma 1980: 47–59, 134–43, passim). Both Sharma and Hershman use history sparingly, if at all, and make only the briefest mention of female infanticide or adverse female sex ratios as relics of the past when explaining the intense preference for sons among Punjabis.

Hershman explains why the poorest and lowliest Jats, who pay bride-price, resort to a form of polyandry in which the eldest brother's wife is shared among all the brothers although only one is ritually married to her.[13] He found twelve instances of this practice in the village of 486 households, of which 165 were Jat. He argues that a number of factors are closely correlated with this practice, and he unquestioningly sees infanticide as something that was prevalent in isogamous, bride-price-accepting peasant households.

> [F]irstly, female infanticide reduced the number of available wives and so necessitated more than one man sharing a woman; secondly because men were absent in military service, wife-sharing was sensible in terms of the protection of family and land; and thirdly, because a proportion of marriages were arranged according to hypergamous principles, this may have caused a scarcity of women amongst groups of the social hierarchy and thus reinforced the practice of polyandry. (Hershman 1981: 178–79)

Hershman's reasoning is puzzling: wife sharing occurs among groups that pay bride-price for the wife, where the woman becomes the property of the husband and by extension that of his brothers. But why would bride-price–paying peasants commit female infanticide and cause a scarcity of women when they could, by the logic of the marketplace, receive cash and cattle for their daughters? If that logic was indeed operative, then polyandry would be untenable, and normal sex ratios and even polygamy would have been prevalent in Jat peasant society.

Hershman's acquaintance with the colonial construction of these matters appears to be limited; he offers a single quotation from an 1881 report he found cited in the 1904 *Punjab Gazetteer* to support his own explanation for adelphic polyandry among the Jats. In the many villages around Jullunder, "under the Sikh regime, they used to kill female children to escape the expense of marriage ceremonies and looked upon themselves as high caste Jats . . . if the crime does exist it is merely among Jats who look upon themselves as something *superior in caste or Got to their brethren*" (cited in Hershman 1981: 178; emphasis added). Colonial Department of Infanticide reports contain numerous references to marriage expenses and hypergamy among "superior" clans of Jats as well as the equally emphatic though contradictory exoneration of Jats from committing female infanticide because they received bride-price (instead of spending money on dowries) for their daughters (see chapter 2 for a lengthy discussion of this contradiction).[14] The British waffled about the culpability of the Jats, since they were essential as soldiers for their army and as frontiersmen to cut down Punjab forests and settle new arable revenue-producing lands; the indispensability of Jat brawn probably overrode concern for Jat female infants. The shortage of low-caste Jat women, and therefore adelphic polyandry, will remain inadequately explained unless we move beyond marriage expenses and high-caste prejudice as the only motives for committing female infanticide and begin to understand the traditional reliance on Jat men for the defense in the Punjab and their greatly enhanced role in the development of the colonial political economy.

Hershman appears to treat female infanticide and skewed sex ratios as things of the past. Yet his own fieldwork on polyandry led him in another direction entirely. After questioning the village residents, including those who actually practiced polyandry, he received what he considered a plausible and practical answer (because, I believe, he spoke fluent Punjabi): "The normal explanation of Sikh Jat polyandry given by Punjabis is that 'it keeps the land together.' . . . According to the villagers it is mainly practiced by the poorer families whose land just verges on subsistence level" and would not be viable after subdivision in the next generation. So, without refuting the historical explanation or his own earlier argument, he was happy to accept their rationale "by which polyandry is described simply as a device to maintain a basic economic solvency" (Hershman 1981: 179). These two contradictory explanations—the culturally determined one with caste hypergamy as the familiar lead player and the economically determined one offered by Punjabi farmers—cause him little consternation.[15]

Mul, it should be pointed out, has not seen the same dramatic changes over time as has *daaj*, as it is tantamount to a commercial transaction and is uncomplicated by notions of status or ritual. In the mid-nineteenth century, it was confined to a wide range of low-caste or menial groups in the Punjab, such as sweepers, tanners, and poor or landless Jat peasants. It has lost much of its following even among these groups (Sharma 1980: 138; *Towards Equality* 1974: 70). In several conversations with twenty-seven Jat women construction workers who work with their faces fully veiled, on house construction sites in an elite housing colony in Gurgaon in Haryana between 1996 and 1998, I was surprised to discover a fairly uniform and frank distaste for marriage customs such as polyandry and bride-price. These were regarded as a symptom of poverty and straitened circumstances in Gurgaon district in earlier times, where drought and saline soil had plagued the region for decades. The women now invested their savings in household goods for their daughter's dowries. They fully expected that their daughters would be married with some pomp and circumstance and receive clothes, cash, and consumer durables as gifts to take along to their conjugal homes. They expected little help from their husbands and none from their kin; they were proud that they had the wherewithal to afford to do this themselves to make up for their own past, when they were "sold" for 500 rupees to their husbands.

Klas van der Veen noticed the same marked tendency among lower castes in Gujarat and called the process "Brahmanization" (van der Veen 1972), much as M. N. Srinivas called lower-caste emulation of the higher castes "Sanskritization." Neither of them, however, discusses the historical factors that induced this shift away from *mul*; it is instead explained as behavior integral to the caste system. *Mul* was then, and it is now, a one-time payment to the father of the bride, a modest sum compared with the gifts and cash that are involved in a dowry. The amount of a *mul* payment has increased with time but has barely kept pace with inflation, and the sums given may thus actually represent a decline in the "value" of women so exchanged. The bride-on-offer can be examined and rejected by the purchasers, and in the marriage transaction the woman is reduced to the status of a chattel, a commodity in the most vulgar economic sense; the bargaining match between the two parties is not known for its delicacy.

Although their ahistorical treatment of dowry is problematical, I would argue that anthropologists on both sides of the dowry debate are partially right. Tambiah was probably correct in insisting that the rights of women to property are irrefutable, since the *Dharmashastra* gives us the vocabulary and the notion of *stridhan*; both men and women enjoyed the fruits of the land on which they lived rather than the power of ownership in precolonial times. This conception of women's property rights no longer corresponds to the practice of dowry described by Hershman, Sharma, Vatuk, and other ethnographers at work in north Indian villages in the 1960s to 1980s. Both sides neglect to mention that a great deal changed in the centuries that elapsed between the original formulation of *stridhan* and its practical reality now, particularly the last 250 years under colonial rule. Madhu Kishwar laments the lack of historical research done "to show how *stridhan* was transformed into dowry payment gifts. All we know is that there is little mention of exorbitant dowries causing the ruin of families in the literature of pre-British India. Ruin due to exorbitant dowry payments became a major theme in nineteenth century literature" (Kishwar 1993: 9). An understanding of the colonial context wherein dowry and property changed radically can liberate the current dialogue from the ahistorical mire in which it is stranded.

Towards Equality contains a fairly accurate description of the present-day malaise that afflicts the custom of dowry: the report tells us that the settlement of dowry "has all the characteristics of a market transaction."

> There are more or less well-defined grades of dowry for men in different regions and in different professions. For example men in the I.A.S. [Indian Administrative Service] and I.F.S. [Indian Foreign Service] in Orissa, Bihar, Uttar Pradesh and Punjab, belonging to well-to-do communities, can easily expect in cash and kind, at least a lakh of rupees [in 1975; it is now supposed to be ten times this much]. Business executives rank next. Engineers and doctors stand lower than the business executives. This class seems to expect that marriage would bring them not only a partner but also all the things needed to set up a modern household, such as a car, refrigerator, radiogram. These groups function as pace setters and naturally influence those below. Thus a peon or a clerk would demand such things as a bicycle, a transistor [radio], and a wrist watch. A [motor] scooter is a common item of gift to the son-in-law in groups at the middle level. In villages too there are similar demands. (p. 72)

The authors go on to say that these inflationary trends in wedding gifts, while not termed "dowry," are also commonly noticed among Muslims and Christians of many regions. Dowries, they continue, may also be demanded in the form of residential property, particularly in big cities such as Bombay or Calcutta, cash to underwrite the expenses for a groom's education abroad, or capital for setting up a business, mainly in large cities.

But the worst development, in the committee members' view, is that young women themselves are complicit in making their dowries bigger and fatter. "It is a disturbing trend that girls themselves aspire to have their household[s] set up in a grand style by the parents and to have clothes, jewelry, furniture and vehicle, etc. . . . It is disconcerting education has hardly had any liberalising influence on the minds of the people in respect to dowry. On the contrary education increased dowry both in rural as well as in urban areas." Middle-class girls themselves, they suggest, are encouraging these changes, since they take up teaching, nursing, or other jobs to "earn their dowry in urban areas" (p. 74). This statement stands the work-equals-worth argument on its head! It need hardly be pointed out that the report's half-hearted blame of hypergamy as the motive force behind rising dowries has been replaced by the modernity-and-materialism argument, in which the motives are believed to be products of Westernization. Despite the committee's disapproving tone about women who are compounding the dowry problem by insisting on taking more and more consumer goods to their future homes, it is important to recognize that women are not passive victims of dowry but may be actively involved in getting a fairer share of their families' resources. This may eventually lead to women realizing that they have a lawful and equal share in their father's postmortem property, as well, and their insistence on obtaining it may begin to level the playing field. Ultimately it will also organize a social consensus on a single inheritance law that incorporates both men and women of all creeds and castes as equals.

In order to understand why dowry changed (albeit unevenly) from voluntary gifts or the birthright of the bride to a demand from the groom's parents, we must trace how status relations changed to contractual ones in the sphere of arranged marriages, when dowry began to be redefined as compensation for accepting a bride who would not be materially productive for the family. And in this, as in many of these conundrums, history and context will be come to our aid.

What affects the life and happiness of most women after marriage is not caste ranking but gender and generational relations, and the ingenuity they bring to manipulating these in the relationships they forge with their husbands. It is no accident that a bride will let herself become pregnant soon after she enters her marital home to live with her husband; she can thereby erase her probationary status as the "virginal gift" and *paraye ghar ki ladki* (daughter not of this home) and join the ranks of other mothers of sons in the family. Becoming the mother of a son is the first step to power in her husband's household, as she becomes the perpetuator of the her husband's lineage. Caste hierarchy may be relevant for male clan groups; for a wife in her many roles in her conjugal home, it is of little meaning. Caste ranking becomes irrelevant to the dynamics of power inside a marital relationship because a woman has no independent caste status. The rituals of marriage automatically erase the status of the *gotr* into which she was born and bestow upon her the status of the *gotr* into which she marries. Caste, anthropologists will tell you, is an ascriptive category, forgetting that this is only true for men, for a woman belongs to the caste of her father at birth and then that of her husband. Anthropologists' emphasis on hypergamy is similarly misplaced. The dynamics at work *within* a family are those of gender and generation (or age), not caste.

The discourse on caste has so dominated the understanding of marriage and dowry—a trend set by colonial scholar-bureaucrats and followed by anthropologists of South Asia—that gender, the indisputable constant in a marriage alliance, is virtually ignored. What makes bridegivers and bridetakers behave in ways that suggest that all marriages must indeed be hypergamous when in reality they are isogamous is the implicit asymmetry in gender relations. Why must a bride's family have to show deference to the groom's family during the wedding ceremonies and unhappily ever after? This is a virtually universal experience for women everywhere. Village women put it with a clear-eyed directness, as Gloria Raheja found in Pahansu. An older woman, in whose house she lived while conducting her research, said that "girl's people" (*larkivale*) are considered to be "little" (chota) and the "boy's people" (*larkevale*) are considered to be "big" (*bara*), and that the grand-father loses at the birth of a granddaughter and wins at the birth of a son (Raheja 1995: 26). I have heard women talk of caste as *jati* and speak of only two *jatis*: the male and the female. It is the only way to make sense of hypergamy.

I would aver that this is the universal common denominator in the patriarchal construction of gender and marriage in almost all cultures. In Western societies, for example, this is best seen when the bride is "given away" by her father and changes her "maiden" name to the husband's surname—before feminists began to resist this arbitrary switch in lineage. A male does not change his *gotr* or family name, for he is the very embodiment of it in patriarchal societies. The inequality lies in women being construed as essentially without individual identities or sub-jecthood, and subsumed by the status and qualities of their husbands' social exis-tence. Therefore, in the deepest cultural sense, there is no choice for women but to seem to be marrying "up." The colonial brand of modernity only aggravated this inequality in the cultures with which they interacted and which they unevenly transformed.

This alleged melding of the female into the superior male does not create a simple, integrally inferior female, however. Her position is more layered and de-serves to be unpacked, because factors such as age and kinship complicate the power relations of men and women in Indian society. A woman's lesser power as a wife or daughter is balanced by her greater power as a mother, widow, or sister. A senior woman may have power over junior men in a family (as in the case of mother and sons, or wife of senior brother over her younger brother-in-law); this same woman had a very different place in the family when she entered it as a young bride. Even a new bride, though, may claim some power. A twenty-year-old educated and employed bride is quicker to challenge her mother-in-law or re-sist subservience than the fourteen-year-old child bride who was (and in rural Haryana still frequently is) married off and expected to adapt herself to a family that she begins to see as her own. As the age of marriage and the threshold of ed-ucation have climbed steadily higher in the last hundred years, relations between the generations show greater friction. An educated daughter-in-law can be per-ceived as a threat to the authority of her mother-in-law, and she may conform less to the rules of deference expected by the older woman. Her education, however, does not temper her preference for sons. If anything, education enables younger women to plan their families even more aggressively as they seek out new tech-nologies that will give them the gender-targeted family that the existing power dy-namics make it "sensible" and desirable to produce. Monica Das Gupta (1987: 94) makes this point forcefully. Sex differentials in the Punjab have persisted, her re-search shows, despite the decline in overall child mortality rates, the rise in in-come and nutritional levels, the improved health care delivery, and rapid increases in female education. Family-building strategies, in her view, sustain the discrimi-nation against female children.

For all these reasons, it is unacceptable to see modern dowries as an artifact of hypergamy, or as "compensation" to the groom's family for an unproductive new member, with little or no relation to the sensibilities of women who play the lead roles in both giving and the receiving of these gifts. More than ever, dowry serves as a safety net to ensure a daughter's well-being in the vulnerable and distant situation in which marriage has put her. Apart from their practical and material value, a bride's clothes, jewels, and household effects constantly remind her parents-in-law that they have a loved and valued member of another family with them now. The new bride and her dowry were and in most cases still are the locus of the groom's family's sense of status in their own village, the hope for the continuance of the male line, and a powerful new ingredient in the very flavor and texture of the family. As prices and property values increase and more and more consumer goods flood the market, expectations escalate and so do dowries. In extreme cases, the situation may balloon into ugly demands, but these should not stubbornly be called "dowry demands" but actionable extortion and blackmail. Women are not passive or indifferent to their dowries, particularly women who are older and better educated than their forbears a few decades ago, and some of these expectations and demands are their own as they are better able to appreciate the implications of virilocality and their entitlements in their natal homes. But it is useful to bear in mind that moderation (or even abstinence) in the giving and taking of dowries, the norm in India even today, as ethnographers will attest, arouses the least comment. We hear little of the cultural behavior that does not engender conflict during the arranging of marriages or the giving of dowries.

It is now time to engage in that much-needed historical exploration of these timeless concepts and theoretical constructs to see how culture, in its multifarious dimensions and the dynamics of gender interacted to both create and explain dowry deaths.

2

The Just-So Stories about Female Infanticide

There are two causes alleged for female infanticide; the one is a religious one, founded on the peculiar tenets or considerations of caste; the other is a pecuniary one, arising out of the habitual expenditure of large sums upon marriage ceremonies.
—*J. P. Grant, Officiating Secretary to the Government of India, 7 September 1853*

The doctrines of the Hindoo religion have been singularly careful to protect the female sex and infants from violence; and it is unlawful to put a woman to death for any offence whatever. . . . "Let all the four castes of Brahmun, Khetry [Khatri, the diminutive of Kshatriya], Bys [Vaishya], and Sooder [Shudra], know that the killing of a woman is the greatest of crimes."
—*James Peggs, Cries of Agony*

Beva mat jalao; beti mat maro; kori mat dabao.
[Do not burn widows; do not kill daughters; do not bury lepers.]
—*Sir John Lawrence, Commissioner of the Jullundur Doab*

An East India Company officer made the earliest causal link between the dowry system and violence against girls in 1789, when he discovered female infanticide. The finding added powerfully to the company's description of the exotic, "cruel," and "barbaric" culture encountered in the process of its conquest of this strange land. On the backs of such discoveries rode the moral imperative of imperialism—its famous "civilizing mission." This served as the most compelling justification, both to the company itself and to a critical public in England, for the conquest, pillage, and domination of Indian peoples and the destruction of their local cultures. It was in this context too, that Hindu women's apparently degraded position in an allegedly rigid caste society became a central preoccupation of colonial rulers and the subject of endless debates, reform rhetoric, and legislation.

British official scholarship on the caste system, once considered to be a marvel of empiricism and objectivity, has been steadily and rigorously demolished in the last three decades. Most pertinently, Ronald Inden tells us that "[w]e cannot be sure that caste had multiplied and crystallized by the time India gained independence, but I think we can safely say that empiricist accounts of caste had. Caste had become essentialized and turned into the substantialized agent of India's history" (Inden 1990: 66). In this erudite and excellent archaeology of British knowledge of Indian society and religion, Inden does not allege that the British invented caste, as some critics have insisted, but that they transformed it by misrepresenting it as a rigid, unchanging, inflexible structure and by promoting the idea that caste was the essential core of Indian society. Nicholas Dirks, following the trail Bernard Cohn blazed in his many influential writings on British colonial institutions, has persuasively argued that caste was embedded in a political context of kingship, not in the context of religion or culture, and that it reflected notions of power, dominance, and order (Dirks 1987; 1989). Colonial imaginings about the role of caste in Hindu society, religion, and culture have finally been repudiated. My own exploration of "cultural crime" ascribed to high-caste Hindu practice affirms that colonial discursive hegemony emptied caste categories of their *political* meanings and left a purely cultural and religious residue; the alleged structural rigidity of "the caste system" became an intransigent, self-fulfilling prophecy.

What is less actively studied is the complicity of the native informant and his British interlocutor in creating the "thick descriptions" about him (and I use the Geertz's phrase and the male pronouns advisedly) and its effect on the political economy of gender relations. If imperial officers sought the knowledge and authority of Indian men to construct or validate their own theories of the tyranny of caste and to give their rule an aura of legitimacy and benevolence, the Indians themselves colluded in this outcome by acting as informants, not without their own strong patriarchal and limited economic interests at heart. Although the power ratio between the interrogator and the informant was dreadfully skewed, the results of the collusion were symbiotic insofar as a colonial setting permitted.

In the official records we can "hear" the conversations of bureaucrats, translators, and peasant elders and "see" the latter act as the foil for caste, and thereby cooperate in inventing and depicting caste as a socially controlling and inflexible institution. Investigations of cases of female infanticide reveal this collusion by native elders to be "self-interested" for two reasons: first, being singled out for consultations in their local contexts by the new rulers affirmed the elders' own patriarchal authority, and second, it was far safer for them to impute caste compulsion or religious obligation from some immemorial time than to claim individual agency in committing the "barbaric" cultural practices being investigated. It would not be too far-fetched to compare the behavior of a caste elder with that of a criminal who makes the insanity plea in court to elude punishment for a crime he knowingly committed; it could perhaps be called the "barbarity plea."

The alternative was to betray his motives and culpability, and to pay for the crime with fine, imprisonment, or possibly a hanging. Women systematically stayed out of the picture because it was patent that female infanticide could not have been committed without the active involvement of women. They quietly passed for ignorant, passive, obedient creatures, sheltered from interrogation by strange men by the rules of veiling and seclusion. In fact, older kinswomen, as we will see, were the ones who determined which girl child would live and which would perish, bending and breaking moral and religious injunctions such as those that against the killing of female infants; they were not the passively compliant victims of caste dictates that they became in the British imagination.[1] The issue of agency gets complicated when it involves issues of criminality, and it is in these murky waters of cultural compunction that both the conqueror and the conquered fish for their alibis.

In the late eighteenth century in Bombay Presidency, female infanticide was already established as a cultural peculiarity of high-caste communities. This was done by locating its motives in Hindu high-caste pride and marriage expenses; the discovery of female infanticide in the Punjab required similar certification. It is possible, by looking at investigations conducted by the British in the Punjab shortly after their conquest of it in 1849, to explore how they gathered their evidence and why they came to lay the blame squarely on the dowry system, even though they found evidence to the contrary. A careful rereading of the evidence that the British gathered on female infanticide in the 1850s reveals a politically motivated and incomplete investigation, and tells a very different tale from that hitherto told.

HISTORICAL BACKGROUND

Two histories must be meshed to create the proper context for the colonial discourse on and suppression of female infanticide in the Punjab—those of both indigenous and colonial political imperatives, which gave Punjabi society its ideas about the comparative worth of women and men.[2] By the second half of the eighteenth century, through an assortment of snares, stratagems, and military victories of its 150,000-man Bengal army, the East India Company, which had been initially chartered only to trade, had wrested for itself the enviable status of paramount power in a vast, rich, and populous subcontinent. Its culminating conquest, after two bloody wars, was that of the Punjab in 1849, the once proud kingdom of the Sikh ruler, Maharaja Ranjit Singh. It had been long coveted not only for its fertile plains and forest wealth but also for its manpower, which would be aggressively recruited to become the flower of the company's troops. Parliamentary acts and inquiries tried to curb the company from acting as a state more powerful than Britain itself, but the distance and the company's politically ingenious "civilizing mission" blunted the thrusts of even its most acerbic critics at home.

This will to unbridled power and greed of the officers of what was once a mere trading company with a poor balance of payments found a much-needed moral imperative. Its officers discovered "barbaric and cruel" customs and "social evils" rooted in a "benighted heathenism" that it became their "Christian duty" to purge. This became, in essence, colonialism's famous "civilizing mission," which was publicized in Britain as the unenviable task to which East India Company officers were dedicated after bringing vast populations in the subcontinent under their sway. It was the Briton's duty to transform India's heathens into "moral" beings; the rhetoric and the reportage were geared to give what might otherwise be judged as acts of naked aggression and plunder a loftier purpose. Helped along by the economic invincibility Britain had achieved as the world's workshop, and later by the nineteenth-century pseudoscientific production of knowledge on the white master race and the nonwhite inferior races and cultures (which needs no elucidation here), this case was spelled out in a whole range of documents prepared for the British Parliament. Company officers had learned that to quell anti-imperial sentiment they had to reiterate the case that a rational, enlightened, and efficient Raj (administration) was gradually rescuing the natives of India from the tyranny of their own cruel despots and barbaric religious and social customs. Not surprising, therefore, are the official records that detail the discovery of "social evils"—the paradigmatic case being that of self-immolation by widows, a long-known practice that gained notoriety under the British as "suttee."[3] Other crimes of a ritual or collective nature were similarly discovered, one of the better known among them being *thuggee* (or *thugi*). Thugs were labeled a criminal caste, and the word passed into the English language. They were alleged to roam the country in looting bands and commit ritual murder to their patron goddess Kali. Female infanticide has no particular name, although in the Punjab the perpetrators were called *kuri-mar* (literally, girl-killers). These produced as much horror as they did political opportunity, once eyewitness accounts and thick descriptions with ethnographic detail by John Company officers reached the mother country.

In 1813 the "civilizing mission" received an additional fillip when the British Parliament passed the India Act of 1813 to admit missionaries, who had hitherto been excluded from tinkering with the most exquisite brand of heathenism in the wild Indian empire because of their politically volatile denunciations of Hindu beliefs and practices. Christian missionaries added greatly to the self-righteous bombast of this mission. James Peggs, a man of the cloth, made an exhaustive, lurid, and cliché-laden compendium on the entire gamut of "Hindoo social evils." His text was cobbled from pertinent Parliament Papers and it first appeared in 1826 as *Suttees Cry to Britain*, followed by a thicker version with female infanticide added on and tellingly called *India's Cries to British Humanity*. In 1832 this pamphlet was fattened from 110 pages to 518, and renamed *Cries of Agony: An Historical Account of Suttee, Infanticide, Ghat Murders, and Slavery in India*. The Coventry Society for the Abolition of Human Sacrifices in India published an abridgment of the original pamphlet and distributed free copies. It remains in print to this day.[4] It was a great victory for William Wilberforce and fellow Evangelicals in England to expand their operations to the Indian theater. The prime target for reform was the generically hapless "Hindoo woman," curiously both the victim and the agent of these many "barbarities." It was not long before upper-caste, English-educated Hindu men joined the fray as social reformers.

The combined offensive against sati in Bengal made it the best-known thing about the subcontinent in Europe. Lata Mani, in two separate articles, has given us a peerless discourse analysis of the triangular debates on sati engaged in by British officers, Bengali Hindu orthodox intellectuals, and progressive reformers (Mani 1986; 1987). She wrote:

> The scriptures, or various versions of them, provided the basis of arguments for and against this practice. Given that the debate on *sati* is premised on its scriptural and, consequently, its "traditional" and "legal" status, it is little wonder that the widow herself is marginal to its central concerns. The parameters of the discourse preclude this possibility. Instead, women become sites upon which various versions of the scripture / tradition / law are elaborated and contested. (Mani 1987: 151)

This process of collaboration of colonials and progressive Hindu reformers produced serious cultural distortions and served two critical political ends for the British. The paperwork generated on a particular social evil and its eradication by the honorable John Company became the most avidly perused papers in England; particularly popular were those relating to the company as it acted in its capacity of instituting "the rule of law" by the British. These masterly representations of a distant and dangerous world plagued with "Hindoo" barbarities, as they were increasingly called (despite the failure to find them sanctioned in any "Hindoo" texts) rendered India the ideal site for continued and expanding colonial control (Oldenburg 1994a).

In dealing with other "social evils," bureaucratic investigative and discursive practices followed the pattern that had evolved in the campaign against sati. Actions were also prompted and constrained by complicated political considerations—prompted by the need for legitimacy for the company's aggressive territorial ambitions in the subcontinent, and constrained by the fear of provoking a rebellion among its benighted subjects and jeopardizing its deeper purposes. To ensure against the political dangers of intrusive social reform, the East India Company sought native participation in framing the crime as a cultural product, enlisting "progressive" and reform-minded natives to further the cause. Officially this activity culminated in a string of laws that dealt with sati, widow remarriage, female infanticide, and hook swinging, making for a thick, impressive statute book that began with the ban on sati in 1829. Social legislation did *not* end or even slow down, as some historians have repeatedly contended, with the dissolution of

John Company and the passing of the Indian empire to the British Crown after the major upheaval and revolt called the Mutiny of 1857. These statutes served as excellent publicity that reinforced India's image in the metropole as a cruel, heathen land, while their enforcement and efficacy were doubtful. With this in mind, we can now cut to the discovery of female infanticide in the newly conquered province of the Punjab in 1851.

The ostensible motive for waging the two Sikh Wars in 1845 and 1849, as the British predictably and retroactively claimed, was to end sati, which was rampant in that region. After Ranjit Singh's death in 1839, "[s]ix years of desperate wickedness followed, a monotonous story of civil war, assassination, and miscellaneous disorder and cruelty. The barbaric horror of these years is luridly shown by the 310 women burnt with Suchet Singh, after he was slain in attempting the throne, March 27, 1844" (Thompson: 1930: 102–3). In terms of realpolitik, the value of the Punjab was manifold: its revenues, resources, and potential were extraordinary; its people were the virile "martial races" of the subcontinent, so that the Punjab would make a fine recruiting ground for the Indian Army; and strategically it would serve as a strong buffer state and military base for the British operations in Afghanistan.

Therefore, even more predictably, soon after the Punjab was conquered, the British discovered female infanticide. Punjabi individuals and groups engaged in debate, admitted to their communal obedience to the dictates of their forefathers (rather than individual responsibility or guilt), condemned these practices in public fora, and ostensibly collaborated in the suppression of the crime. There were command performances prodded by threats of fines and worse, by caste and village headmen, who agreed to monitor their own communities.

The "mutiny" of 1857 came as a massive shock for the British in India; it proved to be a widespread rebellion, far bigger than anything they had ever expected. They came within a hair of losing the empire entirely. This experience inaugurated an era of acute mistrust of most northern Indian natives, except the Punjabis, who had proved invaluable as soldiers in quelling the revolt. The strategic and financial value of the Punjab was now redoubled. The Indian Army was revamped, its regimental units reorganized along religious and caste lines, with a disproportionately high number of recruits from the "martial races" of the Punjab. The Punjab region was seen as the key to holding the empire, which the British managed to do for the next ninety years. The "civilizing mission" was concomitantly muted, but far from abandoned, in the second half of the nineteenth century, as we shall see.

FEMALE INFANTICIDE

Against this broadly painted historical backdrop we must situate the discovery and suppression of female infanticide in the Punjab in the wake of the British victory over the Sikhs in 1849. It was not a new crime; most officials were familiar with the pioneering 1789 report of Jonathan Duncan, the British resident at Banaras, written when plans to annex that region were being hatched.[5] Duncan's memorable account of female infanticide as practiced by the Rajkumars, politically high-status Rajputs of the region before the British takeover, was to become the model for magistrates in the far reaches of the empire; and his sociological analysis— of culpability grounded in the unique cultural practices of "hypergamy" and "dowry"—became the official diagnostic tool for pathologists of female infanticide.

For the purposes of this investigation—of how dowry and marriage expenses came to be equated with the motive for murder of female infants, and its corollary, how women came to be regarded as a family "calamity"—I scrutinize the official record in the Punjab.

The new Punjab administration quickly generated a paper blizzard. Embedded in the reports are the points of intersection where the ulterior motives of the colonialist and the native informant colluded to create the formula in which the culpability of particular castes rather than the responsibility of particular individuals was hammered out. In this space—between British hammer and Indian anvil—gender relations were reshaped to produce a hybrid patriarchy. We will look at the very processes whereby garbled accounts and excuses were honed into tidy, unambiguous cause-and-effect narratives, or what Kipling might have rendered as his "just-so stories," and why "insatiable curiosity" was vested in creating them. In a profound way these documents capture the conversations of men, of officer and native, and how they talked about matters of political import, of survival and killing in anecdotal ways. This listening will allow us to analyze the complicity of men, albeit unequal in power and effect, which distorted indigenous institutions and rent the safety nets engineered by women for their own protection.

The case against dowry was fabricated in the process of intensive interrogations by ethnographer-bureaucrats of headmen in whose villages infanticide was suspected. Midwives and women, the likely perpetrators, are not on record as participants in these conversations. Since it had been long established from pertinent Sanskrit texts that infanticide was a heinous crime, motives for committing it should have been inadmissible in an honest investigation, and those who confessed to its habitual commission should have been punished as murderers. Yet discussions of the culturally constructed motives for committing the crime dominated the proceedings serially in each province and sabotaged a forthright examination of the true extent of the crime itself.

Alexander Walker, the British resident at the independent princely state of Baroda, near Bombay, in 1808 submitted a widely publicized (and later much emulated) report in which he stated that in an important Hindu text whose title he transliterated as the "Vatim Buwunt Purana," infanticide was considered a perfectly abhorrent act. He cited a translation of the pertinent verse:

It is as great an offence to kill an embryo as a Brahmin; that to kill one woman is as great a sin as killing a hundred Brahmins; that to put one child to death is as great a transgression against the divine laws as to kill a hundred women; and that the perpetrator of the sin shall be damned to hell where he shall be infested with as many maggots as he may have hairs on his body; be born again a leper and be debilitated in his members.[6]

With this unequivocal condemnation in a Sanskrit text, the British could have promptly passed a law forbidding the practice as early as 1789, instead of playing it safe and deliberating on the matter for eighty more years! Torn between his conviction that such deeds should be ruthlessly punished and the political necessity of not antagonizing powerful Rajput chieftains, Walker decided to publicize female infanticide in order to shame the culpable "superior chiefs" into abjuring the practice. He sought to embarrass them by summoning *biradari* (caste or brotherhood organization) meetings, writing them personal letters of admonition, and seeking direct discussions with their mothers and wives. Later, heavy fines that ranged from Rs. 2,500 to Rs. 30,000 (depending on the rank of the infanticidal chieftain), rewards for informers, and marks of recognition for those who reformed their ways were proposed to bolster the system, although the fear of offending "the feelings of the Jharejas" mitigated the fines. The response of several chiefs to these tactics was to request a remission in the British revenue demand, which only confirmed for Walker their "avaricious character" and "caste pride" (Panigrahi 1972: 49). These official actions in Baroda became the nucleus of subsequent actions in the Punjab against female infanticide. Panigrahi gives us a detailed but uncritical account of British policy in the Punjab and all other provinces where it was found. Only after eighty years of ethnographic exegeses was legislation finally passed in 1870 (Panigrahi 1972).

CASTE AS CULPRIT

On 10 June 1853, R. Montgomery, the judicial commissioner of the Punjab, prepared his *Minute on Infanticide* (Montgomery 1853: 391–409).[7] He distilled in "a statement of the facts" the fairly extensive responses generated by his circular (dated 31 December 1851) to all commissioners of divisions of the Punjab, directing them to investigate the extent of the prevalence of this crime in their areas and to suggest measures for its suppression. His own circular was instigated by Major Lake, the deputy commissioner of Gurdaspoor district, who brought to the attention of the Punjab government in Lahore his discovery (on 24 November 1851) of "the prevalence of Infanticide among the Bedees in Dera Baba Nanak in his district" (p. 1). Montgomery's eighteen-page *Minute* is an authoritative abstract of the many responses that "shew, in detail, the classes and the localities infected by this dreadful crime" (p. 392). The divisional reports by these amateur politician-scholar-bureaucrats on which the *Minute* was based are minor ethnographies. They are replete with caste- and tribe-based statistics, detailed descriptions of marriage customs, speculative comments on the cultural nature of the crime and its perpetrators, and self-congratulation at the steps envisaged to eradicate it and raise the erstwhile Indian ruling classes to the humane standards of the British. Infanticide is described in these documents as a crime to which specific classes of natives are "notoriously addicted." Each report consciously harks back to its forebears—earlier reports by British officers in other territories, such as those by Duncan and Walker from Banaras and Baroda.

Montgomery promised that Punjabi infanticide would be seriously addressed, since the expert on the subject, Mr. C. Raikes, had been transferred to Lahore and had brought his zeal to the task (p. 392). Raikes, when he was the magistrate and collector of Mainpuri district in the North-West Provinces, had been alleged to have complete success in inducing the Rajputs of that district to abandon the practice. The publication of these proceedings in November 1851 "has excited a greater interest in the subject throughout the country generally," Montgomery noted.

By the time Montgomery requested his district commissioners to prepare reports on the prevalence of female infanticide in the Punjab in 1851, the business of investigating and reporting on the subject was already a fine art, with models to replicate. Although differences were noted in separate regions, the discernible structure and intertextuality of the infanticide reports created a distinct genre. For instance, the investigations turned up the same causal connections—caste pride, dowry, and hypergamy—but bureaucratic habits kept information on infanticide from spilling over into reports on famine or revenue, even though both types of reports were often composed by the same officials. The practice of compartmentalizing "cultural" and "economic" information, which ought to have been linked to make deeper sense of either, lay behind the insufficient and frequently erroneous analyses of Indian society, customs, and crimes. Discussions of the pernicious effects of the custom of dowry, however, managed to seep into both boxes. This was because it was not only seen as a prime cause of female infanticide but was also blamed as the chief reason for the indebtedness and impoverishment of Punjabi peasant farmers and thus for their default on revenue payments. The limitations of such a diagnosis became manifest when British intentions to "civilize" competed with and lost out to their intention of collecting their stipulated revenues.

Caste became equated with culture, the prism through which all Hindus had timelessly seen their world and to the dictates of which they acted in unthinking conformity. Female infanticide was established as behavior mandated by caste leaders or caste rules: it was the predilection of certain hypergamous high-caste Sikhs and Hindus or a result of the ignorance, improvidence, and folly pervasive among the lower castes (lesser peasantry), who wantonly and habitually strained to enhance their caste status by emulating the culture of high castes, even going into debt to give dowries and celebrate their daughters' weddings. This latter was even more reprehensible because peasant indebtedness was seen as the chief cause of arrears in paying government dues.

For the British, the most culpable group in the entire province of the Punjab were a *jati*, or subcaste, of the Khatri caste called the Bedis, a sacral group by virtue of the fact that the founder of the Sikh faith was a Bedi.[8] This conclusion, as we shall presently see, was derived from the report of Major Lake from Dera Baba Nanak and was confirmed in the reports of Major Edwardes and Major Abbot. Major Edwardes recaptured his conversation with an elder Bedi during his energetic inquiry into female infanticide. His search for unmitigated "caste pride" was richly rewarded, as we see in the following narration.

Dharam Chand Bedi, the grandson of Guru Nanak (1469–1538, the founder of the Sikh faith), had two sons and a daughter. The latter was betrothed to a Khatri boy, but on the day of the nuptials the bride's family suffered a deep affront by the groom's family. The groom's party insisted that the doorway of the house be widened, and destroyed it by force to allow the groom's litter to pass through. "The incensed Bedee prayed 'that the threshold of the Khuttree tribe might in like manner be ruined'" and the nuptial rites were celebrated amid mutual ill-feeling. Finally, when the bride's brothers accompanied the groom's party to bid their sister farewell, "the weather was hot and the party took a malicious pleasure in taking the young Bedees further than etiquette required." The boys returned, footsore and weary, and it was then that the enraged Dharam Chand,

> indignant at all the insults that the bridal of his daughter had drawn upon him from an *inferior class*, laid the inhuman injunction on his descendants, that "in future no Bedee should let a daughter live." The boys were horror-stricken at so un-natural a law, and with clasped hands represented to their father, that to take the life of a child was one of the greatest sins in the shastras. But Dhurm Chund replied, "that if the Bedees remained true to their faith and abstained from lies and strong drink, providence would reward them with none but male children. But at any rate, let the burden of the crime be upon his neck, and no one else's," and from that time forth Dhurm Chund's head fell forward upon his chest and he evermore walked like one who bore an awful weight upon his shoulders.[9]

The Bedi elder, with his permanently stooped mien, appears to have taken on the shame and guilt for generations of Bedis to come, an idea consonant with the nature of caste authority as constructed by the native informant and the curious Edwardes. With "consciences thus relieved," the "race" of Bedis "continued for 300 years to murder their infant daughters, and if any Bedee out of natural feeling, preserved a girl, he was excommunicated by the rest, and treated as a common sweeper. . . . It is difficult to imagine how the parents of a whole class could so systematically stifle the yearnings of nature as to carry out the murderous injunction of their early teachers" (Edwardes 1852: para. 9). Edwardes's rare account of how the infant was murdered is also gleaned "from questioning some Bedees closely upon the actual mode of their infanticide." When a Bedi mother delivered a child, the attendant "nurse" communicated to the family outside the "purda" whether it was a boy or a girl.

> [If a daughter was born] the mother turned her face to the wall, well know-ing the sentence that awaited her offspring; and the silence of disappoint-ment was soon broken by the elder matrons of the family commanding the nurse to put the child to death. Various were the ways in which this order was executed; sometimes the nurse stopped the infant's breath in a few mo-ments with her hand, but oftener the object was effected by neglect; by ex-posing the babe in the winter on the cold floor, and in summer by aggra-vating heat. And as one of my informants remarked, "you see, Sir, they are but poor little things, and, a puff of wind puts them out." (para. 12)

The head of a single Bedi family defied this ritual code of behavior, Edwardes's re-port continues, and was promptly excommunicated by the religious leader of the Bedis; "all but his own family treated him as a sweeper" (para. 14). He goes on to recount that the Bedis "go even a step further in brutality" because the dead fe-male infant's family buries her with a piece of raw sugar placed between her lips and a piece of cotton in her hand while reciting a couplet, which he quotes and translates.

> Goor khaien, pownee kutteen;
> Aap na aieen; bhayan ghulleen.
> [Eat your goor (raw sugar), and spin your thread,
> But go and send a boy instead.]

He continues, "*The Bedees deny this,* but are not offended at the quotation; and one of them corrected me in rehearsing it and explained its meaning" (para. 13; em-phasis added).

Edwardes states that the Bedis denied that the couplet was part of any ritual killing of girls (but were not offended by it), but he chooses to dismiss these de-nials. Edwardes selected his informants mainly to prove his own theory that in-fanticide was part and parcel of their religious beliefs. His presentation of the couplet is inaccurate. It is in fact sung by pregnant mothers—who are at the spin-ning wheel eating raw sugar (since folklore even today has it that a craving for sugar means that the woman is carrying a boy and a craving for sour things means it is a girl). *Aap na aieen; bhayan ghulleen* (*ghulleen* should be transliterated *ko layeen*) means "You don't come but bring a brother." The chanting of the verse and the placing of raw sugar in the mouth of a dead child and a piece of cotton in her hand gives the tale the touch of a heathen ritual that lends it credibility. Ed-wardes's description of the Bedis, with their caste rules rigid and unchanged for three centuries, is clearly what Montgomery urged his other officers to find for other culpable castes. A "just-so story" about Dharam Chand Bedi and a mistranslated verse collected from informants trying to excuse the inexcusable were officially recorded as the founding moment for a caste crime. We are left with two connected questions: what did the elder Bedi's story tell Edwardes? and what does the elder Bedi's story tell us?

The Bedi's story represents for Edwardes the end of a quest; he now has the irrefutable reason for the killing of female infants from a caste elder, and it is unmistakably rooted in caste pride. Such anecdotes from the natives themselves supply the authentic touch to narratives by strangers in a strange land. Edwardes believes, equally easily, that it "is now solemnly affirmed by the Bedees that from the very beginning of British rule, Female Infanticide was checked, and is now almost extinguished" (Edwardes 1852: para. 16). His remarks continually reveal his own credulity, ignorance, and religious prejudice. He accepts the Bedi tale as the direct sanction for mindless cruelty because it conforms to his own preconception that even the wisest natives are benighted and blindly obedient to the alleged dictates of their caste. Infanticide suddenly has an unimpeachable religious provenance—the founders of this brutality are the grandsons of the founder of the Sikh faith, Guru Nanak himself.

The story was an obvious coup for Edwardes; his report was rich with ethnographic complexity that dazzled his superiors. Montgomery appreciated it highly and commented that the "reports are generally very full; pre-eminent among them stands that of Major H. B. Edwardes" (Montgomery 1853: 392). He assumed that these stories (for others were reported) contained all the elements that were needed to fix the constitutive element and underlying motive for the crime. They underscored what the British already believed to be the mindless barbarity of caste rules, the bedrock of an inferior culture, and did not implicate the individual in making the decision to kill a daughter in each case. By the time this story of origins made it into Montgomery's report, it had attained the status of social science, and we thereby receive indubitable proof of that ruthless logic that governs the actions of the highest-ranked members of Sikh society: the pride in their religion and caste dictates both hypergamy among the Sikhs and its fatal results for all their female infants.

As Edwardes goes on to describe the dramatic moral change that British rule has rapidly brought to the Bedis, his gullibility and his inability to see the irony in the elder Bedi's commentary become patent. The Bedi elder, who must have spoken on condition of anonymity, for he is never named, says,

> After murdering our daughters for three hundred years, we are compelled
> by our rulers to abandon the custom imposed on us by our prophets. In
> doing so, let us take steps to make the innovation at all events successful.
> Let us not put it in the power of our enemies to say, that no good has come

of our deserting the old paths. Under the Sikhs, we were a sacred race, honored, and wealthy. In the eyes of the English, a Bedee and a Bhungee [sweeper] are equal. Our jageers are lapsing day by day, and no gifts and offerings are coming in. We shall be poorer and poorer year after year. Why, therefore attempt to vie with the Sureens [a wealthy section of Khatris who allegedly spent ruinously on weddings and dowries] which only a few of us can afford? Let us sink at once to the level of the Bhoonjaees [the fifty-two Khatri lineages that intermarried freely], which the poorest of us can maintain. (Edwardes 1852: para. 23)

Wrapped inside his fabulous tale about the Bedi past is the barbed truth about the Bedi present under the new rulers. The British and their new land ownership and revenue system have ruined a very prosperous and once politically powerful people, and the colonials are happy to equate the Bedis with the lowest sweepers. The Bedis have lost their lands, and therefore their power, so their caste status is now an empty burden. Their actions—particularly infanticide—can have no strategic meaning for the warrior peoples now; it is, indeed, a cruel barbarity. Edwardes, on the other hand, is pleased that the Bedis attribute the destruction of Bedi caste status to the British takeover of the Sikh realm, which, in his view, is tantamount to the destruction of the source of three centuries of entrenched infanticidal feelings toward their own daughters. This first-person narrative stands in as the voice of the clan doubly fraught: they lost their country to the British and now it is their social prestige that is under siege.

Major Edwardes, working separately in Jullundur, but much influenced by the earlier reports on the subject, particularly one by Barnes on the Rajputs, concludes that the Bedi and Rajput cases are almost interchangeable: "Through the mists of this story," Edwardes concluded, "it seems clear that religious pride, and horror of giving a daughter to an inferior caste, and not pecuniary considerations, first led the Bedees to adopt the custom of Female Infanticide." This was his mistaken insight from that long conversation with the Bedi elder. For him caste pride stood clearly indicted as the cause for female infanticide, notwithstanding the fact that Sikh religion explicitly rejected the entire caste system, and Gobind Singh, their last guru, who drew up very strict rules of conduct for the Sikhs, forbade the practice and had his injunction engraved on the entrance of the Akal Takht near the Golden Temple at Amritsar a century and a half before Edwards's own investigation. He goes on to explain hypergamy. "For throughout the East, I believe it is the principle of matrimonial alliances, that girls marry their equals, or superiors, and boys their equals or inferiors in rank. This placed the *descendants of the great Sikh teacher* on the horns of a dilemma, either to abandon their high pretensions, or else get rid of the difficulty by murdering their daughters" (Edwardes 1852: para. 10; emphasis added). So persuaded was the entire British establishment by the argument that caste status and pride were organic parts of Hindu culture and that pecuniary motives on the part of the Rajputs and Bedis were absent that their reports became very repetitive, and some went to absurd lengths to prove the point: "What still further proves that the motive to Infanticide was religious and not pecuniary," states Edwardes, "is the fact that in consequence of the Bedees having no daughters to give to the Khuttrees in exchange, they were compelled to adopt the singular custom of giving *dowries* with their sons, to marry Khuttree daughters. Not withstanding this obvious purchase, the Bedees prided themselves so highly that they never allowed a Khuttree to smoke from the same hooka. . . . How characteristic of the two races [Rajputs and Khatris], this choice between dignity and gain" (Edwardes 1852: para. 11; emphasis added). But the Bedis are Khatris, and so this conversation is not about caste but about their lost political standing, which Edwardes and his interpreters ignore. The coup de grace to the caste arrogance of the Bedis, Edwardes anticipated, was imminent, since the true caste antecedents of Baba Nanak himself would be determined at the forthcoming Bedi *panchayat* (caste council) at Phagwara, also in his district. The Sareen and the Bhunjaee Khatris (of which the latter made up the overwhelming majority of Khatri clans and were regarded as inferior by the Sareens) both had stories and verses to back their claims (paras. 24–26).

So something else is occurring as this interlocution goes on between British officers and native informants. Edwardes, who has made the elder Bedi's story about the origins of infanticide a part of the written record of the Raj, fails to realize that the wily elder has managed to get into a British report an uncontested statement that Nanak was indeed a Bedi, just before the debate about the Guru's origins was to occur! Edwardes has also scored a tacit point, one that his informants enabled: official British reports, including his own, were rapidly becoming an unimpeachable authority for caste ranking. Was it not now beyond dispute or quibble that Nanak was a Bedi (instead of a ordinary Sarin), when it was written thus in Major Edwardes' report? While the Bedis exult at Nanak being a Bedi, Edwardes is thrilled that at the meeting scheduled at Phagwara, the prominent Baba Sohan Singh Bedi "was preparing to betroth his daughter," who had not been cruelly killed, "and as he is a man of influence, the course now pursued by him is expected to become a precedent" (Edwardes 1852: para 26). But best of all, caste (also interchangeably called race and tribe) has been declared the agent of Punjabi history, and local history is nothing more than the practices and customs of local tribes; the Bedis are off the hook for murdering their infant daughters.

Edwardes is deluded into believing that his intervention is the catalyst for change; he is going to break the Bedi habit of killing their daughters just as abruptly and authoritatively as Dharam Chand Bedi had instituted the practice three centuries ago. "All the Bedees with whom I have conversed, have assured me that the abandoning of the practice of Female Infanticide is now fully recognized among them; and that a great agitation is at this moment going on in the tribe for the authoritative establishment of a scale of dowries for the Bedee daughters"

(Edwardes 1852: para. 19). Recall that the Dharam Chand story had no mention of dowry in it, but Edwardes has managed to convince them that it was the dowry problem that needed to be fixed. He believes he has wrought a revolution, for was it not also true, he asks, that on his urging the Bedis and the run-of-the-mill Khatris agreed to share their hookahs [smoking pipes] and to intermarry "as an indication of the change now going on" (para. 27)? If he could review his report today, he would have to note in the margins that female sex ratios were still depressingly low, but there was no dispute today among Sikhs of all stripes that their esteemed Guru Nanak was, indeed, a Khatri of the Bedi *jati* and that the Sareens lost their claim. Also, he would concede that dowries, which were not a problem in 1852, had risen exponentially in scope and scale because of the interventions he (and others like him) made to "fix" their scale to match caste status.

Edwardes was diligent but naïve, to say the least. Modern ethnographers have written about how villagers are apt to give them half-truths or even fanciful and elaborate explanations in a bid to protect their own interests, particularly if the outsider is powerful and therefore has his own axe to grind. Villagers, particularly elder spokesmen, pontificate fictions or suppress information that may reflect adversely on their religious or caste status, "and that which they believed might lead to additional taxation, legal proceedings or other governmental interference" (Berreman 1972: 4; also see xvii–lvii). The elder Bedi knows that his hoary tale cannot be verified; other informants might even corroborate it, as Major Abbot personally found out. No Bedi in the district would contradict anything in Major Edwardes's report, since it established them as the direct descendants of Guru Nanak. The report also makes no criminal charge against any particular family or village. The Bedis were asked to give up the error of their ways, and this they solemnly agreed to do. If they were not judged to be the agents of their own history, they could also not be punished—neither imprisoned nor fined—for ritual murders of their daughters they were enjoined to commit by the tenets of their caste.

The case of overweening caste pride against the Rajputs had already been made in the North-West Provinces about a half century earlier, and we find Montgomery using those data to construct generic Rajput behavior to explain marriage practices among the Punjabi Rajputs instead of ordering a fresh investigation to establish their culpability in the Punjab.

> The practice among the Rajpoots is of extreme antiquity, and arose from the combined motives of pride and poverty. The Bedees were actuated by pride alone as they are generally opulent, and live in affluence.
>
> Amongst the Hindoos an idea prevails, that the bestowal of a female in marriage betokens inferiority, their sons may marry their equals or inferiors, but custom prescribes that their daughters should marry only their equals, or their superiors. Also that a female cannot remain unmarried without bringing disgrace on her family. It is considered, therefore, to be

imperative on a parent to provide, betimes, a suitable husband for his daughter; and by delaying to do so, he is thought to be disgracing her.

It follows then, in the case of the Rajputs, that as we ascend the scale of society (I quote from Mr. Barnes' report):[10] "We must eventually reach those who stand on the highest round of the ladder and admit no superior; these classes find themselves in an awkward dilemma—either they must bring up their daughters unmarried, or they must provide husbands for them and thereby confess that they are not the high and exclusive race to which they lay claim; either alternative is attended with disgrace, and there is but one remedy, viz., to destroy their female infants: and hence we see the farce of conventional rules. Murder may be committed without any stigma attaching to the murderer, but artificial restraints cannot be avoided without loss of caste and honor." Among the Hill tribes, the Jammu and Kutoch (Kangra) clans rank first, and yet Infanticide is not confined to them. The other classes also have high pretensions, and as they are precluded from inter-marriage with their tribe by consanguinity, so they refuse to risk their claim to superiority by giving their daughters to a rival clan. (Montgomery 1853: 395–96)

Montgomery's *Minute* repeatedly affirms that this crime, of great antiquity, was only getting worse with the loss of position and status that attended the coming of the British Raj, which demoted all Kshatriyas—Bedis, Khatris of lesser rank, and Rajputs—to the ranks of common soldiers in the British army. Much like the displaced Bedis, the Rajputs were suffering from increasing poverty and were not able to adapt to their new circumstances under the new regime.

They could no longer "give a dowry worthy of their lineage, and this gives a [fresh] impetus to dooming their daughters to destruction. They are no longer required as formerly [under Sikh rule] in the higher grades of the army [which were now exclusively reserved for European troops], and they will only enlist to a limited extent as common soldiers; nor will they handle the plough; this would be contrary to their ideas. They are in comparative destitution, and the sacrifice of daughters is alike dictated by their position and their poverty" (Montgomery 1853: 398).

The only reason, Edwardes confusedly deduces, that any Khatri female offspring lives at all is *also* authorized by religious writ. "[T]o receive the 'Kuneeadan' [*kanyadan*] is by the *inconsistent* law of the Shastras [Hindu legal texts] a great sin; but to give it, is one of the most meritorious of acts; consequently *to rear a daughter and give her in marriage was necessary to every Hindoo, who had ever been married himself*"(Edwardes 1852: para. 43; emphasis added). The explication of cultural paradoxes was clearly Edwardes's forte, but his methodology apparently did not include checking these alleged inconsistencies. Only a groom receives the gift of the virgin, and if such an act was a sin then marriage itself would be a sinful event, instead of a compulsory stage in the life of all Hindu men except those who choose to leave the social world and become ascetics.

That Edwardes's Punjabi informants were having considerable fun at his expense by inventing patently absurd religious laws becomes apparent when he writes that a "Brahmin tried to explain the sin to me as consisting in this, that 'Kuneeadan' is a form of 'Poon' [*punya*] or religious gift, which none but a Brahmin should dare to receive" (paras. 43–44). Had he been open to any cross-cultural ramifications in patriarchal societies, he would have found that *kanyadan* is not such a bizarre custom after all; in the Christian tradition, as I have said, a father is also required to "give away" or gift his virgin daughter to the groom.

Thus far it would be safe to claim that in Edwardes's careful analysis hypergamy and its correlates, caste pride and extravagant weddings and dowries, emerged as the driving force behind the crime of infanticide. British understandings and constructions of caste as the organic, fixed, and unchanging structure of Hindu society were already cemented in place; caste was indeed accepted by colonial scholar-bureaucrats as the irreducible unit of social agency and responsibility. The hypergamy argument served two essentially political purposes of the colonial regime. First, it morally discredited the classes at the top of the former power hierarchy that they had forcibly displaced—Khatris and Rajputs in terms of caste and Hindus and Sikhs in terms of religion. Second, it highlighted the want of civilization and the barbaric nature of native belief and behavior systems, the cruelty and irrationality endemic in the two religions.

But the profound conclusion that hypergamy and its economic inseparable, dowry, were the motivational force behind the eliminating of female infants was itself curiously contradicted by the colonials themselves as a result of investigations among lesser Khatris and Rajputs, Punjabi Muslims, and lower-class and Jat agriculturists. We must return to Edwardes, who takes a long close look at the non-Bedi Khatris and discovers that even they, who have ever so many clans of equal status among which to find grooms, kill their daughters. So he carefully splits a theoretical hair.

Again, it is not the crime, or life-and-death questions, but the cultural cast of even economic motivation that he wants to grasp. He distinguishes between the common form of female infanticide and the proud, hypergamous Rajput or Bedi variety because "[u]nlike the Bedees the mass of Hindoos were actuated *exclusively by pecuniary motives*." Marriage expenses were now so high, he explains, that either "the father's fortunes or the daughter's lives [*sic*] must too often be sacrificed. The choice lying with the fathers, they chose Infanticide, in preference to beggary or wounded vanity"(Edwardes 1852: para. 40; emphasis added). It is this perception—that a daughter is a burden because of the expense of marrying her off—that becomes the keystone of the official policy for the prevention of female infanticide.

Edwardes found, however, that the Lahoreen Khatris (of Lahore) claimed that their caste ranking enabled them to demand dowry from the fathers of the brides they chose for their sons. This plunged Edwardes into the most complicated part of his investigations: the determining of the precise rank of each Khatri *jati*, or subcaste. It is clear that he did not understand that rankings were contested and fluid and that they changed from village to village, and were reconfigured yet again in large, political centers like Lahore. His informants made him believe otherwise.

He apparently spent many days touring villages with a small army of assistants and laboriously compiled a long and definitive list of all the Khatri clans in the region.[11] That such a list did not already exist among a literate group ought to have indicated to Edwardes that Khatris (and other castes) believed that to draw up such lists would only petrify a fluid system in which rankings were continually negotiated with the political hierarchy. If ranks had, indeed, been fixed in perpetuity, there would definitely have been lists in existence in every village and in the court at Lahore, specially among the literate, aggressively bookkeeping Khatri clans. His informants appeared as zealous to give information (and who would not wish to play a role in compiling the list the officials now wanted?) as he was to receive it, and this very effort to "retrieve" what Edwardes assumed to be irrevocably fixed rankings became an opportunity for wily informants to promote the interests of their own *jati* and to actually create such a list. One informant laboriously named a hundred subdivisions (*gotr*) of the lower branch of the Khatris, the Sareens, an act that might appear quaint and even silly unless we realize that he was looking to the new rulers to assign afresh, after the defeat of the Sikh rulers, political significance to these myriad lineages. Edwardes unwittingly did just that when he decided to select only eight from among them and name them as the principal *gotr* (paras. 45–54). Clearly his choices were not randomly determined but were negotiated by the self-interested assistants. Ironically, these rankings were to have only academic and cultural meaning for the new rulers. When he methodically notes that the Sareens "have no laws regulating the expense of marriages," their extravagance is unbounded, and they will not marry "on any terms" with the Bhoonjaee Khatris "between whom and themselves there is a religious jealousy which can never be overcome" (Edwardes 1852: para. 48), they do appear to be a needlessly fastidious tribe. Described as such, the caste system does look like a frozen, antiquated, rigid social structure devoid of any political significance.

The other, higher branch of the Khatris made up by far the majority and was therefore even more complex. This group had three superior grades of families—the *urahi-ghar*, or two-and-a-half houses; the *char-ghar*, or four houses; and the *bara-ghar*, or twelve houses—followed by a "countless" number of intermarrying *gotr* lumped under the rubric of Bhunjaees, supposedly the number *bawinja*, or fifty-two in Punjabi. Edwardes painstakingly recorded what his informants told him, particularly regarding how these names and groupings came to exist one historic day at the court of Emperor Akbar some three hundred years earlier. Edwardes paraphrased another "just-so story" on how castes became split into so many rival clans: all Khatri *gotr* "were formerly united and freely intermarried, but were splintered into these many segments by a single event: the intervention of the Mughal emperor, Akbar [1556–1605], on behalf of a widow."[12] Taking pity at the plight of a Khatri widow whose husband had been slain in battle, Edwardes is told, Akbar resolved to abolish the law against widow remarriage. He summoned deputies from the Khatris from every town in the Punjab. Multan was the headquarters of the Khatris, and the two most influential leaders there were the brothers Lulloo and Jugdur. The brothers listened to the problem and told the royal messengers "that they must consult their mother, as this was a matter that concerned women even more than men." Their aged widowed mother said she would agree to widow remarriage "on condition that another husband should be found for herself." The sons reasoned with her that a husband of her ripe eighty years of age would be of little use. To this she replies that "she would compound for two husbands of forty years each." The sons were "abashed at these insults to the memory of their father, and a proposition so opposed to their religion." Punjabis who heard Emperor Akbar's proposition for widow remarriage "set off for Hindoostan."

At Akbar's court in Agra, all those who looked for court favor and gave their unqualified adherence to widow remarriage were called Sareens. Those who wished to argue the point with the emperor came to be called the Lahoreens; those who came to the court and kept their silence were called the *char-ghar*; those who did not enter the court but waited to hear the verdict became the *bara-ghar*, or the outsiders; and those who turned back with "faith uncorrupted" are the mass of the Bhoonjaees. Needless to say, "amidst such divisions the emperor could gain no general consent to his new law, and even the Sureens never permitted their widows to practice it."[13]

Edwardes recorded all this information in definitive detail only "to apply this account of the Bhoonjaee Division of Khuttrees to the subject of Female Infanticide," because in this story, he believed, lay "the explanation" for infanticide he had been "at some pains to extract." It is difficult to believe that he failed to recognize the analogy his informants were making about government intervention in social matters or their intent in frankly admitting to committing the crime. Perhaps those castes and tribes who agreed to abandon the practice of female infanticide might receive the same political influence as did the Khatris who agreed with Emperor Akbar on the question of widow remarriage. Edwardes either ignored or failed to perceive the double-edged political import of the story and of caste rankings—yet again. The Khatris rightly perceived a diminution of their status under the British, who privileged Jats and Muslims with respect to the lands and jobs that the Kshatriyas had previously held in the armed forces of Emperor Akbar and Maharaja Ranjit Singh.[14]

There also appears to be a wisely oblique moral inserted into this story told to their British masters and interlocutors. The Bhunjaee Khatri informant appears to be implying in a subtle and cautionary way that Hindu Khatris were united and respected each other until the intervention of Emperor Akbar, who tried to make widow remarriage a law, which divided the community; perhaps this meddling with female infanticide would leave the society even more fractured as the British tried to pin the blame on specific tribes or castes. Politically motivated interventions (for what else could this be coming from Christian conquerors from a distant land?) would lead only to greater fractiousness and divisions among all religious communities and their subdivisions. In all probability, those who practiced infanticide knew who did it and why, so accusations against selected "hypergamous" Khatri clans were misguided.

But Edwardes was not attuned to hearing anything other than "cultural" quibbles in all this political information, even as he meticulously noted the divisions and created rerankings on the say-so of a few very articulate Khatri informants. His own single-track sleuthing ignored the informants' hidden message; like his bureaucratic predecessors, he would conclude that the fine distinctions described by this informant were the hallmarks of a society that believed in hypergamy (why else would they vie for ranks?) and its corollary, dowry, which, of course, made them infanticidal! Another informant spelled out the inflexibility of hypergamy among the Khatris in tedious detail. The Lahoreen Khatris, he asserted to Edwardes, belong to the top grade of *urahi-ghar*, and are custom-bound to give their daughters to a very restricted number of families within this group. Whereas ideally a Lahoreen male ought to marry within the same *urahi* (two-and-a-half) houses, he is at liberty to receive a wife from Khatris of lower rank because his wife acquires the higher standing after marriage. (The implications of gender trumping caste remain elusive for Edwardes in his obsession with only one aspect of hypergamy.) The next in rank, in the same way, receive daughters from the ranks below them but did not give daughters to them, and the three upper ranks of Khatris occupy the same position relative to the mass of unclassified Khatris (Edwardes 1852: para. 60).

Edwardes concludes that he was "convinced that the first thing necessary in legislating for the natives is thoroughly to understand their existing status, customs, prejudices and traditions. In these lies the heart of the people, and through these only, so long as they are Heathens, can they be approached with any hope of usefulness" (Edwardes 1852: para. 83). For Edwardes, his persistence in finding out these details about their caste was the key to their cultural universe. Knowledge of their terrible ways and their culturally inspired cruelties was power, and was the only hope for an alien government to rule them and make laws without provoking an uprising.

This persistent use of what I call "cultural forensics" leads to the discovery of only high-caste "cultural fingerprints" at the scene of the crime. As long as criminal behavior, including infanticide, was seen as rooted in Hinduism and the caste system, little real help or attention would be paid to the asymmetries of power in gender relations, in spite of the British purport to "uplift" the lot of the Hindu woman. Edwardes presents us with a diametrically opposed view, now clearly blaming Sikh rule rather than Hindu culture.

> [T]here exist customs of expense and at the marriages of daughters which are intolerable to parents, and which under Sikh rule, have been avoidable only by Female Infanticide. By general consent and observation, this sad result has been considerably checked by the country passing under our rule, and the dread of our criminal laws; but while the cause [dowry payments] remains un-eradicated in every home, we may be sure that under the surface a sad strife is going on between new laws and ancient customs, between the ruinous consequence of committing crime, and the ruinous consequence of not committing it.[15]

Edwardes had, indeed, uncovered a startling shift in the meaning of dowry in mid-nineteenth-century Lahore, but there is a major problem with his analysis of this shift. He tried to fit the facts into the theories of hypergamy and dowry and did not investigate what else might have caused the kind of violence he describes. Yet in his exuberance as the young investigator, he steers perilously close to another kind of truth about caste rules. He laments that there are too many "self-made Laws" and breathtaking regional diversity even "whilst the same castes pervade the country, spring from the same root, and have fallen into the same absurdities." He recommends that "no patch-work remedies" be tried but a uniform set of laws, "drawn by the Board of Administration, not pecked at by District Officers, who will only produce a mass of incongruous local Laws. . . . The variety of rules will end in all being optional and none binding. It would be far better for the Board to digest the information furnished from the districts, and in consultation with a Grand Punchaeet [*punchayat* or tribunal] to which deputies from all Districts should be invited issue an authoritative scale of marriage fees for every class" (Edwardes 1852: para 82). The chief commissioner did not ignore these suggestions, and such a meeting was indeed held, as we shall see in the next chapter.

It is noteworthy that this obstinately argued case for hypergamy, or more generally for caste-driven behavior instead of human agency as the culprit, was countered to a large extent by the volleys of conflicting data also present in the same reports. Just when we might be persuaded to believe that the Bedi Sikhs and other Khatris were the exclusive offenders and that infanticide was a culturally sanctioned crime, Edwardes is confronted with the disturbing census figures for the rest of the population, who entertain neither caste pretensions nor large numbers of wedding guests. It comes as no great surprise that Edwardes suddenly indicts all Hindus "of what are called respectable classes" who also have enormously skewed sex ratios, "for all suffer from the same causes in exact proportion to their class pretensions" (Edwardes 1852: para. 65).

Having delivered this sweeping judgment, he moves on, only to unravel the empirical case he has painstakingly knitted together. This process begins when he has to deal with dramatically skewed sex ratios among his well-loved peasants, "the unpretending and industrious Jats" (Edwardes 1852: para. 66) and Muslims. The Jats were a numerous and widely dispersed agricultural caste, whose members included Hindus and Sikhs, and the majority of whom practiced bride-price. The Muslim Jats, called Meos and concentrated in Gurgaon and Rajasthan, claimed the same customary practices in the colonial period (Chowdhry 1994: 251), although Islam does not countenance bride-price for marriage and Muslims often marry paternal cousins. Whether or not caste distinctions were important for Muslims, their sex ratios were almost twice as bad as those of Hindu high castes in the figures turned up by Edwardes's enumerators.

Edwardes, pressed for a credible scenario to explain Muslim numbers, unconvincingly decided to pin the blame more widely on all Hindus rather than exclusively on the upper castes. He stated that "all respectable classes, more or less, practiced Infanticide under the Sikhs." They did so secretly, "and not to anything like the extent of the Chowhans [Rajputs] of Hindoostan, but it was generally understood, *and was sufficiently common to be no cause of reproach*" (Edwardes 1852: para. 38; emphasis added). This statement is quite bewildering, after his tangled and persistent explications of the tyranny of hypergamy and caste pride among the Khatris and Rajputs.

Edwardes and his informants seem not to be able to spin a real just-so story that would explain why it was that the very carefully conducted census appended to his report showed the aggregate "among all classes of Hindoos" were "54,095 boys and only 44,909 girls; or one-fifth less" (Edwardes 1852: para. 39). For all their ability to elicit explanatory narratives from the Rajputs and the Khatris, neither Edwardes nor any of the other forty or so district magistrates charged with writing such reports found stories that would explain the practice of infanticide among the lower castes, undeniable in the face of equally skewed sex ratios. That lower castes were capable of telling interesting tales about how they came to be lower castes is clear from the much scholarly ethnography of Indian villages enlivened with such anecdotal embroidery; yet these colonial reports are singularly devoid of any narration at all by lower-status Punjabi Sikhs, Hindus, and Muslims. Perhaps Edwardes and his band of investigators simply ignored bride-price-paying groups or Muslims because they were already convinced that the causes of infanticide were hypergamy, caste pride, and dowry. For what incentive would Jats, who received money for their daughters' marriages, or Muslims, who did not pay dowries, have to murder their infant daughters? Or was it the political importance of Jats and Muslims to the British hold over the Punjab that make it injudicious to explore the uncomfortable truths embedded in the empirical data? It would have undermined imperial purposes to antagonize Hindu, Sikh, and Muslim Jat soldiers and farmers, and the politically powerful Muslim tribesmen who secured the northwestern frontier against the Afghans, so the "civilizing mission" conveniently exempted some groups from its purview. Were these two groups quietly ridding themselves of some of their female offspring because the logic of an agrarian economy and the politics of keeping their landholdings secure made the need for more sons and fewer daughters inevitable? The missing denouement can be pieced together from brief asides and fragments that turn up in the record.

The figures on Jat sex ratios were much worse than any Khatri or Rajput figures. In Jullundur district there were 17,532 boys to only 12,487 girls between one and five years of age, which made for a 40 percent excess of boys in the population (Edwardes 1852: para. 66). Precisely twice as many girls were missing as among the notoriously hypergamous castes. Edwardes made a feeble bid to excuse these shocking figures by stating that "universal opinion assures us that no such disproportion exists, and that for the most part no suspicion of infanticide attaches to them. On the contrary, a Jat looks upon every female as a farm laborer, if he parts with one out of his family he expects to be paid for her, not to give a dowry. In the Cis-Sutlej [east of Sutlej] all Jats are said to receive money for their daughters" (Edwardes 1852: para. 66). Here he introduces what he considers irrefutable evidence to erase all suspicion about Jat gender relations: because Jats "receive money for their daughters," they could not possibly want to murder them at birth. Logical yes, but patently untrue, for such uncomfortably skewed ratios cannot be wished away. But the myth held: the Jats were simple, "unpretending and industrious," frugal, and without caste pride, and they even received bride-price for giving away their daughters in marriage. The census takers must have made mistakes, Edwardes averred.

Mistakes must have also been made in the census figures on Muslims, whom the British regarded as utterly separate in customs and beliefs from the Hindu and Sikh populations. The Muslim boys in Jullundur district numbered 52,538, while the girls numbered a quarter fewer at 38,303 (137:100). These figures were worse than the Hindu total for the district as a whole, which was 120:100. "Such a disproportion could only be accounted for by Female Infanticide, a practice which I believe, to be wholly repugnant to the feelings of the people, and rendered imperative by none of their religious or social obligations" (Edwardes 1852: para. 71). Edwardes, at pains to sustain the official high-caste Hindu hypergamy and dowry theory, finds himself substituting mental legerdemain for rational thought to keep the readers of his reports in awe of his cultural knowledge. He concedes that "Muslims can be just as extravagant as Hindoos in their marriages," but they "do not marry their daughters at all if they cannot afford it; and it is notorious that on this account the daughters of the best Mahomedan families often remain unmarried to the age of thirty" (Edwardes 1852: para. 72).

The generalization about Muslim daughters remaining unmarried was probably as inaccurate then as it is now. Contrasts and comparisons of the cultural and social practices of Muslims and Hindus appear with increasing frequency, but the unflattering representations of Muslims and their treatment of women were not nearly as rampant as those of Hindus. Edwardes shows no social familiarity with Muslims in this report, but it is clear that he has made up his mind that Muslims cannot commit female infanticide because, he believed, that they do not have castes and they do not give dowries. No names, no anecdotes, no confirming evidence are offered at all. His glosses are hurried, his excuses lame. The daughters of sheikhs and sayyads "are usually grown up before they are married. Among Putans [Pathans], about half the girls are married in childhood and half in maturity." He makes excuses for a very populous branch of Muslim Rajputs called the Raeens who "marry their daughters as early as the Hindoos, never leaving them at the age of ten," but he is sure that "no one who has ever walked into a Raeen village, or seen a Raeen harvest, would entertain the belief that daughters were a burden to that industrious people" (Edwardes 1852: para. 72). He says that the daughters of Muslim Rajputs, a "renegade class" whose members are very numerous in Jullundur district, are never married young. He never quite explains what influence the age of marriage has on female infanticide. Furthermore, the Muslim Rajputs are described as recent converts to Islam who are completely in the grip of the Mirasis (a caste of Muslim minstrels), "who have fastened on them as their genealogists and masters of ceremonies, and according to their pedigrees arrange their alliances, and order their expenditure" (Edwardes 1852: para. 72). This may be so, but it still does not explain the sex ratios, or why some Muslim converts might adhere to their Rajput affiliations and behavior to distinguish themselves from low-caste Muslim converts. It would have detracted from the force of Edwardes's argument to acknowledge that Muslims too might commit infanticide—and not just Rajput converts but low-caste ones such as the Mirasis, who are notorious to this day for boasting that they kill every single female child that is born to them. Edwardes really did believe in strictly compartmentalized and discrete religious and caste cultures.

Edwardes, and others who were zealously compiling evidence in other districts, would not permit a bunch of unruly empirical data to sabotage the grand theory of caste as the agent of female infanticide. He knew that his discussion of the Muslim female infant mortality statistics was going to raise more questions than he could answer, so he suggested that the data were themselves suspect. One wonders why he failed to order and supervise a fresh census to allay his own suspicions or cleanse his data of the doubt they raised.

But neither he nor any of the others changed their overdetermined theories, even though statistical "anomalies" turned up as a regular feature among Muslims and Jats in reports from other districts. Instead, he insisted that "[a]gain, the custom of some [Lahoreen] Hindoos to demand dowries is altogether unknown among Mahomedans. Therefore there does not appear to be that amount of pressure that would lead us to suspect that they practice Female Infanticide, and to doubt the general assertion that they do not. To that I deem the census, as far as the return of female children is concerned, to be below the reality, as was indeed remarked by the Settlement officer" (Edwardes 1852: paras. 73–75). Edwardes's view of female infanticide became increasingly strabismic and communal. Disproportionately high female infant mortality among the Muslims in the Punjab showed up in district after district, year after year, and only worsened over time, but official prevarication or silence prevailed.

A few decades later, it appears, Muslims gave a new spin to a much-beloved legend to justify eliminating their daughters. The popular Punjabi legend of the celebrated sixteenth-century lovers, Heer and Ranjha, was sung by minstrels throughout the Punjab.[16] Ranjha was a handsome Muslim Jat who was smitten by love for the beautiful Heer, of the Sial clan from the Jhang in western Punjab. Heer was forcibly married by her parents to Khaidon, but yearned for Ranjha. The Sials, claiming descent from the Rajputs, refused to countenance their daughter's secret liaison with a Jat, whom they considered their social inferior. The lovers' elopement enraged the families on both sides. Heer's father and brothers relentlessly pursued the couple through the woods of the Punjab; and when the two were accidentally separated, Heer was captured, poisoned, and buried in a tomb. Before the interment was complete, Ranjha arrived at the spot, managed to secrete himself inside the tomb, and died next to his beloved. Their tragic end was blamed on Heer's immoral and unwomanly behavior, which brought dishonor to her clan. The two families—the Sials and the Ranjhas (and therefore Rajputs and Jats more widely)—came to consider themselves as feuding parties (Temple 1885: 177–78, 499–580). The upshot of this tragic story is that women can bring great shame and dishonor to their families, and this became the excuse to kill female infants (Freed and Freed 1989: 149).

The popular meaning of the story of Heer and Ranjha was severely distorted to fit "just-so" as the cultural and religious basis for committing the reluctantly admitted female infanticide among Muslim warrior clans. The plot of the story contains is an obvious case of "caste pride," but this was interestingly ignored because of the perception that Muslims did not make caste distinctions, and the imbalance was blamed on improperly converted Hindus who had not acculturated to true Muslim ways. Only a century later, after Partition in 1947, when Punjabi Hindus fled to India and left Pakistan with a population that included fewer than one percent Hindus, and international agencies collected fresh statistics on sex ratios, these glosses were exposed to reveal an unambiguous picture of the extent of murder of Muslim female infants. In 1981, according to statistics published by the World Health Organization, Pakistan (which is 97 percent Muslim) led all nations in the Indian subcontinent in adverse female sex ratios, at 1,078 males for every 1,000 females. Nepal (82.2 percent Hindu) had a sex ratio of 1,049:1,000. Bangladesh was not noticeably different from its neighbors. Clearly the political economy of the region created other social and behavioral similarities across castes and religious communities, even though the culture of dowry and hypergamy was not shared across religious lines.

The culture-as-culprit theory hardened into an axiom as more future reports conformed to the Edwardes model, which had reproduced the methods and arguments of his notable forebears in Gujarat and the North-West Provinces. Soon every report was substantially similar, and it became axiomatic to assert that Rajputs, Khatris, and other high-caste Hindus were unable to break out of the financially self-destructive cycle of marriage expenses prescribed by hypergamous caste rules that could not be bent, changed, or broken, and that girl children had been killed in consequence since the beginning of Sikh rule, which the British had mercifully ended. Punjab officers became just as vested in proclaiming the ills of these practices, and passing sumptuary laws to curb wedding expenses, as were their counterparts in other northern parts of the dominion. South India, where female infanticide might have been found as a practice only among the lowest and poorest castes, was never brought into the same net, nor was eastern Bengal, which is now the Islamic state of Bangladesh.

On 18 March 1870, after further tortuous arguments among Lord Mayo's advisers and provincial officials, the government of India enacted Act VIII of 1870, the Act for the Prevention of Murder of Female Infants. It was to be enforced only "in the first instance to the North-Western Provinces, to the Punjab and to Oudh."[17]

The act itself was extremely brief and essentially unenforceable, but never had more socially intrusive legislation been passed in British India. It invaded the precincts of the Indian home. It required heavy surveillance of pregnancies, births, and deaths, and involved hiring small platoons of *chowkidars* (watchmen) whose salaries had to be paid by the residents of suspect villages to report questionable deaths and keep track of the all births and deaths. Every village that had a ratio of female children lower than 40 percent would be "proclaimed" as infanticidal. The fact of being so openly condemned was supposed to shame the girl murderers. Midwives were recruited to help the government keep track of sex ratios at birth, notwithstanding their well-known conflict of interest as hired hands that committed the crime, and the new vigilantes would be paid from an extra cess on the proclaimed population. The amount to be charged to pay for extra personnel was fixed by the government and was recoverable as arrears of land revenue. A police manual detailed the respective duties and penalties of family heads, landowners, police officers, village watchmen, and midwives. The law ironically made no provision for urban families, even though the Lahoreen Khatris were the ones considered most reprehensible in their demand for dowries.

There was also a manual for civil surgeons and public prosecutors that included a meticulous taxonomy of the various ways of murdering female infants. Infanticide by commission included poisoning, bludgeoning, suffocating, strangling, and exposure to the cold. Infanticide by omission included neglect of disease, starvation, and physical abuse. How a stillbirth could be distinguished from a child that had been murdered after birth was also described in detail: change of weight, feel of the lungs that had respired, presence of food in the stomach, absence of fecal matter in the intestines, exfoliation of the scarfskin, and umbilical cord changes had to be scrutinized. All these were to be done by postmortem examination and autopsy (Sriramulu 1893: Chapter 10).

It is easy to imagine that the possibilities for corruption and genuine error under the conditions of the times must have made this law and its enforcement a nightmare for both sides. An inexplicable move only thirty-six years after the passing of Act VIII of 1870 seems only to underscore the political nature of this entire exercise for the British. British officials claimed success in the eradication of the timeless practice, and in 1906 the act was quietly repealed. There appears to have been no public clamor for such an action, and news of its repeal was barely reported in the English or vernacular newspapers. I only chanced upon the notice of the repeal in trying to locate the text of the act itself. In general, reform statutes constituted weighty evidence against Indian society, and once passed, as far as I have been able to ascertain, were never repealed; much of the legislation still exists in Indian statute books.

Why was the Act of 1870 summarily repealed in 1906? The claim that infanticide was no longer practiced was patently untenable—if anything, the British knew well from their own careful monitoring and innumeration that sex ratios continued to worsen in the Punjab. The ratio of 832:1,000 males for 1901 declined to 780:1,000 in 1911 and was 799:1,000 in 1921. The small decline in infanticide posted in some specific areas was due to the fact that criminal and eventually fatal neglect had replaced the outright murder of girl infants. Yet the bigger tragedy that shaped the destiny of east Punjab villages in the last quarter of the nineteenth century may also give us a clue as to why the act was repealed. Given that the human costs of the catastrophic droughts in the second half of the nineteenth century were rendered far worse by the intransigent imperial policies in place, it might have become politically inevitable to withdraw a socially intrusive law that could fuel the engine of revolt in the face of 1.25 million deaths in the east Punjab and its contiguous provinces. Lord Lytton, the viceroy, would not remit the revenue payments or halt the exports of wheat from this region, which had become a captive export sector to sustain England and Europe through their own poor harvests, because the money was needed to finance his expensive and obsessive military adventures against the Afghans. The staggering loss of life was even more tragic because it was avoidable, and the self-proclaimed rational government in the world, with its stout Utilitarian faith, presided over the large-scale pauperization of the peasantry (Davis 2001: 51). The Infanticide Act probably added insult to mortal injury. Political exigency probably forced the repeal of the Act of 1870. Agrarian discontent in the Punjab at the turn of the century had made the situation explosive and its suppression in 1907 is often referred to as the Third Sikh War (Fox 1885: 77–104). With the British nervous about the threatening developments in nationalist politics in general and agrarian unrest in the Punjab in particular, the repeal of the Act of 1870 in 1906 was timed to appease the spreading ferment of ideas and resistance to British rule. The extra police used to enforce the act were redeployed to manage the law-and-order situation in the turbulent countryside.

Besides, the burden of reform had been taken up by indigenous organizations. The Arya Samaj, a Hindu reform organization that grew and spread rapidly in the last quarter of the century, had stepped into the breach, with the elimination of caste, the simplification of marriage ceremonies, and control of wedding expenses on its agenda. Led by a Gujarati named Dayanand Saraswati, the Arya Samaj took powerful hold in the Punjab in the last quarter of the nineteenth century with its stance against the perceived degeneration of Hindu past greatness and the danger of mass conversions to Christianity, Islam, and possibly even Sikhism. It aimed, like similar Muslim endeavors to cope with defeat at the hands of the Sikhs and the British, at the regeneration of Hindu society through the instruments of modern learning and a reformed and simplified Vedic Hinduism. The organization sought to purge society of Brahmanical corruptions such as caste and elaborate and expensive traditional rituals and wedding ceremonies, and it emphasized among other things modern Western education, particularly for women. The Arya Samaj acquired a large urban following among middle- and lower-class Hindus who shared these concerns and, for our purposes here, played an aggressive role in the stripping down of wedding expenses and *dahej*. It even pioneered advertisements for marriages among far-flung Arya families in the Samaj newspaper, *Arya Patrika*, from 1883 on, and was a radical social force that promoted widow remarriage, proscription of child marriage, female education, and a redefined role for Hindu women in modernizing India. The imperial state's distaste for dowries and extravagant weddings ebbed along with its interest in female infanticide, as it turned its attention to the newly fueled political challenges to its rule in the area.[18]

The convoluted politics of motivation on both sides to set up an irrefutable cultural crime have to be understood before we can connect it to the new twists it has taken in our own times. Arguably, the deliberate misattribution of cultural causes to female infanticide had fateful results: it sabotaged the colonialists' own intention to eradicate the practice and prevented them from comprehending the underlying circumstances that actually motivated the practice. If anything, their other far-reaching policies—on land ownership and revenue collection—might have actually pushed selective female infanticide and its pitiless logic to its limits and induced the epidemic they sought to stem. Their claim that the practice had been suppressed (during the period of its legal ban between 1870 and 1906) proved to be an empty boast. The crime continued to flourish in its crueler variant—systematic nutritional and medical neglect of unwanted daughters—until in recent decades newer technologies created the kinder method of aborting female fetuses.

The logic or rationale behind the killing of female infants, which Edwardes and other officials failed to penetrate, becomes patent in reexamining both the historical evidence of the past and the overwhelming amounts of contemporary data on sex selection and sex ratios churned out by international agencies. Selectively murdering newly born female infants seems to have been a primitive but foolproof method of producing the precise mix of sons and daughters that Punjabi families considered right for their existential rather than spiritual or cultural needs. These allegedly fatalistic peoples who decidedly wanted more males than females knew the futility of leaving the matter to chance. They deliberately determined the fate of the newborn: an unwanted female was killed promptly after its sex was revealed. The agents who actually perpetrated this cruel act were women—grandmothers, midwives, and aunts—who acted with the tacit knowledge of the mother herself, bonded by silence and secrecy.

Prem Chowdhry (1994: 47–62) has keenly analyzed the Jat peasants' preference for males in the colonial period, when their military and agriculturalist skills were in high demand and they became a statutory "agricultural tribe" protected from alienation of their land to moneylenders of trading castes.[19] Rainfall-dependent Haryana, part of colonial Punjab, was a region that was prone to drought and had a large section of Jat peasants engaged in subsistence farming. A minimum of twelve acres made a viable holding, and only 28 percent of Jat households fell into this category. The landowners, explains Chowdhry, lacking other resources, were entirely dependent on family labor, "and this situation greatly reinforced, what is perhaps common to peasant economies generally, namely a very strong desire for male progeny. Widely reflected in its folklore and sayings, a male child came to be regarded as essential as life-giving rain" (Chowdhry 1994: 48). The usefulness of girls was also acknowledged, but daughters were destined to be married early and to prove their full worth as wives and daughters-in-law, because no peasant household could make ends meet without a wife's hard work in the fields and her capacity to reproduce male children. But Chowdhry notices a shift in sayings collected in early colonial days and those prevalent today, as the preference for sons deepened during the British Raj. Early sayings included: "A daughter after two sons brings prosperity, three sons in a row bring beggary." Another "more drastic one voiced by women prayed: *beta mariyo par tissar na pariyo* (May a son die, rather than I get a third boy)" (Chowdhry 1994: 50–51). Later the desire for seven sons is expressed in blessings given to daughters-in-law. For our purposes, these sayings not only confirm what masculine sex ratios in the twentieth century tell us but they also give us a vital clue to the birth order preferred by Jat women in that period. A daughter born after two sons would be very desirable and would surely not be exterminated at birth. This preference for sons was not restricted to agricultural tribes, as we shall see, but subsumed all castes, tribes, and religions in the colonial period. Therefore we have to see what conditions bolstered such reasoning in a population that was not dependent on subsistence agriculture. The graph

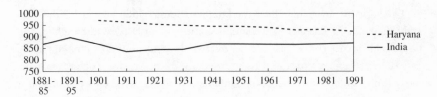

FIGURE I Females/1,000 males, 1881–1991

in Figure I shows that in the districts that make up present-day Haryana, adverse female sex ratios have fluctuated within a very small range hovering between 866:1,000 in 1886 and 874:1,000 in 1991, but always remained well below the national average. The first half of the nineteenth century showed a steep decline to 835:1,000 in 1911 and slow recovery to 869:1,000 in 1941. The post-Independence decades have shown female ratios in the 870s, with the highest point, 874:1,000, achieved in 1991. The national average shows a steady decline in the past century, but Haryana posts a small upturn in its last decade.

The scholarly literature on the subject of a preference for sons grew from a trickle in the 1970s to a torrent by the mid-1990s. A succinct discussion of the best work has been presented by Philip Oldenburg, in which he reviews the full spectrum of explanations offered by scholars for high masculine sex ratios before proposing a central but overlooked factor: "the perception of the need for sons to uphold, with violence, a family's power *vis-à-vis* neighbours (not infrequently including kinsfolk)." He credibly hypothesizes that in regions where sex ratios are more masculine, families want (or need) more sons "because additional sons enhance their capacity literally to defend themselves or to exercise their power" (Oldenburg 1992). Peter Mayer (1999) has a more recent review of the pertinent literature on the subject. In agrarian Punjab, the defense of landholdings, the fight for water rights, and the living to be made in Maharaja Ranjit Singh's army were reasons enough for desiring more sons; the changes in the colonial economy pushed this imperative to its logical limit.

From Edwardes's account we know that killing the unwanted infant female was as prompt as it was pitiless, and that the grandmother, the midwife, and other female members of the family actually executed the deed. By discounting the cultural reasoning, the mystery about why daughters were killed remained. I decided to ask the questions that Edwardes had omitted to ask, and to ask them of women in three villages in Gurgaon district in several trips between 1989 and 1997. The promptitude, I was to learn, was not only out of consideration for the mother's feelings; killing the child prevented lactation and cleared the way for the mother to become pregnant again, possibly to produce a son. Nursing a child was and still is believed to prevent pregnancy and is practiced as a device to space the birth of children. But if two or more consecutive male children had to be produced for the economic security of the family, then time was of the essence, and the decision to kill the infant, if it turned out to be a female, was made in advance if one or two female children had already been born. In order to make it emotionally less brutal for the mother, she never saw or held the infant marked for death; she would be psychologically appeased to think of it as a stillbirth. It was a conspiracy of women to keep their own numbers low for the well-being of their families.

Infanticide worked as the only "sex determination test" available at that time. When the newborn emerged from the womb and its genitals became visible, its fate was sealed; a penis saved the infant. Daughters early in the birth order had the lowest chances of survival, since the priority was to produce an optimum number of five or six boys as early as possible. My informants told me that an obviously deformed or handicapped male child would be destroyed at birth. Similarly, nowadays the absence of a penis in a sonogram is tantamount to a "birth defect," and the fetus will be aborted.

The size and composition of families, overtly referred to as *kismat* or "God's will," are actually the products of human agency systematically deployed. Senior women appear to be the ones who make the decision—grandmothers, mothers-in-law—and the midwife is paid to do the deed to make families "ideal" or at least optimal. Given this reality and the grim mechanics of infanticide, it is hard to condemn the fetal diagnostic technologies that offer a morally less repugnant alternative. But these technologies are powerless against the very discrimination against girls that makes their abuse so popular. Infanticide cannot be legislated against; it will automatically disappear when technological advances allow the selection of the sex of the child before conception. One can conclude that female infanticide, the fatal neglect of infant daughters, second-trimester abortions after "sex tests," and finally, in the future, the conception of sexually predetermined babies are all responses to the same powerful impulse—to control the number and the sex of children so that the goals and interests of the family and the state are met. Monica Das Gupta has compellingly shown that educated women are better able to manipulate their fertility and their daughters' mortality, and are "better equipped than others [i.e., uneducated women] to achieve the family size and sex composition they desire" (Das Gupta 1987). Projecting an efficient and cheap technology-assisted "ideal" into future reality makes the present female sex ratio of 927:1,000 look stunningly favorable for women.[20] My own informal polling of fifty women in a village close to Ambala (in the Indian Punjab) revealed that all but three of them considered an "ideal" family to consist of three sons and one daughter (which would bring sex ratios down to 333, far worse than the current sex ratios in the Punjab), and seventy-five women college graduates in Lucknow in 1992 who wanted three children hoped for two sons and a daughter each. If, however, in the new millennium, if the relationship of women to property and employment does not radically improve, and the sperm separator or similar technology becomes widely and cheaply available, we will see two unequivocal results: family sizes will shrink in a generation, and sex ratios will become more masculine than ever before.

It is not surprising that recent surveys by most major international agencies show that son preference is firmly in place in many countries around the world, which suggests that the ownership of land and most paying jobs are in male hands. A 1986 UNICEF survey (Ravindram 1986: 5, 13) on son preference showed Pakistan at the top of the list; its juvenile mortality rates (ages two to five years) were shockingly skewed at 66.5 male deaths for every 100 female deaths. Nepal, a Hindu country, had the second-highest son preference, but its juvenile mortality rates were far more balanced, at 93 males to 100 females. The Ravindram report also alerts us to a similar situation in Victorian England, citing R. Wall (1981), who concludes that extensive mortality data in England pointed to an abnormally high death rate of girls in the middle and late nineteenth century, attributed to the so-cial and economic disadvantages of women and girls especially at the lower social levels and to conscious or unconscious negligence on the part of their parents. It is not known whether the imperial officials in the field in India had any awareness of skewed sex ratios in their own country that resembled those in the Punjab countryside.

It is obvious that not all female children were killed in the areas where infanti-cide was practiced, nor could they have been: the vast majority were valued for their roles as links between villages and as reproducers of the next generation. So the problem is to disentangle the logic—the economic, social, and political from the cultural—that made a greater number of men necessary for the communities where female infanticide was practiced. The challenge is to dig deeper and disrupt the nearly two-century-long consensus that marriage expenses, particularly dowry, are the reasons for selectively killing infant daughters. And to do this sys-tematically, we must return to the nineteenth century.

3

The Tangled Tale of Twisting a Safety Net into a Noose

After careful review of the cultural interdict against the Rajputs' and the Khatris' "addiction" to female infanticide—the alleged result of their high-caste custom of hypergamy and the concomitant marriage expenses, presented by Montgomery in his *Minute on Infanticide* in 1852—our own investigations have established that the colonial government's seemingly well-caulked case was deeply problematic. In exploring the cultural construction of the crime of female infanticide, we discovered that caste itself was cut loose from its moorings in politics and its transformation into its colonial image was under way. We also discovered that bride-price-receiving groups such as Jats and Muslims of all classes were at least as culpable as the notoriously targeted high-caste Hindus. In examining the process of collecting knowledge, we also saw how native informants, in an attempt to save themselves from fines and imprisonment, became collaborators in the project of the colonial remaking of Punjabi society.

Now we can take our investigation further and follow the steps taken by the colonial government to eradicate the alleged causes—dowry and wedding expenses—of female infanticide. As the British faltered on causes, their experiments to fix Hindu upper-caste behavior were bound to be experiments in futility. In any case, the attempt to persuade the upper castes to join in a war against their own constitution makes a very interesting chapter in Punjabi social history, particularly from a feminist perspective. How did the colonialists propose to wean the upper castes of their alleged lethal addiction to "caste pride" and ruinous profligacy at the time of a daughter's wedding, and what social effects might this have produced in the Punjab?

It is important to tease out a baseline in the mid-nineteenth century from which we can begin to track what happened to a variety of marriage expenses, including the vilified "dowry system," over the next century, particularly the way these changed in response to calls for reform from colonial and local leaders. We will also examine how the radical restructuring of land ownership and the revenue system soon after the British takeover, the accelerated monetization of the agrarian economy, urban growth, and emergent middle-class values all worked to transform the dowry system itself.

I expect to ascertain the material content of *daaj*, how it was accumulated, what proportion of a family's resources was allocated to it, and its separate and changing meanings for bridegivers and bridetakers. What relationship did *daaj* have to the wealth and prestige of a family, and how was this relationship manipulated by the bridetakers? By probing the disparate property rights of women as daughters and wives in Punjabi "customary law" in the mid-nineteenth century, we will better be able to reconstruct the changes in gender relations unleashed in the colonial period. This should bring us to the heart of our investigation on the changing meanings and effects of *daaj* on women and violence.

Major H. B. Edwardes, the deputy commissioner of Jullundur, had made it his business to explore the custom of dowry payments in his now-familiar report on female infanticide. After setting out with a very different premise, he had been forced to conclude that, with the exception of the Khatris of Lahore, the custom of dowry among upper-caste Hindus did not appear to be the cause for alarm it was elsewhere in the Indian empire, although wedding expenses certainly were. The most gratifying portion of his report for him was his ability to persuade the people of Jullundur and Rahon to submit voluntarily a schedule of expenses "that was drawn by the people themselves in their own homes, in consultation with the females of their own families, stimulated by the opportunities afforded them by this enquiry" (Edwardes 1852: para. 79) This is probably the first written account of marriage expenses and dowry compiled in the colonial period in the Punjab, and perhaps represented the only time that women's knowledge of such matters was incorporated into a colonial report. The expenses are noted under five heads, with the expenditure on the first or the "lugun" (or *lagan*, literally auspicious date) that "decides the rate of all other expenses." The bride's father usually sends one-third of the value of the gifts in cash, and two-thirds in property such as horses and camels. If a hundred rupees are spent on the *lagan*, then the bride's father customarily spends fifty rupees on the *milni*, the occasion when the bridegroom's procession arrives at the house and the two fathers embrace. The third head of expenditure is the fee of the Brahmin priest, which would be more that the *milni* but would not exceed seventy-five rupees. The fourth is the "Meeta bhat; for two days all sorts of sweetmeats and fruits mixed up together are set before the assembly, and all the neighbours of the same caste come and partake, but it is etiquette to take only a morsel or two." And finally, the "Duheys [*dahej*]; or as it is called in the Punjab the 'Khut.' This is one-fourth or one-fifth more than the 'Lugun,' and consists of a gift of all household requisites, from water vessels down to a sweepers broom" (ibid.: para. 81). The average expense for a daughter's wedding would therefore have been within five hundred rupees, a not inconsiderable amount. The informants were Khatris, the educated and wealthier section of the population who had traditionally served the government and the army as officers, and who were also commonly involved in farming, trade, and even shopkeeping and moneylending operations. They were also the community widely accused of committing infanticide in all districts of the Punjab.

This urges us to probe whether a daughter's wedding entailed expenses "ruinous" enough to warrant her elimination in infancy. Were sons were so obviously preferred because their weddings cost less? Is this the past we need in order to understand the present?

After fairly exhaustive questioning among his informants, Edwardes asserts that "it is not the general practice, as in Hindoostan [which refers to provinces to the east and south of the Punjab], for the Bridegroom's father to demand a dowry from the father of the Bride, on the contrary whatever the latter chooses to offer, the former is honor bound to accept." The wedding, however, was another matter; the bride's father felt his honor to be at stake and was not past "ruining himself on this occasion. Thus daughters became family calamities, and more than one or two were seldom allowed to live" (Edwardes 1852: paras. 41–42).

We ought to trust what Edwardes's native informants say about dowry and wedding expenses, as little as we trust the just-so story about Bedi infanticides. But there is a significant difference here. In detailing wedding and dowry expenses in 1852 there is no unverifiable past being dredged up, but a workaday report of expenses at that time generated by male householders at home with the help of their wives, mothers, and aunts. Edwardes also makes two telltale distinctions. The first is between Hindustan and the Punjab. Hindustan (literally, "land of Hindus," the name given to the Hindi-speaking regions of north India), where he suggested that dowries could be demanded by the bridetakers, had been under colonial sway for half a century. In Hindustan, dowries were seen as a problem because his bureaucrat forebears had reported them as such. He was quite sure that this was not the case in the recently conquered Punjab, where however little or much the bride's father had to offer, the groom's father was "honor bound to accept" it. Punjabi machismo was deeply intertwined, much like that of the Rajputs of Rajputana or the Pathans of the northwest frontier, with matters of honor.

This is important for the baseline we want to create, because a few decades later, under colonialism, the difference in the attitude toward Punjabi and Hindustani dowries appears not to be remarkable.

Edwardes's observation of this critical difference between the old and new territorial acquisitions of the Raj opens up a new way of thinking about the puzzle of escalating dowries. Did the Raj itself, in its effort to introduce the selected ingredients of capitalist agriculture, alter the economic and cultural chemistry of the regions it brought under its wing and unwittingly change the way dowries were given and received? Edwardes declares that the practice of dowry was bound by rules of honor and mutual respect between bridetakers and bridegivers in the Punjab of the 1850s. This recognition that Punjabi dowry giving did not induce infanticide is a remarkable internal contradiction of the official case. Does it mean that "problem" dowries were a creeping phenomenon that followed the Raj to the new regions it conquered? Is that why this shift is noticed everywhere today, along with the change from bride-price to dowry?

The second distinction he draws is between dowries and wedding expenses, a distinction that is very real in north India even today. There is no doubt in his mind, after surveying his district and reading the reports of other district officers in the Punjab, that the ruinous expenditure was not dowry but wedding celebrations. And this, as we shall see, applied also to the weddings of sons. This insight is drowned out by the official clamor to establish, as had been done in Hindustan, clear and credible motives for female infanticide. What gained uniform acceptance as the cause for the destruction of infant daughters was the high cost of what a daughter must be given (or what may be demanded) at the time of marriage, and in the annual cycle of festivals and auspicious occasions for the rest of her parents' lives.

One of the critical tasks at hand is to determine whether we are looking only at a steady quantitative change—one that inflation and the burgeoning of consumer goods can explain—or whether there was a real qualitative change in the meaning, function, and composition not only of dowries but also of basal gender relations in the colonial period. There is evidence in the codification of customary law and in the documents generated at meetings held to contain the practice of dowry in 1853 to allow us to discern whether "the people"—those who gave and received dowries—considered it as baneful then as it was perceived to be more than a century later, when the custom was banned in 1961. Amid the din of consultations among prominent local leaders in 1853, and later when inquiries were made during the widespread famines of 1878–1879 and 1899–1900, there are dimly audible voices and opinions of women as mothers, aunts, sisters, and daughters that need to be rescued. These will enable us to disentangle the changing customary and legal constructions of gender at different levels of class and caste in the context of the transition from a subsistence economy to a very curious form of colonial capitalism in the Punjab.

To track these changes in dowry and gender systems closely, I had to make some arbitrary choices. With a canvas as vast as the colonial Punjab (which included what is today the most powerful and populous part of Pakistan, and which in India was later divided into Punjab, Haryana, Himachal Pradesh, and the Union Territory of Delhi), I will focus on the areas where dowries and bride-price coexisted then and now, namely, the eastern, Indian (and Hindu) part of the state, although higher masculine sex ratios existed throughout the region.

Although the colonial archives are filled with the reports on famine, indebtedness, and revenue payments that are, of course, useful in reconstructing our own narrative, there seems to be little evidence written by the natives themselves that does not either respond to colonial questions or consciously critique the customs the British had condemned. I must confess to a prolonged bout of misplaced euphoria when I chanced upon an impressive cache of bound Hindi and Urdu documents that appeared to be agreements signed by caste leaders in 1853—especially the castes we know to have directly admitted committing female infanticide—at the India Office Library in London. I spent several weeks painstakingly transcribing and translating these oddly similar, almost repetitive declarations by caste group after caste group repudiating the linked customs of dowry and the killing of infant daughters. This was a real coup, I thought; here were authentic collective confessions of the original "dowry deaths," signed by the culprits themselves, the very things that I hoped would give me a clear idea of what "the people" thought and did about dowry a century and a half ago. As I worked my way through them, however, their purport and provenance became clear: they all contained measures to control and fix marriage expenses. They were *ikrar nameh,* or agreements between caste groups and the administration, signed by the leaders of the caste organizations in Lahore, Amritsar, Ambala, Jullundar, Kangra, and other district headquarters. Soon afterward I discovered that the Urdu documents were mere transliterations of Hindi agreements, or vice versa, and both were based on an English model.

After some further squinting I decided that the content of these *ikrar nameh* were officially inspired, even dictated by the native assistants of British officers, to produce a very homogeneous body of "tracts," reinforced by the archive's classificatory system that had filed translations as original vernacular documents. I was suspicious because the native representatives sounded overly enthusiastic in their self-condemnations, admitting their extravagance at weddings and unanimous on what should be done about it. My hunch proved to be correct. It was relatively simple to catch up with the paper trail produced at the meeting called by the judicial commissioner—none other than Montgomery himself, inspired by Edwardes's suggestion in his report to do just that—where major chiefs of important clans and castes had signed these documents in English on 29 October 1853 in Amritsar. The next step was to compare these with a complete set of vernacular translations appended to the report of the meeting, which were clearly produced to let the literate among the native chiefs and leaders see what they were signing, because not many would have known English in 1853, nor would many British officials have known Punjabi. Even though it became clear that these were not "authentic" opinions of the people, produced as they were under official supervision, unlike Edwardes's summary of marriage expenses submitted by his informants in consultation with their womenfolk, they are dense enough in detail to be useful in reconstructing the ceremonies that were part of the *kanyadan* complex of wedding rituals and exchanges and the expense entailed by each.

The documents are also important because they formed part of the official blitz to saturate town and country with antidowry propaganda. On the single occasion of a meeting in Sialkot alone, "[s]ome 1000 vernacular books and pamphlets, of sorts, having the object of exposing the social evils of profuse expenditure at weddings, and the abominations of child murder" were distributed by Charles Raikes, commissioner of Lahore division and the pioneer of the Mainpuri anti-infanticide campaign against Chauhan Rajputs. All other district commissioners were instructed to follow suit.[1]

Let us return to the orchestrated labors of the senior officials of the forty-six districts in the Punjab in 1853 and their efforts to persuade the "murderous castes" to desist from committing infanticide and to draw up what appeared to be some rather stern sumptuary laws to control extravagance in the future (SPCPA 1854: 423–63). The meeting to achieve this was duly held on 29–31 October in Amritsar, an important commercial center and holy city of the Sikhs with its famous Golden Temple. The top brass of most of the eastern districts of the province—including Montgomery, the judicial commissioner, and Edmonstone, the financial commissioner, who jointly presided over the meeting—accosted the "chief and leading men of the tribes, who practiced infanticide, other rajas, sardars [chiefs], Native Gentlemen of rank and position" (SPCPA 1854: 431). Never before had so large a body of British civil officers collected in their Indian empire to garner the unanimous "consent" of the indigenous leaders to social control.

The invitation, or rather the summons, was issued as part of a proclamation from the governor general of India, the highest British official in the country, and was widely distributed in the vernacular.[2] The proclamation was brief—only four sentences, the last of which was the announcement of the meeting at Amritsar, during the festival of Diwali (the widely celebrated Hindu festival that also marked the peak season for weddings on the ritual calendar)—and was stated with a sense of menace. Although it named only the Bedis as the most culpable community, its scope was indubitable: any persons committing the crime of infanticide would incur the penalty for murder and would forfeit their lands, estates, and pensions. In real terms this might mean life imprisonment or hanging, along with total impoverishment for the extended family or even the clan. The proclamation also promised those who worked actively to suppress the crime that they "would be held deserving of reward, honor and title" by the governor-general of India" (SPCPA 1854: 434).

Needless to say, with a notification that stern, the meeting at Amritsar was extremely well attended, and it produced the desired stack of signed agreements between the chief commissioner and the heads of suspect castes. Two hundred of the most prominent chiefs of the Punjab, Rajput and Khatri, came without heed to the Diwali festivities at home.[3] Several maharajas and rajas of sovereign princely states, such as Patiala, Kapurthala, and Jammu, attended in person or sent representatives, not to apologize for their social customs but in fear for their political futures as independent rulers. Nervously, they had seen how the British Raj had absorbed kingdom after kingdom on the grounds that "social evil" flourished therein or that the rulers were profligate, and they abandoned all thoughts of Diwali to demonstrate publicly their serious commitment to reform in matters as domestic and private as marriage expenses. The Khatri chiefs flocked in great numbers, including "the commercial heads of every City of note within 200 miles of Umritsar."

The venue was, appropriately, on the grounds of the Amritsar Jail, where a pavilion covered a space two hundred by sixty-two feet, capable of accommodating three thousand people. The conviction that Indians cared only about their caste status persisted. The hardest part of the arrangements, according to Montgomery, was to seat the acutely sensitive chiefs according to their social rank and status so as not to offend them, and to create a "Select Committee of Natives, who were calculated by their caste, position, and local influence, to assist the operations." Montgomery, a veteran strategist of the prevention of female infanticide in the North-West Provinces, did not forget that the meeting had to be seen as a compact between the British and the native elite, with the latter having no choice but to actively collaborate for the plan to work at all. Here too the British reduced the point of the seating arrangements to empty caste or tribal vanity rather than affirmation of the political status of independent rulers from neighboring states in the Punjab region.

The spirit of past operations and bureaucratic experience in the North-West Provinces hovered over and shaped the Amritsar meeting. A pair of agreements— the result of initiatives taken by the commissioners of Jullunder and Hoshiarpur a few months earlier—was used as the exemplars for the deliberations. These agreements, in turn, were based on what Charles Raikes had "originated [as] measures for Mynpooree [Mainpuri in the North-West Provinces] for the extirpation of Female Infanticide for the Chohan Rajputs of that district" (SPCPA 1854: 424). At Montgomery's behest, Raikes had been transferred to Lahore expressly to use his experience to subdue the haughty Khatris in the strongly affected district. After these model agreements were read out and distributed to the assembled, "they were all directed to separate, to give the purport of these documents their serious and earnest attention, and to make any suggestions, or modifications which their feelings, or the particular customs of their clans, might dictate" (ibid.: 425). Edwardes's idea that Khatri chiefs be allowed to work at home in consultation with their women was obviously ignored.

The meeting was an intense affair, lasting until long after sunset on all three days. It produced a general written concurrence by the chiefs of their own cultures and customs, along with fifteen separate *ikrar nameh* that listed the ceremonies and the expenses for weddings. The "phraseology" of the general indictment that was "expressive of their horror of Infanticide" was "purposely made comprehensive and brief." Several drafts were necessary and took a longer time than expected, and the meeting broke up at a very late hour on the final day (SPCPA 1854: 428). We can only imagine the quibbling that went on before a succinctly worded consensus could be reached among "all the chiefs and the people, residing in the Punjab."

The first point of general agreement is surprising. Only the Bedis and the Rajputs had been directly accused of killing all their infant girls; yet a whole medley of castes and classes, including independent princes, and Muslims and Jats from eastern Punjab who were deemed not guilty, cheerfully swore and signed the agreements to apprehend and deliver to the authorities any perpetrator "of our tribe" of the execrable crime. They also agreed to "expel from caste" any member who refused to join in the program of reform to uproot the practice entirely in their own community. Clearly the legal threat of fines, imprisonment, and execution made in the official proclamation worked its magic and shaped the complicity of the conquered and the independent chiefs alike to generate what I would like to call a "coerced consensus."[4] Official amnesty for the princes and chiefs would be reward enough.

Serious as this meeting was intended to be, it strikes one as a charade. It is easy to visualize the Indian chiefs and British bureaucrats, after what the bureaucrats saw as much punctilious fuss over seating arrangements according to caste rankings, earnestly discussing (through native translators, of course) matters such as hypergamy and marriage expenses without a single woman in attendance. The British legal world was strictly masculine, and this unilateral structure of authority was now imposed on their subjects in reworking the rules of gender and marriage. This travesty has been more pithily expressed as white men talking to brown men to rescue brown women from brown men. The British had skewed Indian priorities: they respected caste distinctions but studiously ignored the authority of women, their central role and presence in matters such as wedding expenses, gifts, and dowries, not to mention their undeniable agency in committing female infanticide. So the chiefs signed the dotted lines in their *ikrar nameh* and the British officials expressed their confidence that the "extravagant expenditure, hitherto considered indispensable, has certainly been the main incentive for the commission of this crime, and the removal of the one affords the surest hope of the eradication of the other, in the course of time (SPCPA 1854: 432).

In a separate statement of general agreement to extirpate female infanticide signed by all the notables present, the chiefs pledged that they would "at once cause the apprehension of any person of our tribe who may perpetrate the crime in our Ilakas or villages, and bring the same to the notice of the authorities: and we will expel from caste who may refuse or show reluctance to join in the endeavours" to abolish a crime "so hateful to God, and execrable in the eyes of Government and all pious and good men" (SPCPA 1854: 434). What is unexpected is the final clause of this agreement, which aims against the exactions of musicians (*bhat* and *bhand*), genealogists (*dut* and *mirasi*), barbers (*nai*), and beggars (*faqir*, *sadhu,* and *bhikshu*)—all itinerants in Punjab villages customarily entitled to small gratuities from landowners at festivals and ceremonial occasions.[5] Their stylized importuning is depicted with great hostility. They are accused of "clamorously demanding charity" in an "outrageous and harassing manner," often using threats and abuse and even violence "with knives and stones." They were to be refused entry to weddings, and their customary services declined; only the police and the district officers were to deal with them (SPCPA 1854: 435).

This stricture is rather puzzling. It canceled with a stroke the web of customary reciprocities between this category of dependents and the better-off residents of the village. Without music, without recitations of genealogies, without the ash-smeared sadhus and fakirs who lived off the charity of the village, the spirit of a Punjabi wedding would be seriously compromised. Here, as we shall see, is clearly enshrined the dramatic change in attitude toward village servants who had been maintained in earlier times, under the Sikh (and earlier Hindu and Muslim) regime's revenue arrangements, by the common fund of the village subscribed to from the revenue collected.[6] The British viewed these services (music, chanting, and genealogical recitations) and obligatory payments as frivolous waste, and refused altogether to follow the custom of native rulers of contributing a tiny fraction of the revenue they collected to the village common discretionary fund for social occasions such as weddings and funerals and the upkeep of the village *chaupal* or guest house. It is more than likely that such personnel were driven to demand their wonted fees directly from the parents of the bride or groom. Their rude insistence, described in the Amritsar agreements, was therefore ironically a product of the niggardly cutbacks imposed by British revenue collectors on village heads. It is here that one might detect the strident voices of these subalterns who infamously "cannot speak," raucously demanding from village heads their former patronage, and being silenced in the official bid to reduce marriage expenses. The British solution was true to their perception of economic deprivation as a problem of "law and order": the functionaries were never to receive gratuities in the future, and should a problem arise, the *bhand*, the *mirasi*, and the formerly trusted matchmaker/barber, the *nai*, were to be rounded up by the police and duly fined and imprisoned.

The specific agreements signed by the representatives of a wide range of castes and clans—from the Bedis of Dera Baba Nanak, the Rajput princes of Kangra and other hill districts, and the Khatris and Brahmins of a dozen districts in joint agreements with the urban and rural Muslims of Lahore—suggest that no community tried to refute the blanket accusation that wedding expenses and dowry were among the chief causes of infanticide. Rather, they promised to respect the new sumptuary regulations they had expressly gathered to draw up. All of the agreements stipulated that marriage expenses—separated into dowry and wedding celebrations—must be reduced and regulated, but some of the agreements were clearly more negotiated than others. They ranged from curiously perfunctory and spare to highly detailed. Some groups were content to sign agreements that mentioned only the prescribed maximum spending limits, without differentiated allocations imposed on high, middle, and lower classes. The (notorious) Bedis, who had made of Major Edwardes a minor hero and erudite social scientist for the establishment, had already gathered under his auspices at Jullundur and produced the exemplary agreement that was upheld as a model in Amritsar. Higher Khatri tribes agreed to abandon their hypergamous ways and caste pride by pledging to intermarry with the lower ranks of Khatris, including the lowest Bhunjaees. The ceilings adopted for expenses for four classes of weddings were Rs. 500 for the first class, Rs. 200 for the second, Rs. 125 for the third, and a single rupee for the fourth. Other agreements, particularly those authored by Khatris, are obsessively detailed, down to the size and weight of the *pinni* and *laddoo* (sweet balls made from grain, sugar, and *ghi*, or clarified butter) to be distributed on the occasion of the announcement of the wedding. In the clear absence of political power, the princes and chiefs were now forced to quibble over seeming trifles.

On the whole, a fairly elaborate set of written agreements emerged at Amritsar, and the meeting was declared an unqualified success. It became the basis for future proceedings in the western districts and in neighboring princely states, and signing agreements with presiding British officers became quite the vogue, probably producing the cachet that attending Akbar's court had three hundred years earlier.

When one analyzes the statements and figures available from these written engagements, it is clear that the assembled chiefs had to work within specific caste groups to arrive at their customized agreements. The Khatris and the Brahmins of Lahore, Amritsar, and Rawalpindi appear to have resisted the rigid compartmentalization forced on them and worked together to produce joint agreements accepting what must have been the definitive list of ceremonies prevalent at the time for *kanyadan* (SPCPA 1854: 433–37, 439–46). The effect this exercise had on the assembly was to make the longer engagements with many ceremonies detailed in them the products of the culturally more sophisticated communities. Ironically, the allegedly most culpable "tribe," the Khatris of Lahore, emerged as the elite reference community for all Punjabi Hindus at that time. The joint Khatri-Brahmin agreements underscored what had long been a feature of Punjabi society: the Brahmins were deemed neither ritually exclusive nor socially superior to the Khatris and were content to follow their leadership, probably as a mark of respect to the economically powerful Khatris.

The British insistence on treating castes as if they were hidebound ritual groups with little in common would only serve as a self-fulfilling prophecy. The Brahmin-Khatri agreements reveal the regional and political significance these caste alliances had in precolonial times: the assorted upper castes in a particular locality or region shaped and shared customs more than a single caste did across regions. This is corroborated by the volumes of customary law codified by district, in which hundreds of customs are shared across caste and religious lines. The Sayyad Muslim Rajputs of Panipat, for example, "while admitting the license [to have four wives] given by the Shara [Shariah or Islamic Law] state that customary law forbids a man to marry a second wife unless his first wife fails to give birth to male issue," much like the Brahmins, Khatris, Rajputs, and other upper-caste Hindus who lived in the same region (Garbett 1910: 6).[7]

Another agreement, signed jointly by the "Zemindars and Lumberdars," or small landowners and village heads, of numerous castes of Amritsar district, regulated the expenses of a daughter's wedding fairly simply. "All persons in a low state of life, and not living in easy circumstances, will spend from 1 to 125 rupees; those in easy circumstances and occupying a middle station in life, will incur from 125 to 250 rupees, while all persons of substance and consequence will be at liberty to expend from 250 to 500 rupees, on the marriages of their daughters" (SPCPA 1854: 437). It is interesting that although the British expected the representatives of different castes to consult with their own and conclude caste-specific agreements, the representatives themselves chose to regroup on the basis of class and custom. They preferred to differentiate themselves in two ways: as regional-political elites belonging to a locality or subregion such as Lahore or Amritsar, and as economic elites, falling into three to five income brackets, to determine the outlay for marriage expenses. The ease with which joint agreements were generated and signed points to the possibility that the caste leaders saw this official intervention as an opportunity to restate their own political ranks in relationship to the new rulers.

Information about money actually spent at weddings by the various income groups is sparse or vague, and the agreements do little to tell us precisely, except in one case, what the notions of improvidence or extravagance entailed. There are passing references elsewhere to the exceptional prodigality of 1.7 million rupees (ten rupees were valued at one pound sterling at this time) spent at the marriage of Kunwar Nao Nihal Singh with the daughter of the "Ataree chief," and eight lakhs of rupees (one lakh or lac equals 100,000) at the wedding of the late "Raja of Aloowala."[8] This information, even if accurate, only confused the issue: such vast resources remained only in the hands of the few independent rulers in the Punjab, whose marriages were political alliances, and the money was spent at the weddings of royal children of either sex, not of daughters alone. The British closely monitored the extravagance of independent chieftains, for they perceived it to be an unfailing symptom of misrule. Such big spenders could be forced either into signing subsidiary alliances (defense treaties whereby native rulers underwrote the entire cost of British military protection offered to them) or into having their territories annexed outright. For the preponderance of their subjects, we have to be satisfied with pronouncements such as "[p]eople live to save money to marry their daughters; others impoverish themselves for life to outvie their neighbours" in the very same letter. In actual terms, the entire exercise at Amritsar amounted to reiterating colonial power over Punjabi Hindu and Sikh elite groups and rulers of neighboring independent kingdoms. As a way of dealing with female infanticide, it did little more than create sumptuary guidelines with prescribed but unenforceable spending limits.

It is possible to extract from these regulations the proportional amounts designated for the dowry, wedding celebrations, and gifts for the groom and his party from the total permitted outlay. Except for Lahore Khatris and Brahmins, most of the castes and classes reckoned marriage expenditures in four discrete clusters. The first was the betrothal (*kurmai* or *dharam sagai*), an engagement ceremony in which the bridegivers do not accept gifts or cash in consideration for the bride, to be distinguished from the engagement ceremony of those who accept bride-price. The second was the *milni*, or gifts for the close kin of the groom, and the expenses for the hospitality and entertainment of the groom's party at the time of the wedding; the third group was what could be deemed obligatory giving by the bride's parents to their own kin with whom reciprocal arrangements existed, and handouts to various traditional servants, including the *pandit* (Brahmin priest), the barber, and the musicians and professional entertainers (the *bhand*, *mirasi*, *bhat*, and others who had formerly been on the village payroll). The last but not least of the expenses was the *daaj*, the gifts to the bride herself from family and friends. No monetary value or maximum limit was stipulated for the *daaj* in any of the agreements, and it was left entirely up to the means of the bride's family and kin to supply her clothes, jewels, household furnishings, and milch cattle, horses, and camels. The fact that dowry went unregulated after all the fuss made about it tells us that it was a discretionary expense and not the crippling burden that altered attitudes toward female children.

Most of the groups put the entire *daaj* at between 55 and 60 percent of the cost in all classes of weddings. There is a consensus in these documents that household utensils, furniture, apparel, and jewels are the kinds of articles that constitute *daaj*. Cash was not mentioned as a *daaj* item in any of the agreements in 1853. The representatives of the people were willing to compromise and draw up schedules of wedding expenses and gifts given to the groom and his relatives at the time of the betrothal and marriage, but they quietly managed to keep *daaj* as a cluster of items that the bride's parents alone would decide according to their own private means. The Khatris and Brahmins of Lahore seem to have been particularly in favor of keeping this a discretionary and jealously guarded category.

The most dependable picture of *daaj* in its particulars emerges from the Amritsar Khatris and Brahmins, a product of the deliberations, as Edwardes tells us, of the women in their families. *Daaj* at the highest, or first-class, level was presumably the pecuniary cause of infanticide and so warrants closer inspection. It included apparel for the bride: thirteen sets of *tewar*, or three-piece outfits consisting of long skirt, bodice, and *ohrni*, or ornamented veil; and thirty-one sets of *bewar*, or two-piece sets of clothing, such as *sari* and blouse, or *suthan-kameez* (sal-

war, or baggy pants, and tunic) and *orhni* (veil). This would make about forty-four sets of clothes made of silk, brocade, and embroidered cotton for the bride of a well-to-do household. No limits appear to have been set on the cost of these clothes. The jewels for the bride would simply be "according to the circumstances of the parents," giving a great deal of flexibility to the parents to determine what they could afford. Only a single set of clothes for the groom was stipulated in the *daaj*. Beds for the couple, a pair of wooden stools, and cooking utensils and storage vessels were also mandatory items. These would be used in the household or become the nucleus of the couple's new home should their circumstances dictate the setting up of a separate home (SPCPA 1854: 439–43). Nothing at all is said that the bridegroom or his family had any say in the composition or cost of the *daaj* and no cash is stipulated.

The Lahore Brahmins and Khatris, who were accused of being the most extravagant, signed an agreement identical in all its particulars to that of their Amritsar counterparts. In fact, one can assume that the two groups consulted together until they could accept precisely the same ceremonies, cash values of gifts, and limits on everything including the powers and responsibilities of their *biradari*, or brotherhood organizations; final discretion in matters of *daaj* was left firmly and unambiguously in the hands of the bride's parents. Whatever else might be suspect, one thing comes through again and again in the dozens of agreements; the men who had assembled to agree with everything the government said resisted precise instructions on what to do about *daaj*. They wanted their own discretion in this matter and did not want to be told what to give their daughters, or to agree to generally acceptable limits, as they seemed ready to do for wedding expenses.

In Prakash Tandon's evocative and charming memoir of the Punjab, the furnishings included in a well-to-do Khatri daughter's *daaj* go on to embellish her marital home. Describing his granduncle's house in Lahore in the first quarter of the twentieth century, he says,

> It was sparsely furnished, with spring charpoys [cots] or niwar cotton tape beds and low sting and niwar stools called pirhis. They all had gaily lacquered legs. In the main bedroom, faded with age, was a rather elaborately worked pirhi with a high back. It had a coloured seat and ornately turned sidestand back studded with mirrors and ivory pieces. It was the pirhi which grand aunt, like all Punjabi brides, brought in her dowry [circa 1870]. Near it was an old bed of elaborate design, which had been her bridal bed. This furniture was very like the style still seen in Gujerat and Saurashtra. In our own house we had a very old bed on which our father's grandmother had lain on her wedding night. The rest of the furniture consisted of many steel and wooden trunks; there was the very large steel trunk in which grand aunt brought her dowry. They contained clothes, linen, blankets, shawls,

quilts, utensils of copper and silver, jewellery and ornaments, and tapestries [embroidered by family women] called phulkaries. (Tandon 1968: 20)

Prakash Tandon's granduncle was a lawyer and represented the upwardly mobile urban professional class of the period with homes that emulated, more and more, the lifestyle of their colonial masters. The furnishings available in Lahore were distinctly more elaborate than those described by Edwardes in 1850, and it can be said that these new articles in the market, mostly imported from England, were going to push up the outlay for a daughter's *daaj*, which consisted of all household items, from water vessels to brooms. Beds had to be complimented with bed stands, and sofa sets of many designs begged inclusion. Water vessels and cooking utensils, and metal *thalis* (plates) and cups would now be supplemented with china dinner service and tea sets. As wealthy Punjabis, across caste and community, vied for imported British luxuries to embellish their lifestyle, dowries naturally followed suit.

Dowries might have already cost many times more than all other wedding expenses put together. Why then, in 1853 or later, did the British officials not insist that dowries be regulated just like the expenses associated with the wedding itself, confirmed as they were in their belief in its causal relationship to female infanticide? What might explain this conspicuous omission at a meeting convened expressly to curtail wedding expenses, and therefore dowries, is that both sides had divergent reasons to let the matter go unregulated. For Punjabis, a daughter's *daaj* was simply not negotiable, even for the most pliant and ingratiating subjects. It was where many of the assembled groups drew the line. Marriage was the time for which women aggressively saved and invested. On the British side, it is possible to speculate that it must have been clear to them that the wealthy urban groups and neighboring princes were the potential consumers of the British-made household goods and textiles, and to limit this consumption, specially in the form of dowries, seemed economically self-defeating. Discretion was certainly the better part of valor here. This conclusion is endorsed by the deliberate vagueness that shrouds the language on *daaj* (compared with the clarity and calculation of all other expenses) in the various agreements of 1853. I was to comb in vain through voluminous documents in search of precise limits set on the values of dowries in these extraordinary agreements that were drawn up expressly to establish those limits in the first place.

These conspicuous lacunae in otherwise purposeful agreements also point to a subtext. They eloquently represent the wisdom and caution of the women who were excluded from attending the deliberations. The men knew that they never determined the selection of clothes, jewels, and household goods unilaterally. At these meetings, they not only debated the minutiae of marriage customs that could be summarily disallowed by English civilians, but also had to bear in mind the interests and dictates of their women—their mothers, grandmothers, wives, and indeed, the daughters themselves—who were the principal actors in questions relating to arranging marriages and weddings. The women might even have foreclosed the possibility of discussions of *daaj* per se, except in the most general terms, since women controlled the decisions regarding the arrangements and expenses of marriages. The men must also have sensed the trap in accepting strict monetary gradations of dowry. It would inevitably have caused disputes about the economic rank of a family and laid it open to the charge that it had given too little (a social embarrassment) or too much (a criminal danger). It would certainly have resulted in unhealthy competition among clan members and imitation by the lower classes of the upper, all ultimately leading to the very escalation in dowries that the restrictions would have sought to avoid.

In the Amritsar agreements of 1853, there is no evidence that bridetakers ever demanded goods or cash above and beyond what the bride's parents presented to them as *milni* gifts and to their daughter as *daaj*. There is no mention of curbing demands by bridetakers, only curbs on the voluntary spending by bridegivers. This is critical information for the baseline that I am trying to establish, because it makes it possible to assert that until the middle of the nineteenth century dowry was not a bargaining chip in the negotiations to arrange a marriage. Although it is fair to assume that dowries are not actively bargained for by the vast majority of Punjabi Khatris and Brahmins even today, there is a growing minority of bridetakers among these groups who actually demand bigger dowries than the bride's parents can comfortably give. The gradual mutation of dowry into a social pathogen is complex. It entails not only the interaction between bridegivers and bridetakers but also colonial social and economic interventions. The late nineteenth century presents a different picture.

The Amritsar covenants are the place to look for some of the earliest clues to this transition. They reflect at least three areas in which *daaj* could easily have gone on to become a far larger proportion of marriage expenses than hitherto. It is noted in parenthesis in Appendices G and H that the expenditure on the distribution of sweets and presents to the groom's party on the second day of the wedding (called *vadhai* and *beyee vadhai*, or congratulatory gifts), valued at three times the gifts made for the *milni* on the first day, was a custom that many did not observe any longer, choosing "in lieu of the presents made on the occasion . . . [to] give [more] jewels to the Bride on marriage" (SPCPA 1854: 440–43). This suggests that if the government did not want bridegivers to squander large sums of money on gifts for their wedding guests, this customary allocation could best be diverted into the bride's *daaj* itself, for which no limit had been proposed. This impetus to increase the *daaj* probably came from both sides—from the bride's mother, who was always looking for ways to increase her daughter's *daaj*, and from her in-laws, who would rather have the resources reallocated to the bride than miss out altogether.

A standard feature of weddings today is the colorful presence of the groom's female relatives and large entourages that have to be entertained, feasted, and housed for the two to three days of the wedding ceremonies, and who also have to be received with welcoming *milni* gifts. This was obviously not the case in 1853, when *milni* gifts were described in almost all the agreements as rather small cash tokens for the male relatives of the groom who actually attended the wedding, ranging from five to twenty rupees. Women relatives of the groom customarily stayed at home, where they feasted and made merry while waiting for the *baraat* or the groom's party to return with the bride. What changed the symbolic welcoming gesture of *milni* into an elaborate gift-giving occasion by the bride's male and female relatives to their counterparts in the groom's family can be traced to the gradual inclusion of women in the *baraat*, as conditions of travel eased and women could no longer be denied the pleasure. The number of relatives who attended the ceremonies appeared to grow as travel became cheaper and easier with the coming of the railways in the last quarter of the nineteenth century, raising proportionately the expense for hospitality borne by the bride's family. If the groom's female relatives and fictive kin accompanied him to the wedding celebrations, it was only natural that they should also be welcomed with saffron-stained envelopes of money and enjoy the hospitality of the bride's family and village. Although this added considerably to the wedding expenses, it must have also have happened at the urging of women themselves. From early in the twentieth century, a set of clothes and jewels was added to the *milni* for the principal female kin of the groom (such as his mother and sisters), and clothes or cash for other women relatives became customary.

Today *milni* gifts can be a major wedding expense, sometimes bargained for in advance between the two parties—an escalation that is more material than cultural. Sometimes, of course, *milni* can become the occasion for mounting greed. The cash and clothes for the *milni* may almost rival the bride's trousseau, as the bridetakers assemble all their surviving kin for the ceremony. In chapter 6, we see that in one case the demand for a set of jewels for a *milni* for a deceased mother-in-law nearly brought the betrothal to an end. In cities, the gift giving is now staged at the beginning of the festivities as an important theatrical moment watched by the wide-ranging circle of friends and officials who attend the wedding. The sumptuary regulations of 1853 had little effect on containing costs; on the contrary, outlays for token and auspicious giving have steadily ballooned in Punjabi families that now equate status with material gifts.

The only area in which a reduction was actually achieved appears to be the traditional dues paid to the *pandit* or priest, and to *bhands*, *mirasis*, beggars, and *hijras* (groups of transvestites who sing and dance at weddings, births, and other auspicious occasions). The *purohit* or *pandit* (always a Brahmin) who is the ritual specialist for performing the wedding found his fees sharply reduced as time went on, and today it is a negligible fraction of the cost of the wedding. Recall that the British disapproved of paying for what they considered to be the noisy and meaningless activity of idle rascals—the many drummers, dancers, and singers who traditionally received small amounts of cash and partook of the wedding feast after the wedding guests had eaten. Although this expense was not proportionately a large one, a utilitarian and austere-minded officialdom strongly urged that it be discontinued entirely as one of the appropriate places to trim waste. Over time, the presence of such traditional performers tailed off, but the expense of entertaining the *baraat* has gone up considerably. The far more expensive English-style brass bands, often rented from the army or the police forces, began to replace local traditional musicians.

The British also wanted the wedding feast to include only the kin and affines of the bride rather than all village artisans, the poor, and the menials. "Another large item of expense, that of the Bhajee Kurahhee, or food distributed occasionally to the whole village, has been reduced to the proper limits and the relations and more intimate friends of the two families only be entitled to partake. The Nurizee, a distribution of food and money to bramins [*sic*], has been suppressed, as regards the poorer classes, and greatly reduced as regards richer people."[9] The entitlements of village servants, too, were gradually eroded until these functionaries were regarded more as criminals to be dealt with by the police than welcome and necessary adjuncts. Again the modest success at excising traditional generosity to village servants to reduce marriage expenses was more than offset by the far greater expenditure on nonvegetarian food and European spirits (scotch whisky, rum, beer, and wine) the British introduced into Punjabi society.

The only agreement that mentions sums actually expended on the various stages of a marriage alliance is one signed by Khatris of the town of Batala in Gurdaspur district, bordering Amritsar. This agreement—which does not follow the approved format—gives us some sense of the actual sums that people thought fit to spend even in a small town; we can extrapolate from Batala to Amritsar and Lahore with less difficulty with the help of these figures. The *milni*, for instance, which was restricted to the amount of one to eleven rupees in the agreement, was "in lieu of from 21 to 250 Rs. hitherto expended." Similarly, the *vadhai* (gifts to the groom's party) was scaled down to Rs. 11 to 125 from Rs. 100 to 3,100, and the cash gift of Rs. 700 given at the *teeka*, or the marking of the groom's forehead with saffron or sandalwood paste at the betrothal, was reduced to range from Rs. 11 to Rs. 51. There is little doubt about the expenses that came under the paring knife: the cash and gifts for the bridegroom and his kin were dramatically cut, but not the money spent on feasting, and the *daaj* was, once more, left solely to the discretion of the bride's parents (SPCPA 1854: 453–55).[10] The underlying conviction in these various agreements seems to be that the enforced reductions in expenditure should impinge not on the rights of the daughter but on the gifts given to the bridegroom and his kin. It would be possible to conclude that it is not *daaj* but the wedding itself that makes the girl the "burden," and that the objection lies not in dowry but in the gifts given to the groom and his kin. What makes this conclusion problematic is that identical or larger amounts of money were spent on the weddings of sons, at the funerals of males, and at Hindu tonsure and Muslim circumcision ceremonies for young males. Social expenditure was part of the fabric of society and was not occasioned by females alone, thus warranting female infanticide.

What these agreements did not acknowledge was the existence of customary giving, which distributed the "burden" of wedding expenses throughout a web of reciprocal relationships. Most of the gifts for the bride were also collected over time by the bride's own family, particularly the mother, who, virtually from the day a daughter was born began to collect clothes and jewels that the daughter would take with her to her new home. The dowry did not have to wait to be bought until the profit from the last harvest, salary, or trade was available; it was, and to some extent still is, accumulated gradually and rather less painfully, in the course of the young girl's maidenhood. The bride's mother—in consultation with elder female kin and affines, particularly her own mother, aunts, and mother-in-law—was and is the principal decision maker, economic manager, and actor in putting the *daaj* together. In fact, among families with even small surpluses the strategy is to fill the *pitara* (a wooden chest, often carved and with ornamental brass trimmings and latch, in which *daaj* was given), continually over the twelve to fifteen years from the time a daughter is born, with the clothes, bedding, and utensils that she will eventually receive. Today the receptacles may be suitcases and tin trunks or modern steel almirahs, but there is not a Punjabi household of some means where children are being raised where a hope chest for a daughter and a *vari* (the gift to the bride from the groom's family) for a daughter-in-law are not being accumulated or set aside. Only uncustomary demands can actually transmogrify a daughter's wedding, the most anticipated event in a parent's life, into a nightmare.

Neonda (also *neondra*) or the premise of reciprocity came into play on all ritual and social occasions, and still does in some parts of the Punjab, at all levels and across religions in Punjabi villages and towns alike.[11] All life-cycle events, including births, tonsure and circumcision ceremonies, betrothals, birthdays, funerals, and local Hindu festivals such as Diwali, activated the network of reciprocities among villagers and city dwellers alike, but the centerpiece of social and political transactions was the marriage of sons and daughters, and the gifts given on such occasions reflected the status of the giver and his relationship to the recipient. This elaborate web of social giving was never casual. A *behi khata*, or account book of what was received and from whom, was maintained by every family, because proper reciprocity involved calculating not just the market value of the gift but also the status of the giver, the number of sons and daughters in his family, and the degree of the relationship.[12]

Once the custom of *neonda* is factored in, and its nature as a dependable resource at the time of marriage understood, the financial impact of dowry giving on the family is greatly diluted. The anthropologist's diagram with arrows representing the flow of gifts in dowry-giving families appears hopelessly unidirectional, but the sources are wider than the illustration indicates. What goes on is complex and burdened with emotional and gendered meaning, with mutual and unequal obligations that shape the nature of kinship and affinal connection. Hershman observes that "[t]raditionally a great deal of the money towards the bride's dowry and also towards the entertainment of the marriage party was collected through the institution of *ninda* [a linguistic variant of *neonda*] amongst the *biradari* of the bride," and he defines *biradari* to mean "an agnatic *rites de passage* group" (Hershman 1981: 202). He defines dowry quite properly as the "money [and goods] collected by the institution of *ninda* and "contributions from the bride's father, brothers, mother's brother, mother's sister's husband, etc." The nucleus of the bride's jewelry comes from her mother's own *daaj* and *vari*, and the grandmothers and aunts from both sides supplement these ornaments. Among Khatris and Brahmins, a ceremony called the *chura* ceremony is designed to bring together all the bride's gift-giving relatives to give the bride and her parents the gifts intended for her and other gifts and cash to help defray the costs of the wedding itself. This occurs only a day before the wedding, although what is going to be given by the close kin is already clear by the rules of reciprocity from the day a daughter is born. The wife's mother's brother (*mama*) leads off the ceremony by presenting the *nanki bhat* (gifts from the bride's mother's family, especially the bride's maternal grandparents and uncles). The *mama*'s own gift varies in value according to his circumstances, but minimally consists of the *chura*—a set of ivory bangles embossed and dyed in red—and the set of clothes and jewelry the bride will wear for the wedding ceremony. The cumulative, and assuredly intended, effect of the system was to benefit all; it made events such as a daughter's wedding a shared responsibility and far less a burden than the British believed it to be, because much of the dowry and the provisions for the feasts were contributed by the direct kin and the fictive family in the village.

The principle of reciprocity defined the bounds of this group to include maternal and paternal kin, fictive kin, and virtually all other residents of the village, who may have been members of other castes. Even estranged kin had to be invited to attend a girl's wedding so that they could be given the opportunity to reciprocate in terms of gifts; to fail to do so was a moral lapse. The parents of the bride coordinated and arranged these matters well in advance—and these traditions greatly reduced the need for loans even if the season was a bad one. This premise of reciprocity surely weakens the logic that wedding expenses were the cause for the killing of female infants; if anything, it supports the view that dowry was the collectively woven traditional safety net for the bride for her future away from the natal village.

Neonda was equally in vogue among Sikhs of the Punjab. On the groom's side much the same arrangements obtained. In a study of Maharaja Ranjit Singh's revenues and finances, Charles Hall remarks on the political import of gift giving on ceremonial occasions among the principal Jat clans. He found that marriage was the most significant ceremony for the exchange of gifts, and that the amount exchanged and the number of *biradari* members who participated in the ritual depended upon the status and power of the marriage parties. Maharaja Ranjit Singh had expected to spend some 4 lakhs of rupees on his son's wedding but managed with exactly half that amount; his account books show that he received some 2.3 lakhs as *tambol*, or marriage gifts, from high-ranking chiefs in 1812. Most of the gifts were of jewelry intended for the new bride. What is interesting for our purposes is to calculate that gifts constituted more that half the expected outlay for the wedding. This kind of expenditure did not cost the state exchequer anything; the ranked nobles and chieftains essentially financed the wedding and all other social occasions. The gifts would have been even more lavish had it been the wedding of a daughter, to cover both the dowry and the celebrations (Hall 1981: 42–48).[13] Hall cites an analogous situation from 1811, when Raja Sahib Singh of Patiala was married. The Raja of Nabha gave a thousand rupees, Jind gave five hundred, Himat Singh two hundred, "and others gave whatever they could *according to their rank* and position by way of 'Tambol' on the occasion of the marriage" (ibid.:44; emphasis added). This aristocratic model, which was followed on a humbler scale by ordinary families, reinforces my argument that weddings were not affairs that concerned only the parents of the bride and groom, as the British perceived things to be; they involved the entire village, and as one went up the social ladder, all the princely lineages of the Punjab.

Neonda, it can be argued, was the key to understanding the social relationships and status markers in a village with all its layering and stratification. In 1853, however, these subtleties, reciprocities, and customs totally escaped the British, and they defined dowry as a direct, almost individual burden for the bride's father that they believed encouraged female infanticide. These traditional networks were, in fact, tested and weakened or even destroyed when peasants became individual owners of land that was once communally held, and when indebtedness, famine, or a loss of income foreclosed social giving.

It appears from the caveats at the end of some of the *ikrar nameh* that most of the middling and lower-income families spent well below the new scale of wedding expenses, because it was suggested that they should continue to do so without their "suffering in repute." The unspoken fear, of course, was that in trying to curb the few extravagant families by setting limits, the British might push the average sensible families, who married their daughters within their means, into an officially approved and publicly endorsed spiral of escalating costs, causing them to go into debt. In other words, these agreements might not have checked the offenders for whom they were intended, but instead made nonoffenders vulnerable to social pressures or the temptation to aspire to higher status by spending more money to make a "third-class" or "second-class" wedding into a "first-class" one.

Implicit in the arrangements of 1853 was the danger that they gave the groom's family room to demand that the bridegivers spend to the upper limit to protect their social rank, now linked by bureaucratic agreement to the specific scale of expenses. And since it was already a well-honed truth that a daughter's wedding was a crushing burden, there was little official activity either to acquaint district personnel with the customs and expenses that obtained on the groom's side or to limit them in any way. I have already pointed out that the *vari* the bride received from her in-laws often surpassed her dowry, and the absence of limits on the groom's side left them free to ratchet up the costs, obliging the bride's side to match, if not surpass, their celebrations and their gifts. The groom's family could claim that their prestige would be doubly at stake — in the eyes of their kith and kin and in the eyes of the government. The *ikrar nameh* established a concrete and monetized notion of marriage expenses, so precisely proportioned, graded, and ranked that they can be seen more properly as the beginning rather than the end of social extravagance among poorer peasants.

A NATIVE'S ASSESSMENT

In April 1867, the secretary of Lahore Anjuman, a literary society, was directed in a letter by Sir D. F. McLeod, the lieutenant governor of the Punjab, to hold an essay competition on the subject of the suppression of infanticide, for which the government would offer three prizes, of five hundred, two hundred, and one hundred rupees, to the winning entrants. The response was not overwhelming. In June 1868, McLeod received a copy of the entry by Mardan Ali Khan, a former employee who had moved to the service of the Maharaja of Jodhpur, which was, even by the most generous reading, an unexceptional piece that reiterated and praised the government's efforts in suppressing the crime. On 27 February 1869, the president of the Lahore Anjuman selected a second entry by Maulvi Muhammad Husain, an assistant professor of Arabic in the Lahore Government College, and judged it to be "by far the ablest and the best" of numerous submissions. This, too, broke no new paths and said little of value. McLeod remarked that no essay by a Hindu "has been spontaneously submitted to us, though possibly such may have been submitted to the Anjuman. As the crime of female infanticide is confined or nearly confined, to Hindus," he had expected the "good men of that persuasion" to compete for the prizes offered and "to come forward and lend a helping hand towards bringing the commission of the crime to an end" (McLeod 1870: 1). If McLeod was surprised at the paltry response to both the subject and the generous prize money, I, as a researcher, have all these years later been even more baffled at the silence on the subject of female infanticide in the vernacular press, which by the 1860s was a thriving enterprise in urban Punjab. All those meetings summoned in district headquarters and in towns such as Jullunder, Amritsar, and Rawalpindi provoked no comment by otherwise very articulate and opinionated native editors and publishers who spoke up on many social issues and other government policies. After minutely scanning some eighty years' worth of politically important selections from vernacular newspapers culled, translated, and compiled by the Punjab government, I found fewer than a handful of perfunctory notices on the official effort to suppress female infanticide—all in the year 1876, some half dozen years after Act VIII of 1870 had been put into effect in the province.[14] This silence was not peculiar to the Punjabis; the people of the North-West Provinces and Bombay Presidency, where the crime was supposed to be rampant, said next to nothing about it in their newspapers. The tracts and pamphlets available on the subject were, as already noted, products of the official and missionary drive to eradicate the crime rather than of native initiative.

The essays for McLeod's competition are no longer extant, but we do have one sharp, clear voice that breaks the silence. Having failed to elicit a spontaneous "Hindoo response," McLeod solicited Pundit Motilal Kathju, an extra assistant commissioner and *mir munshi* (chief clerk) of the Punjab Secretariat in Lahore, to provide one. He did, and his "Memorandum on Female Infanticide" was entered into the sputtering competition. This "very able" and "singularly outspoken" document authored by a Kashmiri Brahmin official was of special interest to McLeod because it represented what the establishment had been previously loath to elicit: the frank and liberal views of a "Hindoo gentleman, who thoroughly understands and appreciates our aims, yet unhesitatingly asserts that our policy in this matter has been mistaken and ineffectual, if not positively injurious, and urges in forcible and earnest terms the necessity for its entire reversal" (McLeod 1870: 2). The memorandum was promptly reprinted and circulated among the officers who were to draft that climactic piece of reform legislation, Act VIII of 1870; it is no accident that the resemblance between Kathju's memo and the Act for the Prevention of Murder of Female Infants is uncanny.

Kathju's work was so impressive, his revulsion toward the crime so untutored, that McLeod recommended him for the first prize in the contest even though his memorandum was not a formal entry. For our purposes, it provides a counterpoint to the many mechanical *ikrar nameh* the chiefs and leaders of various groups agreed to sign and a valuable note of dissent against the cultural analysis of infanticide implicit in all of the officially sponsored initiatives. It also gives us enough firsthand evidence to further etch the baseline on dowry that I am in the process of establishing. Kathju's memorandum offers an uninfluenced glimpse of what educated natives in this period really thought of those presumed twin causes of infanticide—caste pride and marriage expenses—and of the view of gender relations among upper-caste Punjabis.

Kathju systematically refutes the idea that "pride of race" and "the heavy expense attending the marriages of daughters" are the causes of the crime in question. Of the first, he says, "if this were so, there should never have been a time when female children were preserved in the families where they are now killed;

whereas by all accounts, the practice wherever it originated, was adopted in consequence of such pride having been injured" (Kathju 1868: 1). He explains that he does not mean to quibble by making a distinction between pride per se and the injured pride or humiliation that results from the alliance of a daughter, which causes—in a very few families—the destruction of that daughter. Men in such families were not behaving according to the rules of their caste but were "unhappy sufferers, in a moment of frenzy, and the dupes of an unfortunate hallucination" who resorted to murder to prevent such ignominy in future. He cites the example of the proudest of Rajput kings in the time of the Mughals, who

> gave their daughters in marriage to the Mahomedan Emperors of India—aliens to them in race, country and religion. The giving of daughters in marriage to men of their own tribes was not considered dishonorable by the majority of the Rajput families of acknowledged rank. The same is the case now. Not all Rajput families, nor all the Khatri tribes, . . . destroy their daughters. This false pride of race, then, influences a small portion of certain tribes, into whose families it found admission by the mad caprice of some depraved mind . . . wherefore it was handed down as a family practice rather than one that involved an entire caste or race. (Kathju 1868: 1–2)

The echoes of the Bedi stories that Edwardes collected reverberate through the text even though Kathju's was ostensibly a dissenting voice. It is quite likely that Kathju did not know of any families who actually killed their daughters and that the idea of female infanticide was more rumor and abstraction than practice among his social cohort. He was extrapolating from the wealth of speculation the Punjab magistracy had generated in the early 1850s and neatly bound up in the volumes in the Infanticide Department. He was the only official who actually went over to the Lahore Anjuman and read through all the other submissions that did not qualify as entries, and he found only one among them to have any original suggestions. He complained

> that all others who have written on the subject have taken their cue from the apparent action of the Government in the matter. . . . [A]ccordingly, it will be observed they all follow a beaten track, enlarging on the measures which [already existed]; or if they have suggested any new measures, they are of a nature chiefly conciliatory, or which cannot produce any results. . . . Some few of the measures seem to me to be positively injurious . . . and place the Government in a powerless attitude, entirely dependent on the action of the people themselves—a most unenviable situation, and one unworthy of a powerful and humane government. (Kathju 1868: 4)

On the subject of marriage expenses, however, his writing is informed with a directness of social experience and a conviction that rings true.

> The expenses attending the marriages of daughters are pleaded as an *excuse* for the destruction of female children only by those who practice the crime.

The anticipation of such expenditure is not a *cause* [emphasis in original], in fact. There is no Hindu family of respectability where heavy expenditure is not incurred on occasions of marriages of daughters or where the desire does not exist of incurring a considerable expenditure on such occasions. I think the desire not only laudable, as indicative of a wish to secure respect for the daughter on the part of the family of her husband, but the feeling, I think, is natural. It is admitted on all hands that the practice of demanding and receiving presents from the family of the bridegroom for the hand of the bride [bride-price], on part of the parents of the latter, is mean and dishonorable. The reverse of this practice, or giving suitable presents on giving a daughter in marriage, is, on the other hand, *honorable* [emphasis in original]. In the great majority of families of all classes the birth of a daughter leads the parents to habits of economy, to lay by a sufficient amount to defray the expenses of her marriage. (Kathju 1868: 2)

Here Kathju confirms what I have observed earlier, that dowries were not bought overnight in the nineteenth century but were gradually accumulated and recycled, and forced fiscal discipline on the family. This flatly contradicted the British dictum that dowries were symptomatic of a thriftless people who were then obliged to kill their daughters.

He also unequivocally tells us that among Punjabi upper castes, particularly Brahmins and Khatris, dowry was the preferred and decidedly honorable practice, and bride-price its shameful opposite, tantamount to selling a daughter. Kathju's writing also affords us a rare glimpse of how upper-caste parents regarded their daughter, and considered providing an adequate dowry a voluntary expression of love and duty that would translate into esteem for her as a bride. This was not an uncommon sentiment in the 1860s and can be widely found today. But unlike the situation in recent times, nowhere in Kathju's candid and thoughtful critique does the idea arise that the groom's parents could demand a larger dowry than the bride's parents had chosen to give. The dowry demands complained about in the 1960s (when the Dowry Prohibition Act was passed) were nonexistent in 1868. They would have been considered shameful, just as they are today among the majority.

The pressure, if any, to be lavishly hospitable at the wedding and to give a large dowry was generally exerted by the bride's family's perception of its own standing in the town or village and her parents' own wish to appear—at this very public opportunity—as people of greater substance than they really were. But this self-serving extravagance, which pushed up marriage expenses at a son's wedding as much as it did at a daughter's, was not the general state of affairs that would account for the missing female children deep in the countryside. The Khatris of Lahore had been noticed to be crass enough to make dowry demands, but this was certainly not a feature of the vast majority of villagers and townspeople who married among their equals and spent according to their means.

Despite the admonitions and agreements the Khatris of Lahore submitted to, they appeared not to be able to curb the appetite for bigger and better dowries in their community. Being conspicuously successful and quick to avail themselves of the opportunities English education and government jobs opened up for them, they emerged as the leading elite urban community in the Punjab, one that was apt to be imitated by those who aspired to higher social status. (For a history of this community see Tandon [1963] 1968 and Malhotra 1998.) They had also profited from British revenue policies, which made many of them into prosperous moneylenders and absentee landlords when the British auctioned off the lands of revenue defaulters.

In 1916, a revised and updated version of the 1868 Customary Laws of Lahore District was published. In a description of the "usual ceremonies" at the weddings of Khatris, Brahmins, and Aroras (a trading caste), a suspiciously new one has made its appearance. "On the date fixed for the return of the marriage party [*baraat*], which is usually the second or third day after its arrival according to the wish and means of the girl's father, *the articles that form the dowry are gathered together and shown to the marriage party as well as to the girl's brotherhood.* . . . The boy is then again called inside the house of the bride's father and *the dowry gifted to him*" (Bolster 1916: 15; emphasis added). There are two startling changes to be noticed here. The first is about caste. Aroras, who came by great wealth as moneylenders in the second half of the nineteenth century, who were then seen to be free from dowry problems and not summoned to sign an *ikrar namah*, are now clubbed together with Khatris and Brahmins. This supports my earlier assertion that the Khatris of Lahore became the trendsetters, the reference community for all other Punjabis, and other castes and communities imitated their life style and large dowries, once these were declared as part of high-status, first-class marriages.[15] The other key change recorded here for the first time, and widely practiced today, attests to a qualitative change in the nature of *daaj* from the private, volitional giving of a traditionally defined set of gifts packed in a chest and sent off with the daughter as *her* property to one that is publicly displayed and formally made over to the son-in-law. This custom appears to have emerged among the Lahore Hindu elite, led by the Khatris, and reflects the desire to display the new wealth generated by them as opportunities for trade and moneylending increased in the Punjab. It also suggests a diminution of the control women exerted over their dowries when they were simpler and of less value.

That a public display of wealth should be dignified as a "ceremony" and be recorded as such in the revised edition of the handbook of customary law in 1916 in Lahore was probably instrumental in creating a new standard and meaning of dowry. The act of public display and comment, which can commonly be overheard today as stage whispers of approval, envy, odious comparisons, or taunts, probably instigated the highly competitive trend in dowries in the early 1920s. Instead of weighing what was affordable for them and appropriate for the bride, families were now coaxed to take into consideration what they had seen at a neighbor's daughter's wedding and what the groom's people might expect or want. Not only would bride's dowry be judged when the bride wore her clothes and jewels in her new affinal home but also the status of her family was up for reevaluation at the sensitive juncture of the wedding itself. The steps in the process of converting a beloved daughter into a social and economic "burden" become easier to trace. That these elaborate and wasteful ceremonies came under sharp attack by native reformers, particularly the members of the Arya Samaj, who saw these innovations as a corruption of tradition, is noted in the same update of Lahore Customary Law. The Aryas resorted to a very simple Vedic wedding ceremony and deplored dowries altogether. "Arya Samajists," the update of the law went on to say, "as well as other Hindus of advanced views do not strictly observe all these ceremonies with the exception of the circumambulation of the fire which is essential in all cases" (Bolster 1916: 15).

An even more ominous change was the apparent gradual shift of control over *daaj* from the woman to her husband and his parents. The abrupt appearance of this new custom in 1912–1916 in Lahore, in which the bride's father led the bridegroom into his house and presented him with the dowry, captures the transition more generally of the relationship of women to their property in the colonial period. It appears to signal that women's customary authority over their own property seems to have declined or become nonexistent.

The contrast is vivid with the picture we have of women and their relationship to their *daaj* and other property in the 1880s, sketched in the many volumes of customary law compiled in the last quarter of the nineteenth century. Diminishing control on the part of wives can be traced through the successive revisions to these compendiums of customary law made every two or three decades, along with the revised and updated assessments of land revenue. And to these compendiums we will turn in chapter 5.

So the promised baseline can be drawn in 1850 with serviceable clarity for dowry and marriage expenses. Dowry was a collection of clothes, household goods, furniture, and draught animals or milch cattle voluntarily given to the bride at the time of marriage, which reflected the status and means of the bride's family. Many of the items included in the dowry were collected over time; they included items given as reciprocal prestations by kinsmen, neighbors, and others, and therefore were not a burden to be discharged at once. There is no evidence in this period that the groom's family either bargained for a dowry or made dowry demands; it is emphatically seen as a matter of honor for the groom's side to accept what is given as a dowry to the bride. In fact, it might be fair to say that even British officers, who had an insatiable curiosity about native customs, were unable to find tribes that haggled over this matter. Natives did not blame dowries or marriage expenses for female infanticide; they blamed instead, as the Bedis had to Major Edwardes, the loss of honor that may prompt such brutal action.

4

Engineering a Masculine World

The whole movement of progressive societies has been from status to contract.
—*Sir Henry Maine*

The time has come for the denouement of this long historical sleuthing. We must resolve the paradox that has haunted our investigation: that in the very decades (1850–1870) when female infanticide was discovered, investigated, and legislated against, the marked preference for sons progressively deepened. This occurred even though social legislation enacted in the same period ostensibly tried to protect and uplift the condition of women. The resolution of this paradox is to be found by examining the concomitant activity of the colonial state and the large-scale, long-term effect of its agrarian development and revenue policies that purported to modernize the world of the Punjab peasants, yet succeeded in transforming it into an even more unambiguously masculine domain where, of necessity, fewer women would survive. Declining female sex ratios during the last century affirm this assertion (Mayer 1999). Although British statistics on certain groups were already skewed in the second half of the nineteenth century, we have to bear in mind that much of the data collected in the early decades of colonial administration in the Punjab was flawed by the colonialists' own theory of who committed female infanticide and why (as we saw in chapter 2). By the turn of the nineteenth century, the Punjab would become a region where sons would be even more fiercely desired than traditional Hindu, Muslim, or Sikh brands of patriarchy had ever imagined or ordained. [1]

This paradox, I believe, is grounded in the anomalous position of the colonial state itself. The political economy of colonialism, as David Washbrook and others have pointed out, was decidedly "Janus-faced and rested on two contradictory principles with different social implications" (Washbrook 1981; also see Gilmartin

1988: 11–38). On the one hand it promoted the emergence of free market relations in land and its produce, and on the other it codified religious law to preserve ascribed status and, I would add and will be at pains to prove, stiffened the patriarchal framework of Indian society. The "free market" was in reality hobbled in colonial India; Indian merchants were never actually free to trade directly with any international partner, since the British controlled all imports and exports, and even land, the newly created commodity, was fettered by political conditions for its alienation or sale. The "modernity" the colonial state bestowed on India was strictly selective and deeply flawed. Little or no modern industry was encouraged, in a period when Britain was reaping the economic fruits of a revolution that the manufacture of cotton textiles in Britain had launched. Indian resources and wealth would have comfortably paid for importing British machines (as did the countries of Western Europe), but the government preferred to keep India as a captive market in their own economic self-interest rather than face the potentially disastrous consequence of seeing its empire grow into an industrial competitor. While Punjab land tenures were modernized into proprietorships, its economy became increasingly agrarian in the age of industry, producing food and raw materials for exports to Europe. Neeladhri Bhattacharya points to the contradiction that beset agrarian policy in the Punjab. "On the one hand there was the need to enhance revenue and augment the financial resources of the state," he writes, "and on the other the desire to maintain the purchasing power of the peasantry in order to expand the market for British manufactures. The short-term attempt to maximize revenue demand also militated against the object of ensuring the long-term reproduction of the of the conditions of appropriation" (Bhattacharya 1992: 120).[2]

Instead of trying to evaluate the ideological grounding of the colonial economy and state, which has been exquisitely theorized by every generation of scholars beginning in the nineteenth century until the present in works of awesome rigor, I will concentrate on the social ramifications of these policies. Modern capitalist ideas in their attenuated form seeped unevenly through the mesh of colonial needs and priorities, and infiltrated Punjabi society via two major colonial initiatives—the ryotwari system and the codification of "customary law."[3]

The first, discussed in this chapter, followed the manner in which the entire subcontinent that came under British sway had been "settled": land was declared a marketable commodity capable of private and determinate ownership, so that a fixed and settled land revenue in cash could be recovered on every plot of land in two annual installments on two fixed dates. Annual assessments, which had been customary in preceding native regimes, were abruptly discontinued for being cumbersome and expensive, and for providing the opportunity for corruption. The British, in striving to put the administration on a rational, efficient, and economic footing, ordained that their revenue settlements for various districts stay in effect for two or three decades without regard to the situation that obtained in any given year, be it drought, famine, or plenty. This was the policy in a nutshell, and rationalized, in the British view, the jumble of competing shares, the varied annual collections, the bargaining matches and corruption that had plagued the revenue collection of the Sikh regime. We will also reconstruct a competing view of Sikh policies from British sources.

The policy favored the government in planning its tightly budgeted profits and outlays far into the future, but made the newly created zamindar, as all proprietors including peasants with small holdings were called, vulnerable to the risk of losing his land. The land he now owned through his proprietary title could be alienated if circumstances conspired to make him unable to tender the government dues on time, an eventuality that was difficult to comprehend in a land where collective ownership and flexible annual assessments, bargained for with the revenue authorities and paid for in kind on the threshing floor, had protected individuals from such a fate when nature visited his crops with an unseasonable hailstorm, drought, or disease. The flexibilities of the old system, including remissions granted in bad years, had insured families against the vagaries of the weather and human and crop diseases that affected yields and, therefore, the ability to pay the revenue demand. Small, unsecured loans of grain helped tide over the crisis. Under the new system the inability to pay could have far more serious consequences, since sale, auction, and foreclosure of the land were all possible, as we shall see.

The second initiative, discussed in chapter 5, is the codification of "custom" as adjudicable law in the Punjab countryside. These two processes worked in tandem and illuminate how the equation in gender and power came to be skewed further. By tracking the enormous changes that took place when the world of the peasants of the Punjab became decidedly more masculine and as land, a hitherto communally held resource, became private property, we can recapture the moment women's voices and customs were erased as men's rights and voices were recorded with singular clarity. The shared control formerly accorded to all those who worked the land came to be replaced by the arbitrary privileging of tillers as owners of the soil.[4] Women—as those who sowed, weeded, hoed, harvested, threshed, and milled grain and vegetables, looked after dairy cattle, collected fuels, processed produce, and prepared it as food—who had been implicit coparceners in precolonial landholding arrangements, found themselves tenuous legal dependents of men, with their access to economic resources subordinated more and more to the control and will of their husbands. The British had not granted their own women rights to property, so it was highly unlikely that they would shed their prejudice while introducing this "progressive" notion of private property to the Punjab (and progress meant an assimilation to modern European norms). They granted these rights exclusively to men so that they could collect their taxes from male proprietors, who could be taken to court or sent to jail if they defaulted. Clearly women, already hindered by the custom of seclusion and veiling, could not conveniently interact with the legal machinery of the new rulers, so their husbands and male kin quietly subsumed their rights. A robust patriarchal mentality was reinforced in this collusion.

What made these two initiatives doubly powerful was the fact that they were deployed simultaneously. At the same time that land titles were formalized and revenue settlements made for each district, revenue officials (earlier called settlement officers) went further by collecting, organizing, and constituting oral, informal *rivaj* (literally, "custom") from male heads of each "tribe" or "caste." The officials themselves redefined these categories and reworked the information into a formal set of laws adjudicable in the new court system. Punjab acquired a fully codified set of "customary law," which was laid out in a manual for each of the thirty-one districts of the province with a three-volume methodological introduction and history by the scholar-bureaucrat C. L. Tupper. These laws were gathered from the heads of households on the same day as a district's revenue was settled, and by 1880 the revised recension of these laws was completed. They were to operate in lieu of the Muslim and Hindu personal laws that had already been translated and instituted in the rest of the empire by Warren Hastings in 1772.

SETTLING REVENUE, UNSETTLING PEOPLE

A contentious and confusing debate over colonial land revenue policy and its implications extended throughout the nineteenth century among British officials themselves and later with Indian nationalists, and is recapitulated in several fine agrarian histories, but it is tangential to our concerns here. (A lucid summary can be found in Stein 1992: 1–32). Stein cogently reiterates the irrefutable conclusion dozens of scholars of the colonial state have reached on why it failed to produce a defensible land revenue policy: "because at all points from the beginning to the end of the nineteenth century, commercial, military and political problems dictated that a large 'surplus' be appropriated for imperial needs in India, in Britain, and in extending the British empire in Asia and Africa. *In none of this was the welfare of the rural population of India as important as the interests of colonialism*" (ibid.: 17; emphasis added). It is imperative for us to grasp this statement of British priorities before I can further my own argument, which assumes this base.

> A general objective of colonial policy was to enhance agrarian commercialization and its link to world trade. The following changes are widely agreed among scholars to have been directed toward this objective: (1) the establishment *in law* of private, alienable property, not only in Bengal, with the zamindari settlement [whereby Mughal revenue collectors were created into landlords], but *everywhere* in British India and its client 'princely' regimes; (2) the reinforcement of class differentiations among rural people through legal and administrative protection to the richer section by privileged ownership-rights and local administrative offices; (3) the *monetization*

of the heavy revenue demand and the *timing* of its collection in such a way
as to require a massive expansion in the rural credit and money-lending by
professional lenders and rich peasants, which resulted in crisis borrowing
for small producers; (4) direct compulsion in the cultivation of indigo and
opium, but even more widespread indirect pressure for the cultivation of
jute, sugarcane, oil seeds, and, very important, irrigation schemes intended
to increase the acreage under cash crops, the cash returns to the state and
private investors, such as those to the Madras Irrigation Company. (Stein
1992: 17; also see Bharadwaj 1985)

What varied over time and space was the class of persons chosen as proprietors of
the land, such as zamindar and *taluqdar*—former revenue collectors who were
transformed into powerful landlords in Bengal and Oudh, respectively—or the
ryots, or peasants, who became individual proprietors in Madras Presidency and in
the Punjab. *Ryots* were now called zamindars, along with the big landowners of
the northwestern part of the Punjab.

Along with these four sharply drawn general rules, I would make explicit a
fifth: that everywhere ownership was recorded in individual titles, and the owner
or owners were invariably male; the implicit rights of women before land became
defined as private and alienable were summarily erased. As British legal notions of
landed property were gradually established in the subcontinent, including the
princely states not directly ruled by the British, women came to be legally construed without determinate property rights across region, class, and caste, and
were dependent on the goodwill of their husbands, sons, and brothers. In the
Punjab, matters took an even starker shape as the physical attributes of Punjabi
men, which had attracted British attention before the conquest of the region, became the foundation of an exclusively masculine economy in which individual
men, and men alone, now owned and managed a family's resources. The shift
gave the word "patriarchy" a new and denser meaning, altering the balance between gender and power in profound and enduring ways.

The results of the revenue "settlements," which consisted in creating (and periodically revising) a record-of-rights and making a general assessment of the revenue demand, were profoundly unsettling, to say the least.[5] On the same desks
where the reports on female infanticide had been reviewed and pigeonholed grew
reports of the disaster perpetrated by the newly implemented revenue system.
Lists of severely indebted peasants, who had defaulted on their revenue payments
and were forced to mortgage their holdings and faced foreclosure, backed these
reports. Why suddenly were peasants not able to pay the British revenue demand
and forced to court landlessness, a condition they had hitherto never known? The
epidemic of land alienations that swept unevenly through the Punjab grew from
a small surface irritation into chronic eczema on the body politic, and no British
civilian (as he was called after the creation of the covenanted Indian Civil Service

[ICS] in 1853), could ignore the problem as several inquiries into famine, poverty, and indebtedness were conducted until the end of the century. This was more and more seen not as a matter of bad policy with stubborn requirements, but a "communal" problem (or a problem between religious communities, particularly the Hindus and Muslims in official parlance), where clever Hindu moneylenders were successfully replacing their indebted Muslim proprietors as landowners (for details see van den Dungen 1972). It also had, in the official view, a cultural dimension. In the official mind the dowry-infanticide connection, so painstakingly constructed just after the conquest of the Punjab, also conveniently explained the new blight; the default in revenue payments came about because the culturally ordained "improvidence" and wasteful social expenditure at daughters' weddings that drove despairing families to favor sons and murder their infant daughters also led to crushing indebtedness and a inability to pay the revenue owed to the government. The average civilian relished the power that such "cultural knowledge" of peasant behavior provided, and utilized it on all occasions to solve all puzzles. But once again the data did not fit the theory. Uncomfortable and persistent questions, frequently raised within the administration, remained. How had Punjabi peasants managed to survive the reigns (and centuries) of allegedly worse native Sikh, Hindu, and Muslim despots without sizable debt or dislocation? What had created this crisis of indebtedness and foreclosures now under the first enlightened rulers this region had ever seen?

Culturally induced peasant "improvidence" was imputed but could not be proved to be the leading cause of indebtedness; on the contrary, its role was soundly refuted by the colonialists' own inquiry into the subject of famine and poverty, as we shall see. The suppression of politically inconvenient data and results of investigations, wide extrapolation from a small sample of statistics, the miscarriage of meanings in translating from one culture and language to another, and other forms of denial and deception were integral to the colonial process of selecting what would eventually pass for "knowledge" and represent native motivations and behavior. To try to answer the riddle of escalating dowries and wedding expenses and the worsening discrimination against women, we will have to look harder at the process of selecting information along with the timing, methods, and categories used by the colonial authorities to produce significant bodies of knowledge, such as the codes of customary law. Information that was willfully ignored, suppressed, or invalidated by pseudoscientific explanations of Punjabi "tribal" culture must be reconsidered to evaluate its effect on gender relations.

PROPERTY AND ITS MEANINGS

The idea of "landed property" underwent a sea change under the new regime. The notion of private property, although not widespread, was not new to the Punjab countryside, but its peculiarly English and modern legal constitution certainly was. Punjab civilians brought up with the ideas of Sir Henry Maine believed in cultural evolution as the dominant if not the sole approach to the analysis of society, according to which institutions in backward societies were earlier versions of their counterparts in advanced, modern societies. "On this hypothesis India became a storehouse of 'survivals' from the earliest stages of Aryan civilization, miraculously preserved by the caste system and the superficiality of India's invasions. . . . Societies were placed on Maine's evolutionary ladder according to the extent to which individual property rights were emancipated from collective constraints. . . . Each SO [settlement officer] agreed upon certain basic essentials. It was an article of faith that there had been no 'absolute freeholds' before the coming of the British" (Dewey 1991: 27).

The substantial and legal differences between the local meanings of land holdings in the precolonial world and the notion of "private property" promoted by the British Raj constitute the unwritten history of gender and property rights. Unless "property" itself is regarded as a dynamic concept that varied among Hindus and Muslims and changed abruptly after the British takeover, we cannot make sense of whether Punjabi Hindu and Sikh women had "property rights" and how treating Muslims as members of strictly patrilineal "agricultural tribes" denied many Hindu men, and women of all communities, participation in the "free market" the British created for land. It is imperative to historicize the meaning of property before we can begin to calculate who could possibly own, control, buy, or sell it, and how the coercive power of the law could change that. Tupper, who produced the three magisterial introductory volumes of *Punjab Customary Law* in 1881, had already revealed in his summary history the efforts of his predecessors' that had created the tribal codes, later called *Punjab Customary Law*. This circulated as a district manual and "was certainly acted upon as though it had been substantive law." And there were many provisions "intentionally made, which are not in accordance with Hindu or Muhammadan Law, and are not supported by any general custom or usage prevailing in the Punjab. . . . In other cases rules are borrowed from foreign laws, on the grounds of their supposed adaptation to the wants of the province" (Tupper 1881: I, 5). Tupper, also a faithful student of Sir Henry Maine, conceded that the government's aims were utterly inconsistent. On the one hand, it wanted to modernize agrarian relations, which meant "the breakup of primitive groups and the disentanglement of individual from corporate rights, whether as regards the personal relations or property" and tribal practices such as "slavery and chronic war" and "forcible abduction of women, the . . . habitual purchase and sale of women, and female infanticide." On the other hand, the government wished to sustain and stabilize the "essential organisation" of the tribal clans. In fact, Tupper strongly urged a revival of tribal leadership to ensure the administration's own political security by creating a set of loyal and committed leaders, because "the representative men selected would owe their position to the British administration exclusively." It was only "through the tribe and clan that the government can gain its firmest hold on the inclinations and motives of the people. The people can be led by their own leaders. It is much easier for a foreign government to deal with organized bodies of men, through those who can be trusted on both sides, than with miscellaneous hordes of individuals."[6] Such a policy, he was convinced, would preclude the danger of disaffected coalition and replace it with "animosity between different tribes." It was thus that the British decided, as Gilmartin has also pointed out (Gilmartin 1988: 14–16), that "tribes" in "village communities" should prove central to the recording of customary law. With no women consulted to settle disputed understandings or to stress the implicit day-to-day workings of their society, a staunchly patriarchal reading of the principles of clan, caste, and tribal organization inflected the codification of customs. Women's property rights in the Shariah and as constituted in the concept of *stridhan* were therefore either admitted perfunctorily or relegated to the margins of this newly created "legal" rendition of custom, wherein only men held titles of ownership and other implicit or tacit rights of usufruct.[7]

In weaving in the momentous changes of the colonial period into the narrative of women's rights in Punjab, I expect to demonstrate that land was not simply "landed property" and that women's rights in land existed most strongly in their affinal homes and were greatly diminished when land was indeed constituted as "property" in its modern capitalist sense.[8] British perspectives on women's property rights in the mid-nineteenth century need no comment: women not only did not own property in England at that time but were themselves construed as property of their husbands. Such attitudes clearly flavored the British interpretation of custom and produced similar-looking effects in the Punjab countryside.

In the case of both Hindoos and Mahomedans, as the British call them, women had never been so unambiguously excluded from the right to hold property. The Muslim Shariah absolutely stated that women could hold "property" and legally inherited half as much as any brother.[9] One can also argue that Hindu women, particularly wives and widows, in precolonial Punjab had other rights, including rights in land, in ways that need some complicated explicating that I do in the next chapter. The Punjab is the best place to comb out the tangle of women's customary rights since, as we know, the British compiled a corpus of "customary law" only in this province, for which they collected village-level data from village headmen. This will make it possible to historicize the meaning of the word "property" and the rights of men and women in these codes, since "property" as we think of it today as a modern capitalist construct was not understood in the Punjab countryside in Ranjit Singh's time. Our exploration will determine what was customary about women's control of property, and in the process will lay bare the mechanics of codification that reveal much about the assumptions and biases of the colonial regime and its close collusion with the males of the castes and tribes for whose alleged judicial benefit these codes were "retrieved."

The other obvious area to examine is the new job opportunities that British defense and development needs brought to the "martial races" of the Punjab, which created both prosperity and poverty in patches, while engendering a thoroughly phallocentric economy, if I may borrow a term. Punjabi manpower filled the ranks of Britain's Indian Army, slashed primeval forests to add some fourteen million arable acres to enhance the revenue base, and constructed canals, railways, and roads. But these opportunities created by the modern economy virtually excluded women and brought both prosperity and tragedy to Punjabi peasant households.

In a perverse move, I plan to read selectively from the prolific work of Septimus Sept Thorburn, a civilian and yet another disciple of Henry Maine, and a vigorous defender of the "primitive" precolonial arrangements of land tenure. I wish to discern from his blunt retelling the dislocations experienced by the average peasant under the colonialists' own new system. His was not a lone voice—most civilians had been won over from their laissez-faire position to the side of government intervention in the matter of land alienations—but it was a passionate one, because he critiqued British policies as fervently as he could hate Hindu moneylenders or crave protection for Muslim landlords.[10] He had an axe to grind, but it was the imperial axe. He feared, as virtually all prominent members of the establishment were tending to do, that the logical consequences of these policies would whittle away the stable rural base on whose loyalty the Raj precariously rested, as indebtedness drove Muslim landowners into the crushing embrace of Hindu moneylenders. His is the trenchant critique of a loyal insider, and it deserves a fresh reading. Malcolm Darling, who was obviously influenced by Thorburn's reports and who adopted some of his monomaniacal attitudes about peasant indebtedness, later wrote in the far more readable diary form that is much quoted by Punjab scholars.

THORBURN'S CRITIQUE

Particularly disastrous, in Thorburn's view, was the British introduction of landownership by title and inflexible assessments of revenue owed on every plot of land. This reduced the peasantry in the Punjab to levels of indebtedness and poverty that would have been reprehensible even by the standards of the alleged "Oriental despots" who ruled the land before them. Thorburn's research methods and sources were impeccable, and he had the added advantage of access to his colleagues' private correspondence and views, and the privilege of personal interviews with the peasants in the many districts he served. He was to become the financial commissioner of the Punjab. His naturally racist and loyalist tone makes his critique the more credible—he was decidedly not a "convert" or a partisan of the natives but was concerned about the damage the impoverishing and alienating policies might have on a martial people whose support and loyalty were the anchor of the British regime and gave it its legitimacy.[11] He was afraid that if the Punjabi soldiers mutinied there would be no hope of quelling the uprising.

Impressed by the "paternalistic" form of government shaped by Sir John Lawrence, Thorburn immersed himself in reading the reports of his predecessors and mastering the nuts and bolts of the administration. In the course of learning the ropes, he discovered a very distressed peasantry in the northwestern districts. Muslim cultivators were heavily in debt to the Hindu moneylenders. Rural indebtedness was rampant and growing, not only in the districts he investigated but in the entire province as constituted in 1849. To find the reasons and remedies for this situation became nothing short of an obsession with the ardent young civilian in the 1880s.

In the course of his investigations—which were sometimes responses to official orders and sometimes bold initiatives taken on his own—Thorburn diagnosed the agrarian malaise with reasonable acuity. In his study of pre-British conditions, under which rural indebtedness was virtually nonexistent, he became a reluctant but honest admirer of the Sikh revenue system, even though he disliked the Sikhs as a group and found their conquest of the western, almost exclusively Muslim, tracts quite unforgivable (but note that he wanted British rule entrenched in the same districts). He learned the Pashto language and developed a paternal affection for the indebted Muslim zamindars and a corresponding loathing for the Hindu moneylenders (Thorburn [1886] 1983: xiv).[12] Since he was the man on the spot, his work, in spite of all its racist, contradictory, and angry rhetoric, can be carefully mined for the serious insights it provides into the deepening preference for sons in that era and the essentially masculine ethos and economy created in the British Punjab.

Unable to rouse his fellow civilians to action, he distilled his findings into a book and published it (Thorburn [1886] 1983). Thorburn's reconstruction of the Sikh revenue system that had lasted until 1844, is reliable, well documented, and has remained unchallenged by later scholarship; an annotated summary is presented here.

Although he was usually contemptuous of what might have preceded British rule, Thorburn became—in his passionate recapitulation—an unwitting defender of the precolonial system and therefore of Ranjit Singh, whom he described as "wholly illiterate and already addicted to the vices of his time and countrymen," continuing, "there was nothing to indicate that the short, ugly, one-eyed, pox-pitted boy was the possessor of a master mind and had the force of character to use it" (Thorburn 1940: 21). An even more virulent hater of Hindus than of Sikhs, Thorburn saw a growing gulf between Hindus and Muslims, since certain groups of Hindus (particularly Banias, Aroras, and some Khatri clans) were moneylenders and traders, and Muslims were constrained in this respect on religious grounds (although these normative constraints were flouted in many instances). He wanted the Muslim chiefs to be the anchor of the Raj.

In sketching an account of agrarian conditions in the Punjab before the British conquest, he discerned a strong administrative structure underneath the apparent "anarchy." Ranjit Singh had consolidated his hold on the Punjab by 1823 and was to remain its ruler until he died in 1839, bringing a very large and disparate number of feuding "tribes" under his control. Thorburn did not differ from other civilians of his time in seeing the Punjab as a "tribal" collectivity, warring within but presenting a united front against danger from without. Despite their animosities, Hindu traders and shopkeepers were an indispensable cog in the wheel of agricultural society, serving "as humble dependents and servants of the strongmen of the day" (Thorburn [1886] 1983: 42).

In this picture, painted with broad brush strokes, the detail of and variation over the vast expanse of the Punjab is dimmed, but it becomes clear that the land was held collectively, by patriarchal families whose members all held shares. In these villages, called *bhaichara* (literally, "brotherly relations") villages, the idea of "individual rights" in land as private property—in the capitalist definition as a commodity that could be readily bought or sold by an individual owner, or alienated from that owner in lieu of revenue or other debt owed—was wholly alien. This view has been confirmed by later scholars, including those who have made the Sikh kingdom the focus of their study. The "control" of land signified the political *defense* of land, and it was, indeed, defended by men alone.

This did not imply control of the produce of the land, however. There were many co-sharers in every field, from the king to the lowly village menials, and these patently included women. No one had "a field of their own" in the current bourgeois sense, and it was not the aspiration of men or women to "own" a field. Land was best controlled, protected, and tilled in the plurality of relationships, its produce shared as was determined by customary practice and the ebb and flow of people who occupied it. The control of land, then, was the basis of politics. The only ways to "lose" land were to lose control over it in an internecine fight, to suffer defeat by invaders (a frequent happening in the Punjab, which made the political control of land a bloody business and able-bodied men to defend it an imperative), or to abandon one's rights in it by moving away to settle elsewhere (which women customarily did at the time of marriage, and some men did as well, though less frequently).

Thorburn described the Sikh revenue system as sensitive to the annual vagaries of the weather in a particular growing cycle, and allowed the hefty 50 percent share of the government to be paid in either cash or kind. When cash was taken, the assessment was advanced by the village moneylender, or by some local contractor who squared his accounts with the cultivators after the harvest. In most cases, Thorburn emphasized, the demand was limited by the ability of the cultivator to pay and of the tax farmer to coerce without raising an insurrection, which would cause him to forfeit either his life or his post. No rights between those of the cultivator and collector were recognized except in cases where policy

made it expedient to use middlemen—generally influential locals—as subcollec-
tors. In such cases, remission of a quarter to a tenth was made to them in order to
repay the cost of collection (Thorburn [1886] 1983: 44).

In Punjab land was plentiful, with wide tracts of jungle and pasture that were
not taxed, "and 'individual rights' was a term hardly yet comprehended: what
were understood were those of the tribe and village collectively." Ranjit Singh extended this widely accepted rule by also levying other cesses, such as taxes on the
date and mango crop and on cattle, a poll tax on artisans, and town duties. However, Thorburn informs us, the Banias never paid a tax at all, "because they were,
except in towns, *merely poor dependents of the cultivating classes*. I draw particular attention to that" (Thorburn [1886] 1983: 46; emphasis added). This relationship also
changed dramatically under the British system.

We also know from more recent scholarship of this period that the contrast of
Sikh and British regimes did not end here. For example, neither Mughal nor Sikh
imperial revenue officials penetrated directly down to the village level; instead
they had to deal with the *muqaddam,* or village headman, aided by the village elders, who made up the village council (*panchayat*), and with the *patwari,* the village records keeper, who was paid from village funds and had the interests of the
villagers (and his own) rather than those of the imperial administration at heart.
Village *panchayats* were held in full view of the village and were open to inter-
ruption from those who watched them in action, including women (see Saran
[1941] 1973, Habib 1963, Hall 1981).

The new colonial administration, with its forcefully penetrative nature, replaced this indigenous version of democracy, in which villagers had representatives who dealt with the state, with mechanisms of direct control. The first step
that the British took to ensure that their system would perforate the crucial village
barrier was to make the *patwari,* who kept the village records, a paid servant of
the colonial revenue establishment. This conferred enormous power on a once-
amenable servant of the farmers. Record keeping could now become a source of
profit for both parties. The British courts of law, shortly thereafter, replaced the
authority of the village *panchayat,* making *muqaddams* no more than decorative
emblems of the past. On occasion they served as informants with historical memories of customary practices, since revenue assessments done directly by British
settlement officers were no longer seasonal affairs but were expected to last at
least two to three decades, or even permanently. These radical structural changes
that struck at the root of village government went unremarked by Thorburn, except for the corruption that developed in the *patwari* in the system. These scribes
now wielded enormous power as salaried officials who kept land records of titles
of ownership and land holdings, and it was this record that was presented in court
as the final word on land disputes.

That these changes were already in place in 1853 is confirmed by the existence
of a *wajib-ul-arz* (administration paper) from that date of the village of Ghausgarh

in Ludhiana district in eastern Punjab. In 1853, the local shopkeeper and money-lender, Ram Kiran Sud, was still a very trusted man. The headman dispensed the common costs incurred by village residents at the moneylender's shop, and the *patwari*, the recorder of landholdings, was in charge of recording these disbursements (Smith 1996: 417–21). The revenue for the summer harvest was fixed to be paid in July, and for the *rabi*, or winter harvest, in February—months that appear to be too early to complete the harvest and convert the produce into cash in order to meet the revenue demand. What is really telling is that the common costs, including those incurred for weddings, funerals, and festivals—for maintaining the *chaupal*, or guest house, sweeping and watering the common areas, lighting extra lamps, and contributing raw materials, such as sugar and wheat, for the occasion—were to be strictly limited:

> The village expenses must not exceed a proportionate expenditure of 3½ per cent. If in any year extra expense becomes necessary because of more travellers coming and going or more weddings, or for some other reason, we headmen should go to the district officer and make an application on plain paper [as opposed to stamp paper which cost extra money] for the additional amount required, in order that the district officer may pass an order of approval or non-approval. (Smith 1996: 417; he translated the entire text)

This 3½ percent represented the slashing of the common village fund to a third of the customary amount allowable during the time of Sikh rule, which was bound to shift some of the common costs onto the already tight budgets of individual families. Since application for an increase in allocation was subject to approval, we can imagine a British collector turning down an application for what had already been condemned as frivolous and wasteful—money for village bards or musicians. The time limitations for presenting such applications also meant further discouragement, and this provision in the *wajib-ul-arz* was more window dressing to appease the elders who were allegedly the authors of this document than an actual source of additional funds.

It is not surprising that the earliest British tax assessments were completely outrageous, since the district officers in charge were mainly young officers trained at Oxford and Cambridge who had few surviving records to consult and little administrative experience to fall back on, and who had the arrogance to believe that anything they calculated would be more reasonable than the exactions of their despotic predecessors. Fresh reassessments had to be very rapidly conducted to save the countryside from ruin. Thorburn defensively explains that the exorbitant claims were made because the few Sikh records that had not been destroyed in the years of warfare between the British and Sikh armies showed only the gross demand, but the details of remissions, deductions, and arrears were irretrievable.[13] So he tells us that the British "retained the cattle tax, abolished all other cesses and dues, substituted individual for collective ownership of land, and converted the share of each harvest paid by the cultivators, which he had generally paid in kind, into a fixed cash assessment" (p. 47). He omits to mention, however, that the British administration imposed several new and far higher cesses than the ones they discontinued, such as excise on alcohol, octroi duty at entry and exit points of all towns and markets on goods in transit, and legal fees and stamp duties for the endless possibilities for litigation the revenue system had itself opened up.

The demand was calculated as the average of the preceding three years and was converted into cash at market rates of the day, less a deduction of 15 to 20 percent, and it was applicable for a fixed term of years. The two annual cash installments were due on fixed dates in the Georgian calendar. "In most cases, the committee of village elders accepted the demand and contracted to pay it for a short term of years" (Thorburn [1886] 1983: 47). With a fixed revenue demand, the scheme would have worked equitably had prices remained stable, but other factors, such as cyclical drought and bad harvests, among others, made this introduction of capitalism go terribly awry, and a tragedy awaited much of the Punjab peasantry. The cultivated area was expanded enormously; "but the presence of a large military force in the Punjab, together with the undertaking of great public works, such as the Grand Trunk Road and barracks doubled the money in circulation. Those causes reduced the money-value of agricultural produce from 50 to 100 per cent. The result was the ruin of cultivators, indebtedness for tens of thousands, and the beginnings of a hold on land for astute and wealthy middlemen" (Thorburn [1886] 1983: 47).

Thorburn's account is verifiable from other sources, and far from being a cranky exaggeration it is, in fact, neither as grim nor as exhaustive as the descriptions of disastrous fate of the Punjab countryside graphically documented in the summary assessment reports of the region. Ibbetson wrote of Karnal district (which is in present-day Haryana) that revenue for lands that had become "absolutely and obviously unculturable was remitted" between 1859 and 1861, and no allowance was made "for the impoverishment due to an ever increasing burden to be borne for so many years" and "no intelligent review of the whole circumstances of the villages was ever attempted. No remissions have ever been made, so far as I can discover, on account of general deterioration" (Ibbetson 1883b: 69–70).

This deterioration was largely caused by the salinity of the soil produced by the canal system built by the British in this region. Quoting from an earlier report of Karnal district made by a Dr. Taylor in 1850, Ibbetson tells us that 60 to 80 percent of the inhabitants of villages worst affected were suffering from "fevers, enlarged spleens, languor, depression of manner and stunted and shriveled forms." The doctor speaks of the shock of finding "malarious exhalations of the soil, of the spectacle of sick women and diseased children crouching among the ruins of the houses; of haggard cultivators wading in the swamps, and watching their sickly crops, or attempting to pasture their bony cattle in the unwholesome grass." His own tour in 1871 confirmed that not much had changed in Karnal and that many of the inhabitants of these villages had moved to Jind, a neighboring princely state, to find relief. Whole stretches of countryside had been laid waste, and "there is really hardly a cultivable acre to be found" in "the area affected by swamps, salts, barren 'snow covered fields.' Picked villagers would tell ever more dismal tales" (Ibbetson 1883b: 68–70).[14]

Another misstep, Thorburn believed, was the making of "summary settlements." And since the "object of such settlements [was] fiscal, no authoritative investigations into tenures took place. As a rule, the person found in cultivating possession was treated as the proprietor and settled with" (Thorburn [1886] 1983: 47). This created further hardship for those who could not assert their rights, and the revenue was again reduced by 10 to 20 percent over a couple of years, in spite of the enormous extension of the cultivated area. Following on the heels of these patently ill-judged moves were "regular assessments," whose prime object was to create a permanent record of rights after holdings of every sort were investigated. "The result is a sort of elaborate Doomsday Book, which permanently fixes individual rights in land and water" (Thorburn [1886] 1983: 48). In other words, the profound transition from collective shares to individual ownership of land was now a matter of record. Land had become private property, but the new meaning this had imbued into the relationship of land to those who now held title to their lands was to become painfully clear over the next few bad harvests. Peasants now stood to lose their rights as summarily as they had received them if they were unable to tender the revenue demand on the due date in cash.

This entire process was, in Thorburn's emphatic estimation, arbitrary, corrupt, and a "grave error" that generated a great deal of peasant indebtedness.[15] The lag between the announcement of the compilation of the new record of rights and its actual happening in every village gave a great advantage to those who grasped the implications of such a move, and this "greatly assisted dominant tribes and families, and sagacious individuals, in perfecting titles to proprietary dues, which if investigated immediately after annexation, would have found to have been either non-existent, or of uncertain continuity." As the regular settlement "fixed government demand for the next 20 to 30 years, and, above all, defined individual rights, and so gave each person with any recorded interest in land, a clear title, the effect of such settlements was everywhere both to largely appreciate the market-value of land and the credit of those whose titles to marketable interests had been established" (Thorburn [1886] 1983: 48).

To think of this new system as a "grave error" was, as we begin to comprehend its effects, almost too generous an assessment. It was also cripplingly inflexible. Fixed rent and revenue systematically replaced the notion of elastic assessments made seasonably at harvest time and payable in grain rather than in cash, with fluctuating prices that were lowest at harvest time. This feature is verifiable from the dates for payments given in settlement reports for all districts.

What compounded the already "grave error" was the simultaneous conferral of what Thorburn sarcastically called the "gift of full proprietary rights in land to individuals" and the right to alienate it at pleasure. "It is difficult for us now to realise the revolution effected in the status and relations of peasants and shopkeepers by the innovations introduced in 1849–50." These transformed the basis of a peasant's borrowing power, formerly limited to the surplus of a good crop, to the market value of the land to which he held individual title. Until then the proprietary unit had been "the tribe," and alienation of the right to cultivate could not occur except with the approval of the entire body of shareholders, and only very rarely did. A peasant (or his family) could borrow only a few rupees; "his Buniah was merely his humble servant and accountant; he himself in worldly wisdom was as ignorant as a wild beast. . . . Such terms as 'individual rights,' 'property,' 'the purchasing power of money,' 'credit,' 'attachment and sale,' were incomprehensible and meaningless to him. In one day the old order passed away, and gave place to a new one" (Thorburn [1886] 1983: 49–50).

Invoking the trauma of the Mutiny of 1857, Thorburn warned against rebellion by the discontented northwestern Muslim landholders, as Hindu moneylenders systematically despoiled them. Muslims "outnumber the trading Hindus, whom they despise as their former dependents and individually unwarlike, by 6 to 1. If the Government by inaction permits their expropriation, is it conceivable that they will remain loyal should an opportunity for regaining their lost possessions occur?" But this was not all. The windfall of the Raj, Thorburn rued, went to the despised Hindu moneylenders, who were actually the villains of the piece. Thorburn railed on:

> With inherited business habits, their want of sympathy for Mussalmans, their unscrupulous greed for gain, their established position as accountants and factors for the agricultural populations, their monopoly of education, of general intelligence, and of trade—most particularly of money-lending (the taking of interest being unlawful for a Mussalman)—prospects of wealth and position, never before attained in their history, were opened for the bunniah class. (Thorburn [1886] 1983: 51)

Here Thorburn's prejudice becomes patent. His warning against the potential for rebellion among the cultivators against the new system is matched by his mistrust and seething indictment of the Bania caste. He now berates the Bania, who he at first described as the once "humble servant" in a comfortably symbiotic relationship with the intellectually inferior Muslim peasant, "the short-sighted and long-suffering animal" (Thorburn [1886] 1983: 50). The benign Bania was suddenly transmogrified into a greedy Hindu demon taking advantage of the Muslim peasant—which describes the upsurge of communal or religious animus among peasants and servants after the interventions of the British Raj rather than *before* it. This classic rant actually indicts bureaucratic obduracy.

The government was pleased that it had expanded the zamindar's credit, since it had rationalized the revenue system and lowered the demand from what it had been in the closing years of Sikh rule. Moneylenders exploited the change to fixed cash assessments that gave them the opportunity to raise interest rates. The introduction of civil laws and procedures, framed on European models, to enforce the repayment of debts and the foreclosure of mortgages favored creditors against debtors. Besides, illiterate landlords were no match in court against the moneylenders and the books they kept. Unyielding about fixed cash payments on fixed dates, the government blamed the growing indebtedness on the thriftless zamindars and their marriage customs that put them at the mercy of the moneylenders. And not only did those officials deliberately disregarded the economic hardship for peasant families and the entrapment implicit in their own policies, they were also entirely blind to the social consequences that they had set in motion for women.

Thorburn and other civilians saw the harm plainly, but their remedy for the harm done was to aim, perforce, at the symptoms rather than the causes of the widespread malaise. Thorburn persistently urged that the administration act to make further alienations of land from cultivators to moneylenders illegal; the laissez-faire attitude of the government in letting market forces decide the winners and losers had to be stopped. His pleas for legislative intervention were ignored until the indebtedness crisis of the late nineteenth century precipitated a serious debate. Thorburn's side eventually won and their basic reasoning, laced with the familiar cultural prejudice, was incorporated in a piece of legislation that endeavored to save the "agricultural tribes" from the "nonagricultural," moneylending ones, carefully eliding their own finding that the inflexibility of the British revenue system was at the root of the indebtedness of the peasants. This was the Land Alienation Act of 1900. It stood the already lopsided free-market commercialism introduced into the Punjab (and elsewhere) squarely on its head and confirmed the alleged "thriftlessness" of peasant culture and the inherent evil of moneylenders.

Nothing could be done about this outcome, although it hobbled the principles of the political economy the government had introduced into the Punjab. The very real political dangers from a disgruntled peasantry were now visible enough to outweigh "progressive" or philosophical considerations. Ignoring the overwhelming evidence in the British settlement reports, N. G. Barrier perceives the illiterate peasant to be at the root of his own problem, because "the *very moderate demands* played a much more significant role in the alienation process by making it much more possible for the cultivator to extend his credit" (Barrier 1966: 11; emphasis added). This argument does not work. The peasant's credit was expanded by virtue of his newfound ability to mortgage his individually owned piece of land, and not "the very moderate demands" of revenue on it. It was also not, as we shall see, the size of the demand, which was lowered after disastrous results with higher assessments, but the rigid rules of collection and payment in cash that actually strapped the peasant to a debt he could never wrestle off his back; and it was the British legal apparatus—laws, procedure, court and lawyers's fees—that sent the unfortunate ones into tenancy or landless penury.

Barrier is content to shrug uncritically. "Most of the Punjab administrators thought that peasant extravagance was the key factor in the indebtedness process. *This narrative is based primarily upon British sources and therefore reflects their opinion.*" Only in the footnote does Barrier admit that there were factors other than peasant extravagance, "such as capital expenditure and unexpected expenses such as death of cattle that played an important role" (Barrier 1966: 12, 24n; emphasis added). This presumption that "British sources" were of unified opinion is difficult to sustain unless one refuses to look beyond the general reports, which collated the similarities across districts and papered over the sharp differences revealed in the detailed empirical work on which they were based. In fact, as my own analysis demonstrates, British sources are probably the best places to look for contradictions, contending narratives, confessions, and even occasional soul-searching, but larger political ends always edited these out in the overall final summary reports.

More pertinently, the act did not bar transfers of land altogether but restricted moneylenders from purchasing or foreclosing on land belonging to "agricultural tribes." Hindu moneylenders were "outsiders" in the eyes of the British, according to Gilmartin, "men without connections to the tribal political fabric of rural society." "Agricultural tribes" were gazetted by name in each district, and land sales and transfers were restricted to those who appeared to belong to essentially agricultural groups (Gilmartin 1988: 30–31). Besides its communal implications in the making of Pakistan, the act also contributed to the creation of rigid and untenable boundaries between the agricultural and trading castes, and of an essentially agrarian world that was relentlessly masculine and "tribal," with primacy placed on agnatic kin in a kin-based society. Its mentality persists and continues to hobble Hindu women's rights in agricultural land in India today.

Peasant indebtedness and land alienations, which sound as if they are Thorburn's personal fixations, had in fact become a widespread reality in the entire Indian empire including Burma, but they are also critical to our pursuit of whether or not marriage expenses were actually the reason for this widespread distress. The problem had persistently nagged provincial administrations and haunted the central government as a succession of reports from different regions of the country streamed in throughout the nineteenth century. The paperwork on this subject had run into volumes in every province where pertinent "Selections from Papers on Indebtedness and Land Transfer" were compiled for the Government of India secretariat in 1894. A further culling from these selected reports was collated and finally published in a single volume entitled *Note on Land Transfer and Agricultural Indebtedness in India*, which ran to four hundred pages, detailing the history of this problem. Warnings of the worsening stress of revenue defaults, foreclosures, and sales, such as those contained in the *Report of the Famine Commission, 1877–78*, poured in.

Between 1871 and 1891, 2.9 million acres of land exchanged hands by sale for nearly Rs. 55.5 million, at an average of Rs. 20 per acre. This represented 10 percent of the total area of land in the Punjab and 11.6 percent of land revenue; another 9 percent of the land was under mortgage. It was also admitted that although it was "a matter of great importance," the figures given in administration and other inquiry reports were grossly understated, because until "1884 the record of transfers was, as a rule, very laxly supervised, and when the matter was taken up zealously after that date, it was found that a very large number of sales and existing mortgages had never been brought on to the record at all" (NLT 1896: 401). There was also "unrecorded debt everywhere mounting up under our present system, and sooner or later the money-lender will be able to utilize it as a means of obtaining possession of the land." And in addition to the unrecorded debt "we must take into account the unsecured debt, which is large," warned another settlement officer in Ambala (an eastern district that was supposed to be better off than the west, where Thorburn was at work). The sheer mass of detail is quite numbing. These dry figures give us some idea of the existential incubus of debt, mortgage, sale, landlessness, and possible migration that Punjab peasant families found themselves in that memorable half century of British rule. The place to look for the palpable results of this desperation is in those other statistics pigeonholed in the Department of Infanticide files. Peasants had no option but to use drastic measures to plan more sons, many more sons, to get them out of the nightmare in which they suddenly found themselves.

Finally, after more than four hundred foolscap pages of single-spaced statistics in small print, this wearying document presents its findings. These tell a very different story and represent a profound reversal of official thinking by 1896, when this *Note* was compiled. After repeating the familiar argument that "the real causes of [the peasant's] indebtedness lie deeper and are to be found in his improvidence and his ignorance—factors with which the State can but feebly cope," it astoundingly reverses itself in the very next paragraph.

> The improvidence of the Indian agriculturalist is often mentioned as the cause of the debt, more specially when his improvidence takes the form of marriage and funeral expenses out of proportion to his income. . . . The results of the Commission's [1876] Enquiry show *that undue prominence has been given to the expenditure on marriage and other festivals as the cause of the Ryot's indebtedness.*
>
> The expenditure on such occasions may indeed be called extravagant when compared with the Ryot's means; but the occasions occur seldom, and probably in the course of the years the total sum spent in this way by any ryot is no larger than a man in his position is justified in spending on so-

cial and domestic pleasure. The expenditure forms an item of some importance on the debit side of his account, *but by itself it rarely appears as the nucleus of his indebtedness.*

The sums usually spent on these occasions have probably been overesti-
mated, *or the operation of other causes in producing debt have been overlooked* by
the officers who have attributed the ryot's burdens so largely to this cause.
(NLT 1896: 96; emphasis added)

Voila! Finally an official admits that the whole case against peasant improvidence
is overblown, a gross misrepresentation of reality. It is admitted that the fault, all
along, has lain in the revenue system that was too insensitive to the agrarian calendar, *"too rigid, and not sufficiently elastic"* (NLT 1896: 102; emphasis added). The
British could, if they sincerely meant to improve the lot of the encumbered peasants, have used the patented remedies of the Sikh regime, but it was not to be.
These findings did not produce instant results, nor did they muffle the strident imperial discourse about both marriage expenses and the cause of female infanticide
in rural society. That belief had acquired a life of its own.

Another major empirewide "confidential" inquiry was ordered to counteract
the persistent view that poverty was increasing among India's peasants. The viceroy,
Lord Dufferin, ordered senior officers of all the provinces of British India to find
answers to his two cleverly worded questions and submit them confidentially:
"1. Is the assertion that the greater proportion of the population of India suffer
from a daily insufficiency of food wholly untrue or partially true? 2. If partially
true [there was no option for it to be wholly true!], can you suggest any remedy?"[16] Answers duly poured in, in the form of summary reports from all corners,
and so too in the Punjab. Some interesting new symptoms of poverty were
noticed.

This inquiry produced even more startling results, but the tenor of the official
chorus remained unchanged. There was a grudging acceptance that the profligate
peasant could not control the costs of weddings, since inflation had increased
these costs. The growing indebtedness of the individual peasants was only partly
a consequence "of *increasing* expenditure on social ceremonies and customs
among all classes," and even though "tribal characteristics and social customs,
such as the seclusion of women, also laziness of character, constitute a very large
cause of poverty where it exists," the *new* causes for impoverishment were far
more important: "[d]isease, which prevents or enfeebles work is often the cause of
insufficient earnings and consequent poor diet" (Poverty Report 1888: 418). The
new canals had become breeding grounds for mosquitoes (although the role of
vermin was not fully understood then) and epidemics began to take a toll in peasant lives as malaria, typhoid, cholera, and other diseases spread during the monsoon season. Better standards of sanitation and migration to less populated parts
of the province were suggested as remedies.

Other hitherto unreported reasons for poverty dotted these reports, and they disagreed with the old official stance. For instance, the report of Ghulam Ahmad, extra assistant commissioner of Rawalpindi, claimed that large pockets of the Punjab countryside and townships did indeed suffer from an insufficiency of food. Although he seemed politely to go along with the official idea of sumptuary regulations, Ahmad judiciously pointed out that funerals were often more expensive than weddings and that nothing had been done to curtail the expense of those. But, most dramatically, he added an astute new litany of expenses that seemed to be of recent origin—indeed, inspired by the colonial regime's policies and procedures. A drought could now bring a zamindar to ruin since he had to pay his revenue in good times and bad on a fixed date. The spreading use of mill-made cloth imported from England and "longcloth and calico, which is expensive, instead of cheap native cloth they used to wear" certainly was another cause of extravagance not known in former times.

But Ahmad's broadside was aimed at the British courts, which had brought most landowners into the ambit of ruinous litigation for the lands they were desperate to keep in their possession. "Litigation and party feeling [sic] have increased to such an extent that the zemindars are ruining themselves by heavy expenses and pleaders' fees on the one hand, and not looking after their lands properly, but wasting their time [in the courts]. Thus the people are involved in debt, and the Moneylenders get nearly all the produce of the harvest, leaving very little for the cultivators" (Poverty Report 1888: 480–81). The high costs of litigation emerged as a key factor in peasant indebtedness, but litigation was chiefly connected with new titles to land; it thus became an economically vicious circle for the landowning peasant whose ownership was threatened by debt. This tallied exactly with the general conclusion drawn in the "Note on Land Transfers and Agricultural Indebtedness" (NLT 1896) that the costs of litigation were often the largest part of an encumbered zamindar's debt and were bringing a vast majority of Punjabi peasants to their present state of impoverishment. A zamindar's only hope of getting out of debt, I would add, was to depend on the labor of his sons, and many more sons would be needed to accomplish this task.

This fact-finding exercise elicited many more uncomfortably trenchant critiques of the various departments of the imperial state, rather than proof of the peasant's wasteful habits that were creating a deepening poverty in the countryside. From Hoshiarpur district came another confidential complaint from Deputy Commissioner Harris about the exponential rise in grain prices that had brought wage earners—day laborers, artisans, and coolies—to the brink of starvation. As a remedy, he recommended cutting down the proliferating government expenditures. "Our Government is already far too expensive, and gets more so every year. The departments to cut down would not, in my opinion, be far to seek. Native industries should be more protected to the exclusion, for instance, of the Manchester trade" (Poverty Report 1888: 466). In another similar communication, reviving a dying native institution was proposed as a remedy for poverty in bad years.

> In times of scarcity or of bad crops the pinch is at once felt, and in times of failure [of] the harvest starvation ensues. There is no reserve as it were and no poor law, and no poor houses to which the lowest may resort. The operation of caste is in this respect beneficial. It rescues from actual starvation caste fellows, and operates to supersede the necessity of a poor law. I propose an extension of the "Malba" village funds system [an emergency fund that was curtailed under British revenue collectors] so as to provide a means of subsistence in each village for the poor. This is an idea I have kept very much to myself, and indeed the entire correspondence. (Poverty Report 1888: 468)

Village headmen had controlled *malba*, and their timely intervention in emergencies in the past is recognized here. The imperial state had a very cost-conscious famine relief policy in place, but popular and scholarly indictments against its substance and spirit were so energetic that it was seen, as in Ireland, as a policy that greatly increased mortality in the populations that it was meant to relieve (see Davis 2001).

The critiques were harsh, and they came alike from civilians and native officers. Rai Karam Chand, a Punjabi officer, pointed out that in adjacent kingdoms ruled by native rulers, the peasants were far better off, as were peasants in the Punjab before the British takeover, "simply because they could not borrow any money on land or interests in land, and even now in the Native States, where they have no power of alienation, they are not so much in debt as in British territory. . . . The lands are daily changing hands, notwithstanding the extension of cultivation, improvement of productive power, high prices of food grain and low rates of revenue" (Poverty Report 1888: 470). He also pointed out that since money was borrowed to pay the revenue demand on time or to pay the costs of litigation, rates of interest were much higher than under Sikh rule. Since the "limitation period [to repay a debt] had been reduced to three years, Moneylenders compounded their interest every year," leaving no recourse to the zamindar but to involve his land as collateral and finally to lose it. Under Ranjit Singh, "when there was no limitation, the interest of grain could not exceed 100 per cent and on cash 50 per cent, under any circumstances," and this still obtained in adjacent native princely states. Needless to say, Rai Karam Chand strongly recommended that the power to alienate a person's landed property be restricted, that the period of limitation be extended to six years or longer, that the tax on wells and canal water be reduced, and that there be a return to the remission of revenue in bad years, as there had been under the rule of the Sikhs, so that the Indian peasant could truly prosper (Poverty Report 1888: 470). Also remarked upon was the fact that increasing monetization under British aegis and government export of grain from the

Punjab had caused a steady rise in base prices, so that wage earners found that their cash "purchases very different quantities of grain in different seasons and in different years." A peasant who had borrowed in a time of need when grain was dear could only repay part of the loan at harvest time, when he had a surplus but grain prices were at their lowest. So the grain loans repaid in grain that had been far more equitable for borrowers in the past became capital gains for lenders even before the much higher interest rate was reckoned. The dismay with the unbending ways of the imperial policies was pervasive.

This provides a critical insight into the material difference between precolonial and colonial imperial systems. The security that Punjabi peasants had in precolonial times was the assurance that land was unalienable; they could migrate away from it but they could not be forcibly evicted from it. Timely remissions, grain reserves, and village *malba* were instrumental elements of this insurance policy and prevented or lessened migrations from the land in times of dearth. In an era of land auctions and revenue arrears, as the colonial period proved to be, the guarantee of their right to the land was abolished and nothing was substituted except the aforementioned "free market" proprietorship. The threat to losing one's proprietary right was now seasonal, and either the magistrate's auction block or the courts did the seizing. The entire context in which zamindar families lived their lives and planned their families was altered, forcing a greater reliance on a larger number of sons to supply the safety net for their future. The growing preference for sons is better read as an obsession for security in a time of new insecurities than as a cultural diktat.

The peasant's notorious "want of thrift" did crop up in the pages of this report, but only as a side issue to the real demon of the fixed revenue demand that had to be tendered in cash by the deadline twice annually. This time it was not the Hindu but the Muslim who was guilty; J. Wilson, the deputy commissioner of Shahpur, had carefully researched the matter and was left with no doubt that "the want of thrift" for weddings, funerals, and circumcisions was decidedly a Muslim trait. "A Mussalman," he wrote,

> yields to temptation, and in order to make a show on the occasion of a marriage or a death, borrows heavily on the security of his land. . . . This way the Mussalman peasantry of the West Punjab are fast alienating their land to the thrifty Hindus, and this, apart from the present question [about insufficiency of food] is a grave political evil loudly calling for remedy. Thrift however can be learnt only by bitter experience, and the severity with which our laws enforce contracts teaches the lesson even too forcibly. The Jats of Rohtak and Sirsa [Hindus] show wonderful prudence by storing up grain or jewels in good seasons and keeping out of the money lender's hands. (Poverty Report 1888: 474–77)

Such a curiously reversed analysis demonstrates that two departments of the same government could happily contradict each other's cultural findings about the natives without any consequences for the state. It need hardly be pointed out that this stands in profound contradistinction to Montgomery's *Minute on Infanticide* (1853; see chapter 2), in which Hindus were described as social spendthrifts and Muslims as prudent and thrifty, because they did not give dowries to their daughters. At the time of Montgomery's writing, the British were purportedly doing their disinterested best to teach the former important lessons in judicious expenditure to save female lives; now they were on the mat to explain the immiseration of peasants in many pockets of the Punjab. The internal contradictions do underscore my point that British cultural analysis was politically expedient rather than anthropologically sound.

Wilson's report aimed the hardest blow against the government's revenue policy. He firmly suggested "[g]reater elasticity of revenue assessment. In times of scarcity, the distress of the peasantry and of the labouring classes dependent on them is much increased if a fixed cash assessment be demanded from them as usual." Only a fluctuating assessment, "while it does cause more present trouble to officials," would "save the smaller peasant proprietor from being driven to borrow money from the money-lender in order to pay the State's revenue in seasons of scarcity." He felt, as strongly as Thorburn did, that what was also needed was the "[r]evocation of the fatal gift of proprietary rights in land from those classes of peasantry who have shown themselves unfit to hold it, and who are fast parting with their rights to Moneylenders to their own ruin and danger to the State." He also urged that the government spend money on schools for educating the sons of zamindars so that they could read and write to avoid being duped, and on the creation of "agricultural banks to save the peasants from the exorbitant usury of the Moneylenders." He commented on the ruinous effects of land litigation on the peasants and proposed an amendment "of the Law of Evidence, so as to allow the court to go behind the bond and decree the principal with a fair amount of interest" instead of adhering too closely to "the nominal terms of contract between the unthinking peasant and his astute creditor" (Poverty Report 1888: 477). The obvious remedy of reintroducing elasticity and remissions into the tax collection regimen, which would have spared a great deal of civilian angst and peasant hardship, was studiously ignored.

The British-created peasant proprietor, Wilson demonstrated, was impaled on the horns of a dilemma. If he defaulted on the fixed revenue demand in a bad season, such as a drought, his land would become unrecoverable collateral for a high-interest loan that he would probably never be able to pay back, and if he did manage to hold on to his land, in the next generation it would be divided among his several male heirs, leading to the fragmentation of his holding into smaller plots that would not sustain his sons' families. This latter trend was to develop unchecked in the coming decades and became a major cause for the inefficiency of Indian agriculture that had to be rectified with land consolidation schemes—a trend still silently at work in India today as the fragmentation of landholdings continues apace. And finally, Wilson added, almost as a resigned sigh at the end of his list of telling suggestions, that, although this was the obvious remedy, he did not expect "that the Government can do more to develop manufactures, which are desirable as affording other means of livelihood to the peasant and laboring classes, who are presently too exclusively dependent on agriculture" (Poverty Report 1888: 476–77). His report is infused with the tacit understanding that these periodic inquiries ameliorated civilian guilt rather than the actual distress that their policies were exacerbating.

The point of this extended exposition is to demonstrate that British officialdom understood—implicitly and explicitly—that the root of peasant indebtedness and poverty was its own inflexible revenue policy but continued to harp on the "improvidence," "want of thrift," ignorance, and stupidity of the peasants who found themselves in distress. The flood of information confidentially solicited by Lord Dufferin spoke of the increasing alienations and subdivisions of holdings, the indebtedness that engulfed peasant proprietors even to the point of death from starvation in years of drought and famine, the total lack of British investment in education or nonagricultural manufactures, and even the lack of availability of indigenous hand-loomed textiles, which had been replaced with mill cloth made in Manchester, yet the overt official narratives continued to condemn a benighted peasantry for their incorrigible folly, superstition, and cruel practices. All the nostrums for the uplift of the population of India remained unlinked to the real problems that were making conditions worse during this period and sought only to tinker with the cultural practices of the people.

In May 1895, when "land alienations" (read: foreclosures, bonded labor, and perhaps landlessness for a peasant proprietor and his dependents due to his inability to meet the revenue demand on time) became intolerable and posed a discernible threat of revolt, all divisional heads, including Thorburn, were asked to conduct yet another inquiry. This one was to be conducted very carefully, "holding by holding," in order to discover the chief reasons the Punjab peasantry had grown progressively more indebted. Thorburn's exhaustive inquiry of the indebtedness of 742 households (a far larger sample than I have encountered in most modern academic ethnographies of various regions in India) was conducted in the "three worst typical villages" in four separate assessment circles in Rawalpindi district. The instructions for this inquiry were very detailed, and Thorburn scrupulously adhered to the specific points to be ascertained: the extent and annual progress of land alienations to moneylenders, whether "the increase is proceeding at an ever-increasing rate" or not, and the "particulars of peasant indebtedness" and its "specific causes" (Thorburn 1896: 1).[17]

The Punjab government did not like what Thorburn put so candidly before it, and it did, indeed, summarily halt the inquiry in the rest of the Punjab. This official panic suggests that officials knew perfectly well that the results elsewhere and everywhere would have matched Thorburn's. The remarkable pattern of practices followed by the *sahukar*, or moneylenders, which determined "the incidents of declension from a condition of petty indebtedness to one of poverty and expropriation will be found to be everywhere almost the same," even though the tribes investigated were inherently different from one another and comprised all three religions (Thorburn 1896: 3). Calling off the inquiry and burying the *Rawalpindi Report* in a departmental office was perhaps the only way they could continue to blame the cultural habits of the peasants for their distress and dismiss Thorburn as a zealous eccentric.

The information pertinent to our own inquiry about the role that the expense of daughters' weddings and dowries played in these heavily involved villages (since these expenses had been deemed the cause of infanticide and of the self-inflicted financial ruin of peasant families in general) is, as I had suspected, very sparse indeed. Thorburn's findings on social expenses, particularly those for marriages, are at odds with those established in the infanticide reports, and warrant detailed scrutiny. This is the last musty corpus of facts that I will disinter to demonstrate that culture had little to do with crime, and the official discourse was not grounded in official findings.

After wrestling with reams of information on the 742 families he had investigated, Thorburn drew for his colleagues the road map that the small peasant proprietors followed on their way to ruin.

Ordinarily he [the peasant proprietor] becomes involved by borrowing grain for food after a short harvest and failing to repay his debt in the ensuing rabi [winter crop]. He begins to take grain in small quantities at a time, from 6 seers [1 seer equals 2.2 lbs.] to 4 maunds [1 maund equals 40 seers], in, say, November or December, and continues to live wholly or partly on grain advances until his spring crop is cut. If that crop suffices to wipe out the debt, *pay his revenue* and sustain his family until the next kharif [summer crop] or rabi [winter] all may go well; but if the yield is insufficient for these three purposes he becomes involved, and after that only the luck of seasons plus generally personal resolution and hard work will extricate him. Instead of facing his difficulties he too often slides into greater indebtedness. His creditor takes part of his crop from the threshing floor as part of his payment towards debt incurred, and then accommodates his debtor by paying the man's revenue for him. In that case the involved peasant becomes in five cases out of six a doomed man. His final expropriation may take five, ten or more years, according to the size of his holding, the luck of the seasons, the accident of extraordinary losses of cattle or of civil litigation or a criminal case, but all the time the catastrophe is surely drawing nearer, and all the time he is more or less a serf making over much of each harvest to his creditor or creditors, and constrained to acknowledge as correct any debit balance that may be put forward against his account. He may, as many do, try to change his *sahukar* [moneylender] or open accounts with several at a time, but all to no purpose. The net is closing round him, and whether he resists in Court or submits and mortgages field after field the end is equally certain.

This is no exaggeration. Out of the 742 families whose debt and land histories have been investigated in detail [including the examination of the *sahukar's* account books for each case], only in thirteen cases did a once involved man recover his freedom, and in three of these cases his restored solvency was due to extraordinary causes outside his own exertions, and *in the other ten we have no evidence as to how the debts were paid off.* (Thorburn 1896: 18; emphasis added)

One thing is clear. Thorburn does not find evidence to suggest even remotely that the zamindars borrowed money to underwrite wedding feasts or buy lavish dowries. If anything, there is evidence that peasants were so heavily involved that they had to sell the ornaments and brass vessels belonging to their wives, and as many of the cattle as could be spared. In a few other cases daughters were sold to raise money (Ibbetson 1883b: 69). Such evidence was probably not readily given because it was a cause for shame to have to sell a wife's dowry or to admit that a larger bride-price was demanded.

Thorburn's notes on encumbered individuals confirm in case after case that a small shortfall in the payment of revenue in a poor season, for instance, "when the rabi crop was damaged by hail and no remissions or suspensions were allowed" (Thorburn 1896: 77) was the primal force that pushed peasants into the gradual slide into hopeless involvement, landlessness, and a state akin to that of bonded laborers to one or more moneylenders. Since Thorburn tried to track debts back to their initial incidences, it can be seen that debts were small before 1870, and the loans were raised with jewelry or livestock in these four circles; the first serious embarrassments date from after 1876. Many debtors were carrying the debts of their fathers (like sins) with no relief in sight.

In calculating the debt incurred by the 742 families, which Thorburn based on actual figures taken from *sahukar's* records and verified by interviews, he found that marriage expenses amounted to an average of 8.75 percent in his entire study area. Only fourteen adult bachelors were found, and in the 742 families examined, of "only three [landowners] can it be said that their extravagance on marriages was the chief cause for their serious indebtedness, but in cases of 142 others it is one among several causes" (p. 22). It can also be fairly adduced that weddings of sons were not any more cheaply celebrated than those of daughters, and in fact, it appears that they usually cost more. Even more surprisingly, dowries are not mentioned as a separate expenditure and appear not to figure in the calculations at all. Only exchange marriages, in which a bride was given to a household from which a bride had been taken, were "inexpensive"; in other cases, "the bride in a sense has to be paid for. Thus a *youth's or man's marriage* must generally cost more than a peasant can afford. The bride's guardians must be propitiated, presents and clothes must be provided, and some small rejoicing and feasting must take place." He showed sympathy for the custom, because "after all the show and excitement of a wedding is about the only relaxation a peasant owner has in his life's struggle against expropriation [since British rule began]. In a few cases the girl's parents also incurred considerable expenditure. Expenditure on *tambol* or marriage presents from friends and relations was everywhere very small." He believed that his investigations on subject of marriage expenses had yielded accurate results "as on such occasions the debtor feels pride in letting people know the extent of his borrowing" (Thorburn 1896: 22; emphasis added).

Even the three families who claimed to be in debt principally on account of marriage expenses were apparently stretching the case. For instance, Qutab Din of village Kot Ghumman of Charkhri-Sialkot was a Muslim Jat who owned nine and a half acres, of which only one was uncultivated, and his land revenue demand was assessed at Rs. 16. He mortgaged six acres in 1882 for Rs. 210 for his daughter's marriage, leaving him with "three and a half unencumbered acres that were insufficient for his family (five mouths)." But when we look into his history of indebtedness, we discover that his dealings with two moneylenders go back to 1867 and have little to do with his daughter's wedding fifteen years later (Thorburn 1896: 67).[18]

Thorburn's data also reveal that, on average, by the 1890s debts were now far larger, exceeding several hundred rupees per debtor, the result of the land collateral that made larger loans possible. Clearly dowries, in order to serve their customary purpose of being a resource to fall back on in times of extremity, had to be bigger by the late-nineteenth century to match the increased distress one might experience. Dowries, it can be argued, were transactions that were forced to acquire extra elasticity to accommodate the inflexibility of the new cash revenue payments; they had to rise in value to match the rise in land prices and other inflation to be of any practical value to distressed families or to those who saw an opportunity to buy additional acres at auction.

Try as we might, it is impossible to conjure from Thorburn's data the picture of the notoriously improvident, thriftless peasant who played a large role in the interpretive sections of the infanticide reports; he does not appear to be in these records. There was no case of a man in debt because he had mortgaged his land for his daughter's marriage. Debts were most often incurred to sustain the family, to pay the revenue demand, or to pay for the replacement of cattle that had perished, for seed, and for the repair of implements. Land was willfully sold in a few cases to raise capital for trade, which was more lucrative than farming. The pawning of jewels and their subsequent redemption is frequently mentioned in these 742 case stories, but that speaks for the utility of women's dowry rather than against it. Borrowing for weddings seemed to be small and only occurred in families that were already in debt for all the reasons given above, and even then such families were fewer than one in ten. Enough evidence existed to exonerate wedding expenses from the charge of being the primary cause of peasant indebtedness and female infanticide. The strident official rhetoric against "thriftless tribes" was muted after this. Such cogent findings with a clear-cut refutation of the charge of "improvidence" against the peasant undermined the entire fabrication about hypergamy, high-caste pride, dowry payments, and barbarity as being at the roots of female infanticide. It perhaps explains why in 1906, without much ado, the statue against female infanticide was quietly rescinded.

It must be pointed out again, before I rest my case in defense of the culturally benighted peasant versus imperial revenue policy, that dowry was not the cause for the increasing preference for sons, and that in all this minutiae there is no mention of *dahej, daaj, jahez,* or any other term for dowry as the initial reason for incurring a debt. On the contrary, in most of the cases pawning gold or silver trinkets or livestock raised the initial loan. This had always been the traditional relationship of dowry to debt; women pawned their jewelry to raise small loans in difficult times. This changed, however, in the last quarter of the century. The price of land went up enormously because it was now a commodity that had value by virtue of being alienable. This raised prices generally, as well as the value of collateral acceptable for loans when revenue payments were due. Dowries were sucked into this inflationary spiral. Since no zamindar wanted to mortgage his land while he or his wife had other assets, particularly jewelry or livestock, both the need and the demand for such assets clearly must grow. And these assets had to be substantial to be of use. Under the Sikhs, loans, as we have seen, had been small, and were often unsecured or secured only with silver ornaments; but in the late nineteenth century, moneylenders, who had tasted the sweetness of foreclosure and seen zamindars toil as sharecroppers on the land they formerly owned, were less easy to persuade. They bayed for gold or land, and their reputation and opportunities for unbounded avarice originate in this period.

On the other hand, the Raj also created prosperity in the Punjab, and those who profited under it—the traders, merchants, retailers in Lahore; government contractors for building, timber, and army supplies; even the despised moneylenders and wage-earning soldiers—all could afford to give bigger dowries or bride-price and celebrate weddings more lavishly. Increasing social expenditure was noted in the poverty reports, we will recall, as a mark of increased means for many. The connection between property and dowry has been broached many times, and now that land values were rising even in the restricted market, dowries could not remain at their former level. It was only logical that the cost of dowries would show a concomitant rise; the newly rich men would give large dowries and host expensive weddings, despite their agreement with the government to keep within the prescribed limits. Bigger, fancier voluntary dowries and demands for ever-larger ones—both came into vogue as prosperity and debt provided occasions for this ancient institution to serve new purposes. It was also logical that a brother now saw himself as individual proprietor and would not part with a quarter of his share of saleable land to his unmarried sister, who would perhaps continue to live with her brother's family, but only at his and his wife's sufferance. The return of an unhappily married woman to her natal home thus became similarly problematic.

Badgered by the cumulative avalanche of facts and figures in report after report, and warned and implicitly chastised by some of its own outspoken officers, the government finally came up with a legislative masterstroke, the Punjab Land Alienation Act of 1900. The act enabled the government not to change an iota of its own inflexible revenue policies and to continue to blame peasant proprietors' misfortunes on Hindu moneylenders. It was not paternal concern for the peasants, as often alleged by scholars, but a cold, pragmatic need to pacify the landowning classes and deflect a rebellion, and to aggravate and exploit any tension that existed between Hindus and Muslims to keep their own political grip on the Punjab, that made this drastically ill-judged measure possible. The political implications of this act were also enormous (see Gilmartin 1988: 115–19). Peasant discontent was converted into fresh and deep religious antagonisms that smoldered dangerously in 1907 and then for another four decades before bursting into the flames that ravaged the Punjab during the Partition in 1947. This was another outcome that could have been mitigated if the government had taken responsibility for the dangerous agrarian conditions it had created and given the industrial and educational development of the Punjab some serious, unselfish thought.

This piece of legislation was perhaps as blatant an example as one can find of the process that created a favored, "dominant" agriculturalist class at the expense of other social groups; here the "agriculturalists" were Muslim tribes and Sikh and Hindu Jat zamindars, and the "nonagriculturalists" were high-caste Hindu Brahmins, Khatris, and Banias. It deflected the gathering ire against the government, who took on the role of protector of the interests of the "traditional" agriculturalists against the grasping nonagriculturalists. The act aggressively made "tribe" and caste the basis of landownership to stem the acquisition of lands from agriculturalists deemed an organic group, by moneylenders, who were believed to be genetically evil and greedy; they would not be judged as equals in the eyes of the law. This law expressly contradicted the very principles of modern, rational, even utilitarian principles on which the Raj allegedly rested. But the simple fix—making revenue demand elastic to match the quality of the harvest, with the due date conveniently fixed so that there was time enough for the grain could be bagged and taken to the market to be sold and converted into cash—was disregarded because it would have meant less revenue and greater assessment expenses. Such were the scrutable ways of these occidental despots.

The act also mocked the principle of the market and the legality of mortgages when it prohibited moneylenders, as traditional nonagriculturalists, from acquiring land at auctions or from foreclosures. The Muslim lobby of large landowners in the northwest was particularly aware that the British apprehended its potential for rebellion and political danger. These northwestern tribesmen were also the "martial races" employed in vast numbers in the colonial army, so their loyalty had to be courted. Having branded the Hindu moneylender (whom the British wished to replace with modern lending institutions) as the cowardly, effeminate villain of the piece and the Muslim landholder as his stupid but honorable victim, Thorburn purposely disregarded the more complex realities behind the plague of alienations. He knew only too well that Hindu landowners were also indebted in proportion to their numbers and were treated no better by the moneylenders, and that in many areas the moneylenders were indeed the larger Muslim zamindars of the northwest, who paid little heed to Islamic sanctions against usury and equally zealously foreclosed on the plots of encumbered proprietors. The Raj contributed in no small measure to the full-blown communalism that partitioned the Punjab in 1947 on religious lines, and ensured that this region would continue its history as a militarized zone with a male-dominant ethos and masculine sex ratios on both sides of the divide.

Colonial political expedience had also created a hamstrung capitalism, but there was no reverting to the precolonial system in which people belonged to the land and their varying rights in it were permanent, heritable, and simply inalienable—in which a peasant holding was never wagered as collateral or auctioned by the state to recover revenue. Borrowing and lending had been at a low level and trade had been mostly local, but the peasant family's security that its rights in the land were inalienable had been rock solid. It had been rare that a peasant and his family could be driven off the land they worked, and even in his old age, his sons would support him with their labor on their land. Now sons, even more than before, would have to stand in lieu of the old insurance mechanism; and daughters would have to be given larger dowries if these gifts were to serve anything deeper that a decorative purpose. The new insecurity created by the new revenue policy created the new imperatives of planning a family with ever more boys than girls. Only more sons could ensure an uncertain future, and their wives could bring in dowries with cash and gold ornaments to tide them over in a crisis.

The introduction of capitalist relations in land would not have been as disastrous as it proved to be in the agrarian sector had the state not paired it with an intractable revenue system—with fixed dates for cash payments and revenues assessed and fixed for fifteen to thirty years at a time—that made peasant proprietors vulnerable to the slightest delay in harvesting or the smallest degree of crop damage owing to the caprice of the weather. It was also these twin features of colonial revenue collecting that made the British "civilizing mission" a travesty, driving tillers to debt and finally separation from their land, condemning them to a profound existential insecurity—and by extension of the same pitiless logic—to a steady increase in the numbers of female infants deliberately killed in order to plan more male children who might, in the future, rescue them from the exigencies of the colonial state.

5

Local Customs and the Economy Grow Mustaches

Hand in hand with the recording of proprietary titles and fixed revenue assessments went the compilation and reduction of a universe of customs into a tightly constructed code of "customary law" that altered the grammar of social relations. All three of these operations were conducted by British scholar-bureaucrats and their teams of native assistants on a single day in each district, not only for the sake of economy but also in order to mesh the meanings of the newly instituted idea of modern proprietorship in land with those of all other existent customary rights and laws to make a seamless package. And much can change in a day. From the morass of overlapping tenures and family and community interests there emerged the peasant proprietor—the native subject-agent, third person singular, possessive case, masculine gender. The ambiguities, nuances, and complexities of the world of shared and graded fields were now rendered as the generic private property of a particular male individual who was granted a title to the property and who could say, "I, so-and-so, son of so-and-so, own this land, in its precisely measured and recorded form, and owe to the Raj a fixed amount of revenue to be paid in two installments in cash on the due dates every year for the next thirty years." This male was legally identified as an individual with his given and "family" name. He had not been transformed into the complete and enfranchised "modern man," as in Britain, but into a seriously hobbled, attenuated colonial subject. In most cases, the *jati,* or tribal affiliation, served as the surname—Arun Singh Aluwahlia (a Jat subcaste) and Baljit Singh Talwar (a Khatri subcaste) rather than Arun, son of Karamjit of Gurgaon, and Baljit, son of Ranjit of Peshawar. Even Sikhs, who had expressly spurned caste names and had all taken Singh as their last name, were registered in the army under their *jati* or "tribal" names.

For women, the gulf between the precolonial and postcolonial meanings of their rights and entitlements was incalculable. The claims of the individual proprietor's wife, widowed mother, and unmarried sisters and daughters went un-recorded, and their implicit constituent rights in the same soil were now wholly predicated on the authority and goodwill of their nearest male relative. These ten-uous claims were worthless when the auctioneer's gavel resolved the persistent indebtedness and revenue defaults or when marital conflict made a woman un-welcome in both her natal and her marital "homes." Manu himself might be sur-prised to see how things had gone so awry.

This was not a slow erosion of women's rights but an abrupt erasure, an ab-sence from the written record that would be binding for all official purposes from then on. It also wiped away women's rights of preemption in a sale or foreclosure, and it appears that women could not be owners, except perhaps as widows if they had no sons. Wives and sisters were not considered viable owners or even people with shared rights in the land by Victorian officers, since women's rights in prop-erty were nonexistent; the very idea of such rights was stoutly resisted as a sub-versive feminist one in Britain in the 1870s. "Private property" came to be the sin-gle most important idea in the social and political economy, and the peasant proprietor became its key player in colonial Punjab. Just as the Bengal countryside had undergone a profound change when the notorious Permanent Settlement of 1793 altered the meaning of the word "zamindar" from "revenue collector" to "landlord," the creation of peasant proprietors in the Punjab unleashed a whole social revolution.

Many key terms in the British records acquired colonial meanings, even as they purported to describe precolonial situations, and they were further skewed by translation into English as codes of law. Nowhere is this more obvious than in the codification of customary laws themselves. Let us take a key example: the word "local," which meant "village" (as in geographical locality) before customary laws were written down, was transformed to mean "caste" or "tribe" after the codifi-cation of customary law, because the British chose to understand that Indians all over the subcontinent, and Punjabis in particular, were not identified by "place" but by "caste" or "tribe."[1] This shift in terminology had implications for women; people were now constituted as belonging to patriarchal lineages more than to lo-calities. Smith aptly suggests that "[l]ocal terms could be used for shares, while at the same time land measures were standardized and agrarian relations fitted into an overarching legal vocabulary of ownership and tenancy." He goes on to explain that in the process

> principles of shareholding were altered and forms of village organization changed. This change can be stated most concisely, I think, as a change in the idiom in which agrarian relations had been expressed. Shares had been reckoned locally in ploughs, a key term in agriculture with many connota-tions. When formal weight was given to one particular usage and this was tied to a notion of property in fixed parcels of land, the semantic field was

disturbed. Correspondingly the integrity of the old system of shareholding, which had centred on balancing economic resources in the village, was undermined. . . . The expression [of shares in terms of ploughs] was now merely customary, like an "algebraic symbol" as one contemporary observer put it. The systemic character of shareholding was broken even as a particular usage was preserved. (Smith 1996: 17)

The plough terminology suggests that animals harnessed to the plough rather than tillers were at stake in the indigenous system. These idiomatic shifts were matched by material realities in terms of gender. Land was seldom bought or sold, or even considered independently negotiable as plots, but the shares of a family grew or diminished according to political or economic opportunities as new lands were acquired by the village through politics, war, or fresh settlement after clearing forests. Men tilled the soil but, more important, they defended it against local and external enemies; the army of the larger political unit to which a village belonged had a right to the manpower of the village. Men defended the rights of their family, *biradari*, or clan in the land that they were entitled to cultivate, and they and their wives, widows, and unmarried daughters shared in the "heaps of grain" and other produce it yielded.

I argued in the previous chapter that in the precolonial period the rights and entitlements of men were not qualitatively different from the rights of women in the land. These consisted of a share in the produce rather than the right to own the land and to dispose of it at will or mortgage it for a loan. When a man migrated permanently to another area, he stood to lose his right to a share in the produce of the land or village of his birth, but the rights of his wife or wives and family did not lapse if they remained in the village. Smith states that "in the ideal coparcenary, the land followed the share; shareholding entailed collective liability and a say in the management of common resources, including an individual allotment for cultivation. In the initial stage of transformation, when the boundaries of the allotments were fixed and each plot of land became independently negotiable private property, *shares followed the ownership of land*" (Smith 1996: 248; emphasis added). The rights of the individual proprietor, once created, subsumed the many shareholders to that proprietor—including wives, minor children, widowed mothers, and unmarried daughters.

The registration of ownership of land was the first phase—the foundation stone—of the making the agrarian economy more masculine. The next step taken in each district of the Punjab was the attempt to translate social and customary practice into legal codes. The new regime insisted on consulting only the male heads of a village, caste, or household in order to inscribe the *rivaj-i-am*, the customs of everyday life situated in a place or region, particularizing them into the attributes of a caste or tribe. Once again, new meanings invaded the husks of many familiar words. The complex and plastic universe of oral, implicit, flexible, and informally transmitted customary practices, negotiated and interpreted as much by women as by men, which ordered everyday life and relationships was systematically elicited from only men and reduced, for administrative efficiency, into a written, fixed, judicable, actionable, and enforceable corpus of laws.

The timing of the project was, perhaps, as critical as the project itself. The very fact that customary laws were to be collected and written down for the first time when the record of who owned the land had just been noted, with the power and the danger of individual ownership unleashed, informed much of what the respondents, all male land owners, would call custom, as we shall see. Women's right to share in the produce of the land became meaningless, but traces of what their rights might have been are discernible in these codes. The codes have to be read with this in mind to extract a faint approximation of the rights women had in a society where land was a common resource with varying levels of entitlements. This analysis will also put in relief the process that emptied the female category of older, subtler meanings—of shares, of birthright, and of the other safeguards of the indigenous patriarchal tradition.

The codification of customary law in the Punjab had six distinct stages (Tupper 1881: vol. 1), and it offers a fascinating study of the evolution of "custom" as British political and economic intrusions reconfigured the supple body of local knowledge and practice. My purpose here is, of necessity, tightly focused on how the process of codification itself transformed the meanings and social realities of women's rights, so I will cut directly to the codes themselves in several districts, namely, Gurgaon, Ludhiana, and Rawalpindi. The selection is geographically representative, ranging from Gurgaon in the southeast to Rawalpindi farther to the north and west. The three districts came under British rule in 1803, 1839, and 1849, respectively. The population of Gurgaon is predominantly Hindu and Sikh, whereas there is a fair balance of Muslims in Ludhiana and a dominance of Muslims in Rawalpindi.[2] These areas are on both sides of an international border today, and have among the worst sex ratios of the entire subcontinent. In addition, the Ludhiana records have been expertly studied by Smith (1996), those of Gurgaon by Chowdhry (1994), and those of Rawalpindi by Thorburn; I felt that I could clamber onto their shoulders to try to see farther to solve the puzzles of gender.

C. L. Tupper, under the tutelage of Henry Maine at Corpus Christi College, Oxford, had acquired the appropriate training and historicist orientation to undertake with confidence the magisterial task of writing a three-volume philosophical and procedural description of the customary laws of the Punjab, and he acquitted himself admirably for the purposes of the colonial state. When only an undersecretary in the Punjab government, he was chosen to accomplish the tall order by Sir Robert Egerton in 1878, then lieutenant governor of the Punjab: to update or replace the existing manuals used by judges and officers, called the Punjab Civil Code. These manuals had been compiled from the customs recorded in the *wajib-ul-arz,* or village administration papers, on succession, transfer of property, and related matters created after the earliest settlement operations in 1852. Various efforts had been made from time to time to update and elaborate these notes into separate registers for each district. The whole enterprise was informed by the British presumption that the Punjab, with its distinctive tribes and castes, was unlike the rest of the Indian empire, in which (an equally ad hoc compilation of) Hindu law had been used for the Hindus and the Shariah had been used for the Muslims for civil litigation since 1772.

Tupper turned out to be dedicated to grand theories and master narratives—particularly of the racial and evolutionary variety then in vogue among British intellectuals. He found in his task the ideal opportunity to display his own opinions, his erudition, and his not inconsiderable speculative and analytical abilities, informed though they were with the often pseudoscientific and racist sociology of his time. To be put in charge of such a massive undertaking was a mark of recognition of these qualities by his superiors. With astonishing editorial energy, Tupper, in a three-month-long leave from his normal duties, compiled three thick introductory volumes in which he included his quite gloriously prolix anthropological commentary, inspired by the freshly published works of Sir Henry Maine ([1861] 1888, 1871; for a critical reading see Inden 1990: 137–208).

In his lengthy introduction, for instance, Tupper rhetorically asks, "[W]hat is the connection of inquiries into the origin and history of kinship and society, with the practical business of Indian administration?" His answer smugly informs us of how the strictly scientific research efforts in progress in Europe had brought them to a new philosophy of social development. In a few years a much more complete and credible theory of human advance from naked savagery to national civilization would be enunciated. He believed that "if a scientific account of social evolution can be framed for the acceptance of the public, and more particularly, of statesmen and administrators, the practical business of Indian government will be immensely facilitated." And these subjects who were "at a primitive phase of development," he added, would not only be better understood and governed after the formulation of the social theory but also *"would never suspect that they were despised. Fully to understand a people you must be able to explain its institutions as well as to recount them; and this is precisely what it is the object of the new social philosophy to do. If you can assign a race or tribe its place in social evolution you know very much what to expect of it"* (Tupper 1881: 1.97–98; emphasis added). Such unabashed statements pepper his work, and are alert us to the collective imperial mentality at work in modernizing Punjabi society.

Tupper hoped to create a complete representation of Punjabi social customs as practiced by each of the "tribes," which were perceived as organically discrete in each district in all matters relating to "succession, special property of females, betrothal, marriage, divorce, dower, adoption, guardianship, minority, bastardy, family relations, will, legacies, gifts, partitions, or any religious usage or institution" (Tupper 1881: 1.7) He formulated exactly one hundred questions grouped under these categories to achieve his goal; these questions were retained in the text of the individual codes and were answered, often severally, to accommodate variations of custom, since various caste representatives within a village had to answer the same questions. All previous digests, attempts, and observations regarding Punjabi society were to be incorporated into this body of data, with differences especially noted. If we examine the cracks and inconsistencies over time, our purpose of seeing the changes in women's rights might be fulfilled. Once the compilation was complete, each district would have a tidy clothbound volume of customary laws that would assist British judges in making socially correct decisions, keeping in mind that those customs "contrary to justice, equity and good conscience" could, of course, be overruled (Tupper 1881: 1.7). This was also a recipe for ossifying a living tradition, but no one then was in a position to complain.

Our first alert of the masculinizing trend is in Tupper's insistence on using "tribe" as the founding idea in rural society. We can hardly forget that the reports on female infanticide from the early 1850s were obsessed with *jati* and caste, hypergamy, and dowry, when the conquest constituted the legitimacy of colonial rule of the Punjab; this was the unambiguous mark of "ancient societies" and clearly not the route a modern nation-state could take to justify its rule in India. New and modern bases for legitimacy had to be found, and for this Sir Henry Maine came to the rescue. The usage shifted to "tribe" in the 1870s when his famous ancient-versus-modern dichotomy took hold among the scholar-bureaucrats who served the British Raj in India as the fundamental tool for classifying societies. Ancient communities, he suggested, based themselves on kinship and blood, defining their relationships by status internally and by force externally; modern European nation-states were defined by association and contract and thus could deal with other nation-states. Sir Alfred Lyall had taken this basic construct further and posited that, if Asians had been organized, as Europeans were, into sovereign states, then it would not have been legitimate for Britain's governing class to impose its "foreign" rule on an Asian nation-state. The lack of modern nation-states in India, therefore, made British rule in India perfectly legitimate, since the question of the sovereignty of rude tribes did not arise (Inden 1990: 176–80). The knotty problem (for race-minded Europeans) was that Aryan tribes had peopled both India and Europe. Baden-Powell solved this, Inden points out, by establishing that indigenous Dravidian institutions were at the base of Indian society and had been only superficially modified by Aryans; the danger of Indians becoming like their European cousins was thus ruled out. He completed the linguistic shift in India from "feudal" (which would have meant it could potentially evolve into a nation-state, as the Germans had done in 1870) to "tribal." Thus "the essences that inhabited the scholarly discourse on India in the earlier part of the nineteenth century—utilitarian despotism and oriental feudalism—had been transmuted by the end of the century into the essences of force and kinship" (Inden 1990: 179).

Tupper inscribed the idea of the tribe into Punjab customary law (Tupper 1881: 2.69–70). Roman legal maxims had posited that in a genealogical tree "we stop whenever we come to the name of a female and pursue that particular branch or ramification no further, all who remain after the descendants of women have been excluded are agnates, and their connexion together is agnatic relationship. . . . A female name closes a branch or twig of the genealogy in which it occurs" (Maine [1861] 1888: 148). The essence of "tribe" in Roman law had been agnatic kinship, and this structural element was lifted and transplanted into the customs of the Punjab. It is true that Punjabi society was infused with patriarchal ideas and kinship patterns, but this strictly agnatic cast to customary law originated in Tupper's dedication to the idea, and that of his predecessors who had also imbibed Maine. One of the distillates from the application of agnatic laws to the Punjab countryside was to create hidebound customs for the Punjabis. Tupper assumed that tribal customs included the common prohibition against the inheritance of land by daughters in the Punjab, and the nature of his codification of customs was strongly flavored with this and with the commitment to preserving the rights of the clan or tribe in matters of inheritance. Land was the key to the status of the tribe, and for any of it to pass to another tribe through a daughter who was to be married out of the close agnatic group, Tupper believed, ran counter to the organic constitution of "tribes."[3]

The method used to compile customary law also helped further the cause of indigenous patriarchy. If custom is about the principal relations of family life and the disposition of wealth (succession, marriage expenses), it would have been useful to consult the senior women of the tribes. But the design of this project of gathering local knowledge (in which "local" had come to mean "tribe," not "village") was entrusted entirely to masculine hands from conception to execution, as these law books reveal. In the Gurgaon report, for example, we can take a detailed look at who was consulted and how the customary codes took shape, since this was the first one prepared, and it served as a model for subsequent reports.[4] Wilson, armed with Tupper's hundred questions that were shaped by Maine's agnatic kinship theory and a band of experienced native employees, gathered "village headmen of each of the principal land-owning tribes" from every village in the district to seek their answers. These headmen were deemed likely to be the most "intelligent" men in the village, since they were "members of the most influential families" and represented their villages "in all important transactions." Of the 3,568 headmen of the twenty-one tribes in the district, 2,754 were present at the attestation of their tribal code (Wilson 1881: 100). Wilson personally superintended the attestation of the more important tribes, which he ranked with the help of his native assistant. Needless to say, this round of inquiries included the headmen (or their successors, typically their eldest sons) of the tribes that had been queried before. This ensured a possibly unintended effect: not only did local knowledge and practice become particularized by "tribe," it also gradually became the entrenched preserve of the "important" tribes or higher castes, omitting the customary practices of the marginal and politically weaker ones. For example, the *bhand* and *mirasi*, balladeers and musicians (whose presence at weddings and other social functions was treated as a nuisance in the sumptuary agreements between the British and the upper castes and tribes, as discussed in chapter 3), predictably found no place in the code book at all; they appear to have been erased both from the record and from their practical functions in the lives of their localities. The bigger project of creating uniform tribal codes excluded the perspectives of women and menials or dependents (as did all Enlightenment ideas on equality and liberty). Wilson concluded, as Maine would have approved, that in "the course of attestation the comparative difficulty which the people [headmen] evidently had in following out relationships through the mother, wife, and daughter showed how much more importance is attached to relationship through males than to that through females." He was of course surprised to find that the terminology for relatives was equally well developed on both the male and female sides, which he even carefully diagrammed to form a full picture of kinship (Wilson 1881: 105–9). The "difficulty" in tracing relationships through female kin might have been in the minds of both the British interlocutors and the native informants, who were more anxious about establishing their own rights in property than in drawing an accurate map of social relationships.

After his labors, Wilson proclaimed two principles, which Tupper was to elaborate on, to be equally true for Hindus, Muslims, and Sikhs: "A man must not marry a woman of his own got [*gotr* or lineage]," and "the property must not leave the got" (Wilson 1881: 112). With these principles, he subsumed Muslims, who ideally preferred parallel cousin marriages, under the Hindu and Sikh rule about *gotr* exogamy and created agnatic devolution for freshly created private property. This "custom" proceeded uncontested into the law book, since the male native informants could hardly object that it translated into exclusive legal rights in alienable property at the expense of the rights of their mothers, widows, and sisters, now that land was a commodity.

There is also little doubt that the civilian's objective was to exclude ambiguities from creeping into the vertical grid of patriarchal and agnatic rights in land that would devolve from father to son to grandson to great-grandson. This is fairly obvious as one reads the responses of Hindus and Muslims of all castes. Socially close relationships with the mother's kin (*nanke*) and wife's kin (*saure*) that would otherwise have been readily acknowledged now posed "difficulty," since the entire exercise of creating customary law books was framed by the more crucial tasks of creating property records and noting revenue demands simultaneously.

We can see an even more blatant shift of social responsibility from women to men when the answer to the question "Whose consent is necessary to the validity of a betrothal?" is noted. The mother is assigned a very unlikely third place in a group of six ranked consent-givers, all the others being male agnates (Wilson 1881: 112).[5] Later ethnographies of the Punjab clearly stress the importance of women in marital arrangements. Important female kin, including the father's mother and other female relatives on the mother's side, such as the mother's mother and the mother's sisters, who were and are frequently key players in betrothals, were entirely omitted from the new "customary" ranks of decision makers.

Another factor may have been at play besides the fear of jeopardizing inheritance rights, extending them beyond the patriarchal grid, or blurring tribal formation. The British officials made no secret about their appreciation of manly men, and manliness for the Punjabi male also meant being in charge of making decisions on important matters such as betrothals and marriage expenses. Sumptuary laws could be aimed at the men of Punjabi society. If the tribal nature of society had been diluted over time ("interrupted by invasions," as Tupper saw it), then this was the moment to hand the reins back to the men and reinscribe their customs. It was also useful in getting a betrothed party out of a commitment that had not been properly consented to according to the customary law book; if the matter wound up in court (which it often did, since the civil courts now adjudicated such matters) then only the men would have to travel to the court to give statements or bear witness. Tribal culture was being restored to its pristine origins. Sometimes it becomes hard to decide which was more patriarchal, "tribal" constructs of authority or the colonial variation of "modernity," but together they produced an invincible patriarchy.

Customary practices rapidly reconstructed themselves, as the new objectives, opportunities, and perils inherent in "the rule of law" became intelligible to those on whom it was imposed. Wilson also noted in parenthesis that the devolution of the office of headman was hereditary, with the eldest son succeeding, although "the people often wish the childless widow of a headman to enjoy the emoluments and hold the office for her lifetime"(Wilson 1881: 139). This custom was noted as an aberration and followed the tenor of stripping women of their authority in social or family matters, since these matters were seen as the core concerns of agnatic tribes. The recent abeyance of this practice clearly describes another circle of reason: succession rights were, in the end, a corollary to inheritance rights, and since sons succeeded fathers in their property, it was only proper that they should supersede their mothers in their rights. In the case of childless widows, the successor would have to be the brother of the deceased headman.

Widows were probably the most vulnerable category of women in this revamped codification of customs project. Wilson noted that the only "matter left doubtful" was the widow's power to alienate her immovable property without the consent of her husband's relatives, who had a reversionary interest in it as the next heirs. Although there was vociferous agreement among the headmen (with the exception of one Rajput and one Khanzada) that a widow could not alienate her movable property as she pleased, there were "many instances brought forward in almost every tribe in which the widow sold or mortgaged the immovable property which had devolved upon her from her husband; and it is doubtful whether in all these instances the consent of the husband's relatives was obtained"(Wilson 1881: 143). Needless to say, Wilson did not consult any women—wives or widows—to confirm what he believed to be the custom, nor would he give them the benefit of the doubt. He found that it was "still more common to find the widow gifting the land, or a part of it, to her daughter's son or husband, and thus preventing it from reverting to the husband's relatives on her death." Wilson willfully struck another blow for patriarchal rights. He wrote—and this might well have been inscribed in stone—that

> it is the almost universal [read: male] feeling that the widow should not be allowed this liberty. I would consider it *the universal custom, both among Hindus and Musalmans* (for in no tribe does the Muhamadan law on this matter prevail) that the widow cannot, except in case of urgent necessity, when her husband's relatives cannot, or will not, help her otherwise, or when they agree to the alienation, sell, mortgage, or give away by gift or bequest any of the immovable property which has devolved upon her from her husband. (Wilson 1881: 143; emphasis added)

Other significant colonial emendations resulted in a hardening of the categories of inheritance rights. Muslims, Sikhs, and Hindus could customarily marry more than one wife, although only very few married more than one wife concurrently. Members of each of these groups claimed that only the lack of a male heir persuaded them to remarry during the lifetime of the first wife. Yet, in cases in which a man had more than one wife and sons from all of them, there were two ways in which inheritance devolved. The somewhat more frequent practice was for all sons to inherit equally (*pagvand,* or *per capita* succession). The other form of succession (explicitly endorsed in the Laws of Manu in his discussion of inheritance rights), called *chundavand (per stirpes,* or uterine, succession), "where the inheritance was divided among the sons according to the number of mothers, the sons however few, of one mother taking as much as the sons, however many, of another, existed particularly among Rajputs, Khatris, some Jats, and Muslims like the Khanzadas" (Wilson 1881: 138).

The British had little tolerance for women as the focus of heritable rights, as I have already noted. Tupper speculated on this as an atavism, perhaps a survival of the custom of polyandry that had prevailed among many Punjab tribes, particularly as one moved north into the mountainous regions of Kangra and to Tibet and beyond, where uterine succession was still the rule. Tupper saw the custom as "plainly unjust now" and seeming "to serve no useful purpose whatever" (Tupper

1881: 2.96–97). His distaste for the idea of any property devolving downward from women hastened the end of this custom in the law books. Wilson also repudiated uterine succession by noting that the custom "seems contrary in a sense to equity, and no reasonable ground can be assigned for the anomaly; very clear proof of the custom should be required before it is allowed" (Wilson 1881: 139).[6] This would have affected a great number of Jat peasant proprietor households, whose members subscribed widely to the custom of the remarriage of the widow or deserted wife to her husband's brother, even if the brother was already married. This, among other things, made the once-assured equality of wives and widows increasingly tenuous and was rapidly overtaken by the proprietary rights vested in men (the sons). Wilson also grudgingly noted that a widow who had no sons was entitled "to a life interest in the share of her husband's land which would have gone to her son had she any." Here were visible elisions in the gendered meaning of rights.

We can see that the customary equality of wives, overriding the rights of individual males as sons, had been the indispensable security for widows with no sons. The life interest in land that sonless widows had enjoyed in the past was gradually disallowed, as a "rare" custom, since sonless widows, by definition, had no male to represent their interests in a critical time when the alienable and salable potential of land became increasingly real. Sons would inherit and be in charge, and their widowed mothers would be their dependents-at-will; women who had no sons would have no rights and would become dependent on the charity of their stepsons or the husband's other agnatic kin.

In Ludhiana district, the presiding officer put it even more bluntly: "The rule of chundavand, under which property was divided according to the number of wives, is clearly a barbarous and unjust one, and is fast disappearing . . . with the growing scarcity of land the right of every son to an equal share in his father's property is insisted on. This was the way in which most of the representatives of the tribes and gots put the matter to me when questioned. . . . There is such a strong presumption now in favor of the equal right of a man's sons in his property that the fullest evidence should be required to establish the contrary [chundavand] succession" (Walker 1885: 56–57). This is another example that illustrates my argument about the loss of control over landed property by women in even the few situations that allowed them to succeed to it—as "appointed" daughters (without brothers) and widows—in the very process of recalling and codifying "custom" and "tradition." Such was the insidious nature of the attestation of Punjabi customs.

Mr. Wilson here, and countless other officials elsewhere, interpreted customs or clarified doubts about customs in ways that privileged the rights of men over women in every instance that came up. They ensured that these fresh interpretations and emendations would supersede the oral precedents in the living memory of their male informants. Wilson, in collusion with his native assistants and the village headmen of important tribes, overrode not only existing custom but also

Muslim and Hindu laws to separate sonless widows from their right to mind their own lands. A native assistant commissioner, Pandit Maharaj Kishn, framed the custom for Rohtak district much more flexibly in a memorandum, however: a widow could "alienate her late husband's property in cases of necessity, such as paying his debts, providing the necessaries of life, paying the revenue, and marrying her daughters." Agnates could object to this "but are bound to arrange to supply her necessity" (cited in Tupper 1888: 2.176). Needless to say, it did not make it into the law book.

We see a similar further slippage in the rights of daughters. Tupper had posited, as we noted earlier, that daughters were prohibited from inheriting land in the Punjab because they were generally married outside the clan, although within the looser circle or tribe of origin, and allowing daughters to inherit would have allowed land to pass outside the clan. He had, in all fairness, also listed the exceptions and caveats to this simple construction of a daughter's rights. "Daughter" meant an unmarried woman, because the married daughter was in the past, by the fact of her marriage and virilocality, admitted to share in the rights and entitlements of her husband's family's land. Tupper also listed the exceptions that earlier records of customary rights had shown. "[I]n Kangra such a daughter, or even an orphaned daughter has the same rights as a widow; in Sialkot unmarried daughters may hold property on a life tenure until marriage; in Rawalpindi a daughter did not inherit only if she married outside the clan, in Hazara the claims of an unmarried daughter stand on the same footing as those of a widow; in Bannu she is generally entitled to an usufructuary interest in half of a brother's share, and in Dera Ismail Khan they are entitled to manage the property and enjoy the income from it for the rest of their lives" (Tupper 1881: 2.81–82). But because "an absolute power of alienations in one member of the family was not to be found in customary law," and therefore all members who lived on the land had a similar lifetime connection to it, the shares of the unmarried daughter should have been reckoned at least at a quarter of that of each of her brothers, as we have noted was found in the *Dharmashastra*. This customary right of unmarried daughters was a casualty of the British vested interest in protesting the importance of the clan and the tribe and agnatic devolution, and in making men responsible for paying their share of the revenue.

Wilson decided that a daughter who was not marriageable could not inherit but was entitled only to lifelong maintenance out of the estate of her deceased father. A woman unable to marry because of serious physical or mental disability had the right to be maintained for life, unless she decided to leave her natal village. Muslim and Hindu headmen readily agreed that the "right of the daughter to be maintained is lost by her marriage or residing in a strange village" and that "it is her absolute right to be suitably married." Wilson observed, "[n]aturally the male relatives are more ready to consent to the daughter taking the moveable, acquired property of the father than his immoveable or ancestral property." The tradition of village exogamy ensured that a married daughter's marital home would be in a "strange village" (Wilson 1881: 146). The two patriarchal ideas fit like hand in glove.

The case of the married daughter was even more complicated. There were far too many jokes and sayings that shamed a son-in-law for being his wife's economic dependent to think that this situation was rare or nonexistent in precolonial times. The disparaging term for a man who came to dwell in his father-in-law's home is *ghar jamai*; uxorilocal residence is clearly anathema in a patriarchal setup. Yet the hostility underlying the jests appears to have had its roots in sexual rather than in material matters, although it certainly had material repercussions for the daughter.[7] In fact, in colloquial Punjabi, Hindi, and Haryanvi, the bride's brother is called *sala*, a word that is not only the kinship term but also a common term of abuse, since it implies the taunt (pardon my literal translation) "I fuck your sister." The word therefore expresses an acknowledgment of the privileged relationship the *ghar javai* enjoys with his wife's brother, or *sala*, and it is an insult for a man to be called *sala* by any other man, for it implies that the man is in a sexual relationship with the addressee's sister. In compiling customary laws, sexual meanings and tensions in society were excised or ignored, and the resultant "custom"—of village exogamy—described only the material aspects of a relationship. The extensive lore on the subject signifies this (Chowdhry 1994: 340–50). It is patent that the rules of virilocality and village exogamy, which were prevalent throughout the subcontinent among Hindus, were undisguised attempts to control the sexuality of women.

In cases in which a daughter inherited land, her interest was "almost equivalent to that of a male owner, subject, however, to the control of her husband. The land does not on her death lapse to her father's relatives but descends to her sons" (Wilson 1881: 146). There were cases then, and are cases now, in these male lineal succession families in which daughters and sons-in-law made the woman's natal village their home. Wilson also noted that generally "in no case is a daughter entitled to inherit; but there is more chance of a married daughter's succeeding with the tacit or express consent of the father's relatives if she live with her father and have a son." This tacit consent was admitted only in a note, and since it was marked as a rare and exceptional occurrence, it carried little weight in the eyes of an adjudicating magistrate, who would—following custom—favor distant male agnates over a daughter.

"Customary law" flatly stated that a daughter was not entitled to inherit. This was far more unequivocal than the existing reality and would, over time, have the effect of becoming a petrified, incontestable patriarchal fiat robbing custom of its elasticity to deal with particular cases, even in ways that were uncustomary. Wilson acknowledged this by saying that daughters, "although never *entitled* to inherit, . . . are *often* permitted to succeed their maternal grandfather by gift or by the simple consent of the heirs. The custom of allowing a daughter's son in default of a son is increasing" (Wilson 1881: 146; emphasis in the original). Weeding out customs that supported daughters' rights where no sons existed was tantamount to bolstering the rights of male agnatic kin; they could now challenge such customary arrangements in a court of law, which would automatically favor the rights of kinsmen over those of the daughter.

The other side of this coin of daughters' rights was the complete absence of any customary law or even notes on customs regarding the rights of wives (which all daughters were raised to become). The most common destiny of a woman was to become someone's wife, but the rights of this category of women merited no attention in Tupper's allegedly exhaustive scheme. Tupper has sections on the rights of widows, remarried widows, and unmarried daughters, and he even poses a question on the rights of a mother and on the rights of sons in the case of multiple wives, but astonishingly, the most common, most customary relationship of all is left out of the customary code entirely. A married woman's existence was apparently merged with her husband's, but without his right as a proprietor of land. There are several ways of interpreting this silence. The first is that a married woman had to be under the control of her husband. As an only wife and the mother of sons, she was the centerpiece of the patriarchal family. Her rights in the land were part and parcel of those of the family unit and therefore needed no explication. Another way to think about this is that since land was not readily alienable in precolonial times, all that mattered to a woman was her control over its resources, which was probably, in practical day-to-day living, as great as or even greater than her husband's. Most decisions were made jointly, with mutual approval, in most families. But the married woman who had been deserted, abandoned, separated, or otherwise abused had absolutely no recourse in customary law or in the civil law courts. And her parents had responsibility for her only if she had never been married. As a widow, she had rights even if she had no sons. (Jats, who made up the dominant agricultural tribes, handled this by their custom of *karewa*, or marrying the widow to her deceased husband's younger brother, as mentioned earlier.) It is more than ironic that, in the customary code, the married woman who actually reproduced the lineage and gave the tribe its continued longevity was neither assigned a category nor given rights to maintenance after marital conflict separated her from her husband. A married woman who reproduced the lineage clearly depended for her insecure existence on her rights as the mother of her sons. A preference for sons became a matter of her survival, particularly in cases in which the husband was abusive, unfaithful, or habitually drunk. The son was the centerpiece of the mother's world whether her husband was living or dead, and it was through controlling him that a woman found security and power.

Sons not only gave their labor to the family plot, now less secure and inalienable than it once had been, but served as construction workers, soldiers, or migrants to the new canal colonies. There were more opportunities than ever before for men to earn a living or even to buy a piece of land, but there was also more in-security for landowners because of the fixed revenue demand. Both conditions—increased opportunity and prosperity and financial insecurity—spurred the plan-ning of large families with more male children than ever before. The more male-oriented the economy became, the more it intensified the desire for more sons, as one can deduce from the worsening sex ratios. It also exacerbated the practice of killing female infants, and a larger number were killed than had been customary. The demand for Punjabi males, particularly Jats and Muslims, trans-lated into more sons per family than ever before, and this demand increased as the colonial government recruited them aggressively to join their army and con-struction works and to clear and cultivate the many millions of wooded acres in the Punjab.

In spite of concluding that Punjabi women had no rights to property, Tupper decided to establish whether or not Punjabi custom admitted the right of *stridhan*, or as he termed it in English, the "special property of females," since this category of wealth appeared to be widespread. The final section of every volume of cus-tomary law is devoted to the subject. The answers that Tupper received to his questions on the "special property of females" from the different districts in which Punjabi Hindus lived contained only small variations. Those who practiced the *kanyadan* and *daaj* form of wedding believed that a woman had unequivocal rights over her movable property—clothes, jewelry, chattels, cattle, and, in special cir-cumstances, over land. In Lahore, for example, "all tribes" had claimed in 1856, 1880, and 1910 that the gifts made before or after a woman's marriage by her par-ents and her husband's family constituted *stridhan*, over which "the husband has no power." This was particularly true among the Khatris and Brahmins of Lahore, where "the husband has no power to sell the property bought by his wife out of her *stridhan*" (Bolster 1916: 44). To the question of whether a married woman could alienate her *stridhan*, the answer was unequivocal: "A married woman could alienate her stridhan by sale, gift or mortgage. . . . The presence or absence of sons makes no difference. A married woman has full power with respect to her property acquired out of her stridhan." A widow, too, had rights of control and alienation, but she lost them if she was "unchaste" (Bolster 1916: 44–45; also see Chowdhry 1994: 96–100). In Peshawar, the same was admitted in even more strongly flavored language: "A husband cannot alienate or otherwise deal with his wife's *stridhan even for urgent necessity without her consent*. A woman has full power to deal as she pleases with her own *stridhan*, provided only that she does not apply it to a vicious or dishonorable purpose, as by spending it on a paramour" (Lorimer 1889: 34; emphasis added). The word "mortgage" invariably appears as one of the things a woman can do with her *stridhan*; jewelry clearly was used as collateral to raise small loans. *Stridhan*, it must be remarked, remains a very tena-cious idea that even men concede while they are being reinvented as strictly ag-natic tribes.

Unequivocal as a woman's power over *stridhan* seems, it was restricted to movable, and probably unproductive, property. Cattle, horses, and camels that had formed part of the dower in 1850, as we noted in chapter 3, are mentioned only a few times in the eastern districts, and not at all in the western districts. Milch and draft animals, once more valuable than land itself, and a productive, movable resource intended for daughters appear to have vanished by the time the 1880s recension on customary law was prepared along with revised settlements in distressed areas. Control over land and houses—that is, any form of productive wealth—seemed by now to be reserved for men. Women acquired rights of maintenance to such property only through their relationships to men as their daughters, wives, mothers, and widows. A daughter could share in her father's estate only if he died before she was married; her brothers saw it as their urgent duty to marry her off so that this stipulated outcome was avoided.

The revisions and updates of customary law undertaken in Ludhiana, Ferozepur, and other eastern districts produced the same shift from women's control over their own property, even more markedly among rural populations than among the urban Brahmins and Khatris. In 1885, T. Gordon Walker, the assessment officer of Ludhiana district, in inquiring after the customs of the Jats, discovered that there was "no clear class of property belonging to females, and over which a husband has no control," although there was disagreement over who controlled movable property, particularly cattle. "The sense of the male agricultural population (of all native society, I may say) is strongly against anything that would tend to give the wife the power of acting apart from her husband; and there is certainly no necessity at present for protecting the special property of married women" (Walker 1885: 73–75). The only items over which peasant women still had control were the jewelry and clothes they received at the time of their marriage as *daaj* from their natal family and *vari* from her in-laws, but this was paltry or nonexistent among the bride-price-paying Jats.

Similar declines in the position of women were uniformly recorded in the dozens of volumes of *rivaj-i-am* compiled and updated with every fresh settlement of land revenue throughout all the districts of the Punjab, particularly among peasant proprietors and large landowners, regardless of religion or caste. Muslims came out as bluntly against the notion of women's special property as did Sikhs and most Hindus; only the dowry-paying castes of Hindus still admitted that women controlled their own *stridhan*.

Wilson affirmed that he found no such thing in Gurgaon, even though his notes are replete with examples. The preponderance of bride-price-paying agriculturalists (particularly Jats) in the region might also have led to his conclusion. Neither Wilson nor Tupper made any effort to ask about dowries per se, which is amazing considering that they were thought to be an ingrained tribal custom that brought ruin to peasant families and had been determined (by Wilson, Edwardes, and other officials) to be the leading cause of female infanticide. Wilson admitted that even among Jats and Gujars (pastoralists) "some little difference is made with regard to ornaments &c., given to a wife by her father and his family." Among Brahmins, Banias, and all other tribes, "gifts made to a wife by her father or her relatives, or property acquired by herself, are considered more or less at the disposal of the wife; and her husband does not make use of it, except in case of necessity, or with the wife's consent. She can dispose of it as she pleases, so long as the disposal is not improper" (Wilson 1881: 147). It is hard to believe that a wife who had implicit rights in her husband's landed property (unless they were estranged), in which she had traditionally maintained a life interest by living with her sons in the family home, and who had exclusive rights to her jewelry and other movables, including cattle, would not merit a category of her own in the customary code books.

In looking at the answers of various tribes in various districts to Tupper's questions about *stridhan*, a distinct pattern emerges. Some subgroups of Jats and lesser agricultural tribes seem not to have known about or acknowledged *stridhan*, but Brahmins, Rajputs, Khatris, and Banias thought of it as the movable property of females over which they had exclusive control. The husband could call in *stridhan*, only with the wife's consent for most tribes, and only in times of crisis. The real reason for ascertaining this from the tribes, of course, was to ensure that a woman's wealth would not be beyond the revenue official's grasp if the husband or sons were in arrears with their payments. There is no doubt that the first collateral offered to obtain a loan was a woman's jewelry, but moneylenders themselves now hungered for land and were willing to lend larger sums at high interest rates to give the borrower an opportunity to default on his loan repayments and become vulnerable to foreclosure.

By the 1850s, the idea of property in the subcontinent had acquired all the refinements of the English idea of property: it was classified as inherited or self-acquired, and as movable or immovable, and very different conditions attached to its disposal depending on its classification. In defining the "special wealth of females," the British were able to ignore the implicit wealth of married women in the family land and the lapse of their shared rights occasioned by the creation of individual proprietary titles in land given to the male head of a family. Wilson's penchant for anachronisms, in which he read the future into the past, and his zeal for minimizing any customary rights of women that had existed in precolonial times, were echoed in most of the other volumes of customary law, since his methods, categories, and final report on Gurgaon were treated as a model to be emulated by personnel in other districts. Wilson ended the ambiguities concerning a daughter's rights by phrasing the "custom" unequivocally: "a father cannot, without the consent of his sons or near kindred (males related through males) make a gift of any part of his immovable property, ancestral or acquired, to his daughter, daughter's son, or any other relative related through a female" (Wilson 1881: 164). The categories of immovable and moveable, ancestral or acquired are English anachronisms because they had not existed in prior usage.

The concept of property stood altered in the most radical way in that universe of swift changes brought about by the British, and on this central concept were predicated the new equations of rights of women and men. The fact that dowries gradually incorporated "movable" liquid assets such as cash and gold made them exceptionally useful in acquiring productive and "immovable" assets, and that this possibility of conversion was instrumental in changing the contents of a dowry and in shifting its control from a woman to either her husband or his father.

We can clearly see Wilson welding the patriarchal strictures of the past and modern capitalistic ideas of individual rights to create hybrid meanings that transmuted into law. It emerged that wives did not have any special or ordinary wealth, and daughters could not inherit. This custom contradicted the colonial fact of having endowed an individual with rights in agricultural land, which he could dispose of as he wished; he could "will" away his property but obviously not to his daughters, and only to his sons or his agnatic kin. This generated a great number of legal disputes in families, particularly between fathers and sons and between brothers, even as it hermetically sealed any loopholes that existed in customary patriarchal law to permit daughters to inherit. It virtually dictated the corollary that daughters could get only movable property as dowry. A father could, in his lifetime, exclude one or more sons from the division of his property, of whatever kind, but after his death, all sons became entitled to share in the father's estate. With some exasperation, Wilson noted a "great confusion [among the headmen] between gifts, inheritance, and (to some extent) sale," as well there might be in a time of such enormous changes (Wilson 1881: 164). The colonial state had made sure that once the title of a particular property and its revenue liability were pinned together onto a determinate owner, he should take full responsibility for the payment of government dues, first and foremost, or lose the property registered in his name.

Finally, it might be said that the whole corpus of local patriarchal "customary" laws was recast into an alien mold. It betrayed traces of Roman tribal law in its devolution of property to the tenth degree among agnates, as well as the Anglo-Saxon obsession with laws of inheritance. The codification of these laws forged an instrument of alienation and adjudication in default of revenue rather than a depiction of the social and economic guidelines, or customs, that had been negotiated daily by Punjabis in the process of living. The codification, clarifications, and precedents were intended for revenue officers and the courts; titled landowners would have to learn what their customs meant in their newly translated form, mediated through the minds of officers who knew a very different kind of "property." They would also find out, as litigiousness became the latest vice (according to the British) on which they squandered their resources, that they could be left powerless, digging themselves deeper in debt, against a savvy moneylender or the state, both of whom were far better prepared to use the laws than the landowners were. And with no recourse but the courts—for the local *panchayat* had no jurisdiction over property titles or land disputes—the proprietor knew he was doomed. A court verdict could overturn generations' worth of inherent rights in the product of ancestral lands. The more people became discontented with the new meanings of property and challenged the existential finality of alienations, the more the government exchequer was enriched with court fees, and the more lawyers fattened on the profits of litigation. Stripped of the substance and glue of social life, particularly the direct mediation of women, the "customary laws" gathered by the British become a strictly male-oriented, self-serving code that was a monument to government priorities of tax collection and social control.

Soon the initial pretense fell away that these volumes of allegedly everyday customs were anything more than a ready-reckoner to help revenue officials find the next heir in line should the original titleholder be dead, in arrears, or, as was increasingly the case, *mafrur* (literally, "absconding"). Precedents involving property disputes were added to later editions of these volumes, so that they contained brief case histories for revenue officers to consult. Many of these only grounded more firmly the rights of agnatic kin over those of a widow or a daughter in the event that there was no son; sons were the key to unperturbed succession. In fact, so closely were the customary law volumes tied to revenue collection in official practice that they were not only revised with each new assessment but were soon relegated to serving as mere appendices in the revenue assessment volumes printed in the late 1880s. New assessments, the Punjab government was loath to admit, were carried out only when previous assessments proved to be universally steep to the point of driving the landowning peasantry into debt and to the brink of rebellion.

These major misunderstandings and convenient reinterpretations of the dynamic of Punjabi society would not have become a codified reality that in turn changed the reality on the ground if the British had included women and ordinary men (who were not headmen) in their consultations, polls, and information-gathering ventures. The deliberate omission reflected their own anxieties founded in the erosion of upper-class male bastions in England, where women had won limited rights to property in 1880 and working-class men a wider franchise in 1882 after heroic and protracted struggles against the British government and Parliament.

So how do society and economy become more masculine? By allowing only men to dictate, interpret, change, and amend the laws, customs, and practices, and doing so on a single day so that consultations with wives and mothers are not possible. A strongly tribe-based, muscular-smelling, hirsute (mustaches and beards being the fashion on both sides) customary law code emerged at the end of this day. It is interesting to note that no tribe brings up the matter of sati, or "suttee," the custom of widows immolating themselves; no hint is given of anything except the increasing notice of "forced marriage of widows" among landowning Jat peasants. There is also no discussion about the killing of daughters, which *was* customary, and it does not help to speculate how the village headmen would have handled a question from Tupper on the topic. This total lack of articulation among the departments investigating "social evils" and making social legislation such as the Infanticide Act and those gathering data to codify customary law is in itself an interesting disjunction. If social legislation was allegedly to protect the rights of women; the tribal customary laws went a great distance to negate these rights.

But there were other major changes making society more masculine, and it is to these we must urgently turn.

PUNJABI MANPOWER: MARTIAL, MIGRATORY, AND SELF-EXPLOITING

For all the imperial pretensions of having created a modern administration and instituted the rule of law, state power still largely depended, as it had done in precolonial kingdoms, on the twin pillars of land revenue and the army. Native manpower—micromanaged to remain loyal and self-exploiting as never before—was the key to the stability of the Raj. If the meanings of property, revenue, and a customary way of life had been brought into the legal domain, colonial patriarchal values had been cross-pollinated with indigenous "tribal" values to create a stouter, more woman-resistant hybrid. The expansion of exclusively male opportunities for employment and migration and the half-baked "free" market in commodity production and land were the final turn of the screw in the ambivalent modernization that the colonial state offered. Beginning in the second half of the nineteenth century, Punjabi men were used to bring forest and scrubland under the plough, to develop and inhabit the uncharted acres within the Punjab so as to expand the revenue base of the government, to build a network of canals and barrages on the five rivers that flowed through some of the most fertile land on the globe, to lay railway lines to facilitate commodity and troop movements, and to form the largest standing army in the world in order to defend the frontiers of the empire in India, quell internal unrest, and expand the African empire. Punjabi men were, in addition, exported as migrant labor to South Africa, Canada, and Australia. Since there are some excellent treatments of the development of the Punjab under British rule that cover these subjects, I will concentrate more on the effect of these changes on female infanticide, the marriage market, and marriage customs and expenses in order to conclude my argument on the masculinization of the Punjab economy.[8]

The Punjab had always been well stocked with martial lore and tales of astounding heroism to match the almost continual warfare that plagued this region and shaped the men and women of all three major creeds that inhabited it and fought for power. Geopolitics had made military skills part of the workaday repertoire of Hindu Kshatriyas, Jats, and even Brahmins long before Islam and

Sikhism produced their own more hirsute and religiously inspired contingents. Muslim Pathans, Afghans, and the militant organization created by the tenth and last guru of the Sikhs, Govind Singh, had battled fiercely as Mughal power declined in the late seventeenth century. For the population of the Punjab, which was both the gateway and the path to the fertile plains of Hindustan, being martially adept was a matter of political necessity rather than racial pride. The Punjabi soldiery found itself duly admired in a typical nineteenth-century racial construction of their prowess as "the martial races of India," and the British were quick to sort out the "martial" from the "nonmartial" Punjabis, classifying whole castes rather than individuals into these categories (Cohen 1971: 32–87). British appellations, one might add, came only once they had empirical proof of the warworthiness of these Punjabis after fighting the famous pairs of Sikh and Afghan wars in the nineteenth century, as they extended their northwestern frontier and played the Great Game with Russia.[9] Fortunately an insightful ethnohistory of the military labor market in Hindustan is available for a detailed understanding of how Punjabis evolved into distinct lineages, tribes, and races in the perceptions of imperial scholars and bureaucrats (Kolff 1990).

In keeping with the racist mentality of the colonial administration, a much-decorated lieutenant general of the Indian Army, Sir George MacMunn, studiously culled all the pertinent racial thinking of the previous century into a brazen compendium (MacMunn 1933). It was written at the height of the nationalist movement and Gandhi's challenge ("the gentle and merciless race of hereditary moneylenders, from which Lala Ghandi [sic] springs") to the Raj. "Indeed to understand what is meant by the martial races of India," he declared, "is to understand from the inside the real story of India. We do not speak of the martial races of Britain as distinct from the non-martial, nor of Germany, nor of France. But in India we speak of the martial races as a thing apart . . . because the mass of the people have neither martial aptitude nor physical courage," which was, by and large, a product of the degenerative "effect of prolonged years of varying religions on their adherents, of early marriage, premature brides, and juvenile eroticism, of a thousand years of malaria and hookworm, and other ills of neglected sanitation in a hot climate, and . . . of aeons of tropical sun on races that were once white and lived in uplands and on cool steppes" (ibid.: 2). Of the 350 million Indians, he reckoned that perhaps there may have been 3 million "manly" males between the ages of twenty and thirty-five, thus explaining the oft-subjugated nature of the subcontinent (ibid.: 2–3). The entire book is studded with such gems, and the connection made between degeneracy and effeminacy is reiterated so often that it is clear that being "manly" and capable of inflicting violence to resolve conflict was so admired that it must have encouraged this behavior in domestic situations, as well.

After the nigh-disastrous Mutiny of 1857, the armed forces of the East India Company were drastically reorganized into Britain's Indian Army with vastly improved conditions of service and a host of political safeguards. One of the principal changes was the discontinuance of recruitment of Bengali soldiers (Bengal had contributed twenty-eight infantry units to the army, as the Punjab had in 1862) and the stepping up of recruitment from among the "martial races," chiefly from the Punjab, which had not quite been gripped by rebellion and with whose help the mutiny was quelled. The Punjabis were classified as a "martial race"—a serious tribute in terms of nineteenth-century British racist perceptions and quite the opposite of the British view of the "cowardly" and "effeminate" Bengalis (see Sinha 1995). The British built on the already existing proud self-perceptions of a variety of Punjabis. Muslims of the Punjab and elsewhere had thrived on their belief that as meat-eating, hairy-chested, strong men from the hardy climes beyond India, they could easily defeat the weakling Hindu armies in the subcontinent. This rhetoric, bolstered by the British discourse on martial and effeminate races, informs the views of the rank-and-file Punjabi soldiers in the Pakistani and Indian armies to this day.[10] An informal state of war has intermittently existed between these two nations since the violent partition that was also the parturition of Pakistan more than fifty years ago.

By the late nineteenth century, Punjabis made up fifty-seven infantry units (not counting the Punjabis poached by the Bombay Presidency to supply their eighteen units), and Bengal (which included Bihar and Orissa), fewer than fifteen. Bengalis, always "effeminate," were now dismissed as "hopeless poltroons," while the Punjabi Muslims and Sikhs were seen as real men with hair on their chests who could be counted on in the battlefield (Cohen 1971: 43–47).

At the start of World War I, in which the Indian Army was to play a large role on behalf of the British masters, the ranks of Indian combat troops swelled to well over a hundred and fifty thousand men, and two-thirds of them had been recruited in the Punjab. By the Armistice of 1918, Indian troops numbered over half a million, of which four hundred thousand, or four out of five Indian soldiers, were Punjabi *jawan*, or young men (the preferred sons), serving in the infantry. There were another hundred thousand Punjabis enlisted in the noncombatant forces called the Imperial Service Troops, serving chiefly as regimental porters, muleteers, *syces* or horse keepers, and *bhistis* or water carriers, the last made famous by Kipling in his ballad *Gunga Din*. The census of 1921 records 190,078 Muslims, 83,515 Hindus, and 97,016 Sikhs as combatants. The Sikhs were recruited in disproportionately large numbers, as they made up only 12 percent of the total Punjabi population, whereas the Muslims hovered around the 50 percent mark and the Hindus along with a smattering of others made up the 38 percent remainder. Rawalpindi became the district from which the greatest number of recruits was drawn, contributing some 114,202 by 1918; not far behind were men from Jullunder, Ambala, and Lahore districts (Ellinwood 1976: 43–47). Even though Sikhs were proportionately the most numerous, they were discriminated against and began resisting recruitment as the militant Akali Movement began gathering strength in the countryside in response to their many grievances against the British in the early part of the twentieth century (Fox 1985: 78–104).

The colonial Indian Army offered greater inducements than previous rulers had, since the former had to recruit fifteen thousand men a year and nearly twice that during the war years. Indians served mainly as sepoys (a corruption of *sepahi*, or foot soldier). A few were promoted to the rank of viceroy's commissioned officers late in their careers, but they could not hope to become part of the top brass, the king's commissioned officers, whose ranks were reserved for Europeans, with rare exceptions. Gone also was the upward mobility that had been possible in the days of Ranjit Singh and the Mughals, when to be a *naukar* (armed adventurer-soldier-state servant) was indeed adventurous, and a brave man could become a *sardar*, a leader of men, to win recognition and play an active part in the politics of war and the royal courts (Kolff 1990).

The inducements, which included the pre-British practice of awarding land grants to officers, were the perquisites of a modern standing army—having a fixed tenure as a soldier with a fixed cash salary and receiving a pension after retirement from loyal service, or a smaller pension for the widow if death intervened. In war years this did not prove to be a sufficient lure, so the colonial state added cash bonuses, free rations of food and clothing, and free burials (although nothing is said about cremations, the custom of Hindus and Sikhs alike) to stimulate recruitment. The notion that these were dazzling improvements might be difficult to sustain, but in the hard times created by the very revenue policies that generated the money to pay for them, a military career brought the peasant family the security that had been compromised by making its lien on land so tenuous. The salary for a sepoy in wartime was eleven rupees a month, plus the perquisites of subsidized board, lodging, and uniforms; this permitted savings to be remitted to the sepoy's family, which could be very useful to pay revenue, get out of debt, or buy more land. But one must not forget that for the British this was defense of the empire cheaply bought, since Indians served as cannon fodder, keeping costs in European lives and salaries to a minimum, and they traveled wherever they were ordered to go.

In 1917, sepoy remittances were in the range of 4 to 5 million rupees (although it is sobering to remember that this was coming from the pockets of the brothers at home who were toiling to make the very revenue payments that constituted the state budget!). News of casualties was daunting, with thirty-five thousand dead and seventy thousand seriously injured in World War I, and the countryside was simmering with economic and nationalist disaffection. Confinement to a life lived by strict rules in one's own regimental quarters in the cantonment (a purpose-built area for the army in each major town of the Punjab and elsewhere in India), in deliberately segregated religious or caste units, drilled and disciplined into obedience, marching in lockstep, and perceived continually as inferior in all considerations to Europeans, made for a very different martial ethos from that fostered by the political contract between ruler and soldier of old (Kolff 1990).

To prevent the kind of mutiny they had experienced from their sepoys in 1857, the British organized religiously segregated regimental units from the alleged "martial races"; Sikhs, Pathans, Rajputs, and Gurkhas each had their own discrete cavalry and infantry units. This severely restricted Hindus of other castes who wished to join the army, particularly the Khatris, who had served in Maharaja Ranjit Singh's forces. Although none of the military histories bring this up, it is important to mention that Hindus, particularly Khatris, who were acknowledged as Kshatriyas but were arbitrarily lumped together with the "trading castes" in the British census reports (since large numbers of them were educated and also engaged in trade), were seldom accepted into the British military service. Under the British, Khatris, who had also been landholders, acquired further vast acreage in auctions and by foreclosure as agriculture became profitable, until the Land Alienation Act of 1900 forbade them to do so as a "non-agricultural" tribe. They had always been much more occupationally diverse than their origins in the "warrior caste" suggested. Educated, entrepreneurial, and opportunistic, they were shown in the 1911 census to be in a wide range of occupations including the military, trade, and agriculture. By other accounts, such as in Prakash Tandon's *Punjabi Century*, they appear to have become the core of the emergent English-educated middle class whose members were to be found in leading positions in Punjabi society as lawyers, doctors, military officers, bankers, farm owners, and money lenders. In Lahore, Punjab's premier city, elegantly built by the emperors Akbar and Jahangir, enlarged by Maharaja Ranjit Singh, and expanded and embellished by the British with a large cantonment and civil lines traversed by a tree-lined canal, the Khatris were the preeminent elite. Their fine bungalows and lifestyles closely imitated those of the highest and most strictly endogamous and hypergamous caste of all— the British rulers themselves. We are already familiar with Thorburn's vitriol about the Banias in Rawalpindi and Ibbetson's particularly jaundiced and communally charged view of the Khatris in general.

These Khatris were not considered suitable recruits for the army—unless, of course, they acquired the markers of the "martial races." Many families in the late nineteenth century and even until Independence got around this artificially imposed caste barrier by raising one or more sons as Sikhs, chiefly by having them adopt the name "Singh" and grow hair and a beard to match. In other words, the British invented the hidebound compartments for Punjabi tribes not only in discursive practice but also in the actual implementation of their own policies, particularly in the army. The British enforced rigid occupational boundaries by creating "traditional agriculturists," "martial races," and "trading castes." They could not trust the educated Khatri to be as obedient a soldier as the Jat, and certainly they missed the rationale for the many male children being produced in these families. Each son could be directed into a different occupation to hedge the family's bets for the future.

The true draw for the young men who flocked to the army was the steady pay, the pension after ten years of service, and the promise of one day owning a few well-watered acres in the fertile new canal colonies. The colonial government had decided that the native practice of giving land grants for heroic services ought to be tried after all, and this promised land, like all proverbial such land, was as effective a recruiting device as any invented. This is what made the soldiers eligible husbands, far more so than those who did not have jobs or who had land that was in danger of becoming encumbered. Any Punjabi family interested in improving its condition in life could plan to selectively raise more boys, while committing the most heinous of sins defined in their own culture and by the laws of their British rulers.

The colonization of western Punjab is unique among the developments under colonialism in the subcontinent, since in no other part of the country were such land resources available (see Ali 1988 for an excellent account of the canal colonies). It was not just an extension of the canal building in already settled agricultural tracts, such as the western United Provinces or eastern Punjab, to supplement facilities in *barani* (rain-fed) agriculture. This particular colonization— now mainly in Pakistan—actually increased canal-irrigated lands in the Punjab almost fivefold, from some three million acres to fourteen million fertile and productive acres. It entailed intensive hard labor and a vast migration of Punjabis of all three faiths from the settled parts of the Punjab. It also led to an enormous assault on the ecology of the region, since these acres were forest and grazing areas, only sparsely populated by nomadic tribes and their herds of goats and cattle. Cutting down forests, opening up new lands to agriculture, and building, for more than half a century, a new and intricate system of irrigation canals employed large numbers of Punjabi men and boys who were imported as migrants from other parts of the state.

The colonization of these lands provided a much-needed safety valve that allowed resettlement of the "well-to-do yeomen of the best class of agriculturists" from overpopulated districts, who would exploit their own wives, sons, and menials, and would "constitute healthy agricultural communities of the best Punjab type" (cited in Ali 1988: 29). A portion (between 7 and 15 percent) of the newly available acreage in each canal colony was put up for sale at auction at an ever-increasing market price to recover any costs the state might have incurred in the development process. The buyers at these auctions were "men of substance" from commercial, professional, or landed groups. The remaining acreage was distributed as civil and military grants (the army fought for larger and larger pieces of this pie) to three classes of men with allegedly bona fide agricultural backgrounds: the peasant (*abadkar*), who received between one-half and two squares of irrigated land (one square equaled 27.7 acres), the yeoman (*sufedposh*), who received two to five squares, and the capitalist (*rais*), who received six to twenty squares. Peasants had to remain occupancy tenants of the state and were disallowed proprietary rights, "designed by altering their status [from proprietors to occupancy tenants] *to protect settlers from the consequences of their own want of thrift and foresight*" (Ali 1988: 19; emphasis added).

The dramatic reversal in British policy toward peasants was striking, particularly as the allegations of the peasants' incorrigible improvidence persisted, and the British refused to make changes in the rigidity of their own revenue system. Instead, as Imran Ali has so persuasively argued and, indeed, as my own research has verified, claims of British munificence or even "paternalism" (Bhattacharya 1992: 113–39) to the Punjab peasant ring hollow, since their policies were grounded in profit and political expedience, and "reflected both the type of society the British wanted to create in the canal colonies and the class of people they wished to appease . . . hereditary agriculturists belonging to land-holding lineages" (Ali 1988: 19). Each colony, as it was developed, became an invincible political weapon that entrenched conservative interests by creating a strong band of agricultural and military families who owed their existence to the state and were unswervingly loyal to and collaborative with the colonial authorities in turbulent times. Such policies made for "dominant" agricultural tribes, particularly in the Muslim and Sikh communities, since the Land Alienation Act of 1900 was based on a belief in organically constituted tribes—and agriculture even today is referred to as the "culture" of the Punjab. Even though Brahmins, Rajputs, and Khatris had always owned land, their access to land was now legally restricted because they were not "agricultural tribes." But there were judicious exceptions made for some members of the Khatri professional and military elite. One such exception was that made for Baba Khem Singh Bedi, who received a rare knighthood and was allotted 7,800 acres because he was the head of the Bedis, a Khatri "clan" with enormous influence among the leading Sikh families, whose loyalty was seen as paramount to imperial interests (Ali 1988: 17). As we saw in chapter 2, these same Bedis were singled out as infanticidal villains in another set of reports. This blatant contradiction underscores the point that development had little to do with beneficence or with the Raj's professed "civilizing mission," and much to do with keeping the rich and powerful natives loyal by systematically vesting them with an interest in colonial rule.

In reflecting on the nexus between the military and the rural elite in Pakistan today, Ali tracks its roots back to the unprecedented dimensions of soldier settlement in western Punjab. To cite but one of his many illuminating examples, it is useful to look at how military and strategic considerations came to dominate the selection of grantees and the allocation of colony lands. Jhelum colony, with a total of 540,000 acres, was settled between 1902 and 1906, and initially 75 percent of the acreage was reserved for peasant grants. All these plans were swiftly set aside, though, when the official Horse and Mule-Breeding Commission, a body convened to explore the possibility of raising Indian horseflesh to replace expensive imports from Australia, recommended that the Punjab canal colonists "be required to maintain mares for breeding horses and mules for the army," and the government of India seized the idea with alacrity. "The outcome of the Horse-breeding Commission's recommendations was that the selection of grantees now depended not on population densities and agricultural skills," Ali tersely states, "but on the possession by applicants of mares suitable for breeding remounts for the cavalry." Ultimately, it depended on the imperial state, "whether it wished to utilize the potential of colonization for economic development or distort it for purposes of its own survival. One of the roots of underdevelopment in the Punjab lay in the fact that the latter option was adopted" (Ali 1988: 22–23; also see 190–57).

The canals brought prosperity to newly opened colonies to which the hardest-working peasants were cajoled to migrate to till the soil, and the state and the peasants shared in the profits of their toil. But the canals also began slowly to create a terrible ecological backlash, which is still in process in the once-fertile fields, most of which became part of Pakistan. Two foreseen tragic consequences—malaria epidemics and infertility of irrigated lowlands due to an increase in the salinity of the soil—cost lives and caused revenue defaults. An early example of this fate, whose effects would continue into the late twentieth century, was the opening of the Western Jumna Canal in 1840–1841, which raised the water table and made some of the contiguous eastern districts of present-day Haryana, including Panipat, Gurgaon, and Karnal, a barren waste of waterlogged, saline land that looked like "snow-covered fields." For thirty years there was no reassessment of land revenue, and appeals from the distressed peasants were not heeded. Acts of last resort—desertions, vagrancy, and immigration to fertile districts to serve as bonded labor—became routine. The small proprietor was now driven from his land in stages: he first landed in the squeezing embrace of the moneylender, then he was forced to the district courts to even more fiscally ruinous litigation, and perhaps took to drink; eventually he submitted to the hammer blows of the state auctioneer's gavel.

These few sentences tell the tale of a great deal of eastern Punjab and how its social exchange was affected. Quiet desperation built pressure to exploit customary ways of obtaining cash, gold, or silver to buy land elsewhere, or to replenish a herd—and dowry was a logical place to look. The will to obtain larger dowries from the families of daughters-in-law, to demand more in cash, gold, and other liquid assets, becomes vivid as one leafs through dozens of official reports that dutifully recorded the effects of indebtedness, foreclosures, barren plots, and deaths of cattle for lack of fodder. A sample statement from one of these reports submitted by revenue officials gives us a flavor of the peasant's lot in 1872–1880, after three decades of British rule in the Punjab. A Mr. Sharer was dispatched to examine the complaints of the peasants in Karnal district. His investigations showed that the water table had risen sixty feet to barely two or three feet below the surface, causing the tract of land to become totally barren.

> The possible resources of the biswadars [peasant owners] of several estates are now exhausted. They have borrowed money at extravagant interest; they have become farm slaves of some Bania [money lender] residing in their village; they have sold their trees on their estates; they have sold their daughters; they have sold silver ornaments and brass utensils [presumably the dowries brought by their wives or daughters-in-law] and as many of their cattle as was possible to spare; and no conceivable source of income is any longer available. . . . No remissions [in revenue payments] have ever been made, so far as I can discover, on account of general deterioration [of the soil]. (cited in Ibbetson 1883b: 5, para. 165)

Ibbetson calculated the area of land rendered uncultivable because of increased salinity at 507,974 acres in 1878 in Karnal district, increased from 1,255 acres in 1820.

Thus the difference between the security of the rights in land that sons inherited and the "movable property" that daughters inherited as dowry was greatly reduced. The dowry became as great a prize for men as their inherited rights in land had been. If anything, dowry was more valuable and versatile in a situation where the land was barren. The devastation of the land was not the expected outcome of a dark colonial plot—it was just a tragic and unintended ecological and etiological disaster that undermined the ability of the peasants to pay their fixed dues on fixed dates. So indebtedness and poverty grew in the midst of the new prosperity, and dowries, the traditional safety net for women, now served the interests of the husband's family to purchase more land, pay revenue in a bad year, or bail themselves out of the hands of loan sharks.

One other feature that made the masculine thrust of this economy ever more pronounced has been little mentioned in the colonial papers and even less studied by scholars, since its major effects were on the lower agrarian classes. This was the rise in drinking that was to overtake the countryside as a scourge. The colonial state had a uniform policy on liquor and excise taxes in the Indian empire; the excise taxes grossed countrywide were second only to land revenue, which speaks volumes. What David Hardiman discovered in Gujarat, and what my own work on Lucknow and the liquor policy enforced there revealed, would obtain as well in the Punjab (Hardiman 1985: 165–228; Oldenburg 1984: 125–31). The colonial government banned the production and consumption of the more nutritious indigenous brews, which used the tapping of the toddy palm or the blossoms of the mahua tree to make toddy and *daru*, or country liquor, which were neither highly intoxicating nor addictive. In their place the government introduced Western-style distilled spirits, which were strongly intoxicating and addictive, preserved the manufacture and distribution of liquor as a state monopoly, and ordained that liquor must be sold and consumed only on licensed premises. This had another, even less studied effect—violence against women by men who drank and became disorderly, which in fact had already become the "besetting weakness" of the soldiers who were entitled to rum rations in the army. "The Sikhs' love of drink is, of course, notorious," observed the ICS officer Malcolm Darling; he really objected to it for the even greater extravagance it implied because it was served at weddings. Drinking was expensive both because it was addictive and because the price of liquor was high as a result of the new excise duty on it—this being the government's excuse to collect vast sums of money while claiming to discourage the habit they had introduced. We know today the role that liquor and controlled substances play in the commission of crime and the social havoc they wreak, and in the absence of a detailed study of the drinking habits of Punjabis, one has to extrapolate from the scattered anecdotal evidence in Darling's work.

Darling reported several anecdotes that suggested growing alcoholism among Sikh Jats in central Punjab. One Sikh landlord confessed to loving his drink to the extent that he stole money from his father to keep up his habit. Another "had drunk most of his substance away when he received a visit from his married daughter. He took her jewellery and sold it for drink. When she went back to her husband he was so angry that she returned to her father and begged her ornaments back that she might not be dishonoured. Overcome with shame, the father went to his well, tied his puggaree [turban] around his neck and, binding hands and feet, hung himself" (Darling 1934: 114).

Some women, particularly those whose husbands were weak or habitually drunk, took business into their own hands. Darling reported that Sikh women in particular, and some women among the Khatris and Aroras (a trading caste), had taken to moneylending since they had withdrawn themselves from agriculture. "There are over fifty who do it in Attari and a sprinkling of them in the villages round Kasel [in Ferozepore Division in Central Punjab]. Most are in the smallest way of business, but [one] had accumulated 'a very fine estate.' She took to it finding herself married to a worthless fellow who drank." The explanation that husbands' drunkenness provoked their wives to take on moneylending was also cited in two instances in Bhakna and Kalan. Darling's informants "tittered" as they spoke of weak husbands. "No accounts are kept, nor are they necessary since the loans are nearly always against jewellery. All that is done is to tie a ticket to the ornament and fix a date for the redemption. The rates are the same as those charged by men, viz. 18 and ¾ per cent for secured loans and 25 per cent for unsecured loans" (Darling 1934: 112–13).

Darling also reported on the spread of other expensive and sometimes destructive habits. Official estimates of those who took opium (which the British had forced to be cultivated and produced on a large scale since the early nineteenth century so they could exchange it for Chinese silver) was about 20 percent of men over thirty and 70 to 80 percent of those over fifty years of age. About half of these were supposed to take the stuff "habitually." This was true of Hindus and Sikhs, who also indulged in chewing tobacco, taking snuff, and drinking tea. He also reported that people had taken to eating white bread instead of whole wheat unleavened *chapati*, and these "little piles of white loaves three or four inches square, are now to be seen in the bazaars" (Darling 1934: 114). The last item was again more expensive than the traditional homemade bread and far less nutritious, but most of these changes in consumption were seen as marks of progress that represented a rise in the standard of living. A more recent survey conducted in the Indian Punjab showed that a household with even one male who drank heavily spent an average of 40 percent less on food per capita and less also on education, clothing, and medicine than a household without this disability (Harriss 1990: 49–68). The strain on the household budget and overall indebtedness were caused chiefly by land revenue payments in bad years and by new addictions that cost far more money than old ones; in addition, women seem to have had less control over spending decisions as household resources came to be held more exclusively in male hands.

These many pieces of policy and prejudice added up to an almost pathologically severe "preference for sons" among all castes, tribes, and creeds because men—strong young men—were the only avenue to status, wealth, employment, and land. Women receded into the background as total dependents in the eyes of the law, the polity, and the economy. Gender differences were now more material than ever in the past.

PUNJABI WOMAN THROUGH COLONIAL EYES

It is not difficult to conjure up a vivid image of the Punjabi peasant, soldier, or urban dweller by reading the reams of descriptive material found in reports, census volumes, and famine investigations, or even from what has been selectively presented here. What remains elusive is a matching profile of the Punjabi woman from these same sources. Women are seldom mentioned, and when they are, they are portrayed with little sympathy as illiterate, superstitious, and overly fecund, with unclean and cruel habits, and submissive to the point of mindlessness—totally in need of civilizing uplift. They appear chiefly as victims who are killed at birth—unwanted, generally shadowy beings with little or no education, a sexual danger and a financial burden, whose "worth" is determined by dowry or brideprice. The average British bureaucrat did not "see" Punjabi women; their veiled faces became the metonym for the backward culture they represented. The officers were imperious and aloof, and Punjabi women quite literally remained out of the sight of strangers to their villages or, in towns, to their homes; if they appeared at all, they kept their faces covered and did not speak. Covering the face and not appearing before male strangers were cultural practices that had evolved in this war zone largely as means of self-preservation, rather than innate modesty, as conquerors were often abductors and rapists, and women were often treated as the booty of war.

In spite of the concern about female infanticide, we find little empathy for Punjabi women and even less investment in their education or health. We get a fairly close look at the rural woman in the early twentieth century in works of two well-known Punjab civilians, Malcolm Darling and Frank Lugard Brayne.[11] Both had idées fixes: Brayne, the tireless "improver," had memorably said, "[T]he routine of defaecation goes to the root of citizenship. . . . Let me ordain where the nation shall defaecate and I care not who makes their laws" (cited in Oldenburg 1984: 96). Darling, more the scholar and the analyst, believed that "fragmentation of [land] holdings blocks the way [of progress]; and it cannot be too often repeated that, till holdings are consolidated, no great advance can be made. Till then all that can be done is to induce the cultivator to use better seed, perhaps buy a Meston plough, and, if possible, join a village bank" (Darling 1925: 185). With the rise of the Indian nationalist movement, which had galvanized around the issue of the widespread poverty created by the British Raj, ICS men were no longer free to critique imperial policies as Thorburn had done; that would only add fuel to the fire smoldering around them in the 1920s and 1930s.

The varying impressions that Indian women made on these two men during their incessant forays into Punjabi villages, though mostly unflattering, certainly deepen and complicate the picture of the generic Indian peasant woman victim and "burden" that was widely recognized by British officials and India reformers alike. All his bigotry aside, Brayne did not underestimate the power of Punjabi women. He understood that they were the chief decision makers in their homes and therefore were a key factor in village uplift that had been overlooked by his colleagues. He pointed out that when he and other officers addressed meetings attended only by male villagers to propose reform and found them unresponsive, "we curse what we think is their amazing stupidity because they do not immediately agree" with the suggestions. "How can they agree," he writes, "until they have gone home and talked to their wives?" (Brayne 1937: 120–21). In one of his Socratic-style dialogues on the subject of female education, he asks the villagers, "Who rules your homes?" and then supplies the answer: "You do not rule your home any more than I do mine. . . . You know very well that you cannot change a custom without their leave and you cannot start a new custom without their leave. Is that true or not?" "I am afraid it is Socrates." Although he understood the dynamics of the Punjabi household, he also thought these female decision makers to be the true bane of the countryside. Women had to be educated to save the household, to nurture good citizens, to create "the peace of happy homes, of empty jails."[12] Punjabi society, with its uneducated women who raised their sons to be liars, felons, and murderers, was in Brayne's view unredeemable because "a community reared by ignorant women is doomed."[13] The government, however, seemed to have no problem with violent men, for they made the best soldiers. A magistrate in Jhelum confided to Darling that he would find thieves south of the Jhelum River and murderers to the north of it: "[A] thief is a timid fellow, a man of smiles and wiles; but the murderer, having a more passionate temperament, is bolder, straighter, simpler, and when disciplined by military service, makes a first rate soldier" (Darling 1934: 37).

As Brayne instituted his famous uplift scheme, the Gurgaon Experiment, he badgered Haryana women to clean their homes, make them attractive, dig trenches for pitting night soil, build latrines, and keep their children clean. He did not question the abject poverty in which the majority of Haryana Jats lived. On the edge of the Rajasthan desert, its canal system in ruins and with its soil saline and barren, its landscape desolate except for thorny acacia trees, the region offered little hope of even marginal subsistence. According to Brayne, the miserable living conditions of the peasants were due to their own dread habits of extravagance and apathy and could not be blamed on the government. "Nor can it be blamed on poverty and the nearness of so many people to the brink of famine. People who have lost all fear of hunger have no higher standards than the rest. The raising of wages does not lead to improvements [but] the very reverse."[14] He strongly urged that "the Budgets of Government must cease to be used for 'men only'. . . . The women must have paid services, institutions and departments to enable them to carry out their jobs, be it farming, crafts, animal husbandry or bayonet fighting." He concluded that "[f]or a century [the government of] India has been trying to spread the light and progress by means of 'men only'. It has been a huge and costly experiment and everyone realises that it has now failed." He lamented that the hundreds of thousands of soldiers who had been taught hygiene and sanitation and who had retired on their pensions "do not teach hygiene at home. Why? Because the women of their home and village have not been taught also."[15] His nostrums were ignored because they would have meant a large investment in women's education; social legislation had a high profile in Britain and cost little more than the paper it was printed on.

Brayne was paternalistic, not feminist. His inspiration for urging women's education came from Alice MacLeod, the wife of another Punjab civilian, who directly supplied Brayne with her ideas on the terrible harm a society suffers from the neglect of its women. She seems to have brought him to the realization that women matter, and she gives a sharp answer to Brayne's question: Why have women not been included in the schemes of development and education by the government? Her answer in a letter to him must have deflated Brayne's conceit when she put his almost rhetorical query into broad perspective to expose a far more universal gender problem: "I imagine why men shrink from the idea of educating women is that most men do not *want* [emphasis in the original] an equal in the home to share their authority . . . c/f the horror with which in England a young man regards the woman he has been dancing with who has been to the University or the alacrity with which he terminates the acquaintance if possible."

She goes on to say that a man hates the idea of a wife whose education may enable her to best his own knowledge in science or the classics. "The idea of her [the wife's] helplessness and incompetence was irresistible to male vanity. If I am right that there is this attitude of mind to be overcome before we can get men to welcome the idea of education for women, you will have to think out some way of talking about it, for your talks [frequent and repetitive lectures to administrators and villagers] as they stand do not allow for the fact that this might be the ultimate stumbling-block."[16]

Brayne did not envisage the kind of education Alice MacLeod advocated in her letter. All he ever expected women to learn was housekeeping skills—sweeping, washing clothes, the practical "home science" popular in women's education in England at the time. He visited Punjabi women's homes but showed little skill in imagining their already laborious days that left them little time or energy for additional housework. He also wanted women to knit and embroider cloth, and little girls to skip rope. He organized a competition for "pretty homes." "The home is the centre of civilisation and we can judge the progress of any country by the niceness of its homes." [17] The response to this was not overwhelming, since most parents were too poor to afford the pretty colored pictures, furniture, equipment in the kitchen, and level of dressing that Brayne advocated.

The historian Clive Dewey rightly finds Brayne's schemes unrealistic under the circumstances: "There was no hope of improving childcare or housekeeping until economic development took place. The reservoir of underemployed female labour which Brayne hoped to draw on simply did not exist." Women in Gurgaon were already overextended, as they were chiefly the wives of market gardeners, and they would have had to give up income-generating activities, which they could only afford to do if their husbands produced more. "All over the Punjab," observes Dewey, drawing on the many illustrations of this that Darling offers in his travelogues, "there was correlation between the peasant's prosperity, the extent to which women withdrew from agriculture, and the care they devoted to their children and homes" (Dewey 1993: 85).

Darling himself was to point out that Brayne's critiques of most Punjabi women were unrealistic and exaggerated. He saw far less squalor and more endless toil on their part. He also realized that a woman's labor kept her husband out of debt. The reason Jat wives in Haryana were happy and virtuous, a husband informed Darling, was that they were "the slaves of their husbands and think it their duty to do their bidding in everything." His own wife, he proudly averred, rose at 4 A.M., ground approximately twenty pounds of grain in a hand mill, milked the buffaloes, cleaned the house, and cooked the morning meal. In the course of the day she spun cotton, drew water from the village well and carried it home on her head, and worked in the fields doing everything except ploughing and sowing. Education would only wreck this willing servitude that women thought it was their duty to perform. Darling found these to be fairly typical conditions for the Jat peasantry in this drought-prone area (Darling 1934: 118). In the new canal colonies, where the fertility of the soil and irrigation had led to prosperity (and the ecological disruptions had not yet surfaced), women refused to work as menials in the fields and spent much more time in sprucing up their lodgings. They saw menial toil as degrading, and had well-tended children and homes (Darling 1930: 50–52, 207–9; also see Dewey 1993: 85).

In truth Brayne, like many other civilians, understood very little of the existential pressures on Indian peasants. He baited them mercilessly in real life and in all the Socrates books that he compiled. At least one such "dialogue" has to be reproduced *in extenso* to give the flavor of his propaganda against the main elements of peasant extravagance, which he wanted broadcast into every village to be received by battery-powered radios—leaven to raise the whole mass of village India. At a large meeting summoned by "Socrates" (Brayne's name for himself in his writings), he hears a few landowners grumbling about their impecunious circumstances. Socrates expresses surprise and tauntingly adds that he thinks they must be the richest people in the world since they "can afford to throw away [their] wealth with both hands."

> "We throw away nothing Socrates." "Yes you do, all day and everyday." "Then tell us what we throw away." "First of all you throw away money. The other day I followed [some people] and found myself at the District Law Courts. The noise was of a big fair and I counted over two hundred people there." [Socrates goes on to say that there were two other courts in the district and there, too, similar crowds could be found.] "Now tell me, how much do you think each person spends each day, on average, in getting to and from court, and on his legal business, and on everything else connected with his visit to the courts, including of course the loss of his time." [This would include court fees, the pleader's fee, the stamp fee, and the incalculable mental and material costs of a process that could take several years to resolve; such was the price of colonial justice.] "Several rupees for certain." "Shall we say about ten?" "Ten would be a very low average." "Well, call it ten, and now tell me how many people on average attend court daily all over the District?" "Not less than several hundred, certainly." "To be on the safe side should we say three hundred?" "That is a very moderate estimate, Socrates." "Then allow two hundred and fifty days in the year, on which the courts are open, and the total thrown away on litigation is—?" "Seven and a half lakhs (750,000) of rupees, Socrates." "Correct! Your arithmetic does you more credit than your methods of business. Seven and a half lakhs a year is more than the total amount of the land revenue that you pay for the whole District. And that is a very low estimate of the cost of litigation, but we must not err on the side of exaggeration." (Brayne 1932: 12–13)

This was, indeed, a startling sum paid to the government in the form of various fees to litigate, but it was also an unwitting indictment of the judicial system that had made justice so costly. It could hardly be called willful extravagance, because for the most part the lawsuits were about titles to land used to secure loans to pay revenue, and therefore were in legal jeopardy.

The propaganda against dowries took an unintentionally comic turn in Brayne's eager hands: the worst addiction of all, in his view, was the Punjabi's love of jewelry, and he deplored the fact that both men and women bedecked themselves: "How much jewellery do you suppose is stored in the people's houses all over the District?" By the same process of educated guesswork he allows a hundred rupees' worth of jewelry per house, and one lakh (a hundred thousand) of houses for the half million population of the district. "That gives us one crore [ten million] of rupees locked up in jewellery, lying idle, wearing away, or getting lost and stolen. Allow the ladies half a crore—we must not be too strict or no one will listen to us." The villagers agree that they "wouldn't have a moment's peace at home if we allowed you to lay hands on all their beloved trinkets." He goes on to reason that the five million rupees could be deposited in the cooperative bank and would produce 700,000 rupees in interest that would pay more than half the annual revenue demand. Asked how much they continue to spend on jewelry every year, they concede that five rupees per household would not be an exaggeration. "Well, that makes another five lakhs for the whole District" (Brayne 1932: 13–14). His revulsion for earrings—which in his view epitomized the villagers' extravagance and barbarity—is noted in virtually every draft of every essay he ever wrote in connection with village uplift. Not only were people not to wear ornaments, he also totally forbade the boring of more than one hole in each ear for women, and men were to have none. He boasted that not only did he forbid men from appearing before him with earrings on but also ordered them torn out of the unsuspecting victim's ears if anyone did so (Dewey 1993: 81–83).

These facile vignettes really did little to reflect the reality in which these villagers' lives were enmeshed. As Darling realized, based on his encounters with villagers, jewelry was more than mere ornamentation for the average village woman, and he found Brayne's crusade against jewelry more than a trifle idiosyncratic. Darling spoke to many village women on his tours and gathered that they would never sell their jewelry but would only agree to pawn it if necessary, because it was their "surest defence against widowhood and separation." Jewelry was also the best collateral for a loan, and actually saved many peasants from mortgaging their land to their village moneylender. "All my informants agree that jewellery has been freely used in the last year [1929] to replenish resources mainly for the payment of government dues, and that much more has been pawned than sold. . . . Goldsmith's confirmed that recovery from the peasant is so difficult that loans without security, commonest of all before [British rule], have all but ceased. Jewellery is like insurance to keep land in times of stress"; and further, "loans were made against only jewellery [an asset controlled by women] and land [an asset controlled by men]" (Darling 1934: 30, 37, and passim).

Dewey has pointed out that owning bullion also acted as a "counter-cyclical force in the economy as a whole." During booms, peasants' savings were invested in jewelry; during depressions, pledges and sales cushioned the service sector and manufacturers against the collapse of peasant demand. "If it had not been for the cultivator's ornaments, the halving of crop prices between 1927 and 1933 would have caused far more disruption than it did" (Dewey 1993: 81–82). And given the scale of the shock, this kept the British government from having a major insurgency on its hands. The bumper harvests between 1922 and 1929 allowed India to absorb 3.6 billion rupees in gold, or 40 percent of world production, of which 40 percent wound up in Indian villages. Richly bedecked village women made Brayne furious, as he was in the midst of his anti-jewelry mission at this time. Then came drought and the world depression, with the collapse of grain prices (but not of fixed revenue demand). Villagers scuttled to the moneylender, whose terms quickly reflected the hardship of the times: interest rates zoomed up to 22 percent. Drought persisted, and pledges could not be redeemed. The value of gold increased sharply as Britain went off the gold standard in September 1931, which brought more gold from farmers' cottages to the moneylender's scales and from there to the towns. "'Prudent' villagers who took Brayne's advice," remarks Dewey, appropriately caustically, "to sell their ornaments at the bottom of the market and put the proceeds in a cooperative society which went bankrupt— must have envied their extravagant neighbours' folly" (Dewey 1993: 82). I would add that the reluctance of women to sell their gold actually saved them in the end. Their dowries indeed proved to be the safety nets they were intended to be. It would have been disastrous if Punjabis had paid attention to the British bureaucrats who had endeavored to abolish dowry practice through the agreements signed by the heads of tribes and castes at the meeting in Amritsar.

However, these large-scale, visible, and crucial benefits of dowry—for what else were ornaments of gold and silver?—must have also been the most influential inducement for families to give to their daughters and demand for their sons more gold or cash in order to own such insurance. Darling calculated in 1934 that dowry inflation rose tenfold in the previous fifty years (Darling 1934: 141). It had indeed become a burden on the bride's family. Sharma (1980: 134) has noted that bride-price had shifted to dowry in parts of the Punjab, a process that, Darling reported, had been under way since the late nineteenth century and had accelerated in the post-1919 years, when there were bumper harvests. He notes the cost of rising marriage expenses at Jat peasant weddings for daughters. Jats came increasingly to be included in the anti-dowry propaganda by bureaucrats and reformers alike. Jat soldiers who had served in the war abroad came home and called on local *panchayat* to implement ideas that they had encountered abroad. "[I]t was decided that there should be no more funeral feasts, that dowries should not exceed Rs. 100, that village servants should get only Rs. 11 instead of the customary Rs. 75, and that Jats should no longer sell their daughters [accept bride-price]" (Darling 1934: 185). One old retired captain reported to Darling that he "told the people that to sell their daughters was as bad as being dacoits [thieves]." Jat women, along with their men, welcomed the shift to dowry, since they understood perfectly that gold ornaments could be sold to buy land—and vice versa. They were an active force in acquiring the wider range of household accoutrements now available in the larger markets and town bazaars for their dowries, and they demanded gold jewelry instead of the silver they had accepted in the past. Retirees from the army, rich peasants who had helped create the canal colonies, soldiers returning from service in World War I—all had an appetite for the British mass-produced consumer durables that flooded the market in the central Punjab, and they invested in better equipment and cattle or simply bought more land (Darling 1930: 207). The Punjab economy was now tied to the world economy. Wedding costs were tied to the market prices of land and of grain, and they rose and fell with them.

After the crash in grain and land prices in 1929, Darling noted, the cost of a wedding for a son had declined to fifty rupees from the three to four thousand rupees spent only eight years earlier. Marriage parties with five members instead of a hundred set off for the bride's place. Jewelry was pawned to pay government dues, so a bride had to bring in this asset in order for a family to prevent its land from being mortgaged or sold (Darling 1934: 3, 30). Darling told of a woman abducted from her field who was found with eight hundred rupees' worth of jewelry on her, and he was horrified that a poor peasant would have invested such a substantial sum in his wife's jewelry. If the average holding had a twelve-rupee annual revenue demand, then this was sixty-six times that amount, which clearly spelled the most reckless extravagance, in his view. He also found Muslims spending more than a thousand rupees on each circumcision and celebrating them as lavishly as weddings (Darling 1934: 20) But the shadow of debt also lengthened, and woven into Darling's text are the ominous shades of a growing number of moneylenders in every village, with women actively joining their ranks, along with rich peasants and market farmers. There was increasing violence against moneylenders; Darling reported the killing of thirty-four in 1930 (Darling 1934: 17).

The troubling question is why dowry costs rose tenfold in the Punjab, when it declined in a formerly dowry-conscious Britain in the same period? According to Marion Kaplan, at least until World War I saving for her dowry was an important aspect of a working woman's life in Europe. "Only when women began to reenter the economy on a large scale as paid workers in advanced capitalist societies did the pursuit of dowries decline. Still the dowry system is in evidence in less industrialized areas of Europe" (Kaplan 1985: 6–7). The Punjab (and the rest of the British Empire in the subcontinent, for that matter) would have been a different place and its men and women as prosperous as anywhere in Europe had the

British not been primarily self-serving in introducing a restricted instead of unfettered capitalism to the region. I have emphasized before that they resolutely withheld, from the Indian empire (as they did from Ireland) the very kernel of modernity—the industrial revolution—while generously broadcasting its chaff in the subcontinent. The Punjab economy remained staunchly agrarian for the century under the Raj, and, indeed, it was run as economically as possible in an extractor-receptor mode. The extraction of raw materials, grain, and revenue continued apace (with allegedly infallible rent and wage laws at the command of the British) while mill-made consumer goods from Britain were off-loaded onto a captive market in India. Britain was the leader in Europe, but sovereign European states, which bought or stole the same technology, were able to catch up and experience the same prosperity as the British did. Rural populations in Europe declined, as peasants became urban dwellers and factory workers in the rapidly modernizing economies. Punjab, meanwhile, labored mightily to both produce and consume for the benefit of the Raj, growing exponentially in the newly opened canal-irrigated colonies. Urbanization was very sluggish, and only service industries critical to the survival of British power—military, construction, and administration—added to the jobs available in agriculture. In comparison to Europe, the economies of colonies became examples of what we call "underdeveloped societies" or the third world. Such a fate was far from inevitable for the Punjab; it was carefully engineered. Women's education was an expense the British government was happy to spare itself, leaving Catholic missionaries from Europe and religious reformers in India to make tiny dents in the vast numbers of the uneducated. Women's employment too, remained of the unpaid variety in the fields and in their homes, and dowries had an entirely opposite trajectory (see Ali 1988).

CONCLUSION

The diverse and detailed evidence in this and the previous chapter has been woven into a parallel and contending narrative that shifts the focus from Hindu high-caste dowry culture as the prime motive to murder selected female infants to a political economy that produced ever more skewed gender relations and therefore sex ratios. We saw that a new era of gender relations was inaugurated as the British rulers decided that the Punjab countryside would receive a less disastrous revenue policy than the one they had pursued in the once-rich Bengal and older parts of their empire. They selected a *ryotwari* settlement that gave proprietary rights in land to the peasants (*ryots*) who tilled it, and to traditional large landowners in their soldier-recruiting grounds in the northwest. This policy might well have been less disastrous but for their clinging to the articles of their own rational, utilitarian faith by insisting on fixed amounts and dates for the payment of land revenue in cash. These strictures were unmindful of the vagaries of the Indian climate or past practice, and transformed the newly created ability of peasant proprietors to alienate their land, through mortgage or sale, into their own uncomprehending undoing. It proved as disastrous as any attempt to "rationalize" customary man-land relations that the British had hitherto undertaken in their Indian empire. Moneylenders in the past had advanced small loans, and the object was never to let a debt be paid off entirely, keeping the debtor a permanent customer. With his land as collateral and with land prices rising, the peasant was able to borrow, and was often coerced into borrowing, far more than he could ever before. Interest rates rose to correspondingly unprecedented levels, topping off in some areas at more than 50 percent. The new breed of moneylenders with an appetite for their debtors' land was thus a creation of colonial revenue policies.

The ritual calendar and the harvest calendar in peasant society are intimately linked; betrothals, marriages, circumcision (for Muslims), tonsure ceremonies, and sacred thread initiation ceremonies all occur at "auspicious times" and are celebrated on the small profits of the harvest. British revenue policies never permitted the peasants to accumulate capital, but kept them at their wonted subsistence level. Inflexible British revenue payment timetables proved often not to synchronize with nature—a late monsoon meant a late harvest that would drive marginal cultivators to deplete their savings or send them to the moneylender's door in order to meet their payment schedules. Short-term loans frequently became lifelong debts because land as collateral gave moneylenders the incentive to make their conditions of repayment as difficult as possible. Occasionally the peasant would need a further loan to marry off his daughter—an event that could in no event wait past her puberty for reasons of chastity—because the profits of the harvest had already been pledged to the moneylender. True, mothers, aunts, and grandmothers had already prepared the girls trousseau, but the other gifts to be given to the groom's family, the cost of the villagewide feast, the music, and the drink would possibly drive a family into greater debt. Those with whom the peasant had social reciprocities would also find it difficult to honor them in a late or poor season. This unfortunate constellation of events had reconfigured a daughter's wedding into the proverbial last straw.

The construction of woman as *kanya*, or virgin, a gender problem found in other cultures as well, is at the root of these constraints. A son's wedding cost as much as a daughter's (and this is true even today in Punjabi urban and rural families), but a son's wedding could wait for a more convenient year. Although funeral expenses remained stable, wedding expenses borne by the bride's family steadily climbed. The crucial fact, however, was that neither daughters' weddings nor funerals could *wait*; other ritual events could be postponed, particularly a son's betrothal or wedding day. But the virginity of a nubile daughter was a man's deepest anxiety, and she had to be married before or around puberty so that she could be gifted as a virgin. So it was not the cost of the wedding as much as the constraints of time and the fear of her sexuality that made a daughter's wedding an urgent and exploitable condition in early colonial times.

In disaggregating a farmer's debt, the small and infrequent amounts that pertained to a daughter's dowry were found in only a minuscule number of cases, yet it was a daughter's wedding expenses that were stubbornly seen as the reason for killing her at birth. On a parallel track we also saw that indebtedness was increasing, and involved peasant proprietors clearly might see a son's wedding as an opportunity to obtain cash or gold from the bride's family as gifts either to pay off a loan or even to purchase more land. The British increasingly understood the devastating ramifications of their own revenue policies, but they continued to indict what they saw as cultural crimes rather than their own "rational" reconstruction of the landholding and revenue system—until, rather abruptly, they repealed the act against female infanticide. Yet the unchanging or worsening sex ratios suggest that family-building strategies did not change much thereafter, and as many or fewer girls were allowed to live.

It can now be confidently asserted, on the strength of the evidence presented here and in the last two chapters, that in the colonial period the cost of the wedding of a daughter went up as a result not just of higher tax levels but of other policy decisions, as well. Chief among these was the policy to reduce drastically the allowance that villages had customarily received for social expenses for the community. Although these were still collected as common charges for the village, several settlement reports describe a 90 percent reduction in what the village elders or the headman received, because this fund customarily defrayed expenses on ritual occasions the colonial authorities deemed unnecessary or improvident. The common fund sustained certain aspects of the social life of the village; it had formerly paid for the upkeep of the *chaupal*, or guest house, where the villagers offered hospitality to visitors and passersby and, most important, which was used for events such as weddings, tonsure ceremonies, feasts, funerals, and religious celebrations. Members of the groom's party, who customarily came to the bride's village for the wedding ceremonies, were accommodated in the *chaupal*. Common funds also took care of other expenses such as water, oil lamps, illumination, temple ornamentation, and fees for the *bhand* and *mirasi*.

In the attempt to reduce what was perceived as customary profligacy in the village, this once provident and now "improvident" fund quickly became a casualty of the revenue department to trim the flab in their revenue collections. Once the money was no longer available, the *chaupal* either fell into disrepair or had to be maintained through private funds. When the time came for a daughter's wedding, the formerly shared costs fell increasingly on individual families. The web of communal, filial, and reciprocal obligations was swept away with the new broom of tidy-minded colonial officers, which in turn transformed the structure of gender relations. The custom of dowry slowly attained its status as the key indicator of the subjugation of north Indian women and became ready to undergo quantitative changes to match inflation, the increasing availability of consumer goods, and the growing commercialization of everyday life in the next century.

Enforcement of village exogamy had worked as part of the precolonial mechanism that balanced village resources between daughters and sons, and often daughters were given far more valuable cattle and draft animals and ornaments. Women were customarily married out of their natal villages, effectively exchanging their rights as unmarried daughters for their rights as wives. But the change in the perception or land as property radically altered a woman's right. Land went up in value, as did other kinds of property, and her dowry was no longer comparable to getting a fair share in her natal family's holdings. Her usufructory rights in her husband's holdings existed only at the suffrance of her husband. An unhappily married woman with a drunken and violent husband might find herself literally without rights in any property—either natal nor affinal. Her return to her *peke* or parents' house was also not as fluid as before, because the holding was now determinately owned and her brothers and their wives would see her presence as an unrightful one. Property and dowry came to sit uneasily beside each other.

The long-term politics and wars of this region in the precolonial period had determined the marked preference for sons among all communities; the preference was not the product of cultural pride or cruelty, as the new British rulers chose to interpret it. The economic and social trends unleashed under their rule certainly saw wedding expenses escalate and dowry payments evolve into possible blackmail, but even more desperate were the conditions they created for an ever-deeper preference for sons. The jobs in the army with their salaries and pensions, the promise of land grants for loyal service, the hope for wealth in the enormous migration of peasants to build the canals and railways and to populate the agricultural colonies and townships that would spring up along them, all made a woman's biological capacity to reproduce her most exploited asset. Punjabi men, with their prized sinews and their reputation for grinding toil, were in extraordinary demand, and Punjabi women, caught up in this compelling logic, dedicated themselves to the task at hand with deadly effect in the interest of their own families.

The colonial call for manpower translated into an implicit imperative for Punjabi women. Women made the important decisions in the household, and the most important decision now was to deploy all the science at their command to "plan" the numbers and sexes of the next generation. A gender-targeted family was achieved, in those medically primitive days, by female infanticide. The figure of the shadowy, ignorant peasant woman was in reality society's double agent, acting in concert with others of her own sex, who reproduced and culled the patriarchal family.

For all their inquisitiveness, and their direct contact with villagers, neither Edwardes nor Thorburn nor Brayne nor Darling, nor any of the other civilians who wrote reports on the subject, discovered the pitiless, almost utilitarian, logic of killing *selected* infant girls. The fog of cultural motives blurred what might otherwise have been in plain view. I found the nerve to ask. The actual reason was the prevailing understanding, then and now, of the biology of reproduction itself. Killing a girl infant was absolutely necessary to increase the number of boys a family could have. After the birth of a girl, a mother would insist on breast-feeding the child, as was natural, but this would interfere with her fertility; if she did not, the child would probably die of malnourishment and disease, but worse, it would be emotionally harder for her to lose a daughter she had actually cared for. And the next pregnancy would be delayed. Time was of the essence if she wanted to create a family of four or five healthy sons, at least, before her fertility span ended her hope of creating future security. The decision was made long before the baby was born: if the family already had one or two girls, they could kill the third, then have two or more boys, and then perhaps let another girl live. It was also crucial to raise girls—to ensure the survival of their society as future wives and mothers—so there was a conscious design and purpose that determined which daughter would live and which would die. The mother knew exactly what it meant when she was not presented with the newborn after parturition, when she heard no cry of a baby who ought to have been slapped to life, but only the muffled, hurried, practiced sounds of a baby being taken away from the room to be quickly strangled or suffocated, exposed to the cold, or given a lethal dose of opium or *dhatura* juice (a poisonous plant found all over the Punjab). Invariably the *dai*, or midwife, did the deed quickly and efficiently.

This act of killing the baby was perceived as expedient and justified as an act for the greater good of the entire family unit. Normatively it is morally abhorrent to the Hindu, Sikh, or Muslim ways of life, and that is why all communities readily condemned it and vowed to eradicate the practice. There was nothing heroic or culturally rewarding in this for any of them. Bluntly put, it was pragmatic, it was ruthless, and it was necessary. Women were responsible for the welfare of the family so it fell on them to decide whether a third consecutive daughter would live or die. Birth order, the number of female siblings, the reproductive health of the mother, and economic conditions all determined this life-and-death question. With high infant mortality for natural reasons, no newborn was seen as an established human until the thirteenth day after its birth, when it was ritually named and formally welcomed into the family. Just as Indian women today wait for the results of amniocentesis or a sonogram to decide whether to seek an abortion, they used to wait for the appearance of the baby's genitals to take the next predetermined step. Drums were beaten and sweets distributed if it was a boy; girls were greeted with little or no fanfare and sometimes, when it had to be done to hasten the production of another male child, with the hushed dark silence of death. A woman would try to get pregnant again almost immediately if the latter choice had been made. This, alas, was the extent of the choice allowed to a woman over her body in the service of the patriarchal family. Colonial times, with their rigid revenue policy and masculine economy, only deepened this trend despite the statutory efforts to reverse it. Neither the dire punishments for such behavior called for in Manu's laws, nor other scriptural authorities that pronounced this the worst of all the murders one could commit, nor the culture of vegetarianism and *ahimsa* (nonviolence), nor even colonial fines and imprisonment stemmed the rising epidemic of infanticide in colonial India. Women would not relinquish their agency and their duty in planning the welfare of their families.

I would tease this logic just a little further to remind us that it has indeed been demonstrated that politically motivated East India Company and later imperial civilians deliberately and consistently interpreted female infanticide as the culturally or religiously informed actions of barbarous Hindus. As we uncover the more complex motivations for this crime, female infanticide becomes less puzzling—but was it an utterly and entirely antifemale act even in those rude times? Is female infanticide misogyny, and did men engineer a safe world for themselves with the collusion of women? Or does the logic of gender roles lead us to acknowledge that while Punjabi sons were being reared by mothers in greater numbers to become soldiers, farmers, and wage earners for the economic security of the family, a large number of boys became cannon fodder for the state. In fact, it is easy to see that violence, which meant danger and death for men in large numbers as, in precolonial times, they defended or extended their control over land against outside enemies or local rivals, increased the preference for sons, which begat violence against females through death for selected infant daughters. The manpower needs of the colonial state were far larger than they had ever been in centuries past, and it offered fine inducements for those who joined the army to risk their lives in wars for the defense of the empire in India and abroad—so even more infant girls were killed to quicken the reproduction of the "martial races."

And thus, in a remarkable paradox, women were protected by colonial legislation from cultural harm, but their customary rights and advantages were curtailed in the land of their fathers and husbands. The struggle for unambiguous inheritance and property rights would be fought anew in the late colonial and postcolonial periods. Patriarchal values were simultaneously contested and reinforced—contested by the movement for women's rights, and reinforced by the attempt to run an efficient colonial empire. But the central bias of the colonial period—that women had no rights in land—pervaded the colonial legal universe in India and deeply influenced the future of women's rights to property. The Hindu Women's Right to Property Act of 1936 excluded agricultural land from its purview, effectively denying women a right to agricultural land. The Hindu Succession Act of 1956 made daughters, married or unmarried, equal inheritors along with their brothers, of their father's estate, if he died intestate. But this act is similarly limited in connection with women's rights in ancestral land.

Dowry, in the meantime, lagged in value compared to landed property, but the potential for the custom to be converted into blackmail or extortion had increased in an increasingly male-dominated world. Prosperity had generally increased what a woman would receive for her dowry, and so had the availability of goods.

The campaign against dowry remained on the agenda for reform, and nationalist leaders like Gandhi, who spent a great deal of their time on social issues, had condemned it outright. The Prohibition of Dowry Act emerged from India's parliament in 1961. The legislation was flawed and ineffective, as we shall see, and by the 1970s a new variant of dowry death was stalking the lives of some women: "bride burning."

6

Writing Lives, Underwriting Silences

Understanding Dowry Death in Contemporary India

Kahe ko biyahi bides lakhi babul mora
Bhaiyon ko din ho mahal do mahal
Hamko diya pardes.
[Why did you marry me in a distant land, oh wealthy father of mine?
You gave my brothers a palace or two, and to me you gave exile.]
—*Amir Khusrau (1253–1325); my translation*

Now we can come full circle—and look with informed eyes at the terrible tragedies reported in the news media about the lethal effect of inadequate dowries on young brides in contemporary India. Instead of using a scalpel on what the media have already dissected to a pulp, I want instead to use a series of conversations that span the last four decades to deepen and complicate the understandings of "dowry death" in a woman's adult life. From that unfortunate phrase I now find it easier to accept the word "death" than "murder," because it also subsumes the accidents and suicides that kill married women, but I find the adjective "dowry" to be too restrictive a qualifier and too unproven a motive for such tragedies and crimes, just as it was for female infanticide. A striking but unnoticed resemblance exists between the just-so stories of those interrogated by agents of the state to explain why girl infants were destroyed and the more subtle just-so quality of stories women told about harassment for more dowry and the violence associated with it. I take courage from Beth Roy, a trained psychotherapist, who reflected on her field experience in trying to reconstruct a communal riot in Bengal, which eloquently captures my own.

It is true that the stories I heard . . . were not about "what happened" (itself a questionable concept). What I heard was how people *saw* what happened, or, rather, how people *remembered* what they saw, or, rather, how they *talked* about what they remembered—or, rather, how they talked to *me* about what they remembered—or, rather, what I *heard* people say to me about what they remembered. I was well aware that what I learned from my informants engaged my own history and was transformed in that interaction. . . . After a lifetime of engagement with other people's stories . . . I have come to suspect that all human understanding takes the form of conversation. (Roy 1994: 5–6)

Conversations are also the grist for my mill, and it is to the compelling stories that emerged in conversations, overheard informally, or solicited as part of my research on the subject, that I will turn in order to probe and problematize "dowry deaths."

To begin, we must turn to a conversation on female infanticide that Edwardes had with a native informant, reproduced in his report with which we are all too familiar from chapter 2 (Edwardes 1852). The slowly brewing danger of wives committing suicide or being burned to death was presaged in the interlocution about Lahoreen Khatris, who were ranked at the top of the Khatri pyramid in the Punjab, as we recall. True to the thesis that the quest for caste status underwrites the violence against newborn females, the informant divulges that the ambition of fathers in the lower ranks to marry their daughters to the *urahi-ghar* sons is simply impossible to fulfill unless a large dowry is paid. By virtue of their position at the top of the hierarchy, the Lahoreens were able choose from among a multitude of eager competitors. The groom then "is a good marketable commodity, and the Lahoreen, by all accounts makes the most of it. He employs his advantage to *demand such a dowry as he thinks proper, which no other Khuttree but the Lahoreen does.*" The Lahoreen proceeds to ratchet up his demands in unscrupulous ways, "by artifice and threatened breach of agreement and . . . refuses to advance another step, without all kinds of entreaties and bribes." He threatens to break off the engagement and makes excuses to protract the time for the final ceremony "until the girl's father sees her approaching the age when to be unmarried, is impious and disgraceful," and agrees to pay a higher dowry. "Here alone we see the ordinary elements of Female Infanticide, which exist in marriage expenses, terribly aggravated" (Edwardes 1852: para. 60; emphasis added).

We have to listen carefully here, because greed (a common human failing) is confused with hypergamy (a cultural specific), and dowry is the only excuse offered for murdering child brides. Again, this is not a caste ordinance among Khatris, the informant is saying, but the willful and unabashed behavior of the arrogant and the greedy Lahoreen, who simply choose socially vulnerable moments in the context of gender inequality to extort more cash and valuables from the bridegivers. It emerges as rare and reprehensible behavior, breaking with caste norms rather than upholding them. Edwardes, as a Britisher, is no stranger either to the politics of avarice or the vulnerability of women. He describes the behavior of the groom and his family that leads to violence, even murder. His narrative has a chilling resonance in present-day Delhi, because he has stumbled upon "a more abominable form of Infanticide, which perhaps would more correctly be called murder" (Edwardes 1852: para. 60). In sum: child brides are being ruthlessly eliminated because of dowry. Edwardes tells us that the Lahoreen father, seeing the hundreds of Khatri daughters from ordinary ranks aspiring to marry a boy from a higher-ranked family, "too often proceeds to get rid of the poor girl he has just been paid for receiving into his family, and either systematically starves and neglects her till she dies, or else brings about one of the thousand and one accidents which would kill all children, if kind parents were not at hand to save them. The vacancy thus created is immediately filled by another Bride and another dowry" (Edwardes 1852: para. 60–61). None of the other reports from the far corners of the Punjab portrayed anything remotely like this. The alleged victims sound no older than children, perhaps only a few years old. Although child marriages were rampant in the Punjab, customarily a bride would not be sent to her marital home until she had attained puberty. It is difficult to ascertain, with no other evidence at hand, whether or not the informant had exaggerated the rumor of an event into a trend among Lahoreen Khatris, what his own motive might be in so doing, and whether the ill-treatment of these Khatri brides was for reasons of dowry. Or was the informant merely reinforcing the theory, which the Khatri males had helped the British invent, that whole castes or subcastes were implicated in the committing of crimes, so as to deflect the long arm of the law from prosecuting infanticide as a crime rather than condemning it as a barbaric custom? Equally disturbing is the fact that Edwardes ordered no investigation to affirm or deny what his informant in a village in Jullundur district has alleged in distant Lahore, and left it as an unconfirmed anecdote in his report. His seniors, who read this report and upheld it as a model, also ignored this information. Reform associations that mushroomed a decade later and were vociferous in publicity against the ills of early marriage and dowry do not mention the Lahoreen Khatris or refer to their alleged murder of child brides.[1]

Isolated and unnerving as this rumor was, it had two distinct portents for the future: one, the official insouciance about investigating violence against women in their marital homes presages the attitudes of the police about dowry deaths in Delhi in the last quarter of the twentieth century. Domestic violence posed no threat to the state, so the police were trained to ignore it. And two, the denunciation of dowry is followed by the provincewide efforts to limit dowry and wedding expenses, cultural addictions that had to be controlled if not banned altogether. Edwardes lays these paragraphs down sparely; he tells no stories, gives us no names. Here was heinous crime among the most wealthy and powerful members of Punjabi upper-caste society in Lahore (perhaps the only place that could call itself a city in predominantly rural Punjab in 1850), who appear to commit and condone murder with formidable calculation. Edwardes makes a keen ethical distinction: female infanticide was morally less abominable than the fatal ill-treatment or murder of young brides, but he leaves it at that.[2]

By the turn of the century, this still rare social pathology of demanding a dowry emerged as a confirmed fact in Bengal and Bombay presidencies and the Punjab, and it seemed to be infecting most parts of colonial north India. A thirty-six-page pamphlet entitled *Marriage-Dowry* written in 1914 by Rai Bahadur Chunnilal Bose, a Bengali, gives us a detailed report of suicide by a young girl. This girl, Snehlata, "burnt herself to death to save the family from impending ruin in consequence of an exorbitant demand of dowry at her proposed marriage" (Bose 1914: 2). Bose mingled his horror at the greed that provoked the act with the awe he felt for "the noble sacrifice of a Hindu girl of tender age." He went on to say that although this was not an isolated incident, most other cases of suicide related to dowry demands were "responsible for the self-destruction of not a few fathers having no means to marry their daughters, and of many a young married girl unable to bear persecution in her father-in-law's house for non-payment of promised dowry." If daughters were not married off at "too early an age" to grasp the "desperate position of their parents," he speculated, "the result would be an epidemic of such tragedies" (ibid.: 1).

The Marriage Reform League, of which Bose was an active member, had been at the forefront of the battle against the widespread practice of child marriage and had promoted the raising of the age of consent for women, but clearly the changing meaning of dowry was equally relevant to its agenda for marriage reform. In discussing the causes of escalating dowry demands, Bose first analyzed how the changed political economy applied pressure to benign customs to adapt in a way that made them vicious. In summary, after condemning child marriage as the root of the evil in Hindu marriages, he saw the demand for dowry as a product of the radically changed criteria for the eligibility of bridegrooms brought on by "modern trends." These, he argued, were in growing vogue in families where the "boys" (prospective bridegrooms) have received "University degrees [that] are largely responsible for the growth and perpetuation of the custom [of dowry] in our society. . . . The question of high education [*sic*] never troubled our fore-fathers in making the selection [of a bridegroom], as people had then not so much to depend upon higher education as a means for earning a living for the family. The struggle for existence had not then grown so acute: every family had some landed property, which yielded sufficient income . . . to meet the absolute necessaries of life" (Bose 1914: 8–9). What mattered in pre-British times was the "status of the family, its religious proclivity, the moral atmosphere," which were now minor factors because "[r]espectability now consists of either being a Government Servant or belonging to one of the learned professions, and as University degrees are the passport to them, undue importance is naturally attached to these degrees" (ibid.: 10). A good dowry that included gold and cash became a logical source "for help to defray the expenses of his [the groom's] education. If the young man's father happens to be a pleader or a member of the Subordinate Judicial or Executive service, the position of the bridegroom in the marriage-market becomes a most enviable one and the fathers of marriageable daughters all try to secure him at any cost" (ibid.: 11). Bose was at pains to explain how the very rules of the game of status and power, so much a part of precolonial Indian society, had been suspended. Closeness to the political power in the land always translated into higher status, as we saw in the case of the Kshatriyas and Emperor Akbar. The British Raj ended the relationship of caste status to political power, and its own politically motivated officers ceased to describe castes as anything but manifestations of agnatic lineages arranged in watertight social and ritual compartments. Ironically, with their monopoly of political power, the British rulers themselves lived out their own fantasy about caste and tribe by becoming the most rigidly ascriptive, commensal, and ritually connected tribe in the subcontinent, and proceeded to project their own concerns about social rank and racial distance onto the high castes they had displaced, treating disloyal natives as their own despised untouchables.

Reflecting the protofeminist disposition of the Marriage Reform League, Bose went on to explain what the British analyses of the same situation failed to identify. Since the number of such educated young men was small, it could be safely calculated that "the price of the bridegroom would go on increasing in the marriage market." The search for an eligible match for a daughter had become even more difficult because of "rigidly bound down caste rules," according to which matrimonial alliances were restricted to families of the same caste. This created the pincer action of the old customs and the new that gave young men with qualifications unprecedented power; young women were caught at a disadvantage that they had never known before. Indeed, "[f]or every such eligible bridegroom there are fifty or more fathers throwing baits for their capture. The matchmakers vie with one another in making increased offers of dowry, and the father of the bridegroom must be more than human if he could resist the temptation of selling his son to the highest bidder" (Bose 1914: 12). Such crass commercialization of a process that was formerly dignified and discreet, he lamented, appeared to be rooted in the *"predominating but erroneous idea of women being inferior to men* [which] indirectly helps this evil practice [dowry] to continue in our society, by undervaluing the worth of our girls in the marriage market" (ibid.: 12; emphasis added). From "a nation which worships its unmarried girls (Kumari Poojah) . . . we have so much fallen from this high ideal of womanhood that we now demand dowries for inferior worth" (ibid.: 12). He insightfully recognized devaluation of women in the new order of things. Status now translated into material wealth, since the old basis of status in political power was defunct under colonial rule, where Indians occupied only the lowest rungs of the bureaucracy and the army.

In noting another modern development that encouraged the "dowry-evil,"

Bose contradicted his earlier statement that "hide bound caste rules" were exacerbating the situation.

> In former times, the fact of the girl belonging to a high caste family went far in favour of her selection as a daughter-in-law. It was considered to be a proud privilege and honour in many Kayastha [a Kshatriya subcaste] families to be able to secure a girl of high Kulin [Brahmin] descent for a daughter-in-law. Even dark-skinned Kulin girls were considered precious prizes and were treated with great respect and consideration in the family of their father-in-law. Now-a-days, however, considerations of pedigree have given place to commercial stipulations. Most people are now quite indifferent to the [bride's] antecedents, provided that she brings with her casketfulls of jewellery and bagfulls of cash-money. An inevitable consequence of this is that the father of a dark-skinned girl has to pay a price for the crime of her colour, otherwise no one would select her in preference to her more fortunate fair sister. (Bose 1914: 22–23)

He certainly conveyed the idea that educated men had come to want more say in the arrangement of their marriages, and apart from money insisted on choosing the best-looking women. The premium placed on light skin, valued in Indian society, might have been reinforced under the tutelage of white masters, whose racist disdain for dark skin was well known; park benches, railway bogeys, public spaces marked with "For Whites Only" or "No Indians Allowed" had become a common feature of the urban landscape. Men without university degrees or job prospects were probably not much sought after, either, and would have to settle for women with only customary dowries. Such modern considerations clearly limited the pool of partners for both men and women. Bose's argument, though a trifle tangled at times, firmly attests that traditional patriarchal values were working in tandem with modern patriarchal values to create an ever-deepening sense of the "inferiority" and dependency of women, and that the relationship of power and gender (as we saw in matters of land and law) had tilted further to privilege men over women. Even the adverse sex ratios that created a paucity of women did nothing to improve women's chances, since eligible males with modern qualifications were even fewer than women in any age cohort in both villages and towns. The dowry brought in by a bride, Bose ruefully observes, was no longer preserved as a woman's exclusive wealth but was now used to pay off debts or to marry off daughters in the husband's family, and "if the sum is considerable it is used to cover the expenses of the education of the son in England or to add to family property holdings, and to buy Government promissory notes" (Bose 1914: 27). These were radically new uses for a woman's *stridhan*, and certainly we can mark this as the beginning of a trend. The only mercy was that the percentage of men who could even aspire to a university education was minuscule and that the incipient dowry "problem" was therefore confined to a tiny subset of the population that dominated urban areas; in the countryside, indebtedness, land auctions, and rising land values visited similar havoc on far larger numbers. Urbanization barely crossed the 10 percent mark in the Punjab in the 1930s, and it hovers around 30 percent in the Indian portion of that state today.

The pamphlet concludes with suggestions on how to bring this "evil institution" of dowry under control. Apart from stating the obvious, that marriages should be simple affairs and people curb their avarice, and urging that the Marriage Reform League should continue to expose this evil and hold public meetings to raise public awareness about the matter, Bose betrays confusion on whether modernity was the cause or the remedy for dowry. He felt that if young men had a voice in choosing their wives (a modern development), the dowry problem might begin to decline, as it had in Britain and the rest of the West. He believed that if women were educated, their inability to bring a dowry and their skin color would not be handicaps. He advocated women's education as the panacea, but his rather limited vision of women's education as courses of study that would make them literate and train them into skilled mothers and housekeepers ultimately only underscored the imbalance of power between the genders. His lament about the problem of dowry appears to have been abstracted, perhaps, from the dozens of pamphlets in circulation at that time that had been churned out by imperial officers like F. L. Brayne, missionaries, and indigenous reform societies such as the Arya Samaj in all parts of British India since the last quarter of the nineteenth century.

If Bose could have looked into the future, he would have seen that it looked even bleaker. Seventy years down the line, this pamphlet was to read like an augury. Scores of suicides similar to Snehlata's would be reported nationwide. In fact, it can be argued that the famous proclivity of Hindu women for "noble self-sacrifice" have enabled the murders of women to be disguised regularly in present times as suicides, and encouraged a general reluctance to investigate circumstances which, had men been the ones dying, would have aroused a great deal of suspicion.[3]

It is to these gender-related crimes in the latter half of the twentieth century, the bride burnings and the dowry deaths, that I now turn, examining a few telling incidents that involve both those who died and those who lived to tell their tales. My own account, which I shall tell, is joined by a multitude of others that are represented in this chapter by a few selected from the files and conversations at Saheli. I spent ten intense months in 1985–1986 as a volunteer at Saheli (literally, "female friend"), a women's resource center in New Delhi, which opened a world of women's life histories to me. There, a few women arrived each day for help, in various states of distress, and told their stories of betrayal, violence, and dowry demands. Sometimes parents came to report the suspicious circumstances in the deaths of their married daughters. As a Saheli volunteer, along with half a dozen others on any given day, I recorded these accounts and transformed them into "cases" for legal or other kinds of help. Some of the volunteers had come to work here because they had their own stories; others were women who saw the need to help and had the time and resources to do so. A four-drawer filing cabinet held a variety of files: the unfinished stories of women who had come once, had become "cases," and had disappeared; the files of legal cases that either were pending in the courts or had simply been withdrawn; and the files of current cases waiting for action.

There were also files full of clippings of news reports of dowry deaths and legislative progress. Listening, reading, photocopying, taking notes from these files, sometimes telling snippets of my story to a distraught woman to draw out her own, and eventually discussing all these stories with other Saheli volunteers proved to be a fruitful research method. This remarkable intertwining itself completed incomplete stories, filled gaps, sealed fissures. The stories that emerged in this give-and-take of conversations, rather than in interviews or case files, illuminated the dark edges of womanly silence and its relationship with the overly prolix masculine legal jargon.

A REMEMBERED TRAGEDY

The earliest conversations in my natal home ebbed and flowed into an ocean of stories syncopated with the clicking of knitting needles attached to great colorful balls of wool, the yarn uncoiling and becoming meshed into booties or sweaters at the same pace that the cadences of those stories unreeled to become part of the verbal tapestries woven by the gathered women. A great many of the stories revolved around marital events—the arrangement of alliances, wedding expenses and dowries, the virtues and vices of other people's daughters-in-law, and the insufferable ways and the alcoholism and violence of men. Most were set far away and long ago—in Lahore, Bhon-Chakwal, or Peshawar in the Punjab, or in Kanpur or Lucknow—and were about kith and kin, chiefly women, and the joys and mishaps that flavored their mundane lives, all disrupted by Partition. But every now and then a tragedy was recounted that imprinted itself on my mind and kept me brooding. Mridula's unnatural death in 1958 was such a story; it emerged in discussions over many months. The details are still vivid, and now, in the light of so many other deaths of young women, the story's shadows are darker.[4]

A precocious eleven year old at the time, I remember coming home from school to find my grandmother and her circle speaking in grim, hushed tones. It was clear that someone we all knew had come to harm. I received the news from my mother and *dadi* simultaneously, in answer to my questioning looks. There had been a terrible accident at the house of family friends, and Mridula had just died after being severely burned in a fire that broke out in her bedroom. Mridula was the daughter-in-law of an old Lucknow family that was like kin to our own. She and her husband, Rohit, the eldest son of six children in the family, had barely returned home after the late show at the movies. It was a hot evening, and Rohit was already in bed when he asked Mridula to plug in the table fan. She obliged, but a spark from the defective plug of the fan allegedly flew into her nylon sari, and she was suddenly engulfed in flames. The family doctor was summoned, but there was little that he could do; Mridula had third-degree burns over 98 percent of her body. I remember a distinct detail: it was said that she was menstruating and therefore was wearing a sanitary napkin that conducted the flames to her vitals quickly, proving fatal. This information was always whispered like a secret, and it was this secret that seemed to explain her unfortunate death. Rohit claimed that he had tried to put out the flames, but it was all too rapid for him to arrest. He was unscathed in his attempt to save her. She lingered that night and some part of the next day, heavily sedated against the pain, never speaking another word, and finally she died, leaving behind a six-month-old son. The doctor certified that the death was an accident. These bare bones of the happening were repeated, ever more compactly, several times over several days as friends and family came to mourn.

The family was one of the richest in the city, with influence in government circles, and was understandably nervous about rumors of foul play. The event never made it into the newspapers, nor were the police ever summoned. We visited the family that evening and heard the story again from Mridula's mother-in-law. Rohit, who looked fresh in a starched white *kurta-pajama*, calmly explained that he had been helpless to prevent the tragedy. I was suspicious of his version and believed that he had not made a sincere bid to save her life. The persistent wails of their infant son made her unnatural death even more unacceptable. Mridula's parents arrived from out of town, fortunate not to have seen the horribly charred body of their beloved daughter. Her mother was inconsolable, wiping away tears of grief and rage, while her father sat in stony, frowning silence. At one point the mother yelled halfway across the room to where Rohit was standing, asking why he had not whipped off the sari or acted with alacrity to save his wife, his child's mother, their daughter. Had Mridula not screamed or Rohit not shouted for help until it was too late? The others muttered their doubts. How could such a frightening event take place in the very heart of that large extended family home where many others were sleeping in rooms arranged around a central courtyard? Did her cries not wake the servants, the other siblings, the parents-in-law? Why were all the marks of the conflagration confined to one corner of the bedroom?

These questions about Mridula's death began to erode the plausibility of the narrative about the unfortunate "accident" even as people sat around during the thirteen days of ritual mourning, trying to establish the precise sequence of events, since it was alleged that no one had been present except her husband. At home I heard allied bits of gossip—an uncle reported that Rohit had been seeing another woman; it was likely that Mridula had burned herself in despair upon finding out. Yet it was difficult to believe that a cheerful, bright young woman with a very young child to whom she was devoted would be selfish and heartless enough to commit suicide because of her husband's adultery. Infidelity seemed so trivial next to the enormity of that death. Women, the members of my grandmother's circle argued, had to tolerate infidelity because that was the nature of men, who had little self-control. Didn't Satya put up with a drunken, unfaithful, violent husband? Did not Sushila, Kanta, and Vimla endure infidelity and violence for the sake of their children? These rhetorical questions elicited sighs and nods of affirmation; no one questioned that infidelity among husbands was the rule rather than the exception, but they also did not know of a woman who would choose to burn herself for that. Others said that Mridula had been murdered because the in-laws were unhappy with her and planned to get him married to another woman who would bring in a better dowry.[5]

On sad occasions such as this one, the older women, many of them widows, trotted out clichés about marriage. It is an ethnographer's heaven to attend a mourning session where women express grief through story and analogy. The ideology (or is it myth?) of wifehood (*pativrata*), based on a woman's exceptional power to sacrifice her own interests at all times, was also spun out in these conversations, and it stood in contradistinction to the ideology of motherhood, in which the mother was a powerful agent. As *wife*, a woman had very limited choices if her husband was "bad-charactered" or was a drunk, and she herself was vulnerable to such charges, but her superior moral strength and endurance (*sahan shakti*) enabled her to be a good wife. Alcohol was a scourge and responsible for economic privations and violence, because a husband misspent money on his addiction and fought and even beat his wife when she inevitably accused him of selfish behavior. Marriage was an ancient, scripted, inexorable fate, and it was up to the woman to negotiate the best terms she could within that arrangement. The rewards came when, as an older wife with grown sons, she acquired the power from her mother-in-law to control and shape the future of the family. The bounds of good wifely conduct were iterated and reiterated by the older women for the younger women to internalize; I know they had a subliminal impact on me as I sat there listening. It never occurred to me to ask why marriage was compulsory, why these strong and wise women had forged no alternative order, and why they played such a major and willing part in arranging for their daughters and nieces this inexorable fate.

An unmarried woman was a very rare phenomenon indeed in the 1950s and 1960s, and her singleness was seen not as volitional but as the consequence of some unfortunate "defect," physical or mental, that made her unfit for marriage, since other options were nonexistent. The conjugal home (*saure* or *sasural*) as opposed to the natal home (*peke, pihar*, or *maike*) was a woman's final earthly destination and permanent home, in which she had to adapt her very nature to fit in. The older women never tired of repeating, as if to convince the younger generation that was being schooled for this fate, that a woman was carried into her marital home in a *doli* or *palki* (palanquin) and only left it (in a permanent sense) when her corpse was finally carried out of it on an *arthi* (funeral bier). Ideally, she would never dare to vote with her feet, as in an elopement with a lover or a divorce. In this central dictum lay the conditions that *sometimes* made death (suicide or murder) the only acceptable way to end a marriage.[6]

The wedding ceremony itself signaled the moment of discontinuity in a woman's life, the moving from the temporary natal home to the permanent marital home—a discontinuity marked with ambivalence.[7] It was an occasion that the bridegroom and his party celebrated, while the bride and her family and friends had their moments of joy laced with sorrow over parting and fear of the unknown. The bridegroom's *baraat* would be drunk, dancing and reveling, at the expense of the unconditional hospitality borne by the bride's family. The bride's parents, on the other hand, fasted all day in preparation for one of their most sacred duties—that of *kanyadan*, the gift of their virgin daughter—and they broke their fast only after the wedding ceremony was over. Some mothers did not eat until the daughter had left the household with her husband and his *baraat*. The songs of *bidai* (the moment of leave-taking of the young bride from her parents' home) are very moving, and even the most casual of guests at a wedding will be seen wiping away their tears when the *bidai* is imminent. The wrenching farewell the bride bids her parents, accentuated by the plaintive notes of the *shenai*, an oboelike instrument used chiefly to play the songs of parting and exile, is among the most unforgettable and moving vignettes in an Indian woman's life. It dramatically signifies the emotional, sexual, and material difference between the bride's and the groom's experiences of the same event. There are no norms or mechanisms that ensure a groom's virginity or a husband's fidelity.

But if her death was not self-willed, why did Mridula have to *die*? Divorce, legal for Hindus only since 1956, when the revised Hindu Code became law, carried serious stigma. For the women in that group who philosophized as they knitted and gossiped, it was certainly not an option, though many of them might have wished that it were at some point or another; to admit failure in coping with the exigencies that marriage created was somehow to compromise a woman's innate strength and being. The paradox of women's *shakti*, or power, lay in deploying this enormous female inner strength only for the greater good of the spouse and children and the larger extended family, never for a selfish purpose. This was the ultimate patriarchal trick—to condition women's special powers to serve the family's purposes and its purposes alone.

Speculation regarding the circumstances and background of Mridula's death reared its head frequently in these conversations months later. The marriage, I was to learn soon afterward, was fraught with problems: Mridula was better educated than her husband, a fact that would only produce strife, since Rohit had barely struggled through high school. Her family was less wealthy and socially prominent than her husband's. Mridula had "flaws" that the family had generously overlooked, her mother-in-law often pointed out. She may have been fine-featured and vivacious, but her complexion was dark, and polio had left her with a discernible limp. Rohit had not been enthusiastic about her, but then he was no beauty himself, being short, plump, prematurely bald, and very dull. It was believed that his mother, fearing that he was going astray in the company of men who drank and womanized, had forced him into accepting this match.

Dowry could be eliminated as a factor, as they had already been married for two years and her parents had never spoken of any harassment on that count. The Dowry Prohibition Act had not yet been passed. Nonetheless, the whisper that Mridula had been done away with because Rohit had offers of marriage from far richer families grew louder. It has always been easier to talk about inadequacy of dowry and other money matters than to speculate about the *sexual* or temperamental incompatibility of a couple. Mridula's sudden, cruel death remained unsatisfactorily explained and became grist for the rumor mill. That it might have been murder was even harder to accept because murder should have been the most abhorrent form of violence in a strictly vegetarian family who objected strongly to the killing of goats and chickens. Why was there no investigation to allay the suspicion?

Women, strictly among themselves, are not abashed about talking about sex, although the subject remains taboo in public or in the presence of men. My grandmother's circle surmised that there had been serious friction between the two because Rohit was seeing another woman, although the details were spare. Mridula had confronted Rohit and threatened to leave him, expose him to his disciplinarian father, and bring dishonor to his entire family. It was thought that his infidelity must have been provoked by her physical "shortcomings"; I now understand that this was because it had to be the woman's fault. There was talk that mother-in-law and daughter-in-law did not get along, a common situation, and that they had exchanged angry words only hours before the incident. Something really serious, though, must have been the problem that resulted in such a morbid outcome.

In private conversations, murder began to gain ground as the only plausible scenario, accomplished by a conspiracy involving Rohit, his mother, and a trusted servant. The little boy's *ayah* (nanny) gave a private account to my *ayah* when she was visiting, and I listened to them agog. She had been minding the child while his parents were at the cinema. She heard them come in arguing loudly. A little later, she heard someone in the kitchen and saw him leave with something in his hand, a shadow moving swiftly among other shadows around the courtyard. Rohit then shut the bedroom door and turned off the lights. The *ayah* heard no screams, as would definitely have occurred in an accident, but muffled, guttural sounds, and she said she thought he had strangled her. A little later there was a fire in the room, and Rohit came running out shouting for help. A few hours later, still in the dead of night, the driver had been awakened to fetch the doctor, and he had carried the doctor's bag upstairs. As soon as the doctor said something about the smell of kerosene, he was hustled out of the room without so much as a proper look at the victim. Other accounts emerged to invalidate the "electrical spark" theory; another nanny had seen the can of kerosene, usually kept in the kitchen, in a corner of the bedroom, and she claimed that she had seen Rohit's manservant fetching it from the kitchen. This servant had disappeared shortly after the "accident" came to light, and it was believed that he had been paid off to return to his village and keep out of the family's affairs in Lucknow. Rohit, the only eyewitness to the mishap, had remained silent and sullen after offering his electrical spark story, but he was soon back at work in the family's retail trade. He consented to another marriage not long afterward and began his new life, the slate of the past wiped clean and references to Mridula's death reduced to sympathetic tongue clucking or silence.

Two things stood out for me as I replayed this unforgettable event in my mind. It became clear to me that this kind of sudden, unexamined, allegedly accidental death would become increasingly frequent for women who were in their late teens or early twenties at the time of their marriage and were unable to accomplish a smooth transition into their affinal families—an unfortunate side effect of the otherwise supremely beneficial raising of the age of marriage. And second, the ramifications of virilocality were frightening. Such an end for a man would have been impossibly hard to stage. Were not their roots in their natal homes, among their own beloved familiars, the very source of their worldly power? And conversely, for women, was the relocation to their marital homes not a brutal uprooting that made them vulnerable to violence as defenseless new outsiders with few or no allies inside their marital homes? Is this not the *pivot* on which the imbalance between power and gender rests? It seemed neither logical nor fair that in marriage women and women alone should be systematically removed from the sight and hearing of their relations and friends to be transplanted to the often-hostile soil of their strange and remote affinal homes. Virilocality, this common feature of north Indian Hindu society, created for women and men vastly different destinies and vastly different experiences, as expressed so well by the young girl in Amir Khusrau's *bidai* song (see the epigraph of this chapter). The accelerating transition to urban middle-class nuclear families would, I was to discover, isolate married women even further, robbing them of the company of siblings, friends, confidantes, and partisans.

Thus the layered meanings of dowry—particularly of dowry as a safety net in the virilocal residence or other forms of displacement—emerged in my grandmother's circle among these refugee women from western Punjab, where most Hindu and Sikh families had lost their lands, homes, and other immovable wealth. Satya, a woman who had lost her young son to a violent mob and now had an abusive, alcoholic, and disturbed husband to contend with, spoke of having brought a small packet of gold jewelry tucked in her inner garments that had given them a fresh lease on life in Lucknow. She had pawned a gold chain and twelve gold bangles in order to borrow the capital to invest in a small repair workshop, where her older son and her husband repaired motorcycles, small pumps, and other mechanical items. They had managed to redeem the gold and had also been able to enlarge the refugee quarters they had been allotted. Others had parlayed small pieces of jewelry to furnish their bare rooms, educate or marry their children, get medical help, or just meet the expenses of reestablishing a business in a distant place. The widows of two brothers had even been able to convert their portable assets into a large house on the plot assigned to them in the new refugee colony, Sringar Nagar, on the southern edge of Lucknow, where they now lived on the ground floor and let out the apartment upstairs. The *movable* property had become *immovable* property. Even in the bloody mayhem of the Partition, each woman had managed to secrete a few pieces of jewelry—necklaces, rings, bracelets, earrings, and nose rings—which they now wore, or pawned, or sold, and treasured as their only private resource.

To these women, dowry was the material counterpart of their instinct for survival. But they also conceded that "we" (Punjabis and others) as a people had become very materialistic and individualistic, and that among the refugees, who had lost so much, there was a tendency to acquire wealth through a son's marriage, particularly a very eligible son's marriage. Bose's analysis of dowry had foreseen this growing trend. Without a proper dowry, a daughter would be difficult to marry off, since demands for a larger dowry were becoming more common. Women with daughters scarcely a few years old had begun to put things away for their future dowries; the odd sari, a shawl, gold bangles bought with money diverted from routine expenses, a gift to themselves that they would rather their daughter have was no longer enough. But dowry demands, though not unheard of in the 1960s, were considered repugnant, as they still are. "Only *neech log* (low people) are shameless enough to complain about a *bahu*'s (daughter-in-law) dowry" was the unanimous and unequivocally view of these women who were all mothers of sons. This was the commonsensical view of dowry, and it was widely shared. Respectable people did not ask for dowry, nor did they interfere in the control of it as the woman's private emolument. Dowry was painstakingly collected and affectionately bestowed, and it was fervently hoped that the daughter would always be happy and prosperous and use it for adornment, never having to put its critical underlying purpose as a safety net to the test. A demand for dowry was not to be countenanced, and to kill a bride for an inadequate dowry was unthinkable. And for the overwhelming majority of Hindus, probably more than 98 percent, fortunately, it still is.

Srimati Basu's sharply drawn analysis on her recent research on dowry and daughters, conducted by interviewing one woman per household in low- and middle-income neighborhoods in New Delhi, definitely supports the tenor of these informal conversations with women some thirty-five years ago. "The social illusion that dowry is a voluntary gift of affection from the bride's family was widespread." Her figures indicated a "strong consensus across social classes that leaving it up to the bride's family to do the right thing was most preferable, since it appeared to ensure customary gifts without showing visible greed." Her figures point to a change in the direction of a more common voicing of dowry demands. An average of 20 percent of the households she surveyed made some explicit demand for dowry, but more than twice as many households in the low-income area made these demands than did middle- and higher-income households (Basu 1999: 98–99).[8] That fact that the groom's family can so easily exploit a domain once controlled by mothers for daughters is a reflection of the gradual diminution of the authority of women in social arrangements, and more starkly of the politics of gender that emerged in codified customary law in the colonial period that we traced in the preceding chapter, rather than the timeless effect of hypergamous alliances.

A MISALLIANCE: 1 OCTOBER 1965–7 AUGUST 1966

I have pondered the problems of telling my own story of a desperate, yearlong, partially suppressed, partially revealed phase of my life that continues to haunt and bedevil the breaking of a silence. I am both daunted and provoked by the risks of this unorthodox move in the writing of history. Historians seldom use the first-person pronoun, let alone enmesh their own lives in their writing about those of others. To write an honest, undisguised, first-person narrative and include it in an academic book sounds like an act of self-indulgence or catharsis that belongs elsewhere, since I am not the normative subject of this project; yet the resonance of my story in those that I heard at Saheli finally compelled me to speak.

Let me briefly acknowledge the existence of the current debate still heard in feminist literary circles about the difficulties attendant on interpreting women's voices. As a feminist historian, I am warned that the field of women's autobiography has become a quicksand because of a profound disagreement among feminist literary theoreticians on the subject of woman as subject. Summarily, this conversation, which it is my privilege only to overhear and to understand very crudely, revolves around "the problem we have reading any women's autobiographies: interpreting a text in which a marginalized subject speaks a dominant discourse" (Carr 1988: 136).[9] Those on one side, who are primarily pioneer American feminist literary critics of the 1970s, stress the imperative right of women "to have a 'voice,' their need to express their different experience, and the importance of uncovering suppressed and forgotten female texts." The other side, feminist literary theoreticians influenced by French poststructuralism and Lacanian psychoanalysis, "sees such privileging of the expressive as naive and treacherous realism. Language is a symbolic system in which woman is always inscribed as the other and inferior: texts give no direct access to an 'author' or to 'true' women's experience." To ignore the formation of women's texts within a "phallocentric discourse" is, they insist, to collude with that discourse. For them, it is only in the gaps and ruptures that what is excluded or unnamed in the phallocentric symbolic order may emerge (Carr 1988: 136). While bearing in mind the caveats posed by both these approaches, I must, as Carr does, explore the challenges to Western assumptions found in the stories and texts of these doubly marginalized subjects.

In my own experience stories, conversations, close and private communications of women have the same potential as historical material as do the autobiographies and biographies of men, and historians, feminist or not, cannot afford to ignore them. We must listen to these stories with a sensibility that both acknowledges and reconfigures the inherent linguistic phallocentrism, because the use of stories is in itself a subversion of the male-oriented, teleological drive of history, especially in the very act of writing a new holistic history. We cannot nudge aside the work of South Asian feminist historians, and of scores of "radical pragmatists" (as the feminist political scientist Mary Katzenstein has aptly called them), of the women's movement in India. They are engaged in the task, among many others, of restoring the subjectivity of Indian women by using their voices and texts as a desperately needed antidote to their reification in colonial history, in law, and the mainstream print media. Those who listen know that women have never surrendered the right to speak or to remain silent, to craft their own and others' stories, and it is in their conversations that we find them as subjects of their own histories. We must listen even to the cries of a woman in pain, which in the public world are not "heard" but dismissed as the muffled noise belonging to that private realm of "domestic violence" in which law makers and enforcers deliberately choose not to intrude.

At Saheli I worked with women who came in to tell of their plight—battered women, women who had fled from potential dowry murders, survivors of other forms of violence, wives of mindless wife beaters and alcoholics. I listened to their stories, read cases in the center's files, recorded life histories, and followed up on them on my own time. In their narratives, but even more in their silences, omissions, and secrets, I found strands of my own story weaving themselves into my conversations with these strangers; in listening to their private anguish, I could unobtrusively explore my own.

In trying to write this, I find that my memory of things as they occurred is not chronological. What are most vivid are the sexual trauma, the violence, and the explosive ending; the rest is shrouded in a gray sadness. So I will not privilege chronology and straighten out this tale, as a good historian should. It is tangled and fitful, and I decided to tell it the way I order the main events in my own mind: beginning with the end and then continuing in a spiral that winds down to the beginning. The story is reconstructed here from memory aided by a twenty-two-page account of it I wrote only a month after the breakup of the marriage, by conversations with friends spread over two decades, and by the continual intro-spection and self-analysis that this period in my life triggered.

I was married on 1 October 1965 after a short betrothal, and I abruptly returned home to my parents on 8 August 1966, just shy of completing twenty. I had be-come gaunt, my once-clear skin was blotchy with pimples and scars, and I had angry, suddenly older eyes. The news of my return spread quickly, and in trickled, in twos and threes, family friends and relatives, more curious than sympathetic, to find out what had happened to bring my marriage to such a premature end. I was grateful to be alive and at home, but also haunted by the shame of having come home to all these startled people, of having subverted the social order. The women who came were practiced at mourning with women who had lost their husbands, but they had no script, no songs, no way to deal with a woman who had left her husband's house by means other than the proverbial *arthi*, or bier. I was quite dazed myself, trying to distill the events of those ten interminable months into a sparse narrative that I could use to answer some of the queries that swirled around me.

The first questions anyone asked, since this was the easy part, were about money, and specifically dowry: Were the in-laws stingy? Were they "money-minded"? Did they think my *daaj* was inadequate? Did they harass me for dowry? I remember just shaking my head, when I really wanted to shriek and tell them that they were not asking the right questions; and while money and jewelry were discussed interminably, none of that discussion was relevant to my experience. I was irritated, even surly, and often chose not to speak at all, for my experience was unspeakable. But the less I explained, the more I felt I was the object of other peo-ple's conversations, whispers, and glances.

For days my mother remained in bed with a variety of unexplained symptoms, looking ever harder in her well-thumbed *Ramcharitmanas* (the fifteenth-century poet Tulsidas's version of the famous Sanskrit epic the *Ramayana*) for solace, ad-vice, and parallels. Her eldest sister had arranged the match, and she had given her consent despite her own misgivings. My father was sullen, and he proposed that I join the family business after qualifying as a lawyer. I could see that my un-scripted reappearance was something we all would have to learn to live with. I felt like my parents' handicapped child, loved but without the potential for a normal future.

Postmortems on the anatomy of this failed marriage were performed regu-larly. Why did I say yes? My own reasons, at eighteen, for not resisting the arrange-ment, so compelling then, appear plainly misguided in retrospect. I had been brought up to be strong-willed but had had no social freedom at all: my grandfa-ther, father, and uncles had the sternest ideas of controlling their women, perhaps the more so because they were philanderers themselves. I had begun to resent their control very early, and this bred a kind of longing for defiance, for auton-omy. Complicating this picture was a secret and socially unacceptable relationship

I was in. Acceptance of such a liaison as ours was unthinkable even to us, let alone to our families and the larger world of which we were part. Consumed with longings and impractical hopes, I was indifferent when I had to "choose" my marriage partner. I also naïvely believed that marriage to a suitable boy was the only redemption for one who had so transgressed, and that it would ultimately fix the deep flaw of rebelliousness in my nature. Worse yet, I had no alternative plans for a career after graduating. Housewifery and raising tidy little replicas of this husband sounded purposeful enough to me. The prospective suitor's father had declared that he had found the beautiful *bahu* (daughter-in-law) they had been looking for to fill the void in their household caused by the death of his wife. I reasoned that my chances at happiness would be greatly increased without the dreaded mother-in-law to contend with. Rings, sweetmeats, and a set of fine clothes were exchanged to seal the engagement.

During the short betrothal, our few chaperoned encounters were fraught with misgivings. I sensed his social conservatism and double standards; I smoldered within, but my ingrained psychosocial conditioning underwrote my glum silences. I knew deep down that I was forcing myself to ignore an omen.

Then there was what can be construed as a "dowry demand." Two weeks before the wedding day, my future father-in-law called to say that for purely sentimental reasons he needed a set of jewelry for his deceased wife, which he would place in front of her photograph on the wedding day. My parents were shocked at this request and the dastardly timing of the demand, and they considered calling off the wedding. This request for the dead mother-in-law was inauspicious, our family priest informed us, but he was overruled since the wedding was two weeks away and to break an engagement now would cause enormous social embarrassment. This moment described for me, as I looked at my parents holding their heads in their hands, the inherent helplessness of bridegivers and the vulnerability of an unmarried woman's reputation. My mother dug up another set of jewels from her own dowry and the wedding occurred as planned on the first day of October.

Not long after I returned home (from this still untold "adventure"), I sensed disapproval and even spiteful glee in several members of my father's extended family.[10] I could not tell anyone that my deepest misery stemmed from the discord in our own extended family, and that I felt only relief about the end of my own marriage. My older *chachi* (wife of my paternal uncle), ever plotting to usurp for her husband my father's privilege as the eldest son of the family, actually precipitated the turning point in my own perception of this event: "*Hai baichari* [poor thing], she is not even twenty and her life is over! No decent boy from a status family will ever want to marry her now. She will be a lifelong burden for her parents!" It rudely ended my self-pitying reveries and nail-biting despair. Oddly galvanized by that memorable gibe, I drove off to the admissions office of Lucknow University. I applied to be admitted to the Western History Department, the only department left in the Liberal Arts section with a vacant seat. And a day later my father and I took the train to Delhi to consult the lawyer retained to obtain a divorce.

I found it impossible to articulate my story to my lawyer, particularly with my father sitting there, and after a tearfully awkward interview the lawyer suggested that I write down whatever he needed to know to make a case. He wanted the answers to pertinent questions that related strictly to the conditions for divorce: Were you harassed to bring more dowry after you were married? Can you *prove* that he was unfaithful to you? Did he have a serious contagious disease such as leprosy or syphilis? Did he have a certifiable history of insanity or clinical depression? Can you *prove* that he beat you—any witnesses or physical signs such as a lost eyeball, scars, broken bones, or burns? Did he fail in his conjugal duties by not consummating the marriage? Was he impotent? The courts would require indubitable *proof* of impotence, which was almost impossible to obtain. It looked like a losing battle to me.

Divorce for Hindus had become legal in 1956, but the grounds on which one could be obtained were virtually impossible to establish, judging from that list. Conversion to another religion was a ground, but I dismissed that out of hand. No mutual consent divorce was available then; it had to be an adversarial procedure in the courts, and the woman, I discovered to my (then) amazement, would have to be a perfect saint or a mutilated victim to impress the lone male judge. (There are no jury trials in India.) The dowry demand was briefly considered as a legal point, because the Prohibition of Dowry Act had become law in 1961, only five years earlier. It deemed the givers and takers of dowry equally culpable, though, so that line of argument was also quickly shelved. There was nothing else in the law that favored a woman's case. That day my father presented me with a tome on the 1956 Hindu Code to study to find out what it meant to be a Hindu woman in the eyes of this law.

I set upon the easier task of complying with my lawyer's request to make a list of everything I had received from both sides as gifts of clothing, jewelry, cash, fixed deposits in the bank, and property—all defined as *stridhan*, women's wealth, and to which I had unequivocal legal rights. It was then agreed that I would write my account and my father, a qualified lawyer, would translate my English into the legalese spoken in the courts. He would send it on to the barrister who would plead the case in Delhi, the legal jurisdiction for the dispute. If we were lucky, this would enable me to get a favorable decree within the next five years and after expending a small fortune. All this was numbing, but I sat down to write the story in an exercise book left over from my school days.

My strategy for retelling the story here is this: I have used the account I produced in October 1966, which roughly orders the sequence of what I then saw to be the critical events. There were many things, as we shall see, that I could never bring myself to say, since the readers of this narrative were my parents and the lawyer. It was a brief, tight narrative, something I am proving incapable of writing this time around. I excised the true horror of some incidents, sparing everyone, but mostly myself, the shame of events that involved sex or violence. There were absolutely no descriptions of either, not even of the bruises examined by the doctor next door. Today, more than three decades later and half a world away from those events, I have after much private agonizing found a candid, strong, blunt voice that annotates, interweaves, extrapolates, and reveals the subtexts of that shy, spare telling. Thus I have split the narrator of this story into subject and object, one knowing the end of the story and the other struggling in it, as it were, as it is happening. I am the author in both cases, with a thirty-five-year time lag between the two tellings. Only the style of the font distinguishes my two voices: the parts in italics are an abbreviated version, with pseudonyms, of what I wrote in 1966, and what is interspersed in brackets in regular type is what I omitted to say then and take the risk of saying now.

My masi [maternal aunt] *arranged my marriage to Bikki and we were married on 1 October 1965 with the usual fanfare that attends such an event. We met once more when I developed doubts about our compatibility, but I ignored these feelings because I had made the choice and it was too late to change my mind. I knew the marriage would not work even before the train arrived in Delhi. I felt a quiet nervousness to be alone with this drunken stranger, whose sexual advances were abrupt and clumsy. I pushed him away. The emotional trauma of leaving my family and friends behind had savaged me completely, so I remained resentfully silent.*

He motioned that he wanted to consummate the marriage right away since his friends would laugh at him the next morning if he did not. I felt the indelicacy of allowing the loss of that "most important and precious thing for a woman" in a hired railway compartment while hawkers periodically banged on the window trying to sell us tea or snacks.[11] *What was even more frightening to me was that he was patently not the intellectual companion I had hoped for either. I disliked his Punjabi accent that inflected his speech in Hindi, Urdu, and English, and his complete ignorance of the literature in any of these languages.* These stubborn judgments became a fundamental obstacle to a sexual relationship and I was childish enough to want to giggle at his attempts at conversation. *In the course of that night I discovered that he had a removable dental bridge. I lost my reserve and asked how he had lost his teeth. He said he was injured during a field hockey game in school. I felt a deep mistrust of him because he had not revealed this earlier when we had talked about ourselves.* Dental bridges are common, I have since discovered, but my dismay was more complicated. I sensed that he was lying to cover up something. This was his first subreption of the many that would follow. I would later discover that he lied often, and glibly. The lawyer had marked this passage with the word "fraud."

The next evening at our wedding reception in Delhi, an unexpectedly intense encounter with Bikki's cousin confirmed my suspicion about the false teeth. I was told that it was unfortunate that Bikki had had a brawl over a prostitute "with a bad man" and that the end

result was a badly damaged mouth. And also that Bikki had never finished college. He in-
formed me that Bikki had no interest in his studies. His father had bribed his son's way out
of high school. Then, because his father had the agency to sell Czech tractors, he sent his
son to Prague, where he worked as a foreman in the tractor factory. He was no engineer.
The family had represented him as such. The lawyer boldly underlined this section and wrote "fraud" in the margin.

That night I was to discover his violently abusive and drunken side. When he gruffly
asked me why I was sulking inside instead of enjoying the grand reception I decided to
confront him head on: he slapped me squarely across my face. Lawyer's marginal note:
"Was there a witness who will testify?"

I was stunned. My vague feelings of dislike had turned into revulsion, and I
knew I had to find the courage to grope my way out of this thicket of deception
and hostility. I did not bring up the fracas at the prostitute's quarters for fear of
being beaten. I was revolted at the idea of sex with him, but afraid that my resistance would only lead to more violence. *I lay in bed in all my clothes refusing to turn*
my face towards him; I did not sleep a wink and felt totally exhausted, doomed, and help-
less. It was only the 4th of October, and from then on every night brought on a fresh argu-
ment. Kanta, my husband's sister, would arrive by lunch time and stay until before dinner,
and would try to work on her self-appointed task of trying to mould me, like clay, to fit
into my new family, become just like one of them and forget my family in Lucknow. She
also suggested that a child would melt my husband's heart.

Bauji [as my father-in-law was called] had heard the arguments with Bikki about the
false teeth and nonexistent engineering degree and decided to calm me down and befriend
me. While he had been complicit in hiding these facts from my aunt who had arranged the
marriage, he now became astoundingly frank about his son's shortcomings. He bemoaned
Bikki's drinking, and his utter failure to study, his lack of acumen as a businessman, his
inner rage. He himself was a self-made man. He appeared to be on my side. "I will teach
you how to make him happy so that he will want to please you. You are an innocent and
marriage can bring great pleasure." The sexual implication here was lost on me then.

Soon afterwards, to demonstrate his solidarity with me he ordered that shares in their
business, a car, and other assets be transferred to my name [which also reduced the tax
burden on their declared wealth, as a woman's wealth or income is not combined
with her husband's wealth or income]. *He made me promise that I would not divulge*
any of our private conversations to Bikki, or even to Kanta, who, although his own daugh-
ter, was no longer part of "our family." We played cards together every evening and I
began ministering to his needs—making sure he had his heart medicines on time, and
pressing his head when he said it hurt. His attempt to establish physical intimacy
started with his asking me to kiss him every morning in his room just as he had
seen me do to my father and grandfather, and then holding me in a long embrace.
One day, while his daughter was present in the room, he asked me to assist him to take off
his daytime pajamas and help him get ready for bed as she used to do. He also asked me to
do this later, when no one was present. This became a fairly regular practice. Kanta ap-

peared to encourage me, so I ignored the erotic undertones I now clearly discerned in his responses. Culturally speaking, daughters-in-law are supposed to keep a physical distance from their male in-laws, because this is a zone of frequent and tacitly tolerated adulterous relationships.

The private scenes in our marital bedroom worsened. Alcohol abuse, sexual jealousy, and stout refusal to have sex with him drove him into regular rages. Quarreling, I realize, had become my only shield against sexual demands; my terror of pregnancy, which would make it impossible for me ever to leave this marriage, kept me steeled, even though I was slyly taking birth control pills I had obtained from a gynecologist in Lucknow before we were married. His sexual desire was always framed in the wish for fatherhood; he would sometimes turn to me in sincere humility and plead that all he wanted from me was a son and heir.

After another ludicrous incident, when my drunken husband was both violent and vomiting, Bauji intervened forcefully. *He strongly chastised his son, and told Bikki that if he were ever violent with me again he would kill himself because he could not countenance such cowardly behavior in his son.* The next day, after Bikki left for work, Bauji inquired quite candidly and specifically about the sexual impasse he knew existed between my husband and me. This conversation breached a new frontier. I had never talked to an elder in my own family about sex, and only the most oblique references to it occurred in my conversations with even my own mother. Excruciatingly embarrassing though it was, this conversation came as a great relief for me. I realized I needed him as an ally against further violence, which I dreaded. I became increasingly more comfortable on our long quiet evenings talking about my marital problems.

Bikki went out of town for a few days on business. On 14 February 1966 only the old widow of Bauji's brother, who lived like a glorified maid in a back room, was in her room in the back of the house. *We played the wonted hands of rummy and then he retired to his room. A few minutes later he called me into his room and asked me to remove his pajamas.* I did so nervously since it was obvious that he was sexually aroused. *He then asked me to rub his chest and later to press his legs, and he removed the covers as I obliged.* He told me he longed for my love, for my body. *I turned my face away. He asked me never to tell anyone about what he had just said.* . . . The narrative trailed off with an ellipsis.

I remember vividly why I left those four dots on the page to be interpreted as the lawyer wished. But what happened was unforgettable. After a brief conversation on the subject of a sexual encounter with him, which I categorically refused, he raped me. After this event a dark chill formed between us. The trust and friendship were rudely fractured. I told my husband what had transpired, and he threatened to kill me with a revolver he kept in his cupboard. He told me I was a whore who had seduced his father and that he would find a way of killing me because divorce was not acceptable; it would bring too much shame to our families. I no longer even wanted to go home; so great was the pollution I felt. I thought it might be best for me to die. I implored Bauji to make a clean breast of it and end his son's suspicions. He refused. This untenable situation lingered until I decided to summon my parents to see me before I killed myself. I would exit the house as everyone expected a good wife to do, on an *arthi*.

My notebook had this concluding episode: *On the 3rd of July my parents accosted my startled father-in-law in the courtyard, before I thought they had even received my letter. My father made me stand behind him and exploded in an anger that surpassed anything I had ever witnessed before, but it made me proud of him. He warned that if he set eyes on the man he would be obliged to do what would be the honorable thing to do: kill him. He would rather make his daughter a widow than let her live in that house another day.* Lawyer's note: This implicates Baljit Singh [my father's real name] in threatening to kill his son-in-law. *My mother pulled out the letter that had brought them so urgently to Delhi and flung it at him, calling them "uncivilized brutes." My father then told me to go into my room and get my bags packed for departure, but I was too stunned to budge. My father-in-law now made a very melodramatic and tearful apology and begged me not to leave. I agreed to stay.* To this day I cannot fully explain the residual loyalty I felt to my father-in-law. I astounded myself when I asked for another chance; I did not know what prompted this. Maybe it was because of all those years of conditioning about wifely mores that I agreed to risk my life to prolong this farcical marriage. I knew that if Bikki heard even a watered-down version of how his father had placed his cap (the symbol of a man's honor) at my father's feet to beseech him to leave me behind, he would kill me instantly. But my father-in-law's abject tears made it all very confusing for me. I really did believe then that his remorse was sincere and that he would kill himself.[12] I now know that those words came bubbling up from that inner depth where I had buried the uneasy, subliminal guilt for my own rape.

My parents left without even sipping a glass of water or exchanging good-byes. Bikki got home and berated me for having dragged my parents into this. I deeply regretted my decision to stay and we barely spoke to each other. This stalemate lingered for another month.

On 7th August, after my husband once more tried to kill me with his bare hands, I wrestled myself free and ran into the bathroom, locking the door behind me. I fled from the back door of the bath that led out to the driveway. I remember quickly removing all my bangles, rings, and necklace and leaving them on the bathroom sink. I was only in a blouse and petticoat, I had not yet worn my sari and I was barefoot. I ran into the family doctor's house next door from where I contacted my relatives but was soon fetched by a contingent from my husband's house and locked up. They had distinct plans to burn me to death.

The danger of being burnt to death was real, and my letters to my parents saying that I planned to take my life would be all the proof necessary to establish my death as a suicide. I screamed loudly, the neighbors were already at our gates watching this riveting drama. This was war. I cursed and abused everyone—torrents of filthy, ugly abuse that would drown all the silences in my life came breathlessly spilling out. *The old aunt* had fetched the kerosene tin from the kitchen and ordered the servant to pour it into the room and throw a lighted match in it. My fear had evaporated and I found a ferocious will to live. I said I would burn to death but not before everything and everybody in this house was burnt to death too. My arthi would not be the only one to leave this house, or else I would leave it on my own two feet. Just then the rescue party, consisting of my grandmother and Mahabir the driver, a muscular, towering Rajput who had once been a professional wrestler. A moment later I was in a car hugging my grandmother all the way to the safety of my aunt's home, where this saga had begun a year ago. I noticed that I was now in a torn blouse and petticoat, still barefoot and with very dramatic marks of resisting violence rather than the ritual marks of a suhagin [married woman] that I had had when I first entered the premises. Yet, it was a trifle better than leaving on an arthi. The exercise book narrative ends here. The lawyer's final comment read: "Not much of a case here, but we can get back the dowry."

The last stage of this saga was its transformation into a "case" fit for a legal divorce. After a cursory reading of the account of my marriage, my lawyer was of the opinion that I had no case for a divorce! The narrative was "all allegations" and contained remarkably self-incriminating passages: I had sworn at my husband and even hurled a chair at him, denied him sex, and showed little sincere affection or duty toward the man. Yes, the violence he had committed was real, but it would be difficult to prove beyond a reasonable doubt by the time the case was admitted in court; the bruises would have healed. His threats and attempts to kill me would also have to be clearly established, and with hostile family witnesses this was going to be next to impossible. Even the doctor to whose home I had fled and who had examined me immediately said he would not testify against his neighbors, for they were dangerous people. If the lawyer filed a divorce suit on my behalf, the outcome for me would be grim whether I won or lost the case. If I won, it would only be after prolonged and expensive litigation in the Delhi courts, during which time I would be forced to return to my marital home, for the husband was entitled to "the restitution of conjugal rights" for a whole year before a divorce could be decreed. This possibility shorted out the circuits of my brain. The other alternative was that I could lose (the courts were far more sympathetic to the rights of the husband than to the rights of wives), especially since their lawyer had hinted that it would be "no problem" for them to produce witnesses who would testify under oath that I had committed adultery on many occasions when my husband was away on tour. I would have no recourse but to return to their home, for that is what they wanted. It was not enough to have narrowly escaped being burned to death; the divorce law was such a stark example of a patriarchal vision that I felt a morbid urge rise within me again. And the barrister added kindly that the process would waste my youth.

Having painted these numbing scenarios, he then revealed what he planned to do in my case that would ensure a quick, clean end to the marriage. He was going to claim that we had never been married. He created a legal fiction that was to win me an annulment on perfectly acceptable legal grounds. It entailed lies, intimidation, and calling their bluff. The scheme is worth repeating, since I found it used in a handful of Saheli cases, as well. I was vulnerable on many counts, while they seemed to be vulnerable on only one: I had witnesses to prove that I had left the house with not even a bangle on my wrist. My entire *stridhan* was in their possession, and I had an absolute right to it that no judge in the land would deny. In talking to their lawyer, my lawyer discovered that although they opposed the idea of a divorce, they worried that I would demand the delivery of my *stridhan* by court order, since that was my property whether or not I chose to remain married or to live elsewhere. My dowry and the jewels and gifts from my husband's father were amply documented on film and in photographs; the car and company shares had been transferred to my name, and I owned several fixed deposits held at the local bank. The 1956 ruling on *stridhan* was unambiguous; no one, not even my husband, could legally obstruct my exclusive control over it. Also, after the divorce, I would be entitled to court-approved alimony based on the income and assets of my husband, including the existence of trunks full of cash that I could reveal. They would quickly agree to a compromise if I agreed not to file a claim on my *stridhan*, to forgo everything they had given me, and to recover only my own dowry. To make the compromise foolproof, my lawyer suggested that Bikki be persuaded to become the plaintiff and I the defendant. This would eliminate the risk of his contesting the charges. As the defendant I would lose the case by not contesting the charge that I had never been legally married. This was the only way to win.

The plaintiff's case was to be based on that section of the divorce law that allowed a marriage to be annulled if it could be proved by either party that even one of the four key rituals in a Vedic Hindu ceremony, as defined by the court, had not been completed at the time of the wedding. We were now working in collusion with his lawyer. Bikki's plaint would simply state that one of the critical Vedic rites—the *satpadi* (seven steps)—had never been performed and that therefore the marriage had never occurred. Uncontested suits are quickly settled; the judge would have no option but to grant the annulment after a single perfunctory hearing in camera. A week after the case came up in court in January 1967, I was a free woman again, not a divorcée but someone who had never been married.

What can we learn from this long and complicated story? The answer will become clear as we submit it to analytic scrutiny along with the other stories, the other "cases," that appear in the final section of this chapter. Immediately, however, we must evaluate the role of our prime institutional culprit, dowry, in the case. There was, indeed, that demand for something more than my parents had thought about giving—and they, and anyone else who they consulted, pronounced such behavior as shameless and untenable. The prospective in-laws had broken a cardinal rule of the dowry-accepting culture. Without telling me, my parents had wrestled with it, seriously considered wriggling out of this alliance altogether, but, as I have pointed out, the timing of the request, their anxiety about how a broken engagement might unfairly and significantly hurt my future chances in the marriage market, and family honor hobbled their ability to do so. Incidents like these starkly demonstrate how traditional gender inequalities, made more acute in the past 150 years, enable cultural understandings to be distorted, bent, and disfigured. and gave bridetakers the unwritten, uncustomary right to make demands and, therefore, created the perception of a daughter as a financial "burden." Be that as it may, it is incontestable that the problem with dowry did not make me contemplate suicide nor did it inspire my in-laws' wish to immolate me in that final showdown.

Having publicly committed themselves to the match at the betrothal ceremony, my parents could not escape the pitiless logic that forecloses the bridegivers' options and underwrites the greed of the bridetakers. Rather than go through the unnerving process of being interviewed by another prospective suitor's family, in which the bride's and the bridegivers' "inferiority" would be tested in some other way, I deferred to my elders. Hypergamy—that notorious imperial bogey—is conspicuous by its absence as a problem in this and most cases that I encountered in my research. The contest was between bridetakers and bridegivers of the same caste. The bridetakers *always* have an edge over their counterparts, and the unmistakable relationship of power to gender rather than to social status or caste is exposed. It is in these interactive moments that we can decode the rules of the game and discern the inclination of the playing field.

The reason to tell my own story is the strong resonance I found it had in the stories of women that appeared in newspapers and women's journals and magazines in the 1980s, and with those of the women who came to Saheli for help. In listening to the stories of others, I was startled at the similarity of the motifs that ran through their lives and mine, how sex and death had dogged us. I could not help thinking that women today are better off than in the 1960s, and not only because we have better legal and media apparatuses to hear their grisly tales. Today there is not a woman in a big city in India who has not heard of someone who has suffered brutally in a marriage and has possibly even been the victim of suicide or murder. More than three decades ago, in 1966, I had only the memory of Mridula as a victim and myself as a survivor; and our stories remained family secrets. The era of women who suffered in silence may well be in its twilight.

DISCONTINUOUS LIVES

Perceptions about dowry that dated back to the mid-nineteenth century had over the course of a century become a substantiated reality, and the first legal step to ban the custom was embodied in the Prohibition of Dowry Act of 1961. It stopped neither the violence nor the escalation of dowry. Feminist activists began to demand its amendment almost immediately, and a quarter century of struggle brought some of the desired changes in 1985. The new clauses were to give the old law "some teeth." The amended law made dowry demands an actionable offence, but violations are difficult to prosecute since demands are usually not made in writing. Other changes include harsher punitive measures and a provision for the swift and easy return of the dowry to the woman or her family (if she had died), and this clause has seen dramatic results. Loopholes remain, though, and the law really is hopeless as a deterrent, judging from the contagion of dowry deaths, which are now reported from many more states in India, including the south, than when they were first uncovered. According to the National Crime Records Bureau in Delhi the number of women being burned to death each year has been well over the five thousand mark since 1991, with a 26 percent rise to 6,917 such deaths in 1998, for the dozen or more years the amended act has been in effect. But there is also a growing acknowledgment among feminist activists that dowry is not the sole cause of violence against women or even of dowry murders, and that women themselves resent this ban on the practice when for the majority of them it is the only cushion they will ever receive from their families. If women had not asserted themselves in actually insisting on taking the best dowry their parents can afford, dowries would indeed have become a thing of the past, with the levels of violence against women unchanged or rising. In her study of dowry victims set in Delhi in 1985, Ranjana Kumari (1989: 14–15) shows that the rise in the value of dowries is partly prompted by brides themselves. She attributes this to their selfish interest in their own status and to make up for the denial to them of a share in the natal family property (Kumari 1989: 14–15).

The insistence of women's groups that domestic violence against women was no longer a family affair but called for legal intervention also prompted amendments to three other acts. In 1983 the Indian penal code gained an additional section, 498–A, which made cruelty to women perpetrated by a husband or relatives—and this included both mental and physical cruelty—a cognizable and nonbailable offense. The burden of proof on the victim was dramatically reduced when section 113–A of the Evidence Act was changed; this made it possible for a judge to infer "abetment to suicide," which was deemed sufficient grounds to convict the victim's husband and mother-in-law in the case of a bride's suicide. The third amendment facilitated the investigation of the murders of women. Section 174 of the criminal procedure code made postmortem examinations compulsory in cases in which a woman had died within seven years of her marriage. This stopped the rapid cremation or burial of bodies of women and made it easier for a woman's kin to press for legal action (Nair 1996: 237–38).[13] Although these are certainly positive changes, the paucity of convictions suggests that these laws are not based, as any effective legislation must be, on a social consensus and are not respected by the law enforcement agencies themselves. The colonial court system, unreformed in the fifty years since Independence, still rests on a vast majority of male judges, an almost exclusively male police force, and an absence of juries, and it has yet to be purged of its strongly vested patriarchal interest in maintaining gender inequality and male hegemony in Indian society. This is not to suggest that the exciting new initiatives being taken by feminist lawyers, a growing number of policewomen, and by the activists in the nongovernmental sector to battle gender bias in the legal machinery are ineffectual; it is only to say that the overhaul of a system based and sustained by traditional and modern and hybrid patriarchies is resistant to reform.

I began my research by making the obligatory round of visits to city hospitals and police stations, and gathered armloads of statistics—surveys and reports—but they lacked the differentiating detail that was essential for my project. I then opted for qualitative rather than quantitative data and, most of all, to be in the company of women who would be coaxed into telling me their stories. It was not until I was able to find a niche at Saheli, a women's resource center, that I became immersed in direct personal interviews with women—near victims, activists, lawyers, and family members—to enable me to probe fully the circumstances of particular cases. The few stories that I have selected to retell from my own notes point toward a more complex set of motives and outcomes.

My ten-month-long experience as a Saheli volunteer allowed me to observe and participate firsthand in what appears, a dozen years later, to have been a microcosm of the feminist endeavors that proliferated. I hope simply to capture the ethos and the ideology of an alternative space that women in New Delhi have created, and how the amalgam of their interests, existential indignation, and belief in their own power as women reshaped the identities and remade the lives of a selected few who knocked on Saheli's doors.[14]

In wishing to probe marital discord beyond what may be ascribed to dowry harassment, which I found to be only a symptom of the more complicated and deeper malaise that afflicts marital relationships, particularly the rarely discussed but frequently troubled area of sexuality, I was daring to tread a little-traveled path in 1985. It is heartening to know that only a decade later that wall, with its concrete certainties about dowry's baneful effects on all women, which stood between women and their worlds, has turned to glass. At the same time, some of my questions were seen to be "irrelevant" to the case at hand, and my interpretations were challenged, but I gradually succeeded in instituting a new and detailed questionnaire for use by women when they first came to the office, which did not automatically abridge their complaints into a litany about dowry. As women from different segments of urban society poured in with their stories and we listened, it was hard to ignore what they did not at first say. Although their stories share some features, and dowry is certainly one of them, it is the sharp differences that force us to look at sexuality as a powerful source of marital conflict and violence.

Saheli had its beginnings in August 1981 in the garage of the private house of one of its eight founding members in a south Delhi "colony," a neighborhood that was created chiefly to resettle Hindu Punjabi refugees who had fled Pakistan in

1947. The founders pledged to volunteer their time to keep its doors open seven days a week; it was to be a place to which women in distress could come. The catalyst had been violence against women—made more urgent by the attention the media had recently paid to the reversal of the convictions of policemen who had gang-raped a young girl, and by the first reports of "bride burning." With astonishing speed, contributions of cane furniture and essentials such as a typewriter, a file cabinet, brooms, dusters, a table fan, flyswatters, and tea-making equipment quickly furnished a functional space for the women's collective. Books, journals, and posters gave the place its comfortable yet businesslike air of a resource center sustained by the will and energy of a committed and articulate group of *sahelis* willing to learn on the job.

Much of the center's early history was compiled by several of its founding members in a privately circulated pamphlet entitled *Saheli: The First Four Years*, printed in 1984. Excerpts from a daily diary written by the volunteers from the time of the inception of the center gave me a sense of their mission. I know that the courage, innovation, rebellion, sincerity, and frankness reflected in this document represented the flavor and mood of the place in its fifth year as well.

> We did not start with a manifesto. Too many groups had fallen apart on ide-
> ological differences before they could even get started. There were (and are)
> different levels of feminist consciousness in our group, but all of us share a
> common concern. We had become acutely aware that our actions in cases
> of bride burning and rape were undertaken when it was too late for the
> woman concerned. We felt the need to reach out and link our own personal
> struggles at work and in our families with those of other women seeking
> new ways of regaining their self worth and identity. (Saheli 1984: 1)

Saheli's blossoming in the first five years of its existence was dramatic; its vision was unique, although it was initially inspired by feminist collectives in the West. Its nonhierarchical structure remained fluid and changed in response to its circumstances as volunteers swelled the small founding group, and a veritable flood of women arrived seeking help. Many "cases" were to become *sahelis*, and many of the *sahelis* were still working on their own cases, in their heads and in the courts, when I joined them in 1985–1986.[15]

The name Saheli, which means "woman friend," was chosen because friendship rather than kinship was to be the cement used to build this resource center. I sensed a deliberate effort on the part of the *sahelis* not to fall into the typical Indian pattern of thinking of friends as fictive kin and addressing each other with kinship terms, such as *didi* or *behenji* (sister), but rather to make a point of becoming friends, *sahelis*. The work grew exponentially as Saheli came to be known for the valuable and much-needed support it provided to wives in desperate straits, often survivors of physical abuse, rape, or burns.

In its search for a larger, more independent space, Saheli had moved from the garage of a private home, and was now lodged in two rooms of a soulless municipal market in the underbelly of a concrete bridge. Paid work replaced the voluntary labor of women, which was seen as an exploitation of women similar to that perpetrated by men in families, as one *saheli* explained. This change enabled strict schedules, and the center's doors were open six days a week from 9:00 to 6:00, with a rotating roster of women employees trained as counselors. A small annual grant from the central government paid for basic expenses such as rent, utilities, and telephone, but the group put in considerable effort to raise money from private individuals (it did not accept money from foreign funding agencies) to keep the staff paid and the center's ends met. It was, to my mind, a homegrown model of a women's resource center that could be replicated with ease in all the other cities and towns that desperately needed such a facility.

In 1985–1986, the main service offered to the women seeking help, who had chiefly fled violent marriages, was counseling. Occasionally a young woman would come in who had fled her home because she had refused to marry by arrangement, or whose love affair had been discovered and disapproved of by her family, and she was seeking protection from the wrath of a violent father or other male relative. I was surprised to find that only a small fraction of the women who came in were indeed newly married or had a "dowry problem." Wives of three or four years, who could not accurately be described as brides, were the most frequent customers; others were middle-aged women with children, who had finally found the courage to leave violent or drunk husbands. The women were assured of patient and astute listeners (two *sahelis* were assigned to every "case"), and if the matter needed further action, a file was opened and a worksheet filled with the basic particulars and the bare bones of the story. Feminist lawyers who offered pro bono services were in regular touch to update the *sahelis* on the progress of cases, consult with them about fresh cases, and inform them about the progress of the amendments proposed for the Prohibition of Dowry Act of 1961. Saheli also had links with an alcohol and drug abuse center to which husbands could be referred. In a corner of the center were a few shelves of literature on other women's movements worldwide, important feminist publications in English, and books on family law.

One of the lasting regrets of the founding members was that they had been unable to rent a place that could serve as a temporary shelter for women who had nowhere else to stay. The center did maintain two basic rooms nearby where, in a pinch, women could sleep, but landlords had a bias against these women who had organized themselves to help other women, and perceived the center mainly as a front to run a brothel. The founders worked instead to build a network of contacts with placement agencies and business houses to which they could send women who needed jobs. During my time there, two of the *sahelis* had special liaison duties with the local police to ensure that Saheli clients would not be harassed, and women who needed it would be escorted home, safe from the threats of husbands and in-laws, or other relatives. Prabeen, one of the *sahelis*, to whom I owe my affiliation to the center, was spirited enough to devise police education classes intended to make the officers more sensitive and conscientious in reporting and investigating the "accidents" and "suicides" to which women were so prone. A strong grasp of feminist issues informed the praxis of the counselors, although some of them did not particularly like to use the word "feminist" because of its Western connotations.

Those who came for help found themselves in efficient hands and on their way to a reorientation that would change their outlook and eventually their identity quite fundamentally. Old "cases," now happily rehabilitated, would show up from time to time, and these were the best testimony to the success Saheli was having in changing the lives of unhappy and deeply damaged women. Friendship seemed to be a new political frontier; one no longer had to be secluded in a *kotha* (a brothel or salon) or a convent, two gender-segregated places, to develop a vision that transcended the bonds of family. The potential of *sahelis* to empower themselves and the women who came to seek help lay in their ability to create a viable alternate space (physical and ideological) that neither was defined by nor imitated the family. They had created a close-knit community of friends who related to each other as equals; authority was not structured or exercised hierarchically. It was the pivotal article of their faith as *friends*, and workaday problems and personality conflicts among the *sahelis* themselves were dealt with seriously on Friday afternoons. This experiment in egalitarianism was a radical departure from previous feminist organizations that had been involved in the fight for women's rights, such as the All India Women's Conference with its roster of officers and formal procedures that replicated male social organizations.

The words of one of the several *sahelis* that were quoted in the commemorative pamphlet alluded to above give a qualitative feel of the place.

> Here I was able to say all I felt without fear. . . . They heard me and did not shout, condemn or advise. . . . I was not alone any more. What had seemed abnormal within me became so natural and normal here. I feel elated every time I climb the stairs to Saheli. It means more than words can even express. Saheli makes me like myself.—Maya

Aziza wrote, sparely, "Somewhere inside me I feel these are my real relatives." Rukmani felt that "[a]t the age of 21 it finally dawned on me that I was a faceless, nameless entity—a woman—a wife! . . . It has been possible to become a little bit myself due to the support of women friends . . . [in s]haring ideas, experiences and working in Saheli." And Kalpana ruminated, "I came because I belong. It is not always love and warmth, it is fights and bickerings as well. It is not always the work I think I should be doing—but then I belong, HERE, with all other *sahelis* and so I come." Savita, who had originally come as a nearly burned bride, candidly asserted that when she is "unable to take a decision about my future, find myself alone and helpless, feel totally trapped in the net of my doings, I remember Saheli. Saheli gives me support and strength to face pain and unhappiness"(Saheli 1984: 4).

After immersing myself in the material at the center, I quickly became attuned to its philosophy and ethos. Before I ever encountered a near victim of a dowry-related crime in the flesh, I "met" Ranjana, a woman who had been married for less than three months when she became pregnant, and had written three suicide notes before she took her life on 21 July 1978. The original letters in Hindi, in which the charged emotions and anger seemed transmuted into stilted words laden with apology and regret, were to her husband, his sister, and her own parents to explain her circumstances and her choice of such a drastic way out of her misery (Kishwar and Vanita 1984: 203–5).[16] In Ranjana's three suicide notes we can glimpse the mind of a *pativrata*, a woman brought up to be a tirelessly duty-bound wife.

The most substantial note is that to her sister-in-law, which details the harassment she endured, chiefly from her husband in her in-laws' home. When the marriage was arranged, she reminds her sister-in-law, Babbu Didi, her parents-in-law and husband had insisted that they wanted nothing. Ranjana had four sisters, so her parents' resources were exhausted when it came time for her, the youngest, to be married; the sister-in-law, on the other hand, had received a good dowry since she was an only daughter. Ranjana found her husband's complaints about the wedding insensitive and hurtful. He nagged her about the quality of the food served, the gifts to the in-laws, even the clothes in her trousseau, and disparaged her parents and siblings. "At first I kept quiet, but later, I too started answering back. Since 16 May not a day has passed when we have not quarrelled." She also believed that she was "ill-starred" and blamed herself; as soon as she "set foot in his house," she wrote, "his business began to suffer" (Kishwar and Vanita 1984: 203–4).

An even greater source of conflict, it appears, was her lack of freedom in her in-laws' house. "[I]n my parents' house, I was not used to sitting at home, but in Janakpuri [where her in-laws lived] I never stepped out of the house even to see the daylight." Yet, she says, "I did not complain because it is the girl who has to change herself. Anyway, do fulfill his wish to get married a second time" (Kishwar and Vanita 1984: 204). The burden of having to adjust to her new surroundings caused predictable friction. She apologized for taking along her husband's *nishani* (which means here the child she was carrying) and requested that after her death she should be dressed in her favorite sari and her husband should light her funeral pyre. "Get him remarried, but explain to him that he should never complain to her [his new bride] against her relatives" about money and hospitality. By his relentless harping on these matters, which she considered trivial, "he ruined both his own life and my life" (Kishwar and Vanita 1984: 203).

Ranjana's letter to her own parents is terse and respectfully apologetic as she takes her leave from them and all her siblings, their spouses, and their children. "Please forgive me—only two and a half months ago I made you bear the expenditure of my wedding, and now again I am making you spend on my funeral rites. . . . After this I will never trouble you again." She beseeches them not to take her to hospital if she survives "after being burnt. Instead give me poison so that I may die without too much pain." And her final statement is "Do not blame my in-laws. Do not say anything to them. Otherwise my soul will not rest in peace."

In the letter to her husband, Neelkamal Varma, whom she addresses as her raja, or lord, we discover a little more of their private contentions. He had complained that she had never written him any letters, so now, she said, she was writing to him. She describes her imminent suicide as her "going away" because her coming to his house had proved inauspicious for him, and his "family had had difficulties." He must fulfill his desire to marry again, but this time, she advises him, "examine the girl very carefully, first," implying that the marriage had little physical desire in it, and that he had later found her wanting in many respects. He was to make sure that the girl knew "good English," which presumably she did not (Kishwar and Vanita 1984: 204–5). He was also to determine beforehand that his new wife's family respected all the members of his family, especially him. After Ranjana's death, he was never to visit her parents' home, where he "was not respected." He could either burn the clothes that she had brought with her or give them to his new wife, if she cared to have them. And she was sorry that she was taking his child along with her in her womb. She asks him to tell his uncle that she understood his advice but could not implement it, because "he put all the blame on me alone" (p. 205). And finally, in the most telling part of her letter, she says, "When the new bride comes, try and listen to what she says, and do not quarrel with her. Even if her relatives do not pay much attention to you, you should try to stay happy. You should ignore these things. Otherwise her life would also be ruined. And if she talks to you privately about anything never tell anyone else in the house what she says. . . . Now I have talked enough, I had better go" (ibid.: 205). She reports that she left him after their final quarrel and went to her parents' home, having made up her mind to kill herself. She repeats her wish not to be taken to the hospital and to be administered poison should her attempt to burn herself to death fail, because she did not want any more pain.

These letters may be self-explanatory, but I do want to underline a few points. Although the husband appears to be bad tempered and quarrelsome, he is not violent. He carps bitterly about everything—her inability to speak good English, her disrespectful parents, and also her dowry. The quarrels about money and respect seem to stem from her husband's incompetence as a businessman. It is clear that he suddenly found his business failing and became obsessed with the prospect of a financially insecure future. He unreasonably attributed his misfortune to her, which she accepted, given her repeated references to her arrival's not having augured well for his business. He fretted about money, about having to provide for her and possibly the needs of the child in the future. All this has little to do with the matter of her dowry.

What Ranjana's letters reveal best is the overwhelming financial anxieties and tensions in an aspiring lower-middle-class extended family. The husband and wife's social and economic statuses are well-matched, and both parties are hurting for money. She is one of several siblings, and she had probably attended a local government school and received an indifferent education that included only rudimentary English. She was not trained for a career, and soon after she finished college (or even earlier) she was married to a petty businessman who probably obscured the fact that his business was experiencing a downturn. Her secluded, claustrophobic life was compounded, no doubt, with the drudgeries of housework and her pregnancy. There is no allusion to anything vaguely romantic or even pleasant in their brief relationship; instead a strong sense of mutual dislike and incompatibility is communicated to the reader. She and her husband were married on 10 May, and she reports their first big quarrel on the sixteenth, less than a week later. In those first few days, when she became pregnant, they must have had sex as total strangers. The daily diatribes to which she began to "answer back" do little to encourage us to believe that they ever had sexual relations after that date. What she knew in the relationship was not a day's caring. She saw no other future, no fair chance at happiness in their querulous relationship, so she fought back. She returned to her parents' home to do the deed because she craved to see them and her sisters before she died. Although Ranjana's case was certainly not one of murder, or even of dowry death, the law in 1978 would not have allowed her husband to be arraigned on an "abetment of suicide" charge.

There is almost a wounded formality in the tone of her letter to her parents; perhaps they did not come out in strong support of her leaving the marriage, given their own financial constraints. But their sorrow and anger over her death are manifest in their trips in 1979 to what were then fairly obscure feminist organizations. They took copies of Ranjana's letters to the *Manushi* and Saheli offices, where they tried belatedly to seek advice on how to bring those who had driven their daughter to this end to justice. They could not save her life, but their actions made Ranjana's story known. Otherwise she would have been one more obscure statistic in the tally of dowry deaths, unable to make her story see the light of day.

The lack of any distinctive crisis or even violence in this unhappy relationship makes us focus on the quotidian aspects of this case that mirrors many others. The abruptly discontinuous existence; the severe temperamental and dimly hinted-at sexual incompatibility that can only be read between the lines of the suicide note to her husband; the distant, sometimes hostile virilocal home; the parents whose means do not permit them to interpret their daughter's anguish—all these appear to be constants in the fate of young Punjabi brides, and set the stage for many of the disastrous marriages I encountered. Savita, who came to Saheli seeking counsel, stayed on as a volunteer. She claimed she was accustomed to telling her story, having been embroiled with lawyers and the civil courts for several years now, and she had also dealt with the media. The experience that she described to me is far more complicated than what can be adduced about Ranjana's marriage from her three suicide notes.[17] The first version she offered me was entirely too terse to interpret. "I was married on 11 May 1981 to C. P. Sharma. It was arranged through the president of the Brahmin Sabha, so we trusted him. On 25 May 1981 I was sent home beaten and bruised, stripped of all my jewelry. My story began and ended in two weeks!" I pressed her for more details, asked questions, and finally elicited the account that follows.

> It was a case of total fraud. Fifty thousand rupees had already been given as dowry and my dowry list is attached to the legal file. They demanded a jeep or twenty thousand rupees more! They had told us all lies about their business, about his education. The publicity this case has received is enormous. I went to All India Women's Conference, Nari Suraksha Samiti, Saheli. On 31 January 1982 we [Saheli] had a demonstration before O. P. Sharma's [her father-in-law's] residence.

She also showed me three foolscap pages of a dowry list with every single item meticulously recorded—clothes, beds, other furniture, major appliances, jewelry. It also included marriage expenses and gifts to the groom and his family members. I pressed for more details. Nothing very surprising emerged, except for the fact—and this has to be an exceptional case—that the man she married was indeed mentally deficient. The Sharmas had lied about everything and concealed their son's insanity. They were also in acute financial difficulty.

> Soon after my marriage I discovered the truth. My husband had no job, or any form of remunerative work, his father was suspended from his job while an embezzlement charge against him was being investigated; his brother was also similarly suspended. They *rented*, not *owned* their house as they had claimed. The Supreme Court ordered that they vacate the rented house within three months. There was no printing press that they had also claimed they owned. He [the husband] was educated only till the fifth grade. He was totally mad, insane, "mental," and also had a "loathsome disease" on his legs and always wore socks to conceal it. [Her body language suggested that her husband was completely abhorrent both mentally and physically.] He was treated like a servant and shown no respect. His parents did not allow me to visit or be visited by anyone including my own family members and friends. I was miserable. I cried a lot. Finally I was permitted to visit my family with my husband and I exposed his legs to my parents. Later that night when we came back, my in-laws took off all my jewelry and took me back to my parents' home since I had resolutely refused to obtain another twenty thousand rupees from my parents which they had demanded.

Back at my parents' house I cried; I felt so humiliated that I thought I should kill myself. I asked my parents, how will I face this world, or face them? You have ruined yourselves for this marriage, for my happiness. My father was very supportive. My mother soon had a heart attack. There was total chaos. I stayed on with my parents, but I fretted all the time and felt that the future was very bleak. People came, relatives came, neighbors came and showed their sympathy, but it did not help. How can saying "Hai vichari" [Oh! poor thing] do any good? They came to satisfy their curiosity.

My parents were unprepared for my sudden return to their house. They had already suffered in the past. They had come as refugees after Partition. My father was from Dera Ismail Khan. My mother was from Lahore and was educated up until the eighth grade. I was their firstborn. [Savita was born in 1955.] We were quite well off; my father has changed jobs and is now working as a stenographer in a private firm. We are three sisters and two brothers. We have been brought up with a lot of affection. My parents are quite liberal, but the only thing they did not want is a love marriage for any of us. There was no risk of that since I was very shy and would not speak to any boys. Or we sisters treated them [all boys] like our own brothers. After finishing college I completed the YMCA secretarial training course. I felt very loved by my parents, I was affectionately called "Munna" [little boy]. But I did not think, nor did they think, of higher education or a career for me. I was twenty-four years old when I was married. [Parents begin to panic if their daughter is still unmarried around this age, because the average age of marriage among urban women is twenty-one.] I had looked at several boys but nothing came of those meetings. Finally my parents consulted the president of the Brahman Sabha [this indicates that their family network had not turned up a suitable match] and he checked their membership directory. He fixed up our meeting and I went to see him with my parents. The agreement came very quickly. His parents immediately asked for *roka*. [Originally a token gesture of a single rupee and a coconut, and now a small sum of money, *roka* signifies that formal agreement to marry has been reached.] They told us their son was "BA pass," the owner of a printing press, and a "very good boy." After this we tried many times to see the boy, to invite him over to our house, but he was never available. They now asked for a proper *sagan* [gifts that accompany a formal engagement] in spite of having been given gifts and sweets and cash twice already for the *roka* and the *thaka*. Their demands were continuous; they approached my parents through the mediator, who would then persuade my parents to agree. They demanded twenty thousand rupees in cash on top of everything else my parents were going to give me. I was kept in the dark about these negotiations because my parents feared I might break the engagement or feel unhappy for being a burden on them. At the temple in Model

Town [a predominantly Punjabi refugee neighborhood in New Delhi] people who knew the groom's family began taunting us with "jhalle di shaadi ho gayi!" [The imbecile has been married!] Many things happened [which she did not want to go into] and I finally came home to my parents.

In the meantime my in-laws were evicted from their house and we had to engage a private detective to locate their new address for "dowry retrieval." [She used the English legal term.] They claimed that I had already taken away everything I had brought. So we are now in court for divorce and to get back my things; and we have filed a criminal suit against the fraud, violence, and dowry demands. Then on 30 January 1982 I went to attend my sister-in-law's wedding. My husband again demanded the twenty thousand rupees. The same night he beat me and locked me up. I had marks all over my body. When the police arrived they wanted to delay the FIR [first information report] and said, "Oh, this is a domestic matter." The next day the women's organizations I had contacted earlier were informed that I was locked up and they organized a big demonstration in front of my in-laws' house.

In many ways Savita's story echoed many others that I had heard and had affinity to my own. But I have great difficulty in seeing her problems as related to the custom of dowry, as she appeared to see them herself. Her marriage and the many others whose brief histories I read or whose victims I encountered exhibit the classic symptoms of the pathology of modern arranged marriage in which the fraud that the groom's side perpetrates is greater than the sum of the dowry demands—and indicative of the violence that follows. True, there was the unmistakable dowry demand for twenty thousand rupees and the violence that Savita's husband inflicted was for her refusal not to ask her parents for the money. His family was in debt and about to be evicted from their rented home. It might be cogently claimed, especially if we remind ourselves of the historical indebtedness in the Punjab countryside in the nineteenth century, that indebtedness exacerbated dowry demands, not dowries indebtedness.

In my view, what are critical are the key deceptions that make such marriages possible in the first place. If Savita or her parents had even remotely suspected that the prospect was a certifiable imbecile, the matter would not have proceeded further. The groom's family lied, as Savita repeated a dozen times, about *everything*. They were liars and embezzlers. And the custom of dowry in the hands of liars and embezzlers can quickly degenerate into an extortion racket. Dowry demands to bail the groom and his parents out of their financial difficulties are piled on top of a fundamental deceit about the groom (his lack of education, alcoholism, disease) or about finances (failing business, debt). No parents would arrange such a marriage for their daughter if they knew the truth about the other party, no matter how deep their anxiety to see three daughters married off. Many Saheli cases would not have existed but for the *fraud* (the word my own lawyer had scribbled several times in the margins of my account) involved in representing the circumstances of the bridetakers.

Fraud and mendacity seem to have become increasingly common in negotiating marriage deals because it has become, with the dislocations of urbanization and Partition, increasingly easy to perpetrate. The influx of Punjabi refugees uprooted in 1947 into Delhi and other cities of north India made the careful process of checking a suitor's credentials and a family's reputation almost impossible. As hundreds of thousands of Hindu Punjabi families came as refugees and sought to replant themselves in new soil in India, they had few resources. Exploiting traditional customs that could enhance these resources (such as marriage alliances and dowry) to rebuild their lives, they vied with one another to make the right connections to establish or regain the status they had enjoyed in the undivided Punjab. In several cases—in Savita's story, and in my own, and in countless others in the Saheli files and elsewhere—incorrect information, sly concealment, and outright deceit were used by the groom's side to secure the bride's family's consent in the first place and that created the scenarios of violence later on. The go-betweens, who are supposed to be in possession of such facts, are truly hobbled, and have to operate without the old marriage-arranging networks they once depended on; this makes misalliances all but inevitable.

It explains some of the nastier surprises in Savita's case, in my own, and in a majority of the others filed at Saheli. None of the blatant falsifications made by the groom's side could be checked. In Savita's case, the groom's inflated educational qualifications, the nonexistent printing press, the house that they did not own but rented and their imminent eviction, the concealment of the groom's chronic disease, and above all, the fact that he was mentally unbalanced emerged only after the wedding had been celebrated. The Brahmin Sabha president, who arranged the marriage but had never met either party before, was unwittingly the villain of the piece. His directory had particulars submitted by families, but he made no attempt to verify the information. Many of the "facts" about the "very good boy" were obviously false; did this wily Brahmin accept a fee to find the imbecile a bride? Do we really need a dowry demand on top of all this fraud to explain the violence that Savita endured?

Savita agreed that the way the marriage was arranged was the fatal mistake.

The biggest lessons I learnt were from my own experience: I insisted that my sisters become financially independent before they dream of marriage. My middle sister did a beautician's training course and opened a beauty parlor in her home. The youngest sister works as a typist at *Times of India* [a national daily]. Now they are both married. I insisted on a *very thorough inquiry* before their marriages were arranged. I invited both men to Saheli for a "checkup." I inspected their bank passbooks, went to their offices, went to their houses, and met their mothers. We dare not make the same mistakes in their cases. My parents even agreed to a love marriage for one of my sisters. And they made it very clear at the outset that no large dowry was on offer, and the weddings were simple, dignified affairs.

I am tempted to conclude that it is not dowry that endangers women's lives, but marriage itself. Much has always been said about the "dangers" of marriage, and the position of potential bride and wife, but the institution itself remains robust—the ineluctable and unquestioned destination toward which all young women travel. It is this compulsive unitary vision that severely limits the choices of bridegivers. Here one sees the collusion of three strains of cultures—Hindu *kanyadan*, Muslim sense of family honor, and Victorian hypocrisy and prudery—that made sexual control uniquely obdurate in north India. The real pressure to get a daughter "married off" is generated from the problem that is universally perceived as needing to be controlled: women's sexuality. Making sure that a pubescent daughter remains a virgin makes looking for a suitor a family exigency; sons can simply wait until the right bride is found. They do not have to be virgins and they must be older than their brides. If we also factor in the lack of enough women in a cohort because of imbalanced sex ratios, then the older the sons the bigger the pool of nubile women they can choose from. (In the last two decades the sexual revolution has been drifting into India, making it a little less onerous for women to find mates.)

In talking with a few of the women behind the "case histories," the scribbled narratives filed on the single-page Saheli form, which were suspiciously focused only on dowry problems, it became clear to me that each narrative had a far deeper unrecorded and unspoken subtext. There were clues and hints, sometimes embedded in the text of the "case" file, sometimes dropped in later conversations, that gestured in a different direction. I quickly learned that these signs—silences, awkward breaks, embarrassed pauses, or pleas for privacy—led to the area of troubled sexuality. To unwrap a "case" swaddled in silence, to get beyond money matters and routine harassment, took a great deal of skillful prizing. Sometimes blunt and sometimes gentle, I found myself asking questions that astonished both of us but that could not be avoided if I was to learn anything.

"Did you have sex with this imbecile with the terrible disease on his legs?" I nervously joked with Savita on one occasion. "What did Sita do as a prisoner in Ravana's garden?" she countered. Sita is the Hindu icon of chastity, since she famously resisted all the temptations she faced in her captivity in her demon-king abductor Ravana's palace. She was eventually rescued by Rama, her god-king-husband, and tested by fire to establish her sexual purity.[18] Sita's celibacy is too well known for Savita's reply to have been an evasion. It was far easier for us to speculate on what Sita did or didn't do, and leave the sexual aspect of this brief and terrible marriage to my imagination.

There were at least two other women who had had similarly brief marriages. One was ended because, among other things, it appeared that the man was impotent. This is ground for annulment, but the medical proof is very hard to establish. Not only does it require a doctor's certificate for the man, it also requires a certificate of virginity for the woman; otherwise it is she who must prove her fidelity! A dowry retrieval suit was filed. Sexual incompatibility or even, as in the cases discussed above, finding a man repellent because of the dynamics of the relationship itself are not admissible as grounds for divorce. So sexual incompatibility and other related "problems" such as homosexuality of the husband or wife are frequently left out of the personal accounts found among the Saheli files because they have no legal value. One particular *saheli*, who spoke to me on condition that I not reveal her name, confessed that she had been with her woman lover before, during, and after her marriage. Her husband, who was frequently on tour in connection with his job, had begun to suspect that the "inseparable friends" were also lovers. His discovery of their relationship ended the marriage, and the two evicted women finally dared to live together. At the time we spoke she was legally embroiled in getting a divorce and in the travails of dowry retrieval, and she had obtained a counseling job at Saheli. She swore me to secrecy, saying there was enough fear of lesbianism in our homosocial society, and at Saheli, that any knowledge of her sexual preference would tilt the outcome of her case against her. The drumbeat of dowry muffled the whispers of sexual orientation and clandestine infidelities.

A woman I call Saroj came to Saheli and was sent over to me so I could take down her particulars. She filled out the case file in two minutes flat, thrust a neatly written dowry list at me, and said she was determined to get back the television set and the scooter that her in-laws were refusing to return. Later she accompanied me to a nearby restaurant, where I frequently invited "cases" to get them to relax and speak more freely. I noticed that she walked with a slight limp. Then she noticed that I had noticed it and said, "What are you looking at me for like that?" "Well, you seem to be a little uncomfortable walking down the stairs, are you all right?" "Whatever my problem is will never in my life happen again." "What is the problem, why are you so angry?" "My husband is a very difficult man and the presence of his parents, who came to stay with us for a few months, made him into a demon (*rakshas*)." "But why the limp? Did he hit you?" I asked. Here she hesitated and said that she had not stopped bleeding for three weeks because even though she was pregnant he insisted on "having relations"; when she refused, he raped her and she bled profusely. She went to the hospital by herself, where they induced an abortion, a decision she made without asking him because she knew she could not give the child a good home; her violent drunken husband was not her idea of a father under whose shadow her child would be raised. She told me that her coital injuries (the cause of her present discomfort) had been a fairly regular outcome of her husband's sexual aggression, but she had never discussed this matter with her parents or with her doctor. "We cannot speak of what we really suffer, so we make it a fight about things. Will anyone care if I write that he beats me often when he is drunk and shouts loudly as he calls me filthy names? This is not to say that there is no fight about money; he humiliated me about money matters often, but that is only part of my story."

Some days later, in a more philosophical tone, Saroj said, "You listen to women's stories and you write them down; do you think women really *can* tell their stories?" This, I agreed, was the problem with many of the case histories I had read or had jotted down. "A woman can have no [sexual] desire except for her husband. Fidelity and chastity are presumed. The woman stands to lose not just the case and therefore her dowry, but her reputation and parental sympathy as well. So the truth does not come out." Even when all reserve falls away, sexuality is not something people discuss directly when a marriage is in grave trouble. She then disclosed her own love for a neighbor she grew up with; both sets of parents were outraged at their liaison, and she had been hastily forced to marry her present husband. "I became the wife of a man for whom I felt no attraction. [Her words reminded me of my own doomed love.] My husband knows that I am involved with someone and has been jealous, drunk, and violent. I have been beaten up, insulted, and humiliated in front of our neighbors. I resist my husband's demands for sex, so he rapes me or he beats me and has threatened to kill me. My life is ruined. But I have to get back my dowry so that I can find a job and live independently. I did not want my husband's child but that is now taken care of. I don't know what life has in store for me, but everything looks hard and impossible."[19] I examined Saroj's statement in her file scribbled on the Saheli form in the space for "Life History." It was consisted of three terse sentences: her husband was extremely violent and greedy; he wanted to keep her dowry and had driven her away with his drunken brutality; she had returned to her parents' home and wanted a divorce and her dowry back. So her story was not told for the record. Since her parents were financially well off, she was referred to a lawyer outside the organization, and I did not meet her again.

She had chosen to reveal so much about her own heartbreak in response to my casual reference to my involvement with another at the time my own marriage was arranged. And yet her story—the one that would make its way into the courthouse and win her back her dowry—was about as different from the reality of her marriage as mine had been. And the more I thought about it the more I found this to be true of almost every story I heard and case I read.

Alcoholism recurred as a motif in many of these tales of violent and unhappy marriages. Saheli volunteers were not trained to cope with alcoholic husbands, and these were often referred to a professional clinic nearby, called Sanjivini, where substance abuse was treated and psychiatric and psychological counseling was available. It is true that violence against women is not caused but only aggravated by alcohol, but the obsession with dowry marginalized other very tangible problems like alcoholism and poverty that were clearly connected to the tension and violence. In the 1990s, Haryana women organized Gandhian-style marches and sit-ins at the hundreds of liquor stores and managed to bring about prohibition in the state in 1996. An interview given by the prominent woman leader of the prohibition campaign, Haryani Bai, reminds us that that violence against wives was a far more complicated issue than the single-minded focus on the evils of dowry would permit us to see.

> One of the major problems women face is violence from drunk husbands. I used to be beaten by my husband. My son beats his wife. My granddaughter may be beaten by her husband. My son will not share his income with his wife. Instead, he beats her when she asks for it. He drinks every day and spends most evenings with his drinking friends rather than at home. . . . On top of this, the lopsided government policy tries to raise revenue from liquor. The little cash men earned was spent on liquor. We have to walk three miles to get water. Liquor shops exist in places where there are no roads or schools. . . . One day an attempted rape by drunkards enraged the villagers and drove home the evils of alcoholism. That is how women in fifty-odd villages succeeded in closing the liquor shop. The Rewari rebellion spread to other villages and today it has reached all over Haryana. That is how I became a part of the anti-liquor agitation. My daughter-in-law is even more strict. She refused to sleep with her husband if he came home drunk. (cited in Hayward 2000: 353)

Among the patterns that emerged from these stories, including the many that I did not tell and, of course, Mridula's and my own, is the theme of the "discontinuous lives": the disjunction experienced by almost all the narrators of the Saheli stories. Just as fairy tales invariably seem to open with "Once upon a time" to locate the story in an indeterminate past, the written and spoken stories of the women I encountered began strikingly with "I was married on such-and-such a date." They did not begin, as one would expect an autobiography to begin, with birth, or family, or earlier stages of lived experience—but with marriage. Only one or two stories actually went as far back as the betrothal, because a problem had emerged in this period. Even the stories told by mothers or sisters who accompanied "the case" did not have earlier starting points—they invariably began with "Iski shaadi jab hui to . . . [When she got married . . .]." In the few cases of women who had love marriages (which were few because there are not many love marriages, not because such marriages are more successful), the story sometimes began with the courtship, but not always. Those who were in their teens or twenties and had been married only a few months had very brief stories to tell. Some had compressed their lives into a single anecdote. These narratives expose how marriage becomes the defining moment of a woman's existence, just as her identity is contracted in the abbreviation Smt. (meaning Mrs.) used since the colonial period in India, before the husband's name. Men begin at the beginning because they are rooted in the soil; their lives are continuous in their natal homes. Their stories exude virilocal confidence, and although marriage is an important, even compulsory event, it does not fracture their narratives, dislocate their lives, or change their names. Marriage brings stability and the assurance of further continuity in the birth of their sons. It might well be that women were constrained to reveal only those parts of their life histories that were pertinent to the problems they had come to Saheli to report, but the commonality of this feature was nonetheless striking. We can see why marriage is compulsory in a patriarchal society.

CHANGING REALITIES

One important factor that appears to have been ignored in making sense of the apparent growth in domestic violence is the twofold effect of the age of women: the increase in age at the time of marriage and the greater longevity of adult women. With the average age of marriage in urban areas at eighteen years or higher for women, their sexuality is no longer as easily controlled by their fathers as it was when the average age of marriage was twelve. And men are even older. The indignation of mothers-in-law who struggle to mold their increasingly well-educated, willful, and mature daughters-in-law generates an atmosphere of hostile confrontation that has the potential to produce murders and near-murderous clashes. In addition, that mothers-in-law now frequently live well into their late seventies or eighties has made the time at which a daughter-in-law can inherit her position of command recede far into the future. A young bride now has to contemplate a lengthy four to five decades of overlap with her mother-in-law in the same household, so the urgency to stake out her own turf expresses itself early in the marriage. Friction over raising children or controlling resources is frequent. Daughters-in-law also increasingly have jobs, and the economic and social independence this brings to the younger generation of women is a further threat to the older generation and the imbalance of power.

Some of the most illuminating conversations I had were with seriously aggrieved mothers-in-law in the very neighborhoods that were resettlement colonies for the deluge of Hindus and Sikhs who had come as refugees from the newly created Islamic state of Pakistan. Their daughters-in-law, they complained, were defiant, autonomous, selfish, and rude, without a trace of the deference the older generation had (grudgingly) shown to their mothers-in-law. Their modern ideas and a consciousness of their rights had created the chasm. Family conflicts were an everyday affair, and, in the perceptions of these mothers-in-law, family violence had increased because wives now spoke back to their husbands, as well. In several Saheli cases of unambiguous murder, in which the women were dead before the kerosene and matchstick were applied to obliterate the evidence, were probably daughters-in-law who had resisted a variety of demands on their time and toil, argued back, only to be engulfed in marital discord; the violence had little or nothing to do with dowry. Lower levels of such tensions and violence are common in extended families or in nuclear units when the husband's parents come to visit. I am neither equipped nor eager to paint a larger demographic picture, but I do want to suggest that it is these exceedingly common and mundane causes that explain the growing domestic clashes.

It is a central finding of this study that although the laws that enabled divorce and banned dowries and the amendments that have given these laws greater clout in the 1980s were designed to protect the rights of women, they have had an insidious influence on how women speak of their problems and how these are reported in the media. My own case is perhaps the most dramatic example of transformation via legal discourse that I have cited, but I cannot find a single case in my notes from Saheli nor in my stacks of newspaper clippings in which I do not detect the law's shaping of a woman's "case history" or sometimes even completely substituting it with a legal plaint that rewrites the history. In my own case, the barrister consigned that written fragment of my life, albeit not an entirely candid version of it, to the judicial rubbish bin. It had not one legally salvageable circumstance in it. If someone were to reconstruct the story of my first marriage from the legal case, they would be able to create a plausible scenario, but one that could not be further from the truth. The sexual complications, the violence, the anguish of it all would simply be erased, since the decree states that the plaintiff and defendant were never legally married and that the defendant never left her natal home. But much more frequently, almost invariably, the life stories of women are truncated to describe only their experiences as "brides" and all their griefs are distilled into a single, unambiguous complaint about dowry and violence occasioned by dowry demands; all these stories are translated into dowry cases. A not untypical case in the Saheli files reads, "I was married on the ninth of June, 1985. Soon after that my husband began to make dowry demands, his mother also makes demands and expects me to be totally subordinate to her. When I said I would not ask my parents for more money but would go out and get a job to supplement the family income he began to beat me. He suspects me of being a bad character even if I want to go to Eros cinema next to our house to watch a movie with my friends. After many such occasions of violent fights, when I came to fear for my life, I decided to run away to my parents' home. Now I want to find a job and live independently. I want to file a case to recover my dowry."[20] This terse fragment signifies a great deal to the volunteer who unpacks the text in which the silence is buried. I prodded the writer, whom I will call Rajni, to annotate her short text and retrieved a far grimmer case of sexual incompatibility and jealousy. We can see the complex forces of money and sex at work.

I observed how the journey of this "case" from Saheli to the courtroom reduced the complexity of the woman's story but then firmed up her self-determination as she learned about legal and worldly realities. Rajni showed remarkable composure as she spoke to me and spoke quietly of the pivotal need for all women: financial independence. This key phrase haunted the many exchanges with other women too; it was the mantra of these battered women. The will to economic liberation had shaped my own adult life and my notions of selfhood after that first false start.

The unidimensionality of the dowry legislation has cast its own dappled shadow on the lives of women who desperately need to have recourse to it. It retrieves dowries for women who escape the marital home even as it usurps their voices and reshapes the substance of their tales. It makes the pain and suffering of women invisible, unknowable. I have presented several stories of women, believing ever more firmly now than when I started to collect them that retelling them is important to penetrate the discourse on dowry and show how it stifles the voices of women and obscures the real violence that takes place in their marital homes. In all the stories I have recounted, and in the many cases Ranjana Kumari surveyed, sexual harassment, or rape, or extramarital affairs were common, and the first cause of the tensions within the marriage. The dowry law has created a legal gag that keeps the messy business of sexual violence and gender relations out of the picture.

The naming of dowry demands as the central problem and of dowry retrieval as the solution severely limits the quality of advice that Saheli, *Manushi*, Stri Rakhsa Sangharsh, and other women's counseling centers can dispense. It is ultimately legal counsel that prevails, and therefore the law shapes these "cases." Harassment, violence, lies, cruelties, all have to be tangibly proved, or else they do not count in a court of law. *So the link of "dowry demands" to marital violence becomes the pivotal factor in these cases.* Dowry *demands*, a cultural oxymoron, are unscrupulous ploys that bear no resemblance to the historical and traditional meanings of dowry, but they are not perceived, alas, as simple blackmail, extortion, or insurance fraud—crimes common to all societies, to which they are akin. Domestic violence is not recognized as a separate offence under the law, but it is given cognizance only if linked to dowry harassment. The cultural flavor of crime and violence is preserved in the Indian setting by the media's insistence on calling extortion "dowry demands" and murder "dowry deaths."

The only possibility of redress that the law offers after an egregiously failed marriage is dowry retrieval. The woman knows that she will have little success recovering anything else—her pride, her hopes, or her virginity—and dowry provides tangible material things to help launch a second start. So the case files at Saheli and the stories published in *Manushi* in the early 1980s become brief just-so stories, and remind us of how, in 1850 in the Punjab, state intervention, regulation, and legislation also constituted dowry and wedding expenses, or caste and family honor, as the chief motives for committing female infanticide.

As a result, instead of hearing a variety of honestly told narratives of women, we encounter voiceless dowry "cases" to be won or lost. Stories are internally or legally edited to make the "facts" actionable; the report of violence is not half as grave as a demand for five thousand rupees. Dozens of files at Saheli consist of a story as compressed as the first version Savita told me of hers, followed by an itemized dowry list running into a few pages. A woman who has suffered the pain and the psychological trauma of violence and insults is torn between the necessity of "making a strong legal case" and disclosing the painful, humiliating details of a failed marriage. She chooses the legal case as I, too, had chosen a legal fiction; my marriage ended with the claim that it had been ritually incomplete.

Love affairs or any signs of sexual straying have to be strictly blotted from a woman's story, for an infidelity or a potential lover lurking in the background can utterly destroy not only a woman's case even for dowry retrieval but also her reputation and her character. From this follows the utter paranoia of parents to protect their daughter's chastity and deliver her as soon as they can arrange to do so into the home of a husband, who is then expected to control his wife's sexuality. The violent response of men at the slightest suspicion of another man's sexual interest in their daughters, sisters, or wives, while applying a different standard to their own dalliances, is not unique to Indian society, although it has been greatly compounded by wishful construction of the sexually chaste wife and long-suffering nature of Indian women. I found more than a dozen cases in the Saheli files where the husband's adulterous affair is actually mentioned, and where the marriage ended with either murder or suicide rather than a divorce, but the dead wife's parents were forced to take the only legislative route out of the tragedy by filing only a dowry retrieval claim. No abetment to suicide charge was filed under section 307 of the Criminal Procedure Code even though it is a nonbailable offense.[21] The amended Prohibition of Dowry Act (1985) puts the burden of proof on the husband and his family and makes it by far the most pragmatic course for parents of dead or abused wives to take. It has reduced the entire public discourse on a broken marriage to a matter of dowry.

Sexuality and sexual problems remained a hushed part of the agenda at Saheli in 1985, as cautious conversations about adultery and lesbianism were taken out of the deep freeze and put on a back burner to thaw while I was there. Many Saheli volunteers talked in private of their struggle with probing the reality behind a failed marital relationship but, as one volunteer put it, there would be little use in discovering and disclosing that an unhappy wife was a lesbian or adulterously involved with a married man, when it would impress neither the police nor the courts and would probably prejudice her case for dowry retrieval. Again the complexity of women's stories is censored by the legal establishment.

The undue emphasis on dowry often serves as a smokescreen that obscures other exacerbating causes for marital violence against women. Alcohol has been alluded to both as a major source of revenue for the colonial government and as a drain on a family's resources. Since its creation in 1966, the Haryana state government has leaned even more heavily on liquor vending for revenue. Its policy of auctioning a liquor license within a radius of every ten kilometers and smaller retail vendors in every three, and keeping the taxes low to increase the volume of sales, gave this tiny state a total of twelve hundred country or foreign-style liquor vendors that generated nearly 50 percent of state revenue. Liquor consumption climbed steadily, as did state revenues and commissions shared by the nexus of corrupt politicians, liquor producers, and vendors. The sale of all types of liquor in Haryana went up from approximately 1.62 million liters in 1966–1967 to an incredible 24.6 million liters 1984–1985, although some of this is exported to other states; country liquor, which is not exported and is consumed by the lower income groups, showed a 745 percent increase, although the population increase in the same period was 30 percent (Chowdhry 1994: 254–59). In the early 1990s, a full-scale protest against drunkenness and violence led by women swept through the countryside in Haryana, replicating the strategies of a similar campaign in Andhra Pradesh. This resulted in total prohibition of the sale and consumption any kind of alcohol in the state in 1996, which actually made conditions worse for women as prices of smuggled liquor rose along with the violence against them. It was reversed in 1998, when political interests weighed in to curb the widespread black market in spirits and the loss of revenue.

Other meanings emerged from my several years of research and discussions on the question of gender. It became patent to me that power and authority was neither monolithic nor usurped entirely by men. Power and domination cut across genders and were continually negotiated between them. The expression and uses of power were dynamic, and the construction of male as powerful and female as powerless in a fixed hierarchical relationship was also problematic. The simple man-versus-woman binary had been imposed on the multifarious roles, faces, and masks that are deployed in social situations by both genders. Age and kinship are important parts of the delicate equation on which the asymmetry of power relations within the family rests. I had to discard the notion of a simple universal hierarchy of gender (that is, universal woman as the second sex) and begin to grasp the far more complex and reticulate distribution of power. This involved the realization that adult male or female identity is not that of a single, unitary self (as it is in the model of man that emerged in the West during the Enlightenment) but a more fluid notion of self that describes itself variously in different contexts. In other words, one does not become simply a "woman" who is subordinate to "man," as Simone de Beauvoir claims in *The Second Sex*, but becomes daughter, sister, wife, and mother (and I would add grandmother, niece, granddaughter, mother-in-law, daughter-in-law, and other affinal personae), with assorted levels of power and autonomy, at different times in her life cycle. The Hindu woman is legion unto herself and unto others; her multivalence is often mistaken for a single-dimensional powerlessness.

But dowry deaths, preemptive or after marriage, are not about Hindu women only, as we have seen. Ranjana Kumari's (1989) study showed that out of the 150 cases she studied, 68 percent were Hindu, 17 percent were Muslim, and 15 percent were Sikh victims, disproportionately higher than their numbers in the population of Delhi in the case of both Muslims and Sikhs—a fact that is neither widely known nor acknowledged in the media. Among the Hindus, the upper castes— Brahmins, Khatris, and Rajputs—accounted for all but 8 percent of the deaths. The concentration of wife murders in urban rather than in rural areas can be explained quite easily, in my view. In the countryside, the dreaded inflexible colonial land revenue payments were summarily reduced by the new central government of India after Independence in 1947. This dramatically reduced litigation and other expenses and therefore indebtedness, even while "improvidence," as the British civilians had named social expenditure, has gone up far more than inflation would warrant. This outcome would have astounded men like Thorburn, Darling, and Brayne, whom we encountered in chapter 4, berating men for their extravagance and caste pride, and women for wasting money on jewelry and dowries.

In independent India, agricultural land and profits from the sale of its produce were declared a tax-free sector, and development schemes supported by the authorities were to make the peasants of the Punjab, Haryana, western Uttar Pradesh, and Gujarat far more prosperous than in colonial times. The thrust of the development has remained aggressively masculine, whether under colonial, Indian, or internationally funded programs. But although sex ratios are remarkably skewed, it is rare or unknown for a village woman to be burned to death by her husband and his family. The age of marriage has not yet risen as dramatically, as it has in urban areas, nor is female education as widespread and advanced. It is also not uncommon in rural areas for fourteen- and fifteen-year-old girls, barely educated up to the fifth or sixth grade, to be sent to their marital homes where they mature into women who are better assimilated into the ethos of their conjugal families. The intimacy of the village setting, as opposed to the anomie of the city's, is also a deterrent because such crimes would be difficult to disguise or hush up. This also explains the demographics of the victims of "dowry death": the overwhelming majority of the murders and suicides occur in lower-middle-class or poor urban neighborhoods. The accidental deaths are clustered in these same neighborhoods, since kerosene is the only fuel available to lower- and middle-income homes, and the pressurized stoves are indeed defective in their manufacture and potentially lethal when they explode.

In closing, I would like to suggest that the rising number of dowry deaths paradoxically indicates that, on the whole, Indian women are asserting themselves very early on in their stifling roles as wives, and although I deplore the violence I also honestly propose that *the rising number of violent crimes can be interpreted as an index of progress in gender relations.* More and more Indian women are scorning the long-suffering route to power that consists of waiting (these days for thirty or more years) to succeed their mothers-in-law; they wish to control their own lives and the upbringing of their children, and fewer of them meekly accept the peremptory behavior of husbands as their lot in life. Arguments, confrontations, and all other signs of resistance are countered with violence. Many, many more women are murdered than commit suicide. The growing violence against women is a desperate response to women's growing assertiveness and verbal audacity rather than an indication of a worsening social milieu for gender relations. This is not an implausible explanation if we consider a similar rise in violence against Dalits in India, and homosexuals and African Americans in the United States and other socially disadvantaged groups, as they have asserted their rights and made strides in their move toward equality.

It also contains a strong element of conflict between generations, as the structure of power that rests heavily on seniority in extended families is being angrily contested. This ostensibly sets woman against woman. I risk such an interpretation because my conclusions are grounded in conversations with hundreds of women. The ineffable nuances in the attitude of the survivors or those who came to seek help warrants my optimism, which are difficult to quantify or express as items on a list, as one can a dowry. This is a time of enormous changes, and an ugly but familiar symptom of a basically progressive trend allows us to diagnose this current wave of violence as precisely that.

Add to this already charged drama a player who formerly made only cameo appearances, who is promoted to a supporting lead role by the evolving exigencies of the last fifty years. This is the adult daughter of the house, sister-in-law to the bride. Daughters are in their natal homes far longer, particularly in cities, and virilocality often means changing neighborhoods in the same town rather than moving to villages a difficult distance away; women sustain far closer ties with their natal kin through visits and telephone conversations. They are in continual consultations with their mothers, aunts, siblings, and cousins, but now they know full well that the Hindu Code of laws promulgated in 1956 has changed the stakes for them in their natal homes. They have a legal and legitimate share in their father's self-acquired property after their father's death. Fathers may finesse their daughters' rights by either distributing their property in their lifetime among their sons or by writing a will that excludes the daughter, but the idea that sisters have an equal share with their brothers in urban property is now an incontrovertible, statutory reality.[22] Agricultural land was not to be treated in the same way, so landed property in villages is still "protected" from these new claimants for now. The ersatz modernity that colonialism bequeathed to the Punjab by encoding patriarchal customary laws and legislating control of land by "agricultural tribes" is still awaiting erasure from the statute book.

Dowries have grown in response to the exponential increases in the value of agricultural land and urban property, although clothes, jewelry, and consumer durables cannot compare with the market value of an apartment or house in any of the major cities in north India. Dowry demands are implicitly based on the perception of the financial worth of a prospective daughter-in-law's family, which the daughter herself might be loath to press, though some of these demands are being made by the daughters themselves. On balance this is an affirmative development for millions of women in India, especially at a time when the middle class is expanding rapidly. The line between dowry and property has begun to fade, and the long-standing dispute among South Asian anthropologists is overtaken by history, yet again.

The *arthi* or widowhood is not the only logical conclusion of a marriage. Many more women have left their marriages since the 1980s, since separation, annulment, and divorce have become legal options that are gaining social acceptance. This trend alone induces *greater* violence against women, who have become a concomitantly greater threat to patriarchal control.

The suicides—and they are indeed many—are, in a way, even more troubling to me. Women who cannot assert themselves, or become depressed with marital problems or dowry demands, or see no way that they can return to their natal homes take their own lives. Since I have met a great many survivors of bad marriages, I was not surprised to find that in 85 percent of the "cases" I examined and the personal interviews I conducted, the women said that the thought of suicide had crossed their minds but that a positive signal from their parents (*maa-baap ka ishaara*) had changed their minds. So for the successful suicides I fear that the onus lies equally on the parents who were constrained from encouraging their daughters to return to the safety of the natal home. If a daughter were conditioned from childhood to think of her natal home not as a place where she is only temporarily resident but as her anchor and birthright (as sons do), and to report the first sign of trouble to her parents, suicides would be fewer. Parents know that a wife beater is often only an alcohol-inspired step short of becoming a wife killer who prompts his obliging mother to stage a kitchen "accident." If a woman wants to leave her marriage and her parents are not ready to accept her back, the situation becomes potentially lethal, and she finds the desperate courage to end her own life. Her despair stems equally from the violence of her husband and the fact that she has nowhere to go if she leaves him. Daughters are sensitive to their parents' economic and social constraints and often do not tell them of their marital difficulties. In seven separate cases in which I spoke to the mothers of the deceased women, the mothers told me that they had never had an inkling of their daughters' misery before they committed suicide. The preemptive suicide, such as Snehlata's described by Bose, when a woman kills herself to avoid the humiliation and expense her parents will have to undergo on her account, speaks loudest of the culture of gender, of its power to socialize women into accepting that they are a burden on their parents, that marriage is unavoidable, that the life of a single woman will be socially and emotionally unacceptable. In 1987 a photograph of three sisters suspended from the ceiling in their nooses left me aghast. They had left a joint note to suggest that they were taking their lives to lift the burden of marrying them off from the shoulders of their loving parents. This was their act of rebellion. The picture and the note appeared in all major national and local dailies and a wave of horror passed over the country. A decade later it had been slotted in the collective memory as yet another inevitable dowry-related tragedy. It was patent to me that it was the idea of the ineluctable marriage and not dowry needed radical legal redefinition.

There are many more human universals than cultural specifics when it comes to women's sexuality and violence, and to the struggle of men to control that sexuality through religion, myth, ritual, law, and social mores. Whether the story is about Draupadi's or Sita's erotic power that launched the two great Indian epics and sent the princely heroes first into exile and then to war, or about Eve's plotting with a reptile to engineer the relatively easy Fall of Man by awakening his sexuality, the subtext is about sexuality. The battle for the control of women's sexuality is the bedrock of all cultures, and with the combined forces of Hinduism, Islam, and Victorian Evangelical Christianity we have about as well-drilled a phalanx of sentinels to guard the virtue of Indian women over the last century and a half as any man might wish and any woman dread. To this we must add the growing dominance of material values in a burgeoning middle class of some two hundred and fifty million people, in which the multivalences of gender in Indian society have been overlaid by the binary construction of the first and second sex in the colonial value system. Violence against women can only be expected to grow as women rebel to assert their rights. In the interstices between the home and the state, women are creating institutions, collectivizing and organizing not only for social reform but for social justice and equal rights. Civil society may one day be truly civil.

In stepping back from the portals of Saheli and *Manushi*, it is easy to see that dowry deaths had far more than dowry as their cause, and the preventive legal steps taken against the practice of dowry will not end "dowry" murders or suicides, nor will a ban on sex-selective tests equalize the chances of survival for girls and boys. A whole new activist and legislative initiative for the empowerment of women through education, economic opportunities, and equal inheritance rights to natal property are urgently needed. Faith in the rule of law can only come if the laws themselves are just and equal for all those who come under their purview. Perhaps the next round of lawmaking and economic development should involve the direct and proportional representation of women to make it a safer world for them. Then, possibly, the violence might begin to reverse its frightening upward trajectory.

This book began in New York, and it is there that it ends. It would be entirely too colonial a habit to look at India in isolation, as beyond the pale of comparison with modern Western societies, so I will do a quick tally to put the violence against women and "dowry deaths" in a broader context. I found some astounding parallels to the Indian situation regarding violence against women in the United States, where dowry, needless to say, is not a problem. This report did not make it into the front section of the *New York Times* but was buried in the Metro section, which is often not distributed outside of the metropolitan area (*New York Times*, 13 March 1997: B2). The categories used in India and the United States are too specific to be strictly comparable, but on an impressionistic level they are startlingly well matched. It informed me that "[m]ore women in New York City are killed by their husbands or boyfriends than in robberies, disputes, sexual assaults, random attacks or any other crime in cases where the relationship between the murderer and the victim is known." From 1990 through 1994, a sexual partner killed 484 of the 1,156 women over the age of sixteen; the remainder of the cases had not been solved or a relationship had not been established for lack of evidence. An average of 231.2 women were murdered annually in New York, a city of 8 million, in that five-year span, which represents 28.9 murders of women a year per million inhabitants. And unlike men, who were most often killed by guns, the report went on to say, women were very likely to be "punched and hit and burned and thrown out of windows." The annual "dowry death" figures for Delhi, also a city of approximately 8 million, for 1990–1994 averaged 17.2 women killed by familiars per million inhabitants. The domestic violence rates for New York ought to give pause to those who continue stubbornly to find cultural fingerprints at the scenes of crimes against women of "inferior" cultures. Isn't defenestrating a wife from a high-rise building in New York as "exotic" as burning a wife with kerosene in a bare kitchen with a stone floor in New Delhi? Or just as expedient?

I received an unexpected gift, as I wrote these words, of a conversation with Celia Dugger of the *New York Times*, who called me at home in New York from the New Delhi bureau on 1 November 2000. She was about to write a story on dowry death for the *Times,* having spent several days in Bangalore looking at case files at Vimochana, a women's center there that had systematically studied all unnatural deaths of married women between eighteen and forty years of age. The center had files on 800 women who had been murdered, or had committed suicide, or had died accidentally, 450 of whom had died of burns. Dugger studied 50 murder cases closely, and to her profound astonishment she found no "typical bride-burning" on account of dowry. "Not even one," she said. "What did you find?" I asked. "Well, it seems to be drunken men who beat up on their wives and finally kill them." "It is disappointingly unexotic close up, isn't it? If they did it with guns or baseball bats, instead of kerosene and matches, no one in the West would have noticed," I added. Then we talked for another hour and I gave her the conclusions to which my research, both historical and contemporary, had led me. Her story appeared on the front page of the *New York Times* on 26 December 2000. I am mentioned as the scholarly expert. That brings fitting closure to my own tangled quest that was provoked by a similar telephone call by the CBS reporter a decade and a half ago.

NOTES

INTRODUCTION

1 There are several reviews of the recent literature on dowry murders; the most comprehensive is by Menski (1999: 37–60) and the most spirited is by Uma Narayan (1997:
   105–17; also see Kumari 1989). Srimati Basu's microstudy, based on her fieldwork in
   three Delhi neighborhoods (Basu 1999), makes a solid analytic contribution to the field.
2 These customs include the outlawing of sati in 1829, the Widows Remarriage Act of
   1856, and the banning of female infanticide in 1870—to name only the pertinent laws.
   There are several overviews of the legislative activity, but the best analytical one is by
   Janaki Nair (1996: 49–94).
3 The custom of dowry was widely prevalent in preindustrial Europe, and is still to be
   found in several southern European countries, for which see Marion A. Kaplan (1985).
4 This is true not only in India but also in other parts of the world in different time periods. Extensive work has been done, for example, on female infanticide in China, and
   in Florence in the early modern period. For the Indian subcontinent, see the historical
   study by Lalita Panigrahi (1972), and the anthropological work by Barbara D. Miller
   (1981). The recent explosion of media analyses of female infanticide offers no new explanations; these analyses continue to associate the alleged "spread" of female infanticide to places such as Tamil Nadu with the appearance of the practice of dowry in
   those places. A report in *India Today* (15 June 1986) on female infanticide among the
   Kallars (an agricultural community) in Tamil Nadu claimed that an extraordinary 80
   percent of all female babies born were killed. The reporter estimated that 60,000 female babies were poisoned to death in the last decade in Tamil Nadu alone.
5 In April 1986 in New Delhi, Madhu Kishwar, the coeditor of the women's journal
   Manushi, invited me to share the results of my year-long research at women's organizations and in the archives on the matter of dowry deaths. She tape-recorded my two-
   hour-long account of my research and findings about dowry I was flattered to read
   (even though she characteristically did not acknowledge my material) in July of the

same year, her now famous volte-face on the subject of dowry, incorporating some of my phrases verbatim. Articles that marked a diametrically opposed stance to the one she had publicly taken before followed, including "Dowry—To Ensure Her Happiness or to Disinherit Her?" and, two years later, "Rethinking Dowry Boycott" (Kishwar 1986b, 1988). Scholars have also begun to examine the psychosocial dimensions of marriage, including sexuality and reproduction, to explain violence against women in India (Menski 1998).

6 The major "social evils" identified by the British have been treated adequately by Indian historians and are briefly discussed in chapter 2. These were sati, *thuggee* (the allegedly ritual crimes of thugs), "hook swinging" (the practice of embedding a suspended hook between the shoulders and swinging in front of a temple image to demonstrate devotion to the goddess Kali), and, of course, female infanticide.

7 Srimati Basu's (1999: 81–88) findings affirm much of this in an attenuated form in arranged marriages among the families she studied in three Delhi neighborhoods.

CHAPTER 1

1 It is a common ploy to use this eminently quotable quotation from Manu to describe the true status of Indian women. For example, Elisabeth Bumiller (1990: 16) does her best to perpetuate this impression in her recent bestselling book: "Some time between the years 200 B.C. and A.D. 200, the upper-caste law codifier known as Manu produced the first compilation of Hindu law which assigned to women the status of chattel."

2 Cyclostyled copy obtained from Professor Lotika Sarkar; publication data were not printed on the peport. Emphasis added.

3 This understanding of the relative merits of *mul* and *daaj* stand in contradistinction to Stanley Tambiah's now classic essay, "Dowry, Bridewealth and the Property Rights of Women in South Asia" (1973), which is discussed in this chapter. The controversy was brought to a full boil in Indira Rajaraman's terse little essay, "The Economics of Bride-Price and Dowry" (Rajaraman 1983). She claims that there has been "a major socio-economic development in recent times—viz., the switch of entire endogamous groups from the bride-price to the dowry system," which she blames on the decline of women's participation in the labor force. Shalini Randeria and Leela Visaria commendably refute this premise. They liberally use Tambiah's theoretical formulations along with their field data from Gujarat to demolish Rajaraman's contention (Randeria and Visaria 1984). Other endorsements and rebuttals appeared in the pages of the *Economic and Political Weekly* on 9 April, 4 June, and 3 and 10 September 1983. The debate spilled into the public consciousness with the story "Born to Die" in the influential newsmagazine *India Today*, in which the Kellar community of Madurai in Tamil Nadu were found to be committing female infanticide. The cause was quickly determined to be the switch from bride-price to dowry payments.

4 It is impossible and perhaps unnecessary to list the fairly extensive ethnographic literature on dowry and bride-price in the subcontinent; those interested in a comprehensive review should turn to Stanley Tambiah's theoretical essay on dowry. The work that is most relevant to our concern here is Barbara D. Miller's *The Endangered Sex* (1981). Although its central thesis about differential gender relations in northern and southern India has been trenchantly critiqued in leading anthropological journals, its influence on the subject of female infanticide and unbalanced sex ratios still prevails among pol-

icy makers of international bodies when they wrestle with the vital question of the preference for males in certain regions and cultures. I also rely on two finely detailed ethnographies by Ursula Sharma (1980) and Paul Hershman (1981), and a ethnohistory by Prem Chowdhry (1994).

5 It is interesting to note that *stridhan* is defined in the Hindu Succession Act (one of the five acts that make up the Hindu Code of 1956) as wealth of a woman, which includes her dowry and any other wealth, such as gifts from her conjugal family. The same act states that a woman's income is her sole property, over which she has full legal rights including those of disposal and sale, and a woman's property is not conjoined with her husband's for purposes of tax assessment.

6 Commissioned by the national Ministry of Education and Social Welfare, *Towards Equality* (1974) influenced a generation of scholars and activists who regenerated a women's movement in India, and it is still a much-used work of reference. Members of the committee that formulated the report included many eminent women, such as the feminist lawyer Lotika Sarkar and the feminist scholar and activist Vina Mazumdar.

7 Pranab Bardhan was the first to sketch this theory (Bardhan 1974). His division of northern and western India versus southern and eastern India works somewhat better than the simple and more problematic north-south divide used by Miller, but neither explains the uneven spread of low sex ratios where both types of agriculture are in use.

8 A longer review of Miller's thesis appeared earlier (Oldenburg 1993). Many scholars have followed Bardhan and Miller and are now locked in a debate on whether on not the rise of dowries is directly related to the decline of women in the labor force since 1911, and whether such statistics measure the true extent of women's work in the first place (Kumari 1989: 11).

9 Exchange marriages are common among Hindus of all castes in south India and may well account for the less severe gendering of power relations in that region.

10 This does not happen in every case—only a statistically insignificant number of bachelors' families are willing to manipulate bridegivers—but it certainly accounts for the reputation that the dowry system now has of being an instrument of extortion.

11 I can only present some anecdotal evidence here. In the course of my research in 1985–1986 and 1991–1992, I talked to scores of upper-class and upper-caste women in Delhi, Haryana, and Lucknow who were quite Westernized and had children of both sexes. These women described their haunting fears about their daughters' looks and their sons' economic prospects. One mother explained her anxiety over her daughter's buckteeth and related that several thousand rupees had been spent to achieve her winsome smile. Many talked of what may appear to be trivial concerns: "How I wish my daughter was not so short." "My daughter has become so tall we will never find a suitable boy." "If only my daughter was fair [light-skinned]." Another was going to pay for contact lenses as soon as her daughter approached marriageable age. I found a daughter being forced on a diet and sent to a weight-loss clinic to look "slim and pretty" as the time approached for her parents to consider arranging her marriage. These gender-related problems often determine the size of the dowry. Beautiful daughters, on the other hand, are sought after, and their parents were less anxious about the dowry since they felt they would have a large selection of mates from which to choose. "We will not have to succumb to any demands for dowry; our daughter can have the pick of the town for a husband," beamed one proud mother. The examples in this genre are boundless.

12 Paul Hershman lived in a village called Randhawa Massandan in Jullunder district in

central Punjab for eighteen months in 1972–1973. Tom Kessinger lived in a village he calls Vilyatpur in Jullunder district in 1961–1963 and again in 1966–1968, and wrote its history. Neither dowry nor brideprice features in this study on land holdings. (Kessinger 1974).

13 Polyandry here broadly means a relationship in which a number of men hold common sexual rights in a single woman; the men are often brothers, in which case the term *adelphic polyandry* is used. The Indian epic the *Mahabharata* contains what is probably the best-known case of adelphic polyandry, in which the five Pandava princes, who are brothers, share the beautiful Draupadi as their wife. This model does not conform to the understanding of polyandry today, when it is practiced by small agriculturists with small holdings. In this case, the brothers' having the same wife keeps the land from being divided among them.

14 The Jats, who are numerically dominant in central and eastern Punjab, can be Hindu, Sikh, or Muslim; they range from powerful landowners to poor subsistence farmers, and were recruited in large numbers to serve in the British army.

15 To endorse the Punjabi farmers' explanation of polyandry, Hershman expresses his full agreement with S. J. Tambiah's study of polyandry as a survival strategy among economically marginal families in Sri Lanka (Tambiah 1966).

CHAPTER 2

1 I ought to make clear that I wish neither to defend nor to justify female infanticide; on the contrary, I argue that it became even more widespread in the second half of the nineteenth century than it was at the time of its discovery, and that morally less reprehensible means of building a family with fewer daughters have reduced the incidence of the practice.

2 I summarize the historical background for the general reader who may not be familiar with imperial history in India, and also to situate my own argument about the construction for political reasons of female infanticide as a cultural crime. I also suggest that the mission to "civilize" the natives was a rhetorical stance rather a program or policy. Sangari and Vaid (1989: 2–30) offer a solid argument that focuses on the impact of the "civilizing mission" on gender.

3 In Sanskrit, *sati* is a noun that means a good, pure woman. The British mistook the doer, the good woman, for the deed, self-immolation, and this misnomer has passed into common usage.

4 A historian cannot resist pointing out that comparable Christian and European practices, including barbaric incendiarism against women in sixteenth- and seventeenth-century witch hunts, and the burning of Anglicans and Papists at the stake in England, make the colonial moral stance a trifle hypocritical.

5 Duncan was for a while a lone crusader in the suppression of this practice; company seniors were wary of the political consequences of meddling with the customs of the ruling Rajputs of Jaunpur. The report produced by Duncan on this subject became the benchmark for subsequent reports on the subject and added much grist to the Hindoo-woman-as-victim mill. Reports on new discoveries of the practice and its suppression that were submitted to Parliament along with the dispatches on sati can be found in *Parliamentary Papers: "Hindoo Widows,"* vol. 2, *Papers Relating to Infanticide*, Parts 1, 2, and 3 (1789–1820).

6 Report of Alexander Walker, 15 March 1808. Hindoo Widows, vol. 2, Part 2, p. 48.

7 The minute generated numerous responses that are appended to Montgomery (1853). I will give the page numbers in parenthesis after each quotation in the narrative that follows.

8 The Khatri, enumerated as caste number 16 in Sir Denzil Ibbetson's celebrated and independently reprinted chapter entitled *Punjab Castes*, which he prepared as part of his report on the Punjab Census in 1881, is described at great length as superior "in physique, in manliness and in energy," and is not, like other trading castes, "a mere shop-keeper. *He claims, indeed, to be the direct representative of the Kshatriya of Manu, but the validity of the claim is as doubtful as are most other matters connected with the fourfold caste system.* This caste group has in its grasp the entire trade of the northwest of the subcontinent, way beyond Afghanistan, they are also the chief civil administrators, and have all literate occupations in their hands. They are also the source of the Sikh priesthood, although only nine per cent of them count themselves as Sikhs. They have served administrations since before and during Mughal times and were the chief functionaries of Maharaja Ranjit Singh of the Punjab" (Ibbetson [1883] 1970: 247–50; emphasis added). It is interesting to note how Ibbetson became the self-appointed arbiter and discounted "claims" made by caste groups as dubious, whereas his own unfounded speculations about these claims became established as fact and served as reference material for all future officials and generations of foreign scholars who have worked on the Punjab since Independence. His work has been reprinted for official use by present-day officials of the Punjab.

9 Edwardes 1852: para. 8. The report of Major H. B. Edwardes, C.B., Deputy Commissioner, Jullundur, sent in a letter to D. F. McLeod, Esquire, Commissioner and Superintendent Trans-Sutlej States, Jullundur, 30 June 1852, forms the core of the official thesis on female infanticide in the Punjab; the remedies suggested in it are prescribed for most districts of the province. It was not only excerpted in Montgomery's *Minute* but sent up to the secretary to the government of India and thus directly to the governor general. I cite by paragraph number because this report was printed in other sources as well.

10 Mr. Barnes, who had been the commissioner of Lahore division, had revised and forwarded the report of Major Lake, deputy commissioner of Gurdaspur district. Lake had first brought to the attention of the newly instituted Punjab Board of Administration the prevalence of female infanticide among the Bedis in November 1851.

11 The classifications presented by Edwardes are to be found in subsequent manuals, gazetteers, and even in Ibbetson's allegedly authoritative compendium of Punjab castes.

12 It is interesting to note that the origins of all problems—infanticide practiced by all religions, caste divisions and rankings, and caste pride—conveniently date back to approximately three hundred years earlier, or the reign of the Mughal emperor Akbar, who used marriage alliances with Rajput princesses as a strategy to consolidate his power in the northwest. His son, who became the emperor Jahangir, became the first Mughal emperor of mixed Mughal and Rajput descent, giving the dynasty an indigenous legitimacy in northern India. Akbar also recruited elite officers from Persians, Rajputs, and Khatris, to offset the preponderance of the Turkish nobility from his father Humayun's and grandfather Babar's time. These political moves endeared him to the vast majority of his non-Muslim subjects, and his reign remains, in collective memory even today, as a period of bonding between communities that formerly been antagonistic. This period also saw the ferment of religious ideas and the emergence of a Sikh

minority, followers of Guru Nanak—the only attempt at religious syncretism to survive. The words Hindu and Muslim were not the common currency; and ethnic designations—Persian, Turk, and Afghan (rather than Muslim) and Khatri and Brahmin (rather than Hindu)—were in use. However anachronistic, it is often unavoidable to use terms like Hindu and Muslim, since the British project to etch these communities sharply and distinctly is in the making in the colonial sources used here.

13 Edwardes (1852), paras. 56–58. Clearly Edwardes had found good storytellers in his district; this just-so story explains why there is infanticide among all Khatris, since the tale about the Bedis was too specific to generalize from.

14 Rajputs and Khatris resented being common soldiers under the British because they had been the principal officers in the armies of Maharaja Ranjit Singh. The British therefore recruited disproportionate numbers of Jats and Muslims to restock their army; Jats were described as the "dominant caste" in the colonial period (Ibbetson 1883: 97–131). British discrimination sharpened caste antagonisms; the Khatri-Jat rivalry owed its beginnings to British recruitment practices, just as the Muslim hatred for Khatri moneylenders owed its existence to the revenue policies.

15 Edwardes (1852), para. 63.

16 The preeminent Punjabi poet Waris Shah (1725–1795) made this popular among Punjabi bards. Ranjha he called the body and Heer its soul, giving their adulterous love a mystical aura, as in the familiar Radha-Krishna legend. It is quite startling that Heer's behavior was condemned as immoral enough to justify the killing of female babies.

17 Section 7 of Act VIII of 1870, Indian Legal Proceedings, dated 4 April 1870, pp. 8–9.

18 For pertinent treatments of the Arya Samaj, see Jones 1976, Chowdhry 1994, and Malhotra 1998.

19 The statute in question was the Punjab Alienation of Land Act, 1900, passed to protect Punjab "agricultural tribes" from losing their land to nonagricultural and trading castes and tribes; it is discussed in detail in chapter 4.

20 This figure is taken from the 1991 census. In 1995 the International Institute for Population Sciences in Bombay conducted the National Family Health Survey and found that female sex ratios were systematically more than 4 percent higher than reported in the 1991 census. An underenumeration of women for a variety of reasons in the 1991 census and, perhaps, even earlier decades is very plausible, given that habits of seclusion and child marriage die hard. It cannot be denied, however, that over the last hundred years the sex ratio has declined from 972:1,000 in the 1901 census to 927:1,000 in the 1991 census, even if we figure in a 4 percent margin of error at both ends.

CHAPTER 3

1 Letter No. 89 of 1854 from C. Raikes, Commissioner and Superintendent, Lahore Division to R. Montgomery, Judicial Commissioner for the Punjab; dated Camp Seealkote, 20 March 1854. SPCPA (1854). All commissioners were supplied with pamphlets and books especially prepared for widespread distribution.

2 The entire text of the proclamation in English appears as Appendix A in SPCPA (1894): 433–34.

3 The arbitrariness of this summons was remarkable; it would be analogous to the governor of New York summoning all company executives in the state to Albany on Thanksgiving Day to compel them to limit expenses for celebratory occasions and gifts.

234 • *Notes to Pages 59–79*

4 The building of a "coerced consensus" has its present-day counterpart in the homogeneity of women's stories shaped in the aftermath of the amendment of the Dowry Prohibition Act in 1985, as argued in chapter 6.

5 The nearest equivalent is the gratuity expected in European or U.S. cities by the superintendent and cleaning personnel of an apartment building from its residents at Christmas time. Not everyone is equally generous, but the gratuity is recognized as a legitimate expectation even though these employees are salaried. The musicians lived off these gratuities, and their services, much like those of the other officially vilified groups, were vital to the life of a village.

6 A detailed discussion of the common fund is in chapter 5.

7 There are literally scores of such examples in the forty-odd volumes of customary law compiled by various officers in the second half of the nineteenth century, one for each district in the Punjab.

8 Letter No. 458, from P. Melville, Secretary of the Chief Commissioner of Punjab, to the Officiating Secretary to the Government of India, dated Lahore, 8 July 1853. Proceedings, Home Department. National Archives of India.

9 Report by J. R. Carnac, Deputy Commissioner Rawal Pindee District, to Edward Thornton, Commissioner and Superintendent, Jhelum Division; dated Camp Husun Abdal, 15 February 1854. This is a report on one of the many meetings modeled on the Amritsar meeting; this one was held to induce the Hindu communities, particularly the Brahmins and Khatris, of the Rawalpindi and Jhelum districts to sign similar engagements. These were competently obtained in a brief three-hour meeting at which the Brahmins and the Khatris signed, as was noted above, joint agreements. Only two hundred families of these two castes were suspected of committing female infanticide. The Muslims of Rawalpindi, an overwhelming majority in this district, were not subjected to a census to determine how many girl children survived, nor was it considered necessary to invite them to the meeting.

10 The attitude reflected in these cuts is similar to that encountered in respectable families to this day. At more than a dozen occasions when such matters were being discussed in families I have known for more than thirty years, the groom's parents strongly suggested that they did not want any special gifts for themselves or the groom. What they requested, or even demanded, was a very elaborate wedding celebration—a feast for more than two hundred friends and relations, illuminations, flowing Western-style drinks, and preferably a military band, fireworks, and entertainment that would do them proud. An out-of-town marriage party would have to be accommodated at a hotel for two nights, since *chaupals* or community-supported guest houses no longer existed. The net escalation of expenses in the colonial period is irrefutable.

11 As with much else in this chapter, it is difficult to decide whether to refer to *neonda* in the present or the past tense. The latter would imply that the practice has died out completely, whereas it in fact survives, vestigially in some places but strongly in most others. Anthropologists (Sharma 1980: 40–41, Hershman 1981: 202) testify to its decline by barely mentioning it as a traditional practice in the villages they studied, whereas Alavi (1972: 1–27) reports its robust survival. Based on my own observation of some fifty weddings of well-to-do Punjabis in Lucknow and Delhi, the practice is certainly alive, but has a very different form. I therefore want to show how this premise of reciprocity was impaired over time.

12 Women generally kept this type of account book, so a literate woman would often lend

her services to those who were not. My paternal great-grandmother, Lajwanti, for example, who died in 1972 at the age of eighty-six, was the keeper of the book in our family and had kept the books for many families in Chakwal in pre-Partition Punjab. She read and wrote three scripts—Urdu, Gurmukhi, and English—and was married two years before she would have finished high school. Many women who came to Saheli, a women's resource center where I did research for ten months, showed me such account books kept by their mothers to prove the existence of gifts given as dowry. These notebooks were often entered as evidence in court cases to retrieve the dowry given to a daughter.

The calculation of reciprocal obligation was complex. For example, if A, who has three daughters, receives from B a gift of Rs. 50 for one of his daughter's weddings, he is expected to give a gift of nearly three times that value when B's only daughter weds. However, if A is much poorer than B and his status in the village or town is perceived to be much lower, he may not be expected even to match the gift, and would give only a token sum of, say, eleven rupees. These variables are expertly and sensitively juggled to produce the encoded gift that in turn reinforces the connection between the two families. This system, as we shall see in chapter 4, was impaired as the British revenue system made peasant indebtedness chronic in many parts of the Punjab.

13 Such behavior and custom was not unique to Indian culture. European monarchs and aristocrats were also conspicuously extravagant at weddings, funerals, and other ritual occasions, but they were resentful if their subjects acted in this manner, particularly when that money could, in their view, more profitably be appropriated to the empire's military and civil costs and associated enterprises. It must be recalled that the Portuguese queen, Catherine of Braganza, who married King Charles I in 1661, brought the fishing villages of Bombay as part of her dowry and transformed British fortunes in the western part of India.

14 This act for the suppression of female infanticide, Act VIII of 1870, was debated and amended in its bill form for a quarter of a century before it came into existence. It superseded all earlier legislation on the subject passed since 1795. Panigrahi (1972: 113–54) recapitulates its tortuous history

15 Further discussion of the Khatri and Bania gains in the colonial period follows in chapter 4.

CHAPTER 4

1 It is important to bear in mind that the insistent use of "Hindoo," "Mahomedan," and Sikh to qualify their Punjabi subjects in a cultural sense, particularly in the process of codifying customary laws, as we shall see in this chapter and the next, was not without political fallout. It helped to shape the cultural and religious identities and differences that the existence of alien rule brought powerfully to the surface of Punjabi society. British power sought to anchor itself in the Punjab by playing up distinctions between "Hindoo" and "Mahomedan," while nurturing the Muslim and Sikh Jats as loyal subjects. In fact, even though it is not the object of this study to explore, an overarching patriarchal Punjabi culture found itself fragmented into disparate Hindu, Muslim, and Sikh cultures.

2 This essay also offers a brief review of the debates that beset scholars of colonial agrarian policies. My purpose is to not to analyze the ideology behind the policy but to show

how new policies on land affected gender relations in the Punjab, particularly in the tension created between property and dowries.

3 The creation of the *ryotwari* system was prompted by the colonial state's desire to eliminate "the layers of mediation" between the rulers and producers, to command information—rather than depend on natives for essential information—and to increase the power of the state (Ludden 1993).

4 Why was the tiller privileged, it might be asked, since tilling was only one of the numerous agricultural operations in a crop's life cycle? Tillers were always men. In crudely symbolically terms in the local culture as well, the earth was feminine and the plough was the masculine. It would be reasonable to say that a crop would not come to fruition without the work of both women and men.

5 For a step-by-step chronological account of the Punjab settlements and the vast Hindi, Persian, and English vocabularies in use for procedure and process after the annexation of the Punjab in 1949, see Baden-Powell (1892: 532–608).

6 Disloyalty and rebellion obsessed the British after the mutiny and revolt of 1857, and all their policies were tinged with the trauma of 1857. See Oldenburg (1984) for a full discussion of imperial security and loyalty in Oudh after 1857. The trouble the British took to co-opt North-West Frontier heads of "tribes" suggests that imperial interests were endangered even in allegedly the most loyal of provinces, the Punjab.

7 Bina Agarwal has cogently argued that wherever women in South Asia have had rights to landed property it has been associated with their typically residing, and often having to reside, within the natal village and often in the natal home across the customary checkerboard in South Asia. She also points out, in her encyclopedic tome on gender and land rights in South Asia, that economic analyses and policies have been centered on women's employment and have ignored the fact that the single most important economic factor affecting women's situation is the gender gap in the command over landed property (Agarwal 1994: 140, 9–24). I fully concur with the broad conclusion, but my research in the colonial Punjab, a place and time with strict virilocality, gives us an occasion to historicize the meaning of the key term "landed property."

8 Many Indian historians, most influentially Ranajit Guha in his classic *A Rule of Property for Bengal* ([1963] 1996), have addressed this shift in compelling detail; however, none has sought to explore the shift for what it might have done to the women's rights in land, whatever their extent.

9 Muslims of the Punjab certainly showed an inclination no greater than that of their Hindu neighbors in dividing landed property to include daughters, even though it is clearly prescribed. That neither Hindu, Muslim, nor Sikh women were disbarred from inheriting does not, of course, suggest that Hindu and Muslim daughters always got their fair share in their father's property; most often they did not, particularly if it consisted of agricultural land or valuable urban property. Fathers and brothers simply defy Islamic and Hindu laws, and daughters and sisters are loath to take them to court, where prolonged litigation and financial ruin are the only guaranteed outcomes. This may also explain why virilocal marriage is compulsory for Hindu and Sikh women and why parallel-cousin marriage is reckoned the best match among Muslims: both systems enable male control of land and houses.

10 It is common for scholars of the Punjab to ignore Thorburn as a crank, but I think a great deal can be learned about the contradictions of colonialism by reading him against the grain. By far the finest work on the political economy of the canal colonies

of the Punjab is Imran Ali (1988). Two recent books most usefully read in conjunction with the present study are Chowdhry (1994) and Smith (1996).

11 Gilmartin (1988), a scholarly antidote to Thorburn, gives a full account of the nexus between the Muslim "tribes" and the British Raj.

12 Himadri Banerji has written a fine scholarly introductory essay on the author in a 1983 reprint of Thorburn's most famous work, *Mussalmans and Moneylenders in the Punjab* (Thorburn [1886] 1983: vii–xxxi); it also includes a complete bibliography of the two reports and ten books by Thorburn. The biographical details are taken from this essay.

13 It matters little to the argument how the revenue establishment justified their miscalculations, but we know that this claim was not quite accurate, since scholars such as Gainda Singh, Charles Hall, and others have used extant records from the time of Maharaja Ranjit Singh in their own histories of the period.

14 I can verify, 125 years later, that the ecological devastation reported in Ibbetson's account is unchanged not only in Karnal district but also in the contiguous districts, where the imperial state created its first canals in the Punjab. Gutrgaon district has vast areas of *banjar* or saline wasteland. See chapter 5 for a discussion of the canal colonies created by the British.

15 In the copy of the book that I consulted, a reader had scribbled "Ireland!" in recognition of a similar and more familiar history of Irish tenures and assessments; revenue defaults and migration to England or North America makes this into a discernible pattern for communities in British colonies. The "paternalism" of British rule, suggested by some historians (Bhattacharya 1992), is patently absent here.

16 The request was made in GOI, Confidential Circular No. 44 F/8–1, dated 17 August 1887. This was duly forwarded to every divisional commissioner in the Punjab. The proceedings of the conferences of deputy commissioners held in 1887–1888 were collected in a report that came to be called the Poverty Report and it is cited as such hereafter. It remained a confidential document, particularly since what it revealed was not pleasing to the government. See letter from E.B. Steedman, Director of Land Records and Agriculture, Punjab to all Commissioners and Superintendents in the Punjab, No. 3217, dated 15 September 1887: 444. India Office Records V/27/800/2.

17 The four circles Thorburn selected for this inquiry were the worst in four representative districts in Rawalpindi division: I. Charkhari in Sialkot district (65 miles north-northeast of Lahore), 120 square miles, a chiefly well-watered circle of 193 villages (revenue estates) with a rural population of 108,493 "of mixed Mussalmans and Hindus, Jats, Rajputs and others"; II. Charkhri in Gujranwala district (40 miles northwest of Lahore), 349 square miles, a well-watered circle of 210 villages with a "rural population of 108,469, viz., 74,845 Musalman Jats, 26,736 Hindus, mostly Jats, and 6,888 Sikhs"; III. Behra-Jhelum of Shahpur district, 233 square miles, a riverain circle of 98 villages with a "rural population of 49,245, chiefly Mussalmans, some being Gondals and others mostly Jats"; and IV. Hill (Salt Range) Circle in Shahpur district, 349 square miles, 34 villages, with a "rural population of about 30,000, chiefly Mussalmans."

18 The detail provides a fine-grained snapshot of a peasant's fiscal burdens. "The aggregate of loans for which there is no detail is Rs. 562; Din's grain borrowings (recorded always as wheat by the sahukar to maximize their own gain, since wheat was the most expensive of grains) "is Rs. 736, other produce, Rs. 35; aggregate of petty dealings Rs. 325; purchase of plough bullocks, Rs. 123, fodder Rs. 15, purchase of seed Rs. 53, payment of land revenue Rs. 163 [assessed for only Rs. 16, so these are arrears from bad seasons

that been building up with the money lender], marriage and funeral expenses, Rs. 158; interest on loan, Rs. 1,151,—in all Rs. 3,321." His credits in 1895 are listed as "wheat Rs. 955; other produce, Rs. 300, land mortgaged, Rs. 210, transfer of bond debts due to debtor, cash payments, Rs. 797, cattle Rs. 632; remissions Rs. 102—in all Rs. 3,321."

CHAPTER 5

1 As discussed in the previous chapter, Khatris, Brahmins, Aroras, and other upper castes of Lahore saw themselves as the urban, Lahoreen elite but were forced to sign engagements with the British that restricted marriage expenses as if they were members of distinct castes or tribes with separate religious rituals and social habits. Smith (1996) does a meticulous reconstruction of the changing agrarian lexicon and landscape by combing through the tangle of village-level records in Ludhiana district.

2 Gurgaon came under British rule as part of the conquest of the Delhi region in 1803 and was made part of the Punjab only in 1858; Ranjit Singh ceded Ludhiana to the British in 1839, and Rawalpindi was conquered in 1849. Rawalpindi is now part of Pakistan, and Thorburn (1896) gives us details of that area that we have of no other district anywhere in India at that time. How the Muslims become more Muslim, or differentiated themselves from Hindus over time, in the Punjab civil code is an interesting subtopic, and must be studied as a separate issue. Here, to avoid confusion as I read colonial documents, I am forced to use these constructed categories, since they are very much accepted and substantiated ones today.

3 I am grateful to David Gilmartin for his insistence that I pay more attention to the linguistic shift from "caste" to "tribe" in my discussion of gender. It also highlights how "unnatural" the system of land alienations that the revenue system had brought about was in the eyes of the officers who were the intellectual heirs of Maine.

4 This report was never published separately but became an appendix to the Gurgaon Settlement Report of 1879. Tupper incorporated Wilson's report as a valuable model into volume 2 of his opus, therefore I will refer to it as Wilson (1881), citing Tupper's page numbers.

5 The ranks were recorded as follows: 1. father's father, 2. father, 3. mother, 4. elder brother, 5. father's brothers, and 6. father's brother's sons. Mother's sisters, sisters, and daughters are missing. In all the customary law codes, female relatives other than the mother—who is considered part of the patriarchal lineage—are seldom acknowledged as playing a role in the family affairs of their married daughter's or sister's household. Punjabi women would have resisted these rankings then, as they would be angry now, if they were apprised of these official doings.

6 Wilson discusses this chiefly in his notes as *maon bat* (division among mothers/wives) as opposed to *bhaiyon bat* (division among brothers), terms that make it amply clear that in the former the shares in land devolved on the widow and then equally on each of her sons, whereas in *bhaiyon bat* all the half-brothers (the sons of the deceased) shared equally. Clearly this law existed only for cases in which a man had more than one wife, which were uncommon. It was probably important for Jats and others who practiced *karewa*, or levirate marriage, in which the younger brother of the deceased took the widow as his own wife. For a consummate exploration of how the British enforced *karewa* for Jat widows so that their rights in their husbands' land remained in the family, see Chowdhry (1994: 92–100).

7 The Hindi term is *ghar javai*; in the Punjab both spellings of the term are in use. The anxieties and fears connected with women's sexuality inflect the discourse on property. The founding stone of patriarchy is women's chastity, so that the male descendants she produces are legitimate; the rest follows, including the social and economic construction of gender roles and relations. The purity of the line is ensured with extraordinary mechanisms—child marriage, the "gift of a virgin," village exogamy, and virilocality. Sometimes it is difficult to suppress the conclusion that social laws arise from a compound of male anxieties about sex and money.

8 There were both large-scale agricultural development and prosperity in the Punjab, but the dislocations and poverty inflicted by the new revenue arrangements were also widespread. The development, however, was not a straightforward case of magnanimity, as the two best books on the subject take great pains to explain. Imran Ali (1988) tells the story of the "underdevelopment" of the new canal colonies, and Richard Fox (1985) that of the Punjab in its general dilemma of "development of underdevelopment." My job here is to use their authoritative research and attempt to tease out the influence of the politics of development and underdevelopment on gender relations and the custom of dowry.

9 It should be noted that this faith in Afghan military prowess lives on, and the United States, as we know, finally subsidized the Afghans and the Punjabi Muslims of Pakistan to deal the deathblow to the USSR.

10 The overarching colonial discourse on race in the nineteenth century and British judgments of native character inevitably came to be internalized by the natives themselves. There is little doubt that the British preferred the "martial" over the "effeminate," the masculine over the feminine, and, of course, men over women. Their version of misogyny made the colors of Punjabi misogyny more intense. But the effeminate Bengali babu or clerk, the pen pusher in colonial offices all over the subcontinent, was just as indispensable to British rule as the manly, sword-brandishing, Punjabi soldier and peasant.

11 For a more detailed appraisal of these two men and an exhaustive bibliography of books by and about them, see Clive Dewey (1993). Both Brayne (1882–1952) and Darling (1880–1969) were graduates of Cambridge University. These men joined the Punjab cadre of the elite and powerful Indian Civil Service and wrote prolifically, beyond the requirements of their jobs. Brayne was didactic and condescending, his writing laced with racial slurs and undisguised contempt for those he wanted to "uplift." His writings include *Village Uplift in India* (1927), *The Gurgaon Experiment* (1928), *The Remaking of Village India* (1929a), *Socrates in an Indian Village* (1929b), *Socrates Persists in India* (1932), and *Better Villages* (1937). Darling wrote as an acute observer, and although he, too, passionately believed in improving the lot of the peasant, he wanted first and foremost to befriend those in whose welfare he was interested. His shock at the level of racism prevalent among Indian Civil Service officers made him an exception. His works include *The Punjab Peasant in Prosperity and Debt* (1925), *Rusticus Loquitor* (1930), *Wisdom and Waste in the Punjab Village* (1934), and *Apprentice to Power* (1966).

12 Brayne Papers, "Fifteen Lacs!" (c. 1937): p. 2.

13 Brayne Papers, "Training of Women Welfare Workers" (c. 1940): p. 1.

14 Brayne Papers, "India's National War Memorial," cyclostyled (c. 1943). In the margin of the first page, Brayne noted that he had circulated this widely "up to viceroy and even H.M. the Q., other [illegible] M.P. of the Parl. [illegible].

15 Brayne Papers, letter from Alice (Mrs. A.M.C. MacLeod) to F. L. Brayne, dated Jullunder City, 19.6.43; handwritten in ink.

16 Ibid.

17 Brayne Papers, untitled typescript, unpaginated.

CHAPTER 6

1 The silence on the mode of perpetrating these bride murders is also disquieting.

2 A sample counterpart to Edwardes's discussion almost a century and a half later is to be found in a story in the *Wall Street Journal*, 21 August 1986: "But the ignominy of an unmarried daughter is even more burdensome. There is little room for an unmarried woman and less for a divorcee. . . . Thus, even Laxman Das Goel, a drug addict whose two previous wives had died of burns, could find a third wife and a third dowry. In July, New Delhi police arrested the 26-year-old man—whose neighbor calls him 'a nice boy'—after his third wife also died in a blaze." There is obviously more to these serial murders of wives than greed, but it the success of such men in finding a second, and in this case even a third, wife that is truly frightening. Fraudulent representations that trick the bride's families into consenting to a match are increasingly the case, as we shall see.

3 I refer not only to the innumerable dowry murders that were alleged to be suicides in the last two decades but also to the infamous forced "self-sacrifice" or murder of Roop Kanwar, the alleged sati in Deorala, Rajasthan, on 4 September 1984. For an unraveling of that case, see my review of the feminist responses to "The Roop Kanwar Case" (Oldenburg 1994b).

4 The names and identities of the people in this, as in all other stories, have been changed, and a few identifying circumstances such as the occupation of the family have been altered to preserve the privacy of the survivors, although to disguise such a memorable case seems impossible. The particulars of the story remain essentially as I heard my relatives and others speak of it more than thirty-five years ago in Lucknow. Although intense suspicions and speculations shrouded this story, there was no legal investigation of the matter, nor was it ever reported in the newspapers.

5 Recently, I confirmed a detail from a doctor friend who still lives in Lucknow, who he said he remembered the event clearly as a dowry murder, and affirmed that all other reasons were gossip, not real motives.

6 I wish to clarify that this grim scenario does not obtain in every Hindu marriage; my discussion is confined to those marriages that become acutely problematic. The overwhelming majority may well be happy or convenient ones that see no end except in widowhood or death.

7 There is an overwhelming amount of anthropological scholarship on Hindu marriage, and I will neither try to summarize it nor even allude to it, since I am here recollecting the impressions and understandings that I absorbed and that any other Hindu girl growing up in an extended family would absorb. I have been encouraged greatly by the excellent work by Gloria Raheja and Ann Gold (1994), which also carries a comprehensive bibliography.

8 Basu probingly discusses the nuances of voiced and unvoiced demands. Many other studies on dowry that covered the 1980s and 1990s also endorse this general ideology that seems to have held since it was first articulated by male heads of households to

British officials when customary laws were codified more than a century ago. Madhu Kishwar's "Towards More Just Norms for Marriage: Continuing the Dowry Debate" (1989) is also an important piece that records the social contempt women expressed for dowry demands, although they did not want dowry banned. They reminded her that women were seldom given parental property, and a dowry was all they could realistically expect for themselves.

9 Helen Carr, an exceptionally lucid writer, paraphrases Toril Moi's summation of this debate. A vast literature exists on this contentious field, and the bibliography at the end of this volume can be a starting point for readers interested in the controversy.

10 In India there is never only one story being told; its threads are always entangled in the skeins of other stories, other disputes, other sordid betrayals. A complicated, lingering property dispute that my *chacha* (father's younger brother) and *chachi* (his wife) had succeeded in fomenting had erupted anew. This pair found it particularly satisfying that my parents were now stricken by the unfortunate events in their daughter's life.

11 This bears annotating. In our moral science class in college, an Irish Catholic nun had once posed this question: "What is the most important, the most precious thing that a woman has?" Someone volunteered proudly, "her brains"; other "simple heathen girls," as we were apt to call ourselves, teased her with answers such as "her wit" and "her pet lizard." The correct answer was "her virginity," and thus my wish to impress him that I would not lose this precious thing so lightly. The culture of the virgin bride is common to Hinduism, Christianity, and Islam, among others.

12 He died not long afterward of throat cancer.

13 Since I began my first research stint in 1985–1986, there has been a flood of articles and books on feminist issues, the feminist movement, and social legislation passed in recent decades. An excellent summary that defines the politics and issues of the new women's movement in India is that by Mary Fainsod Katzenstein, "Organizing against Violence: Strategies of the Indian Women's Movement" (1989; also see Agnes 1992). There are also several recent historical analyses of social reform laws in India. Like Nair, Archana Parashar (1992) uses a feminist perspective. Excellent reviews of the pertinent literature are to found in several places (see Agarwal 1994, Menski 1998, and Basu 1999).

14 I have deliberately chosen to avoid discussing cases that were ostensibly dowry cases for two reasons: first, the women who had written these histories could not be contacted to dig deeper into their lives to present a more fleshed-out story, and second, stories of dowry and dowry death have appeared regularly in newspaper reports and in at least a dozen compendiums, and I do not want to go over that familiar ground. This effectively means that I will be ignoring approximately a decade's worth of my own research, but the problematic of gender relations is, in my view, of far greater primacy than the exploitation of that basic inequality in the form of escalating dowries. A popular account of dowry atrocities against women is Jamila Verghese (1980); in addition, individual case histories have been published in many volumes of the leading feminist journal *Manushi* (New Delhi) since the first story appeared in the media in 1979. Ranjana Kumari (1989) conducted a detailed study of dowry. She surveyed 150 cases in 1985–1986 and presented five in detail. Her conclusions are problematic, as we shall see. The study serves more as a tautology: it studies dowry and "dowry deaths," positing dowry as the sole cause of the violence against wives and, therefore, concludes that the deaths and desertions (of women back to their natal homes) must be due to dowry; even she registers her shock at the high incidence of sexual harassment and abuse her study exposed.

15 I confine my discussion to 1981–1986 based on my own research; the center's subsequent vicissitudes have been many and interesting, but my knowledge is both insufficient and indirect to comment on the period after September 1986. I returned to Saheli in 1991, but it was no longer in the business of counseling women. Its activities appeared to be confined to raising consciousness about women's issues.

16 Facsimiles of these letters were printed in the first Hindi-language issue of *Manushi*, a woman's journal that was founded as a collective in 1979, and translations of them appear in Kishwar and Vanita (1984). I saw the Hindi originals and find the translation adequate. *Manushi* became the leading feminist journal in India and played an enormously influential role in informing its readers about the perils of dowry and dowry murder.

17 Savita is not a pseudonym, nor is her story taken from her file at Saheli. This is the story she told me in several separate conversations between 15 and 19 November 1985. Savita is bilingual but prefers to speak in Hindi; she approved my translation of her words. This version of her story differs slightly from the one in her case file; I never did see the plaint that her lawyer filed in court, but Savita assures me that it was "more about the dowry and less about myself."

18 There are many readings of the *Ramayana*, and many *Ramayanas*, as Paula Richman (1991) has famously brought to our attention, but I take the simplest, commonest explanation here that takes Sita to be the paradigm of the chaste Hindu wife.

19 Saroj came to Saheli on 3 January 1986. We spoke a week later, when she came to learn the ropes of filing a dowry retrieval suit. She spoke to me, as the women at Saheli very often did, in a mixture of Hindi and English. I have translated the Hindi parts of her sentences.

20 Interview with Rajni (pseudonym) on 5 January 1986 and a telephone call two days later.

21 Ranjana Kumari (1989: 63–71) describes such a case in case study 5, and other sexual motives in her first case study, but her reluctance to discuss any other motive but dowry has already been noted.

22 Basu (1999: 41–78, 117–58, and 191–232) has a first-rate discussion of this law in all its negative and positive ramifications and a review of recent legal and feminist commentators. The 1956 Hindu Code has had a ripple effect among Muslim and Christian women, and Mary Roy led and won her radical challenge to the infamous Travancore Christian Succession Act (1916) in 1986, which enables siblings to inherit equally. The demand for a better uniform civil code that would give all men and women of all creeds equal rights has been tabled and women must see that it is passed without communal forces disrupting its passage.

REFERENCES

Advani, Poornima. 1994. *Crimes in Marriages: A Broad Spectrum*. Bombay: Gopushi.

Agarwal, Bina. 1994. *A Field of One's Own: Gender and Land Rights in South Asia*. Cambridge: Cambridge University Press.

Agnes, Flavia. 1992. Protecting Women against Violence. Review of a Decade of Legislation, 1980–89. *Economic and Political Weekly* 27(17) (5 April): WS19–WS33.

Ahmad, Shagir. 1970. Social Stratification in a Punjabi Village. *Contributions to Indian Sociology* New Series 4: 105–25.

Alavi, Hamza. 1972. Kinship in West Punjab Villages. *Contributions to Indian Sociology* New Series 6: 1–27.

Ali, Imran. 1988. *The Punjab under Imperialism, 1885–1947*. Princeton, N.J.: Princeton University Press.

Altekar, A. S. [1938] 1956. *The Position of Women in Hindu Civilization*. Delhi: Motilal Banarsidass.

Anand, Mulk Raj. 1946. *Apology for Heroism: A Brief Autobiography of Ideas*. New Delhi: Heinemann.

Anonymous. 1850. *Sirat al Mustaqim* (A Treatise against Female Infanticide). Sialkot. [Urdu]. India Office Library and Records. Words in parentheses were handwritten on title page.

———.1870. *Dastur al'amal-i-zawabit-i-shadi* (Rules for Regulating Marriage Expenses among Kayasths). Allahabad. [Urdu]. India Office Library and Records. Words in parentheses were handwritten on title page.

———. 1874. *Qawaid-i-davat* (Rules for Regulating Expenses for Feasts among Jabalpur Kayasths). Lahore. [Urdu]. India Office Library and Records. Words in parentheses were handwritten on title page.

———. 1874. *Zawabit-i-shadi* (Ajmere Association Rules for Reducing Marriage and Funeral Expenses). Lahore [Urdu]. India Office Library and Records. Words in parentheses were handwritten on title page.

———. 1875. *Rusumat-i-shadi* (A List of Marriage Expenses Agreed to Be Observed by

Agarwala Merchants of Delhi). [Urdu]. India Office Library and Records. Words in parentheses were handwritten on title page.

Anonymous. 1895. *Majmu'a-i-Rasumat Shadi wa Ghami Muta'allka Qaum-i-Miliyat*. [A Collection of Customs for the Muslim Community for Weddings and Funerals]. Rawalpindi: Sarhadi Press. [Urdu]. India Office Library and Records.

————.1930. *Daaj* [Dowry]. Amritsar: Khalsa Tract Society, Wazir Hind Press. [Gurmukhi]. India Office Library and Records.

Baden-Powell, B. H. 1892. *The Land Systems of British India*. 3 vols. Oxford: Clarendon.

Bardhan, Pranab. 1974. On Life and Death Questions. *Economic and Political Weekly* 9 (32–34) August: 1293–1304.

Barrier, N. G. 1966. *The Punjab Alienation of Land Bill of 1900*. Durham, N.C.: Duke University Monograph and Occasional Paper Series, No.2.

Basu, Srimati. 1999. *She Comes to Take Her Rights: Indian Women, Property and Propriety*. Albany: State University of New York Press.

Battenburg, C. A. 1874. *Rifah-i-khala'iq. A Treatise Directed against Prodigality in Marriage Expenses and Other Social Customs*. Allahabad.

Bayly, C. A. 1988. *Indian Society and the Making of the British Empire*. Cambridge: Cambridge University Press.

Beadon, H. C. 1911. *Customary Law of the Delhi District*. Vol. 22. Lahore: Civil and Military Gazette.

Berreman, Gerald. D. 1972. *Hindus of the Himalayas: Ethnography and Change*. New extended ed. Berkeley: University of California Press.

Bharadwaj, Krishna. 1985. A View on Commercialization in Indian Agriculture and the Development of Capitalism. *Journal of Peasant Studies*. 12(4): 7–25.

Bhattacharya, Neeladri. 1992. Colonial State and Agrarian Society. In *The Making of Agrarian Policy in British India 1770–1900*, edited by Burton Stein, 113–49. New Delhi: Oxford University Press.

Bolster, R. C. 1916. *Customary Law of the Lahore District*. Vol. 13. Lahore: Civil and Military Gazette.

Bose, Rai Bahadur Chunnilal. 1914. *Marriage-Dowry*. Calcutta: Hindu Marriage Reform League. [Urdu]

Bourdieu, Pierre. 1990. *The Logic of Practice*. Oxford: Polity.

Brayne, F. L. 1927. *Village Uplift in India*. London: Oxford University Press.

————. 1928. *The Gurgaon Experiment*. Village Gurgaon, Punjab: Rural Community Council.

————. 1929a. *Remaking of Village India*. London: Oxford University Press.

————. 1929b. *Socrates in an Indian Village*. London: Oxford University Press.

————. 1932. *Socrates Persists in India*. London: Oxford University Press.

————. 1937. *Better Villages*. Bombay: Oxford University Press.

Brayne Papers. F. L. Brayne Collection. Mss. Eur. F. 152, file 76. India Office Records.

Browne, John Cave. 1857. *Indian Infanticide: Its Origin, Progress and Suppression*, London: Allen.

Bumiller, Elisabeth. 1990. *May You Be the Mother of a Hundred Sons*. New York: Random House.

Campbell, George. 1852. *Modern India: A Sketch of the System of Civil Government*. London: Murray.

Carr, Helen. 1988. In Other Words: Native American Women's Autobiography. In *Life/Lines: Theorizing Women's Autobiography*, edited by Bella Brodzki and Celeste Schenck, 131–53. Ithaca, N.Y.: Cornell University Press.

Carroll, Lucy. 1983. Law, Custom and Statutory Social Reform: The Hindu Widows' Remarriage Act of 1856. *Indian Economic and Social History Review* 20(4): 363–88.

————. 1991. Daughter's Right of Inheritance in India: A Perspective on the Problem of
Dowry. *Modern Asian Studies* 25(4): 791–809.

Chakrabarty, Dipesh. 1993. The Difference-Deferral of (A) Colonial Modernity: Public Debates on Domesticity in British Bengal. *History Workshop Journal* 3(6): 1–34.

Chakravarti, Uma. 1989. Whatever Happened to the Vedic Dasi? Orientalism, Nationalism
and a Script for the Past. In *Recasting Women: Essays in Colonial History,* edited by
Kumkum Sangari and Sudesh Vaid, 27–87. Delhi: Kali for Women. Reprinted New
Brunswick, N.J.: Rutgers University Press, 1993.

Chatterjee, Partha. 1989. The Nationalist Resolution of the Women's Question. In *Recasting Women: Essays in Indian Colonial History,* edited by K. Sangari and S. Vaid, 233–53.
New Brunswick, N.J.: Rutgers University Press.

Chowdhry, Prem. 1989. Customs in a Peasant Economy: Women in Colonial Haryana. In
Recasting Women: Essays in Colonial History, edited by Kumkum Sangari and Sudesh
Vaid, 302–36. Delhi: Kali for Women.

————. 1994. *The Veiled Women: Shifting Gender Equations in Rural Haryana 1880–1990.* Delhi:
Oxford University Press.

Clark, Alice. 1983. Limitations on Female Life Chances in Rural Central Gujarat. *Indian Economic and Social History Review* 20(1): 1–25.

Cohen, Stephen P. 1971. *The Indian Army.* Berkeley: University of California Press.

Cohn, Bernard S. 1987. *An Anthropologist among the Historians and Other Essays.* Delhi: Oxford University Press.

————. 1996. *Colonialism and Its Forms of Knowledge: The British in India.* Princeton, N.J.:
Princeton University Press.

Colley, Linda. 1992. *Britons: Forging a Nation 1707–1837.* New Haven: Yale University Press.

Comaroff, J. L., ed. 1980. *The Meaning of Marriage Payments.* London: Academic.

Cunningham, J. D. 1849. *A History of the Sikhs.* London: Oxford University Press.

Darling, Malcolm L. 1925. *The Punjab Peasant in Prosperity and Debt.* London: Oxford University Press.

————. 1930. *Rusticus Loquitor.* London: Oxford University Press.

————. 1934. *Wisdom and Waste in the Punjab Village.* London: Oxford University Press.

————. 1949. *At Freedom's Door.* London: Oxford University Press.

————. 1966. *Apprentice to Power: India 1904–1908.* London: Hogarth.

Darling Papers. Malcolm Lyall Darling Papers, South Asia Centre, Cambridge, U.K.

Das, Lala Mathura. n.d. *Jagadpurush-Chatvan Bhag-Vidhva Niyog ke Vishay Mein.* Amritsar.
[Urdu]

Das, Veena. 1976. Masks and Faces: An Essay on Punjabi Kinship. *Contributions to Indian Sociology* New Series 10(1): 3–30.

Das Gupta, Monica. 1987. Selective Discrimination against Female Children in Rural Punjab, India. In *Population and Development Review* 13(1): 77–100.

Das Gupta, Monica, and Li Shuzhou. 1999. Gender Bias in China, South Korea and India
1920–1990: The Effects of War, Famine and Fertility Decline. *Development and Change*
30: 619–52.

Das Gupta, Monica, and P. N. Mari Bhat. 1997. Fertility Decline and Increased Manifesta-
tion of Sex Bias in India. *Population Studies* 51: 307–15.

Dasa, Jiwan. 1891. *Do Hindu Bewa ki Batchit* [A Conversation between Two Hindu Widows].
Lahore. [Urdu]

Dasa, Ramji. 1892. *Nuqsanat i shadi i sighr-sinni* (The Evils of Early Marriage and the Advantages of Female Education). Ludhiana. [Urdu]. The words in parentheses were handwritten on the title page.

Davis, Mike. 2001. *Late Victorian Holocausts: El Nino Famines and the Making of the Third World*. London: Verso.

Desai, A. R., ed. 1986. *Women's Liberation and Politics of Religious Personal Laws in India*. Bombay: C. G. Shah Memorial Trust Publication 16.

Dewey, Clive. 1972a. Images of the Village Community: A Study of Anglo-Indian Ideology. *Modern Asian Studies* 6: 291–328.

———. 1972b. The Official Mind and the Problem of Agrarian Indebtedness in India. Ph.D. dissertation, University of Cambridge.

———. 1991. *The Settlement Literature of the Greater Punjab: A Handbook*. Delhi: Manohar.

———. 1993. *Anglo-Indian Attitudes: The Mind of the Civil Service*. London: Hambledon.

Dirks, Nicholas B. 1987. *The Hollow Crown: Ethnohistory of an Indian Kingdom*. Cambridge: Cambridge University Press.

———. 1989. The Invention of Caste: Civil Society in Colonial India. *Social Analysis* 25: 42–52.

Doniger, Wendy. 1995. Begetting on Margin: Adultery and Surrogate Pseudo-marriage in Hinduism. In *From the Margins of Hindu Marriage: Essays on Gender Religion and Culture*, edited by Lindsay Harlan and Paul B. Courtright, 160–83. New York: Oxford University Press.

DPA. 1961. *The Dowry Prohibition Act, 1960*. Act no. 28 of 1961. New Delhi: Gazette of India, Extraordinary.

DP(A)A. 1984. *The Dowry Prohibition (Amendment) Act of 1984*. New Delhi: Gazette of India, Extraordinary, 2nd ed.

Dreze, Jean, and Amartya Sen. 1995. *India: Development and Social Opportunity*. Delhi: Oxford University Press.

Eden, Emily. [1866] 1978. *Up The Country: Letters Written to Her Sister from the Upper Provinces of India*. London: Curzon.

Edwardes, H. B. 1851. *A Year on the Punjab Frontier in 1848–49*. 2 vols. London: Bentley.

———. 1852. Letter to D. F. McLeod, Commissioner and Superintendant, Trans-Sutlej States. In R. Montgomery, *Minute on the Infanticide in the Punjab*. Lahore: Chronicle.

Eglar, Zekiye. 1960. *A Punjabi Village in Pakistan*. New York: Columbia University Press.

Ellinwood, DeWitt C. 1976. An Historical Study of the Punjabi Soldier in World War I. In *Essays in Honour of Ganda Singh*, edited by Harbans Singh and N. G. Barrier, 337–62. Patiala: Punjabi University Press.

Famine Commission. 1879. Government of Punjab. Lahore: Government Printing Press.

Forbes, Geraldine. 1995. *Women in Modern India*. Cambridge: Cambridge University Press.

Foucault, Michel. [1976] 1981. *History of Sexuality*. Vol.1. London: Penguin.

Fox, Richard G. 1985. *Lions of the Punjab: Culture in the Making*. Berkeley: University of California Press.

Francis, E. B. 1890. *Customary Laws of the Tehsils of Moga, Zira and Firozepur*. Lahore: Civil and Military Gazette.

Freed, Ruth S., and Stanley A. Freed. 1989. Beliefs and Practices Resulting in Female Deaths and Fewer Females than Males in India. *Population and Environment: A Journal of Interdisciplinary Studies* 10(3): 144–61.

Freed, Stanley A. 1982. Book Review in *Natural History* 91 (May): 27–30.

Fruzzetti, Lina M. [1982] 1990. *The Gift of a Virgin*. Delhi: Oxford University Press.

Fuller, C. J., ed. 1996. *Caste Today*. Delhi: Oxford University Press.

Gandhi, M. K. 1936. Marriage by Purchase. *Harijan*, May 23.

———. 1993. *The Collected Works of Mahatma Gandhi*. Vol. 12. New Delhi: Ministry of Information and Broadcasting.

Garbett, C. C. 1910. *Rivaj-i-am of Panipat Tehsil and Karnal Pargana in the Karnal District*. Lahore: Civil and Military Gazette.

George, Sabu M., and Ranbir S. Dahiya. 1998. Female Foeticide in Rural Haryana. *Economic and Political Weekly* 33(32): 2191–98.

Gideon, Helen. 1962. A Baby Is Born in the Punjab. *American Anthropologist* 4(6): 1220–34.

Gilmartin, David. 1988. *Empire and Islam: Punjab and the Making of Pakistan*. Berkeley: University of California Press.

Greenfield, M. Rose. 1886. *Five Years in Ludhiana or Work amongst Our Indian Sisters*. London: Partridge.

Guha, Ranajit. [1963] 1996. *A Rule of Property for Bengal: An Essay on the Idea of the Permanent Settlement*. Durham: Duke University Press.

Habib, Irfan. 1963. *The Agrarian System of Mughal India*. Bombay: Asia.

Hall, Charles J., Jr. 1981. The Maharaja's Account Books: State and Society under the Sikhs, 1799–1849. Ph.D. dissertation, University of Illinois at Champaign–Urbana.

Hardiman, David. 1985. From Custom to Crime: The Politics of Drinking in Colonial South Gujarat. In *Subaltern Studies 4*, edited by Ranajit Guha, 165–228. Delhi: Oxford University Press.

Harlan, Lindsey, and Paul B. Courtright, eds. 1995. *From the Margins of Hindu Marriage: Essays on Gender Religion and Culture*. New York: Oxford University Press.

Harris, Marvin B. 1977. Why Men Dominate Women. *New York Times Magazine*, November 13.

Harriss, B. 1990. The Intrafamily Distribution of Hunger in South Asia. In *The Political Economy of Hunger*, edited by J. Dreze and A. K. Sen, 49–68. Oxford: Clarendon.

Hawley, John S., ed. 1994. *Sati: The Blessing and the Curse—The Burning of Wives in India*. New York: Oxford University Press.

Haynes, Douglas, and Gyan Prakash, eds. 1991. *Contesting Power: Resistance and Everyday Social Relations in South Asia*. Berkeley: University of California Press.

Hayward, Ruth Finney. 2000. *Breaking the Earthenware Jar: Lessons from South Asia to End Violence against Women and Girls*. Kathmandu: UNICEF Regional Office for South Asia.

Henry Lawerence Papers. India Office Library and Records.

Hershman, Paul. 1981. *Punjabi Kinship and Marriage*. Delhi: Hindustan.

Hindoo Widows. 1789–1843. *Parliamentary Papers: "Hindoo Widows."* Vols. 1, 2.

Hindustan Times. New Delhi.

Hirschon, R., ed. 1984. *Women and Property: Woman as Property*. London: Croom, Helm.

Hyde, Lewis. 1979. *The Gift: Imagination and the Erotic Life of Property*. New York: Vintage.

Ibbetson, D. C. J. [1883] 1970. *Punjab Castes*. Being a Reprint of the Chapter on "The Races, Castes and Tribes of the People" in the *Report on the Census of Punjab* (Lahore: Government Printing, Lahore, 1916). Reprinted by Government of Punjab, Languages Department. Delhi: Punjab National Press.

———. 1883a. *Census of the Punjab—1881*. Calcutta: Superintendent of Government Printing.

———. 1883b. *Settlement Report on the Revision of the Panipat & Parganah of the Karnal District, 1872–1880*. Allahabad: Pioneer.

Inden, Ronald. 1990. *Imagining India*. Cambridge: Blackwell.

India Today. New Delhi.

Infanticide. 1828. *Parliamentary Papers: Papers Relating to Infanticide, 1828*.

Infanticide. 1843. *Parliamentary Papers: Papers Relating to Infanticide, 1843*.

Jacobus, M., ed.. 1979. *Women Writing and Writing about Women*. London: Croom Helm.

Jayawardena, K., and M. De Alwis, eds. 1996. *Embodied Violence: Communalising Sexuality in South Asia*. London: Zed.

John Lawrence Papers. India Office Library and Records.

Jones, Kenneth W. 1976. *Arya Dharm: Hindu Consciousness in the Nineteenth Century*. Princeton, N.J.: Princeton University Press.

———. 1988. Socio-Religious Movements and Changing Gender Relationships among Hindus of British India. In *Fundamentalism, Revivalists and Violence in South Asia*, edited by J. W. Bjorkman, 40–56. Delhi: Manohar.

Kabeer, Naila. 2001. Conflicts over Credit: Re-Evaluating the Empowerment Potential of Loans to Women in Rural Bangladesh. *World Development* 29(1): 63–84.

Kaplan, Marion A. 1985. *The Marriage Bargain: Women and Dowries in European History*. New York: Harrington.

Kathju, Pandit Motilal. 1868. *Memorandum on Female Infanticide*. Lahore: Government Civil Secretariat.

Katzenstein, Mary Fainsod. 1989. Organizing against Violence: Strategies of the India Women's Movement. *Pacific Affairs* 62(1): 53–71.

———. 1991–1992. Getting Women's Issues onto the Public Agenda: Body Politics in India. *Smaya Shakti* 6: 1–16.

Kessinger, Tom. 1974. *Vilyatpur: Social and Economic Change in a North Indian Village, 1848–1968*. Berkeley: University of California Press.

Kishwar, Madhu. 1986a. The Daughters of Aryavarta. *Indian Economic and Social History Review* 23(2): 151–86.

———. 1986b. Dowry—To Insure Her Happiness or to Disinherit Her? *Manushi* 34: 2–13.

———. 1988. Rethinking Dowry Boycott. *Manushi* 48: 10–13.

———. 1989. Towards More Just Norms for Marriage: Continuing the Dowry Debate. *Manushi* 53: 2–9.

———. 1993. Dowry Calculations: Daughter's Rights in Her Parental Family. *Manushi* 78: 8–17.

Kishwar, Madhu, and Ruth Vanita, eds. 1984. *In Search of Answers: Indian Women's Voices from Manushi*. London: Zed Books.

Kolff, Dirk H. A. 1990. *Naukar, Rajput and Sepoy: The Ethnohistory of the Military Labour Market in Hindustan, 1450–1850*. Cambridge: Cambridge University Press.

Krishnaji, N. 2000. Trends in Sex Ratio: A Review in Tribute to Asok Mitra, *Economic and Political Weekly* 35(April 1): 1161–63.

Kumari, Ranjana. 1989. *Brides Are Not for Burning: Dowry Victims in India*. Delhi: Radiant.

Lal, Munshi Pyare. 1871. *Jag-upararak* (Rules for Regulating Marriage Expenses among Brahmins and Kshatriyas). Patna. [Hindi]. Words in parentheses were handwritten on title page.

———. 1877. *Dastur al-ʿamal* (Rules for the Curtailment of Marriage Expenses for Kayasths). Bareilly. [Urdu]. Words in parentheses were handwritten on title page.

———. 1879. *Firhist* (A List of [1000] Members of the Committee for Regulating Hindu Marriage Expenses). Bareilly. [Urdu]. Words in parentheses were handwritten on title page.

Leslie, Julia. 1989. *The Perfect Wife: The Orthodox Hindu Woman According to the Stridharma-paddhati of Tryambakayajvan*. Delhi: Oxford University Press.

———. 1998. Dowry, "Dowry Deaths" and Violence against Women: A Journey of Discovery. In *South Asians and the Dowry Problem*, edited by Werner Menski. Delhi: Vistaar.

Liddle, Joanna, and Shirin Rai. 1998. Feminism, Imperialism, and Orientalism: The Challenge of the "Indian Woman." *Women's History Review* 7(4): 495–520.

Lorimer, J. G. 1889. *Customary Law of the Peshawar District*. Vol. 29. Lahore: Government Printing Press.

Ludden, David. 1993. Orientalist Empiricism: Transformations of Colonial Knowledge. In *Orientalism and the Postcolonial Predicament,* edited by C. Breckenridge and P. van der Veer, 250–78. Philadelphia: University of Pennsylvania Press.

MacLagen, E. D. 1892. *Census of India, 1891*. Vol. 19. *The Punjab and Its Feudatories*. Calcutta: Government Printing Office.

MacMunn, Sir George. 1933. *The Martial Races of India*. London: Samson Low, Marston.

Maine, Sir Henry. [1861] 1888. *Ancient Law, Its Connection with the Early History of Society, and Its Relation to Modern Ideas*. New York: Holt.

———. 1871. *Village Communities in East and West*. London: Murray.

Malhotra, Anshu. 1992. The Moral Woman and the Punjabi Society of the Late Nineteenth Century. *Social Scientist* 20(5–6): 34–63.

———. 1998. Pativratas and Kupatis: Gender, Caste and Identity in Punjab, 1870–1920. Ph.D. dissertation, University of London, School of Oriental and African Studies.

Mani, Lata. 1986. The Production of an Official Discourse on *Sati* in Early Nineteenth Century Bengal. *Economic and Political Weekly* 21(17) (26 April): WS32–WS40.

———. 1987. Contentious Traditions: The Debate on Sati in Colonial India. *Cultural Critique* 7: 119–56.

Manushi. New Delhi.

Mauss, Marcell. 1967. *The Gift: Forms and Functions of Exchange in Archaic Societies*. Translated by Ian Cunnison. New York: Norton.

Mayer, Peter. 1999. India's Falling Sex Ratio. *Population and Development Review* 25(2) (June): 323–43.

Mayo, Katherine. 1927. *Mother India,* New York: Harcourt, Brace.

McClintock, Anne, 1995. *Imperial Leather: Race, Gender and Sexuality in the Colonial Context*. New York: Routledge.

McLeod, D. F. 1870. Minute on the Suppression of Infanticide; dated Murree, 22 June 1870. Judicial Department. Patiala Archives.

McLeod, W. H. [1976] 1996. *The Evolution of the Sikh Community: Five Essays*. Delhi: Oxford University Press.

McMaster, Rev. W. 1874. *Ritidarpana*. (A Tract against Pernicious Customs). Ludhiana. [Hindi]. Words in parentheses were handwritten on title page.

Menski, Warner, ed. 1999. *South Asians and the Dowry Problem*. Delhi: Vistaar.

Middleton, L., and S. M. Jacob. 1923. *Census of India, 1921*. Vol. 15. *Punjab and Delhi*. Lahore: Civil and Military Gazette.

Miller, Barbara D. 1981. *The Endangered Sex: Neglect of Female Children in Rural North India*. Ithaca: Cornell University Press.

Milner, Murray. 1994. *Status and Sacredness: A General Theory of Status Relations and an Analysis of Indian Culture*. New York: Oxford University Press.

Mitra, Asok. 1979. *Implications of Declining Sex Ratios in India*. New Delhi: Allied.

Moi, Toril. 1988. *Sexual Textual Politics*. London: Routledge.

Montgomery, R. 1853. *Minute on the Infanticide in the Punjab*. 10 June. *Reprinted in Selections from the Public Correspondence of the Punjab Administration*, vol. 1, no. 16. Lahore: Chronicle Press, 1954, pp. 410–510.

Moon Papers. India Office Records.

Muller, Max. [1886] 1964. *Laws of Manu*. Translated and with extracts from Seven Commentaries by George Buhler. London: Oxford University Press. Sacred Books of the East Series. Reprint. Delhi: Munshiram Manoharlal.

Nair, Janaki. 1996. *Women and Law in Colonial India: A Social History*. New Delhi: Kali for Women.

Narayan, Uma. 1997. *Dislocating Cultures / Identities, Traditions, and Third-World Feminism*. New York: Routledge.

New York Times. New York.

NLT. 1896. Note on Land Transfers. Government of India, Judicial Department. Patiala State Archives.

North-Western Provinces. 1852–1860. *Parliamentary Papers: Selections from the Records of the Government of India, North-Western Provinces*.

Oberoi, Harjot. 1992. Brotherhood of the Pure: The Poetics and Politics of Cultural Transgression. *Modern Asian Studies* 26(1): 157–97.

——. 1994. *The Construction of Religious Boundaries: Culture, Identity, and Diversity in the Sikh Tradition*. Delhi: Oxford University Press.

O'Hanlon, Rosalind. 1988. Recovering the Subject: Subaltern Studies and Histories of Resistance in Colonial South Asia. *Modern Asian Studies* 22(1): 189–224.

Oldenburg, Philip. 1992. Sex Ratio, Son Preference and Violence in India: A Research Note. *Economic and Political Weekly* 27 (December 5–12): 2659–62.

Oldenburg, Veena Talwar. 1984. *The Making of Colonial Lucknow, 1856–1877*. Princeton, N.J.: Princeton University Press.

——. 1990. Lifestyle as Resistance: The Case of the Courtesans of Lucknow. *Feminist Studies* 16(2) (Summer): 259–87.

——. 1993. Dowry Murders in India: A Preliminary Examination of the Historical Evidence. In *Women's Lives and Public Policy*, edited by Meredeth Turshen and Briavel Holcomb, 145–58. Westport, Conn.: Greenwood.

——. 1994a. The Continuing Invention of the Sati Tradition. In *Sati: The Blessing and the Curse*, edited by John S. Hawley, 159–73. New York: Oxford University Press.

——. 1994b. The Roop Kanwar Case. In *Sati: The Blessing and the Curse*, edited by John S. Hawley, 101–30. New York: Oxford University Press.

Panigrahi, Lalita. 1972. *British Social Policy and Female Infanticide in India*. Delhi: Munishiram Manoharlal.

Parashar, Archana. 1992. *Women and Family Law Reform in India*. New Delhi: Sage.

Parliwala, Rajni. 1989. Reaffirming the Anti-Dowry Struggle. *Economic and Political Weekly* 24(17): 942–44.

PCCLC. 1915. *Report on the Punjab Codification of Customary Law Conference. September, 1915*. Lahore: Government Printing Office.

Peers, Douglas M. 1997. "Those Noble Exemplars of the True Military Tradition": Constructions of the Indian Army in the Mid-Victorian Press. *Modern Asian Studies* 31(1): 109–42.

Peggs, James. [1830] 1984. *India's Cries to British Humanity*. 3d ed. London: Simkin and Marshall. Reprint edition entitled *Cries of Agony*. Delhi: Discovery.

Percival, Spear. 1965. *A History of India*. Vol. 2. Harmondsworth: Penguin.

PFC. 1888. *The Punjab Famine Code*. Lahore: Department of Revenue and Agriculture, 1888. (Revised 1908, 1930). Patiala State Archives.

Poverty Report. 1988. Punjab. No. 12. Government of India. India Office Records V/27/800/2.

Pritchett, Frances W. 1985. *Marvelous Encounters: Folk Romance in Urdu and Hindi*. Delhi: Manohar.

Punjab District Gazetteers. 1910a. *Gurgaon District*. Lahore: Civil and Military Gazette.

Punjab District Gazetteers. 1910b. *Rohtak District*. Lahore: Civil and Military Gazette.

Punjab District Gazetteers. 1913. *Delhi District*. Lahore: Punjab Government Press.

Punjab District Gazetteers. 1919. *Karnal District*. Lahore: Punjab Government Printing Press.

Punjab Notes and Queries. 1870–1890.

Raheja, Gloria G. 1988. *The Poison in the Gift*. Chicago: University of Chicago Press.

———. 1995. Crying when She is Born and Crying when She Goes Away: Marriage and the Gift in Pahansu Song Performance. In *From the Margins of Hindu Marriage: Essays on Gender Religion and Culture,* edited by Lindsay Harlan and Paul B. Courtright, 19–59. New York: Oxford University Press.

Raheja, Gloria G., and Ann G. Gold. 1994. *Listen to the Heron's Words: Reimagining Gender and Kinship in North India*. Berkeley: University of California Press.

Rajaraman, Indira. 1983. The Economics of Brideprice and Dowry. *Economic and Political Weekly* 8 (February 19): 275–79.

Rama, Tulasi. 1876. *Jativbhaga* [An Account of the Brahman and Khsatriya Tribes of the Punjab]. Amritsar. [Hindi]

Ramu, G. N. 1977. *Family and Caste in Urban India*. Delhi: Vikas.

Randeria, Shalini, and Leela Visaria. 1984. Sociology of Bride-Price and Dowry. *Economic and Political Weekly* 19(15) (April 14).

Rattigan, W. H. 1929. *A Digest of Civil Law for the Punjab*. 11th ed. Lahore: Civil and Military Gazette.

Ravindram, Sundari. 1986. *Health Implications of Sex Discrimination in Childhood*. Geneva: World Health Organization/UNICEF.

Ray, Bharati, ed. 1995. *From the Seams of History: Essays on Indian Women*. Delhi: Oxford University Press.

Richman, Paula, ed. 1991. *Many Ramayanas: The Diversity of a Narrative Tradition in South Asia*. Berkeley: University of California Press.

Robertson, F. A. 1887. *Customary Law of the Rawalpindi District*. Lahore: Civil and Military Gazette.

Rose, H. A. [1911–1919] 1970. *A Glossary of the Tribes and Castes of the Punjab and North-West Frontier Province*. 3 vols. Reprint. Patiala: Punjab Languages Department.

Roy, Beth. 1994. *Some Problem with Cows: Making Sense of Social Conflict*. Berkeley: University of California Press.

Sahai, Parmatma. 1873. *'Ahd namah o dastur al-'amal* [Rules for Regulating Marriage Expenses among Kayasths of Meerut]. [Urdu]

Saheli. 1984. *The First Four Years* (private circulation).

Saheli Files. Saheli Case Files. New Delhi.

Said, Edward. 1978. *Orientalism*. New York: Pantheon.

Sangari, Kumkum, and Sudesh Vaid. 1989. *Recasting Women: Essays in Colonial History*. New Delhi: Kali for Women.

Sangari, Kumkum, and Sudesh Vaid. 1995. Contesting Claims and Counter-Claims: Questions of the Inheritance and Sexuality of Widows in a Colonial State. *Contributions to Indian Sociology* New Series. 29(1–2): 65–82.

Saran, P. [1941] 1973. *The Provincial Government of the Mughals, 1526–1658.* 2nd ed. New York: Asia.

Sarkar, Lotika. 1983. *91st Report on Dowry Deaths and Law Reform: Amending the Hindu Marriage Act of 1955, the Indian Penal Code, 1860, and the Indian Evidence Act, 1872.* New Delhi: Law Commission of India.

Sarkar, Tanika. 1992. The Hindu Wife and the Hindu Nation: Domesticity and Nationalism in Nineteenth Century Bengal. *Studies in History* 8(2): 213–35.

Sharma, Ursula. 1980. *Women, Work, and Property in North-West India.* London: Tavistock; paperback ed., 1983.

———. 1994. Dowry in North India: Its Consequences for Women. In *Family, Kinship and Marriage in India,* edited by Patricia Uberoi. Delhi: Oxford University Press.

Simha, Hanuvanta. 1893. *Kshatriyakula-timiraprabhakara* (A Treatise on the on the Kshatriya Caste with Suggestions for Their Social Improvement). Agra. [Hindi]. Words in parentheses were handwritten on title page.

Sinha, Mrinalini. 1994. Reading Mother India: Empire, Nation and the Female Voice. *Journal of Women's History* 6: 6–44.

———. 1995. *Colonial Masculinity: The "Manly Englishman" and the "Effeminate Bengali" in the Late Nineteenth Century.* Manchester: Manchester University Press.

Smith, Richard Suamarez. 1996. *Rule by Records: Land Registration and Village Custom in Early British Punjab.* Delhi: Oxford University Press.

SNNR. 1865–1910. *Selections from Native Newspaper Reports Published in the Punjab.*

Souvenir. 1985. *Souvenir of the International Conference on Dowry and Bride-Burning in India.* 30 Sept.–2 Oct. 1995. Harvard Law School, Cambridge.

SPCPA. 1854. *Selection from the Public Correspondence of the Punjab Administration.* Vol. I. Lahore: Chronicle.

Spear, Percival. 1951. *Twilight of the Mughals.* Cambridge: Cambridge University Press.

SPI. 1870. *Supplementary Papers on Infanticide.* Lahore: Chronicle.

SPILT. 1894. *Selections from Paper on Indebtedness and Land Transfer [Home Department].* Calcutta: Government of India Secretariat.

Spivak, Gayatri Chakravorty. 1989. The Political Economy of Women as Seen by a Literary Critic. In *Coming to Terms,* edited by Elizabeth Ward, 218–29. New York: Routledge.

Srinivas, M. N. 1984. *Some Reflections on Dowry.* Delhi: Centre for Women's Development Studies.

Sriramulu, Bhattiporulu. 1893. *The Medical Jurisprudence Examiner.* Masulipatam: Dove.

Stein, Burton, ed. 1992. *The Making of Agrarian Policy in British India 1770–1900.* Delhi: Oxford University Press.

Stokes, Eric. 1959. *The English Utilitarians and India.* Oxford: Clarendon.

———. 1978. *The Peasant and the Raj. Studies in Agrarian Society and Peasant Rebellion in Colonial India.* Cambridge: Cambridge University Press.

Sunday. Calcutta.

Tambiah, S. J. 1966. Polyandry in Ceylon with Special Reference to the Luggala Region. In *Caste and Kinship in Nepal, India and Ceylon,* edited by C. von Furer-Haimendorf, 164–358. Bombay: Asia.

———. 1973. Dowry and Bridewealth, and the Property Rights of Women in South Asia. In

Jack Goody and S. J. Tambiah, *Bridewealth and Dowry*, 59–169. Cambridge: Cambridge University Press.

———. 1989. Bridewealth and Dowry Revisited: The Position of Women in Sub-Saharan Africa and North India. *Current Anthropology* 30(4): 413–35.

Tandon, Prakash. [1963] 1968. *Punjabi Century: 1857–1947*. Berkeley: University of California Press.

Temple, R. C. [1884] 1977. *The Legends of the Punjab*. Vol. 1. New York: Arno.

———. 1885. *The Legends of the Punjab*. Vol. 2. London: Trubner.

Temple, R. C., ed. 1883–1887. *Panjab Notes and Queries, A Monthly Periodical*. Allahabad: Pioneer Press.

Thompson, Edward. 1930. *Reconstructing India*. New York: Dial.

Thorburn, S. S. 1885. Report on Mussalman Indebtedness to Hindu Moneylenders in the District of Dera Ismail Khan. Government of India. Judicial Proceedings. October 1885, nos. 252–254A. Patiala State Archives.

———. [1886] 1983. *Musalmans and Moneylenders in the Punjab*. Delhi: Mittal.

———. 1896. *Report on Peasant Indebtedness and Land Alienations to Money Lenders in Part of Rawalpindi Division*. Lahore: Civil and Military Gazette.

———. 1940. *Punjab in Peace and War*. London: Blackwood.

Times of India. New Delhi.

Towards Equality. 1974. *Towards Equality: The Report of the Committee on the Status of Women in India*. December 1974. New Delhi: Government of India Department of Social Welfare, Ministry of Education and Social Welfare.

Tupper, C. L. 1881. *Punjab Customary Law*. 3 vols. Calcutta: Government Printing Office.

van den Dungen, P. H. M. 1972. *The Punjab Tradition: Influence and Authority in Nineteenth Century India*, London: Allen and Unwin.

van der Veen, Klas. 1972. *I Give Thee My Daughter: A Study of Marriage and Heirarchy among Anavil Brahmins of South Gujarat*. Assen, Netherlands: Van Gorcum.

Vatuk, Sylvia. 1975. Gifts and Affines in North India. *Contributions to Indian Sociology* New Series 9(2): 157–96.

Verghese. 1980. *Her Gold and Her Body*. New Delhi: Vikas.

Vernacular Tracts. 1874. [Five tracts containing speeches and notices of meetings held with a view to curtailing marriage expenses among various Hindu sects]. Patna. [Urdu] *Vernacular Tracts* 1170. India Office Records.

Walker, Gordon T. 1885. *Customary Law of the Ludhiana District*. Calcutta: Calcutta Central Press.

Wall, R. 1981. Demographic Neglect of Females from Mortality Data. *Annales de Demographie Historique* 2: 110–40.

Washbrook, David. 1981. Law, State and Agrarian Society in Colonial India. *Modern Asian Studies* 15(3): 653–54.

Weinberger-Thomas, Catherine. 1999. *Ashes of Immortality*. Translated by Jeffrey Mehlman and David Gordon White. Chicago: University of Chicago Press.

Wilson, J. 1881. *Gurgaon District: General Code of Tribal Custom*. Mss. Eur. D. 188 (1879). India Office Records. Reprinted in C. L. Tupper, *Punjab Customary Law*, vol. 2, 99–172. Calcutta: Government Printing Office.

INDEX

and dowry and bride-price, 11
and dowry murder, 5
and East India Company and cultural
    crime, 10
and family planning, 17, 71, 171–73
forensic detection of, 67
legal penalties for, 17
and Muslims, 63–64
in the press, 93–94
and sex ratios, 6
and variation by caste, 48
Fox, Richard, 13

Gandhi M. K. (Mahatma), 23, 151, 174
Ghar javai (also *ghar jamai*; uxorilocal
    husband), 143–44
Gilmartin, David, 11, 106, 115, 238 n. 11, 239
    n. 3
Gurgaon, 35, 62, 134, 137–40

Hall, Charles J., Jr., 92
Haryana, 10, 35, 70, 216
Hastings Warren (Governor General), 102
Heer Ranjha, 65
Hershman, Paul, 32–35
Himachal Pradesh, 10, 33
Hindu Code Bill of 1956, 19, 23–24, 193
Hindu Marriage Act (1955), 21
Homosexuality, 214, 220
Husain, Muhammad Maulvi, 93
Hypergamy, 30–31, 37–39

Ibbetson, D. J. C., 112–13, 154, 233 n. 8
Ikrar nameh (agreements), 77, 79–80, 87,
    92–94, 97
Imperialism (or colonialism) as key con-
    cept, 13–14
Improvidence, 10, 12, 15–16, 104, 121–22
Indebtedness, 103–4, 107, 116–18, 123–27,
    169–70
Inden, Ronald, 42, 136
Indian Army, 151–55
Indian Evidence Act (1872), 21
Indian Penal Code (1860), 21
Individual rights and private property,
    113–14
Isogamy, 30–31, 37

Jats, 11, 34, 38
Jewelry as women's resource, 3, 10, 16, 32,
    165–66, 180, 191

Kanyadaan, 24, 25, 185
Kaplan, Marion, 167
Karam Chand, Rai, 120
Katzenstein, Mary, 190
Khan, Mardan Ali, 93
Kipling, Rudyard, 47, 152
Kishn, Pandit Maharaj, 142
Kishwar, Madhu, 35, 229 n. 5
Kuri-mar, 44

Lahore Anjuman, 93
Land Alienation Act (1900), 115, 120–23,
    128–29, 154–56
Land grants, 156–57, 161
Land revenue policy, 101–4, 117–18, 123–27,
    168
Land rights, precolonial, 109
Lawrence, Sir John, 108
Legal plaints and women's stories,
    218–19
Legal system, unreformed, 201–2
Lord Dufferin (Viceroy), 123
Lord Lytton (Viceroy), 67
Loreto Convent College, ix–x,
Lucknow, vii
Lyall, Sir Alfred, 136

Macleod, Alice, 162–63
MacMunn, Sir George, 151
Maine, Sir Henry, 99, 105, 134, 136–37
Malba, as emergency fund, 120–21. *See also*
    Chaupal
Mani, Lata, 45
Manly men, 139
Manu, Laws of, 19–20
Manushi, 7, 219, 225
Marital fraud, 194–96, 209–12
Marital problems and sexuality, 196, 202
Marital violence, 195–98, 219
Marriage, expenses of, 74–75
Marriage and illicit liaisons, 183–84,
    191–92
    as "fate," 184